To Howard on
January 4, 2004
Love from
Mom

A NARRATIVE HISTORY
OF THE TOWN OF COHASSET

MAJOR DONORS

Gordon L. and Motoko T. Deane

Robert F. Johnston

Shirley Marten

William W. Park

Carol A. Riley

Margaret B. Rose

Donald E. Staszko

Wilhelmina J. van der Lugt

Anne and Gary Vanderweil

Cohasset Travel

Hub Shipping Company, Inc.

Red Lion Inn

A NARRATIVE HISTORY

OF THE

TOWN OF COHASSET

MASSACHUSETTS

1950-2000
VOLUME III

JACQUELINE M. DORMITZER

PUBLISHED BY THE TOWN OF
COHASSET, MASSACHUSETTS

2002

First published in 2002 by
The Town of Cohasset, Massachusetts
41 Highland Avenue
Cohasset, Massachusetts 02025

Book design by Harold E. Coughlin
Book production by James W. Hamilton
Jacket photograph © Margot P. Cheel
Color photographs © Lynne E. Layman
Many black-and-white photographs from the files
of *Cohasset Mariner* and *Patriot Ledger*
Minot's Light logo from a drawing by Howard S. Reid
Foreword by Wigmore A. Pierson
Maps by Jeffrey A. Donze, Ralph S. Dormitzer, and Michael Thompson
and produced by Technology Planning & Management Corporation

ISBN: 0-9718086-0-0
Library of Congress Control Number: 2002103956

Poem by Roscoe E. Trueblood reprinted by permission
of First Parish in Cohasset, Massachusetts

First Edition
Printed in the United States of America

I predict that on the last day of this planet,
when the sun hangs cold in the sky,
only two men will be left to face it.
One will be a Chinaman, and if you ask the other
he will say, "O yes, I was born at Cohasset."

—Van Wyck Brooks

This volume is dedicated to the memory of these brave Cohasset citizens who, in the Korean and Vietnam wars, gave their lives so that our country and the world might have another chance to live in peace and freedom.

CPL C. David Strout, Jr.
US ARMY ☆ KOREA

TSgt Peter J. Albiani, Jr.
USAF ☆ VIETNAM

PFC Peter Cogill
US ARMY ☆ VIETNAM

SP4 Allen F. Keating
US ARMY ☆ VIETNAM

LCpl William C. Laidlaw
USMC ☆ VIETNAM

CPT John P. Lyon
US ARMY ☆ VIETNAM

BT3 R. Edward Maree
US NAVY ☆ VIETNAM

1st Lt. Dennis J. Reardon
USMC ☆ VIETNAM

PFC Craig M. Simeone
US ARMY ☆ VIETNAM

Article 25, Special Town Meeting, October 28, 1996

(Inserted by the Board of Selectmen, at the request of the
Historical Commission, Noel A. Ripley, Chairman, and others.)

To see if the Town will vote to establish a committee to be appointed by the Board of Selectmen to write volume #3 of the Town history covering the period from 1950 to the year 2000, said history to be dedicated to the memory of those persons of Cohasset who, in the Korean and Vietnam Wars, gave their lives so that our country and the world might have another chance to live in peace and freedom, said committee to consist of not more than twenty citizens; and further to raise and appropriate, transfer from available funds or borrow pursuant to any applicable statute a sum of money to defray the Town history committee expenses, or act on anything relating thereto.

FOREWORD

This book project had its genesis in the spring of 1996 when the Cohasset Historical Commission, under the chairmanship of Noel A. Ripley, drafted, approved, and sent to the Board of Selectmen a resolution establishing a Committee on Town History to write the *Narrative History of Cohasset, 1950–2000*, Volume III.

The resolution, Article 25, was approved unanimously at the October 28, 1996, Special Town Meeting along with an initial appropriation of $5,000 for the project. The resolution provided that the book be dedicated to Cohasset citizens who gave their lives in the Korean and Vietnam wars.

The first organizational meeting took place in January 1997, led by Selectman Peter J. Pratt. Peter is the son of Burtram Pratt, who authored Volume II of the *Narrative History of Cohasset*. This writer had the honor of being elected chairman of the committee and served in this capacity throughout the six-year project, 1997–2002.

The committee is grateful for the support and encouragement it has received throughout this project from succeeding Boards of Selectmen and Town Manager Mark W. Haddad and for the additional appropriations of $30,000 each at the October 1998 Special Town Meeting and the December 1999 Special Town Meeting.

In order to ensure maximum flexibility to produce the best book possible, over $10,000 was raised from individual and corporate contributors. Over 400 copies were sold in advance at a reduced prepublication price and nearly 200 copies of Volume I and 175 copies of Volume II were sold at a profit.

Nearly 50 regular public committee meetings were held over a six-year period with 23 Cohasset citizens serving as official members for varying lengths of time. During work on the book, we lost a dedicated member and beloved friend, Clark Chatterton, to cancer. Clark was a widely known and respected citizen of Cohasset who had been involved in numerous community activities and served as Athletic Director for over 20 years at the high school.

At the top of a long list of organizational, content, marketing, and timing issues facing the committee was the all-important selection of an author. Six candidates presented themselves to our committee. At our May 1998 meeting, the committee unanimously selected Jacqueline M. Dormitzer as the author of Volume III. She also was immediately appointed an official member of the committee. Jackie has lived in town since 1967, holds a B.A. from Wellesley College, and has been involved as a volunteer in many activities in town for over three decades. She lovingly and tirelessly devoted thousands of hours to this project with the enthusiastic support of her editor and husband, Ralph. Their good cheer and dedication have, in turn, inspired all of us on the committee to fully participate and do our part to successfully publish Volume III, *Narrative History of Cohasset, 1950–2000.*

To each member of this committee, I extend my warm appreciation and personal thanks for your commitment and unique contribution to this project. Because of you this chairman's job was easy. Every member of the committee contributed significantly to our effort. Each brought special talents, interests, and perspectives to our mission. And what a lively committee it has been! The following is a short list of their contributions:

Margot P. Cheel took the aerial photo on the dust jacket, contributed several other photos, and was most helpful with photographic questions.

Harold E. Coughlin, professional book designer extraordinaire, was responsible for the layout and overall "look" of the book. Hal's suggestions on many technical aspects were invaluable.

Louis F. Eaton, Jr., has lived in town since 1946 and has witnessed most of the events chronicled here. Lou gave of his wit, wisdom, legal knowledge, and writing skills, serving as secretary pro tem for many meetings.

Julia H. Gleason, a "townie," has been deeply devoted to this effort and has personally distributed hundreds of books to homes throughout our community.

Ernest J. Grassey served ably and enthusiastically as vice chairman and has been especially helpful as liaison to the Cohasset Historical Society.

James W. Hamilton, unofficial town cartoonist since 1988 for the weekly *Cohasset Mariner* newspaper, drew on his knowledge of the print industry to create a budget and guide the committee through the mechanics of publishing and printing a book.

Louis S. Harvey, in addition to being our sales, marketing, and public relations guru, brought his special knowledge of the information technology field to our committee's work.

Ann C. Pompeo, a "townie" and sister of the late Clark Chatterton, made a huge contribution by corralling hundreds of photos of the 1950s, '60s, '70s, and '80s, many of which appear throughout the book.

Hubert P. van der Lugt contributed to this effort in many ways, but was especially helpful in fundraising, which gave us maximum financial flexibility.

Mary M. (Molly) Hochkeppel Pierson, besides serving as secretary of the committee, was also photo coordinator and copy editor of the book, and she brought a special perspective to the project as Cohasset reporter for the daily *Patriot Ledger* newspaper for much of the 1980s and '90s. And yes, dear reader, we were married as the project neared its completion.

Lynne E. Layman, although unable to join the committee officially since she did not live in Cohasset, contributed dozens of wonderful photographs of people, lifestyles, and places in Cohasset at the end of the twentieth century.

Diane C. Sullivan, a selectman from 1997 to 2000, was also an active member of this committee before moving out of town. In addition to serving as liaison to the Board of Selectmen, she spoke eloquently at town meetings in support of full funding for this project.

The Committee on Town History thanks all those who generously donated photographs to the committee or granted their permission to publish the photographs that have been included in this book. We have attempted to give appropriate credit whenever possible. However, the committee does not have complete records of every photograph, and we apologize if we have failed or been unable to give such credit. Please contact a member of the committee if you have any such additional information. We will attempt to include it if a revised edition is published in the future.

This book project has been a labor of love with contributions of time and, in some cases, money from hundreds of our fellow citizens as well as those on the committee who enthusiastically gave their personal and professional time. We believe the final product is a wonderfully readable, accurate, and evocative history of the last fifty years in our special community, Cohasset. We hope you agree.

Wigmore A. Pierson, *Chairman*

Cohasset, Massachusetts
January 30, 2002

Standing: *Ernest J. Grassey, Harold E. Coughlin, Julia H. Gleason, Louis F. Eaton, Jr., Wigmore A. Pierson, Louis S. Harvey, James W. Hamilton, Hubert P. van der Lugt,* Seated: *Mary M. (Molly) Hochkeppel Pierson, Jacqueline M. Dormitzer, Margot P. Cheel, Ann C. Pompeo.* Photo © J. David Congalton

AUTHOR'S PREFACE

Following in the footsteps of E. Victor Bigelow and Burtram J. Pratt, authors of the first two volumes of Cohasset's history, would be daunting for anyone. Bigelow was the pastor of the Second Congregational Church, a learned man for his time, and Pratt was the scion of generations of Cohasset families. I was part of that great wave of newcomers who came to Cohasset in the 1950s and 1960s. Yet perhaps it is appropriate that one of those who helped shape the "new" Cohasset be given the task of recording its history.

The dominant theme of this book is the change in the character of the town from 1950 to 2000 and, having moved here in 1967, I was witness to much of that transformation. During this period Cohasset changed from a small, semirural town with a colony of wealthy summer residents to a more homogeneous, upscale bedroom community. The world changed too, as the cold war came to an end after nearly 50 years of tension and hostility. I have tried to relate external events to the evolution of the town, or at least to place this local account into a larger context.

It was a great privilege to author this book. When I learned that a Committee on Town History had been appointed to update Cohasset's history, I volunteered to edit or help someone write it. But the committee asked me to take on the whole project—and I accepted. I gathered as much information as possible, but found very little in the archives on the fifties and sixties. It was only in 1978, when the *Cohasset Mariner* was first published, that the Historical Society began saving issues of our local newspaper. For most of the earlier period, I depended on the personal accounts of Cohasset residents, as well as on issues of the *South Shore Mirror* and *South Shore News/Scituate Herald* (containing the *Cohasset Cottager*) that the Scituate Public Library, fortunately, had microfilmed. I also used the Historical Society's collection of annual Town Reports. The research and interviews occupied half my time; the writing, by far the most challenging job, the other half.

My interviews with more than 60 men and women, and informal discussions with many others, turned out to be the most enjoyable part of this project. They helped form my perspective on Cohasset, and the pages of this book are filled with their voices. I am grateful to them all. Too numerous to mention here by name, they are listed at the back of the book. Still others, notably Rebecca M. Bates-McArthur, Kenneth R. Jason, Alfred G. Odermatt, Nancy C. Snowdale, and Sarah A.Young, lent me articles, photos, and other items they had saved, and Frank H.White shared the scrapbooks kept by his mother, Cornelia.

Many residents have contributed to the history of Cohasset through their quiet dedication to service and countless hours of volunteer work. I fear many of their names do not appear in this book, either inadvertently or because I did not know about them. I regret the omission. They also deserve our gratitude.

This book took three years to research and write. I could not have done it without the help of my husband, Ralph S. Dormitzer. He was my in-house editor, technology consultant, and right-hand man. He read every word of the manuscript, adding detail and depth where needed and watching for lapses in tone and style. Together we went to the Boston Public Library to read endless microfilmed pages of the *Patriot Ledger* to fill gaps in the coverage of Cohasset news. Ralph also spent hours researching old maps of Cohasset to delineate the estates and collaborated on the maps of the town. His work on this book in many dimensions has been invaluable.

One of my aims was to incorporate the earlier history of Cohasset into this account. I asked David H.Wadsworth, our town historian, to review the first four chapters for historical content, and he graciously did so, making many other useful suggestions. I am grateful to him and to all those who reviewed specific topics. Any errors that exist in the book, and I am sure there are many despite my efforts to be accurate, are my own responsibility.

I want to thank Wigmore A. Pierson, chairman of the Committee on Town History, for giving me a free hand in writing this book. I am honored by the faith he and his committee placed in me, and I hope I have not disappointed them. Members of the committee contributed to this work in significant ways. Mary M. (Molly) Hochkeppel Pierson coordinated the photograph program and wrote the captions. She also did general text editing and wrote the section on the Music Circus in the 1950s. Ann C. Pompeo volunteered to search for photographs and found priceless treasures. Louis F. Eaton, Jr., prepared the list of town officials at the back of the book. A special thanks to Harold E. Coughlin for his superb book design and layout, to James W. Hamilton for coordinating and managing all aspects of book production, and to Louis S. Harvey for his creative marketing ideas. I also appreciate the steadfast support and interest of committee members Clark Chatterton (whose death in 2000 saddened us all), Margot P. Cheel, Julia H. Gleason, Ernest J. Grassey, Diane C. Sullivan, and Hubert P. van der Lugt. Thanks, too, to Lynne E. Layman, our photographer; Jeffrey A. Donze, who donated his time in producing the two maps of Cohasset; and Marilyn Pratt Morrison, our proofreader, who contributed her detailed knowledge of the town as well as her professional expertise.

As I was completing the last chapter, the catastrophic events of September 11, 2001, occurred. The terrorist attack brought an unexpected relevance to the enigmatic lines by literary historian Van Wyck Brooks that I have used as an epigraph. (My thanks to William W. Park for bringing the quote to my attention.) Probably written after World War II, the words suggest the tenuousness of life on earth. But they also affirm, remarkably, the central place of Cohasset in the hearts and minds of those fortunate enough to have lived here. We may not have been born in Cohasset, but we are just as proud of this town as our native predecessors.

Jacqueline M. Dormitzer

Cohasset, Massachusetts
December 27, 2001

CONTENTS

xvii

Cohasset in the 1950s:
ONE TRANSITION

In 1950 Cohasset was a small seaside town of about 3,700 people. The fishing boats of local lobstermen dotted the inner cove of the harbor, while farther out, toward Bassing Beach, the sailboats and yachts of the summer residents tugged gently at their moorings. A few dairy, poultry, and pig farms still gave the town a rural flavor. Children could spend a carefree afternoon playing in the woods or in the green meadows and daisy-covered fields near Oaks Farm on Sohier Street, or they could pick blueberries behind the pastures of Walnut Grove Farm in Beechwood.

Cohasset was not a wealthy town. The median family income was 26 percent lower than the state median ($2,146 v. $2,909); in striking contrast, by 1998 it would be about 68 percent *higher* than the state median ($74,310 v. $44,332). World War II had ended in 1945, but industry had not yet fully converted from wartime to peacetime production and owning a car was a luxury—in those days teenagers did not expect one as a gift from their parents. Some Cohasset families managed without a car, while others had only one, such as an old "woody," or beach wagon. You often got around by bicycle or on foot. Typical of the times, Louis F. Eaton, Jr., a young lawyer, did not own a car when he moved to Cohasset just after the war. He walked to the station in downtown Cohasset each weekday morning for the 7:38 train to Boston, and his wife, Elizabeth, walked to the A & P on South Main Street to buy

1

groceries. Policemen and mail carriers walked their routes.

Looking back to the fifties, people fondly remember Cohasset as a small, neighborly place where everyone knew each other. To Marion ("Molly") Coulter Bowditch, it seemed as if "everyone were family. You knew all the people at the post office, at the grocery store; you knew the policemen; you knew the selectmen." You not only knew who they were, but you knew about their families, their lives.

At town meeting the moderator, Robert B. James, could call on everyone by name. There was no need to announce who you were and where you lived. The police chief, Hector ("the Protector") Pelletier, knew all the children, and so did the other police officers.

Henry A. Rattenbury recalls, "If you had any kind of a guilty conscience and you saw a police officer walking down the street, you'd cross to the other side — because they knew." When a teenager was caught speeding, Chief Pelletier would take the offender to his second-floor office in the police station (the old Independence Building) on South Main Street. He would read him the "riot act," take his driver's license, and put it in the drawer. There it would stay until Pelletier thought he was ready for it. Meanwhile, the youth had to come with his parents to the chief's "Sunday

Police Chief Hector "the Protector" Pelletier behind his ever-neat desk. Pelletier was chief from 1924 to 1967. Photo courtesy of Barbara Conte

In 1950, Rosalie Conte, 20, was the only licensed woman police radio operator in the state. She had been "calling the cars" full-time since age 17. Photo courtesy of Cohasset Historical Society

The 1956 Cohasset ambulance was a Cadillac purchased from Joe Silvia's Garage. Here, Ruth Silvia makes the delivery. Photo courtesy of Cohasset Police Department

Morning Club" at the station for a weekly report. Teenagers stayed out of court.

The affairs of the town were managed somewhat informally by three selectmen, who were also the assessors and public welfare officers. Frances Chatterton, whose husband, Frank, was the pastor at the Second Congregational Church, remembers Mary E. Oliver, the town's welfare agent who worked for the selectmen. "She was born and bred here and knew every family in town. She knew whether or not you were really needy. You couldn't pull the wool over her eyes." The townspeople themselves often looked after each other. Louis N. Simeone recalls that when someone noticed that a family needed food, he would get a voucher from town hall, buy the groceries, and deliver them to the family.

Although a strong community spirit prevailed, the town was divided by ethnicity, neighborhood, and social class. Cohasset was predominantly Yankee. The old families included such names as Bates, Beal, James, Lincoln, Litchfield, Lothrop, Nichols, Pratt, Ripley, Souther, Stoddard, Tower, Wheelwright, and Whitcomb. Many "natives" (commonly understood to mean those whose families went back at least two or three generations in Cohasset) could trace their family tree to the seventeenth and early eighteenth centuries, when Cohasset was still part of Hingham. There were also Portuguese from the Azores, who came here as crew for Cohasset fishing schooners in the mid-1800s and settled near the Cove; Irish, who immigrated here at about the same time and lived mostly on Lincoln Hillside, between Smith Place and Oak Street; and Italians, who came from two neighboring villages in Calabria in the early 1900s and lived on King Street and, later, on Hull Street. By 1950 a number of Canadians from the maritime provinces had also moved to Cohasset.

Most residents in the early fifties were either natives or "townies," people who made their living in Cohasset, many of them longtime employees in town departments. A rapidly growing number of residents were commuters who worked in the greater Boston metropolitan area. The shift from local employment had begun on a smaller scale in the early 1900s, after the collapse of Cohasset's shipbuilding and mackerel-fishing industries around 1895. The railroad, brought to Cohasset in 1849, made it possible to commute to jobs out of town.

Some of the summer "cottages" on Jerusalem Road and Atlantic Avenue, built by wealthy Bostonians in the late nineteenth and early twentieth centuries, had been converted to full-time residences in the 1930s and 1940s. During the tough times of the Depression, it was more economical to move to Cohasset, where taxes were lower and the lifestyle simpler, and commute to work in the city. After World War II the trend accelerated. Some of those who could not afford to maintain the dual lifestyle of their parents chose to winterize the family home and live here year round. But surprisingly, in the early fifties about 400 families still vacationed in Cohasset during the summer, increasing the total number of families by roughly 35 percent; the rest of the year, summer residents lived in places like Newton and Brookline. In winter most shore houses were shuttered and empty.

In June Cohasset grew lively again as children, out of school for the summer, played on the Common and rode their bikes around town. Noel A. Ripley, a native who grew up near the center of town, recalls that kids from each neighborhood had their own hangouts. There were the Jerusalem Road/Atlantic Avenue set, the Beechwooders, the Hillsiders, and the North Cohasset/Hull Street kids. Those who lived in the Jerusalem Road/Atlantic Avenue area sailed at the Yacht Club and played tennis on private courts. The kids who lived on Lincoln Hillside and around the town center met at Call's Drugstore, which had an old-fashioned soda fountain. Another group gathered at the Common, and still others hung out at the Cove. You could always find a more social crowd, a cross-section of young people, down at Sandy Beach.

People look back on the fifties with nostalgia for its easy sociability, with parties every weekend. There were progressive dinners, where different courses were served in different homes; masquerade parties; cocktail parties; Saturday night dances at the Yacht Club, the Golf Club, and Dreamwold in Scituate; and Subscription Dance Club dinner dances during the winter. There was also gossip of "key parties" and swinging times among a group with too much money and leisure. But for the most part Cohasset's social life was convivial and fun, a welcome release from the austerity and restrictions of World War II. Ebullient optimism characterized the mood: "Young people in the 1950s thought that everything was going to be wonderful," says Molly Bowditch. "They were looking forward to the best of everything—great jobs, great homes, and so on. Everything seemed possible." This confidence in the American Dream, the naive belief that greater material comfort guaranteed the "good life," would change within another decade.

Artist Tom Lucas and his wife, Lois, at a Beaux Arts Ball in the 1950s. The cocktail parties and dances so prevalent in the 1950s were a welcome contrast to the austerity of the World War II years. Photo courtesy of Torrey Capo

Glad to be home again and eager to start their families, men and women returning from World War II and the Korean War married young. At its lowest point in 1956, the median age at marriage for men was 22.5, and for women 20.1; thus half of all brides in the mid-1950s were still in their teens. They had children early and usually completed their families by their late twenties, launching the famous baby boom generation (born between 1946 and 1964). Typically couples had three or four children; father was the breadwinner and mother stayed at home. Postwar prosperity, low inflation, and low-interest government-backed mortgages enabled many young couples to leave the cities and raise their families in the secure environment of the suburbs. Cohasset, with its beautiful rocky coastline, wooded parks, sunny beaches, and picturesque harbor and Town Common, was a desirable place to bring up children, and plenty of new homes were becoming available.

Until this time the town's population had been inching up over the years. It had taken 50 years, from 1900 to 1950, for the population to rise from 2,759 to 3,731, an increase of 35 percent. But in the single decade of the fifties, it shot up by almost 57 percent, from 3,731 to 5,840. The number of children in the Cohasset schools more than doubled, from 655 in 1950 to 1,427 in 1960. The number of housing units increased by nearly one-third, and development was just beginning. The small rural town of Cohasset would never again be the same.

RURAL COHASSET

In the early 1950s some Cohasset neighborhoods were like little country villages. This was true of the older section of Beechwood, west of Bound Brook (also known as the Beechwood River). Jeanette C. (Lincoln) Somerville, a native of Cohasset who grew up in Beechwood and still lives there, notes that until the 1960s the neighborhood was much smaller. It consisted primarily of farmhouses and two-family homes on Beechwood, Doane, and Church streets and Mill Lane. The residents were farmers, fishermen, plumbers, painters, masons, mechanics, salesmen, and storekeepers. "No professionals, except for the minister," says Jeanette. "Now the area is much more built up and has attracted doctors, lawyers, and teachers."

Beechwood had its own post office and general store, a fire station, a cemetery, a ballpark, a library, a community center, and a neighborhood church. E. Harold Brown's General Store on Beechwood Street, between Doane and Church streets, sold everything from bicycles to sides of beef to penny candy. It also had a soda fountain, and two gasoline pumps out front. "If we don't have it, you don't need it" was the slogan. The Brown family ran the store until the 1970s (as of 1999 family members still live on the second floor). Inside the store was the post office, which closed in the mid-fifties when the U.S. Post Office planned to start using ZIP codes and shut down many satellite offices. Nearby on Doane Street, you could buy bread, milk, eggs, ice cream, and candy at Tom Cummings's Variety Store.

For several years Leo J. Fiori was the rural mail carrier for part of Beechwood and the west end of Scituate. He not only picked up and delivered mail but also sold stamps and handled packages and money orders while on his route. Houses had been assigned street numbers since 1939, a year before mail delivery service began. Yet a complete address for this neighborhood consisted merely of the addressee's name and the words *Cohasset R.F.D.* (rural free delivery). Leo knew everyone on his route. People could leave money in their mailbox and a note asking him to get them a carton of cigarettes or some other small item. Occasionally he would find a dozen eggs left for him by the lady who lived on a chicken farm. "Those were the best working days of my life," he says.

The Cohasset chapter of the Grange, a farmers' organization, was formed in 1939, with Arthur Somerville as its first "Master." It met twice a month at the Beechwood Improvement Association (BIA) Hall across from the cemetery. Founded to promote cooperation among farmers, the Grange also nurtured social interaction and family life. Men from Beechwood used to attend meetings at the hall and play whist. The Grange was at its height at the end of World War II, when a quarter of U.S. workers were farmers. The family farm declined in Cohasset as in the rest of the country, becoming uneconomical as large corporate farms took over. The Grange in Cohasset functioned until 1971, when the building inspector ordered the hall closed for lack of bathroom facilities.

The largest farm in Beechwood was Frank Wheelwright's Walnut Grove Farm in Cherry Valley. The original farmhouse is still at 312 Beechwood Street. Until 1948 Wheelwright grew market vegetables, which he sold at Faneuil Hall in Boston. When that became unprofitable, he turned to dairy farming, milking about 70 cows. The farm had a milk route in the 1950s, and cows grazed in pastures where the Wheelwright Farm condominiums now stand.

Howard Bates's piggery was at the end of what is now Riverview Drive. As many as a thousand pigs were also kept deep within what are now woods behind Mill Lane. The pigs were sold at market in Boston, and the manure was used to fertilize neighboring farms. Bates, who was also Cohasset's tree warden, collected garbage from local restaurants to feed his pigs, occasionally finding treasures in the slop. His most spectacular find was Eleanor

Bleakie's diamond ring, buried in the refuse from Hugo's Lighthouse Restaurant. Bates stopped raising pigs in the fifties, when the state passed a law requiring farmers to cook the garbage they fed their swine.

1. *Porcine residents of Howard Bates's piggery enjoying their slop.* Photo courtesy of Becky Bates-McArthur 2. *Richardson White loading logs for his sawmill at Holly Hill Farm in the late 1950s.* Photo courtesy of Ed Long 3. *A towering stack of railroad ties for the traditional July 3 bonfire at the Beechwood ballfield.* Photo courtesy of Ray Sargent 4. *Deborah Bates tending crops at her family farm in the 1950s.* Photo courtesy of Becky Bates-McArthur 5. *E. Harold Brown taking last delivery of mail for satellite post office at Brown's Store.* Photo courtesy of Merle Brown 6. *Brown's General Store on Beechwood Street. "If we don't have it, you don't need it" was the slogan.* Photo courtesy of Becky Bates-McArthur 7. *Tom Cummings's Variety Store on Doane Street. Cummings sold staples like bread, milk, and eggs. It closed in 1956.* Photo courtesy of Becky Bates-McArthur 8. *Italian farmer Antonio Rosano plowing his field near Rosano Lane in the 1950s.* Photo courtesy of Ann Pompeo

Beechwood was like an extended family, and in fact many people were related. Everyone came out for neighborhood events. Thomas C. Stoddard has vivid memories of summer fairs with pony rides and church lawn parties at Billings-Pratt Park. Every July third, a huge bonfire was built at second base in the ballpark near the BIA Hall and the fire station. It was a polygonal mound of old railroad ties, piled 35 feet high. As Raymond C. Sargent recalls, "The fire was so hot and so high that you had to water down neighboring houses." The tradition ended when hot embers landed on the roof of Town Accountant Malcolm H. Stevens's home.

Turtle races sponsored by the church and held at the park were another Beechwood tradition. Children would catch five or six turtles in Lily Pond or Bound Brook, receiving a dollar for each. The turtles would be placed in a container set in the center of a miniature circus ring with a board for a floor, surrounded by a three-to-four-inch-high circular metal ring. The ring was about six feet in diameter and had numbered openings. Bets were placed on the numbers. At the beginning of the race, the turtles would be released. One or two would crawl a short distance and then stop, the crowd wildly cheering them on. A few would make their way toward the edge of the ring. Finally one would broach an opening, and the person holding the number of that opening would win a prize. The games were eventually stopped by a minister who took a dim view of the gambling.

The BIA Hall, at 502 Beechwood Street, was the heart of the community. Not only Grange meetings but square dances, minstrel shows, political rallies, bridal showers, dancing lessons, Saturday movies for children, and summer Sunday School classes were held there. The BIA assembled its own baseball team from the neighborhood, and even housed a branch of the Paul Pratt Memorial Library at the rear of the hall. Over time, however, membership in the association declined and, as mentioned earlier, the building was closed for health reasons. In 1978 the BIA sold it to a local couple, who converted it to a residence. The following year members Herbert P. Bates, Percival M. James, and Charles R. Stoddard used proceeds from the sale to set up a $4,000 trust fund to be administered by the Cohasset Recreation Department "for the perpetual benefit of youth from the Beechwood neighborhood."

North Cohasset, at the other end of town, was also a unique neighborhood. Like Beechwood, North Cohasset had its own library, post office, and fire station, the latter two sharing the same building on Hull Street until the post office closed in 1972; the Nantasket Library closed in 1983. In the early 1950s the North Cohasset Fire Station was manned by Edward J. Fitzpatrick and James L. Happenny, who also operated a blacksmith shop across the street. When an alarm sounded, they would dash to the station, don their firefighting gear, and command the fire truck. The station was closed in 1981.

Hull Street, originally settled in the nineteenth century, saw the arrival of Italian immigrants between 1928 and 1932. Typically the men found jobs as caretakers, landscapers, and gardeners for the large estates in town, and many worked at Oaks Farm on Sohier Street. James W. Lagrotteria's parents came to Cohasset from Italy in 1930. Italian was spoken at home, and Jim spoke Italian until he went to school. Children in the neighborhood called everyone Cousin, Aunt, or Uncle even if they were not related. People of his parents' generation brought with them the customs of the old country. Jim described one of the traditions kept by the neighborhood into the early 1950s:

> Families raised pigs on vacant land off Lamberts Lane. Around the first of December, before winter set in, the pigs would be slaughtered. We would set huge drums of water to boil over roaring fires in our backyards. The pigs would be immersed in the boiling water and the skin scraped clean. The kids had to keep the fires going for three days. It was three or four days of hard work as well as singing, drinking homemade wine, and sharing.
>
> The whole pig would be used—the skin as well as the meat. The meat was prepared in the cellar. Families would make sausage and bacon, and lard from the scraps. The sausage would be hung in the cellar or in one of three smokehouses on Hull Street, where the ham was cured.

The meat would last us all winter, along with potatoes, turnips, beets, and carrots grown in backyard gardens and stored in root cellars.

All this faded away in the late fifties as the older folks ran out of energy and the younger ones went to college, married, and moved away. By the end of the decade the tradition was over and gone.

North Cohasset had its own social clubs. The Hull Street Neighborhood Association was a club exclusively for residents of Hull Street and Lamberts Lane, and included Irish and Yankees as well as Italians. The clubhouse was the lower floor of the Nantasket Library at "West's Corner," on the southwest corner of Hull Street and Jerusalem Road, near the site where Charles West had built a department store in the 1800s. It was a social club, hosting potluck suppers every four months, but it also sponsored the building of a playground on Hull Street in 1947 for the neighborhood children.

The West Corner Men's Club (at one time a barber shop) was, and still is, a card club. It began with the first Italians who moved to the area. Since the men who worked for Oaks Farm and the Jerusalem Road estates had little to do in the winter, they played cards and made wine. The Men's Club was a place to meet and "network." The women did not have a comparable club—they were too busy at home.

Beechwood and North Cohasset were two communities that gave Cohasset a rustic quality in the 1950s. Closer to the center of town were the estates of gentlemen farmers, embedded within older residential neighborhoods. Clarence W. Barron, founder of the financial publication *Barron's Weekly* and owner of the *Wall Street Journal*, established Oaks Farm in 1900 behind what is now the Deer Hill School on Sohier Street. It was a dairy farm, comprising several hundred acres of pastureland on both sides of Sohier Street, including the present Fairoaks Lane residential area. At its height in the 1920s, the farm, which produced Guernsey certified milk, had 200 cows, 20 buildings, 60 acres of corn, and 25 full-time employees. Pauline A. Keating remembers when three or four men from Oaks Farm would pick up a new shipment of cows and bulls down at the railroad station on Depot Court and drive the cattle up Pleasant Street to the back fields of the farm. Although operating at a smaller scale in the 1950s, Oaks Farm still produced milk and hired local youths, mostly to pull weeds in the cornfields, clean the stables, and bring in hay.

The other large farm in Cohasset was Richardson ("Dick") White's Holly Hill Farm at 190 Jerusalem Road. White was the fifth generation of his family to own the property, which in his time consisted of 200 acres. His great-great grandfather Thomas Richardson bought the original homestead from Henry Doane in 1845. The homestead has since disappeared, but you can still see its stone gateposts on Jerusalem Road. The farm property is being brought back to life as a "community" organic farm by one of Dick's sons, Frank H. White, who grew up there and shares his father's love for the land.

Most of Holly Hill Farm was wooded with oak, maple, and holly. At the edge of the woods was a large ice pond, framed on one side by a dramatic 50-foot-high granite ledge outcropping. Open fields and meadows provided pasturage for White's horses and a refuge for hawks and owls, pheasant and quail, and songbirds and ocean birds. In 1980 White and his sister, Mrs. Charles C. Cabot, donated 120 acres of Holly Hill's woods, saltmarshes, and fields to the Trustees of Reservations, to be preserved as open space.

In the 1930s and 1940s White cultivated a hundred acres in widely scattered parts of Cohasset and Scituate. He stopped farming in the late 1940s, when it became uneconomical, and began to harvest timber. He operated a sawmill on the farm, sold cordwood, cleared land, and cut hay for farm horses and saddle horses until his death in 1993. Using equipment he made himself, he dragged felled trees from properties off Forest Avenue and Nichols Road, where homes were being built. The lumber from those trees, "still dripping with sap," as Frank recalls, was fabricated into houses on the same land where they had grown. White also made lobster pots for local fishermen and raised and kept horses for pleasure. He is best remembered as a sculptor of small bronze horses, winning three medals from the National Sculpture Society for his work.

Other farmers in Cohasset raised poultry or pigs. Cedar Acres Turkey Farm at 376 North Main Street, owned by Arnold G. Erickson, sold eggs, roasting chickens, and turkey pies. William T. Barnes raised pigs at 336 North Main Street and also had a piggery on Forest Avenue. By the end of the decade, however, few people remained in farming. The number of men who identified them-selves as farmers, dairymen, or poultrymen in the Cohasset List of Persons dropped from 18 in 1950 to 7 in 1959.

Lobster Fishing

In the eighteenth and nineteenth centuries most people in Cohasset made their living from farming, fishing, and shipbuilding. The ship-building industry ended in the late 1800s, and farming all but dis-appeared in the 1950s. Only lobster fishing has continued to be viable. In the fifties, however, you could not support a family sole-ly on fishing. Parker Malley was an electrician as well as a lob sterman; brothers Herbert L. and Kenneth Jason worked for the Bethlehem Steel Shipyard in Quincy; Charles E. Butman Jr. ("Junie") built and repaired boats in his shop on Spring Street. Every winter near Cunningham Bridge you could smell the fragrance of a wood fire and wood shavings from the Chutes' beautiful paneled barn, where Louis Figueiredo was allowed to build boats when the fam ily resided in Boston.

Oldtimers in Cohasset's fishing community can still name all the fishermen of the past half-century. Besides the Jasons, Junie Butman, and Parker Malley, there were several members of the Figueiredo, Grassie, and Silvia families, as well as Ralph Barrows, Ken Boylston, Harry Coyne, Johnny DeRocha, Earle Higgins, Frank Lean, John Pattison, Arnold and Alonzo Pearson, Carl Perry, Bernard and Manuel Salvador, Sheldon Sladen (who drowned in 1996), John Small, Bill Stone, Frank Stover, and Bert Tilden.

Herb Jason has been trapping lobsters for 70 years. In the days before fiberglass, Herb and other fishermen built their own boats from local white oak. These were open boats about 30 feet long, powered by gasoline engines. Falling overboard from one of these could be fatal if you fished alone, because the high freeboard made it difficult to climb back up. Ladders over the stern were added later. Fishing was, and still is, a dangerous occupation. It is rated by the Bureau of Labor Statistics as the single most deadly occupation, with fatality rates 20 to 30 times those of all other occupations.

Herb tells of going out one November with a 15-year-old assistant. They got caught in rough seas with strong northeast winds. Enormous waves battered their boat and swamped it. Herb knew that if they remained onboard, the boat would flip on top of them. The boy was too frightened to jump, so Herb pushed him out and followed him into the sea. He remembers going under the bubbling green water and grabbing the boy by the hair to pull him up. They swam to Brush Island, the waves threatening to dash them against the slippery rocks. They finally got up and later made it to shore—"but I hated to lose that boat," he says.

William G. Stone, another longtime lobsterman, recalls that in the fifties the entire fishing fleet consisted of about 15 wooden boats, all moored at the Cove. Fishing was low-technology: no automatic haulers or modern depth sounders and global positioning satellite systems. You wound your trawl lines by hand around a revolving drum, and you memorized the contours of the ocean floor, relying on information from other fishermen to find the best spots. The men typically fished close to shore along the beaches and ledges. High school and college students, as well as fishermen, would also go out in dories to gather Irish moss, or carrageen, from the ledges, using rakes to pull the fronds off the rocks outside Cohasset harbor. After they dried the moss on Bassing Beach, they would sell their haul to Lucien Rousseau of Scituate. Food and drug companies would buy it from him for use as a binder in cosmetics, medication, toothpaste, and puddings. A. J. Antoine recalls that when he was a child, some local families used to make a cough remedy from moss tea and lemon.

Most lobstermen in the fifties fished alone and handled 100 to 125 wooden lobster traps, which they painstakingly repaired during the slow winter months. Today lobstering has become a two- or three-man operation, so that one boat can handle as many as 1,000 to 2,000 traps. Modern fishermen use long-lasting wire traps, which they drop four to five miles out to sea. "The ocean floor is covered with them," says Stone. The lobstering business used to be passed down from generation to generation, he notes. It took skill and experience to make a living from the sea. Now, with wire traps and electronic equipment, Stone believes it has become almost too easy. It has also become so profitable that overfishing threatens the industry. In 1995 Cohasset was ranked tenth in lobster catch in the state, with 570,000 pounds landed; by 1998 our rank dropped to fifteenth, with a catch of only 350,000 pounds. Cohasset is one of the last coastal towns where people who fish from the town also live here. About 35 fishing boats were registered in the harbor in 1998. If the lobster population crashed, Cohasset would lose its fishing fleet, and much of its color and character.

THE COVE

One of the most popular hangouts for fishermen and other locals was Polly's Sea Grille Restaurant and Tavern at the Cove, adjacent to Gaetano Bufalo's Liquor Store and across from Manuel Marks's Mobil Gas Station on Elm Street. Polly's had a reputation as a

The infamous Polly's Sea Grille Restaurant and Tavern in 1950. The lively barroom burned down in the late 1950s and the site is a vacant lot across from Kimball's-by-the-Sea.

Photo courtesy of Richard Barrow

rowdy place. Gilbert S. Tower, a local historian, cartographer, and engineer, once referred to it as that "vile bar room" in one of his many opinion pieces. It was known familiarly as the Cleaver Club, for the meat cleaver that hung behind the bar, and patrons also euphemistically called it Polly's Tea Room. In the late 1950s it was destroyed by fire and torn down. The lot, directly across from Kimball's-by-the-Sea Motel, has been vacant for the past 40 years.

The Cove was "where the action was," according to Richard ("Dickie") P. Barrow, a police officer who patrolled the area in the fifties. The restaurants, bars, and eateries were packed until 1:00 or 2:00 a.m. In the evening policeman A. J. Antoine directed traffic in his white gloves as customers from Cohasset, Scituate, and Hull crowded the parking lot at Hugo's Lighthouse Restaurant on

Manny Marks's Gas Station at the corner of Elm and Border. Photo courtesy of Pasquale Gentile

Border Street or Kimball's Lobster Shop and Hugo's Shack. Kimball's and the Shack were located on a large, paved triangle of land at the western end of the Cove. The Shack faced Border Street, while Kimball's was directly on the water. Kimball's incorporated a much older structure built in 1823 to house the old Tilden Ironworks, which assembled the iron framework for the original Minot's Ledge Lighthouse. The restaurant, built over a wharf in 1922, contained several trap doors through which local bootleggers hauled up liquor from rumrunners during Prohibition. Nearby was Cohasset's Central Fire Station, at the site of the present Memorial Park, across from the American Legion Hall. At the corner of Elm and Border

The Memorial Day Parade passes the old Central Fire Station located on the present-day site of Veterans' Memorial Park. Photo courtesy of Ray Sargent

streets was Marks's Gas Station. (Most of that area is now occupied by Kimball's Motel and its parking lot.)

John G. Carzis owned and operated Hugo's Lighthouse, Kimball's, and the Shack, having bought them in 1948 from the estate of the previous owner, Hugo Ormo. The Lighthouse was renowned for its "fine dining" and view of the harbor; the Shack, a gathering place for the teenage and college crowd, was a favorite spot for lobster sandwiches and hot fudge sundaes. You could also get ice cream and sandwiches at Grace Silvia's

Seahorse Restaurant at 114 Elm Street, and listen to the latest hits on the jukebox. You could buy groceries and other convenience goods at Annie Silvia's Variety Store at 95 Elm Street.

The Old Salt House Lobster Shop on Border Street sold fresh Cohasset lobsters, clams, and oysters. Owned by Jessie Bancroft Cox, it was run by Frank Stover and later by Charles and Alice Antoine. In its original state the building was Samuel Bates's salt house, dating back to 1750. It was used to store salt from Cohasset's old salt works at Sandy Cove, Quarry Point, and Sandy Beach. Fishermen used the salt to preserve mackerel that they packed in barrels for market. In 1974 Jessie Cox deeded the Salt House to the Conservation Trust, which sold it to Cohasset resident Thomas Eisenstadt in 1988. Both Hugo's Lighthouse and the Salt House are now part of Atlantica, a new gourmet restaurant owned by Cohasset resident Peter Roy.

THE VILLAGE

In the early 1950s Cohasset village was the major shopping center for the town. One could buy most necessities, including groceries, clothing, and hardware, in the village. There were three grocery stores, three clothing stores, and two hardware stores. There were also three restaurants, a liquor store, two drugstores, two beauty salons, three banks, a newspaper store, a real estate office, a jeweler's shop, a shoe repair shop, a dry cleaners, a barber, a dentist, and a doctor's office next to the Community Center. On the corner of Ripley Road and Sohier Street, not far from the Community Center, was the Cohasset Private Hospital, where numerous Cohasset residents were born (the last baby born there, in 1952, was Lynne Pape). The building was later converted to the Ripley Road Nursing Home, and then to a private residence after the nursing home closed in 1992.

You could buy appliances and get your radio or television repaired in the village, buy a new car at two dealerships, and service it at two gas stations. The police station was in the center of town, in the Independence Building; the post office and telephone exchange were nearby, on Deport Court. At the western end of

Depot Court, where the Art Center is now located, stood the New York, New Haven & Hartford Railroad Station. In 1951 the station was moved 80 feet north on Ripley Road, and a portion of the building was converted to commercial use; it still exists, in 1999, as Bernard's Restaurant at 107 Ripley Road.

Two smaller, abandoned stations had been remodeled as

The Cohasset Railroad Station, built in 1885, being moved 80 feet north on Ripley Road in 1951. Photos courtesy of Joel Pratt

Next door, in the "flatiron building," was Bailey's Delicatessen. Proprietors Alden and Betty Bailey stand outside their establishment in the 1950s. Photo courtesy of Betty Ripley

private residences in 1940: the old Beechwood Station is now at 40 Beechwood Street, a few hundred feet west of its original location; the Black Rock Station, relocated from the junction of North Main and King streets, sits next door at 44 Beechwood Street.

It is hard to imagine Cohasset village so crammed with shops and services. In some cases two businesses shared the same space. Pilgrim Co-operative Bank and Rockland Trust, for example, both occupied the ground floor at 48 South Main Street, next to D.S. Campbell, Jeweler. Some businesses were located on the second floor of buildings. William Raymond's Cohasset Radio and Television Sales and Service and the Sarah Lawrence Beauty Salon were above Delory's Drugstore at 56 South Main Street. Elizabeth Bristol's Sportswear Shop occupied the first and second floors at 62 South Main Street, next to Reddy's Garage and his Tydol Gas

Station on Brook Street. The office of Dr. William Matteson, the school dentist, was located above Reddy's Garage. (The Cohasset schools had dental clinics, where Dr. Matteson cleaned, filled, and extracted students' teeth. In 1968, 12 years after fluorides were added to town water, the clinics closed.)

The telephone exchange was on the second floor over the post office at 9 Depot Court. It was a manual system, requiring as many as four switchboard operators to direct calls, until rotary dialing was installed in 1958. The operator would ask, "Number, please?" when you placed a call. Then she would connect you to the number you requested or, if you did not know or could not remember, to a neighbor based on name only. In an emergency she would patch you through to the police or fire station without the number. Operator Pauline A. Keating would serve as a personal call-forwarding system and direct an incoming call to you when you were out visiting a neighbor. She would also provide up-to-the-minute information on what was going on in the center of town.

People could catch up on local news around the corner at Ralph P. ("Pete") Williams's Cohasset Restaurant (5 South Main Street). "Pete's was a real institution in town," says Frank White, whose father, Richardson, had breakfast there nearly every morning, hobnobbing with fishermen and town officials. The restaurant, which Pete owned since 1934, looked like a Norman Rockwell painting of small-town America: Pete would stand at the counter in back, while the local folk sat talking and eating at two booths in the middle of the room or at tables on each side. The business declined in the early 1960s when Pete's son tried to expand it into the A&P's space next door. It got too big, and lost its character and customers.

The Red Lion Inn at 71 South Main Street was a popular restaurant and bar, frequented by Music Circus celebrities as well as townspeople. It was originally a farmhouse, built by Thomas James in 1704. Later James's son Christopher enlarged and converted it to the Red Lion Inn. It was also known at various times as the Norfolk House, the Central House, and the Hillside Inn. According to Robert N. Fraser, former curator of Cohasset's Maritime Museum, the inn was also used as a way station for runaway slaves before the Civil War and contained a secret staircase up to the second floor. In 1949 Murray and Grace Cone bought and restored the old building. Some residents wistfully remember the 99-cent lunches. When the price rose to $1.29, patrons were outraged.

Norman C. Card, a selectman, was the grocery manager at the First National Store, where Tedeschi's Food Shop is now located. In those days there was no self-service. You gave the grocer your shopping list. Norman, known as the Sliding Grocer, would race down the aisles, grab the items, and slide back to the counter on the sawdust-covered floor. As he bagged the order, he would jot down the price of each item on the bag; then he would run his finger down the column, adding it on the fly, and come up with the right total. Norman lived across the street, in half of the two-family home that is now Cards & Shards Gift Shop and Heads-N-Tails Pet Grooming. The Sliding Grocer's life came to a sad but somehow appropriate end on Christmas Eve 1960, when he died skating on Lily Pond.

If you wanted something special for dinner, you could shop at Central Market, now French Memories Bakery (64 South Main Street). It provided personal service and the best meat in town, catering to the wealthy, who often had orders delivered to their homes. Unwittingly these customers contributed to the store's eventual demise. Not wanting to write frequent checks, some habitually allowed their bills to accumulate over several months. The result was a disastrously irregular cash flow, and the market finally failed in the 1980s.

A few stores dating back to the fifties and earlier have retained their identities. Fleming's Marine Hardware, at 24 Elm Street, sold gifts as well as marine hardware. It is Fleming's Gift and Lamp Shop today. A historic building, it was originally a residence built by James Stutson and his son Benjamin around 1762. His grandson added a second floor and then a third. The third floor was fashioned from an old schoolhouse believed to be the North School, which once stood at the corner of North Main Street and Jerusalem Road, one of several district schools that existed in Cohasset before

1890. The neighbors, bemused by the apparently endless enlargement, called the house Stutson's Folly. A storefront was added, and in 1931 it became Fleming's Marine Hardware, owned by Edward, John, and Mary Fleming until 1983.

Across the street, next to Carlos ("Charlie") Tanger's little barbershop, was the imposing Cohasset Savings Bank, on the corner of Elm and Brook streets. This classical building, designed by Cohasset architect Edward Nichols in 1898, is still a bank, now the Hingham Institution for Savings. Up the street, at the corner of Elm and South Main, was and still is the Cohasset Hardware Store. Originally Samuel Bates's Tin Shop, established in 1849, it was converted to a hardware store in the 1880s by Allen Collier Bates. In 1912 the store was sold to William H. McGaw, a local builder. (McGaw also owned the historic Captain John Wilson House at 4 Elm Street, which he donated to the Cohasset Historical Society in 1936.) When McGaw died in 1958, he left the business to his employees Robert and Helen Collier, descendants of the original owners. In 1965 Cohasset Hardware was bought by Louis Watson and his wife, Helen, whose children Tina and James ("Benjie") still run it today.

At 29 South Main Street was Simeone's Liquor Store. In the 1950s it was owned by Nicholas Simeone, who lived in a 10-room apartment above and behind the store. In continuous use as a package store, it is Village Wine & Spirits today (1999). Anna A. Abbruzzese, Simeone's daughter, remembers her next-door neighbor Edith Grassie, who lived in the old Samuel Bates House, built in 1811. Edie ran the Cohasset Taxi Service from her living room. Although she herself did not drive, Edie had two taxis, Dodge sedans, and always rode with the driver. She knew most of the passengers, many of whom were regulars. Her drivers would take people from the train station to their homes. If a driver was unavailable, she would grab anyone off the street and press them into service. She even recruited Anna, who at the time did not have a license and could not drive. Nevertheless, she obligingly took the driver's seat next to Edie and taxied the passengers home.

The village was bustling with shoppers in the 1950s. With all the new people moving into town, why not build more stores? In 1956 Cohasset developer Joseph Kealey bought the old St. John property between Joe Caro's Coffee Shop and the A&P, and built a new Village Shopping Center right in the middle of downtown. It was big enough for seven stores. Rockland Trust moved there from across the street, and new businesses came in: Jay's of Boston, Thayer McNeil Shoe Store, a beauty salon, a gift shop, a five-and-ten-cent store, and Cora Chandler's Ladies Wear. The

Downtown Cohasset, 1955 and 2000 looking north from the corner of Main Street and Brook Street. 1955 photo courtesy of Neil Murphy, 2000 photo courtesy of Ralph Dormitzer

Historical Society even picked a name for the walkway and courtyard in front of the stores: Stagecoach Way, commemorating the fact that before 1850 the stage coach would stop nearby to pick up passengers for the Hingham steamboat. The selectmen, who presided over the ribbon-cutting ceremony, were confident that the new town parking lot, built in 1950 on property acquired from the railroad, would be a great boon to business.

Downtown Cohasset, 1954 and 2000 looking south from the corner of Main Street and Depot Court. 1954 photo courtesy of Neil Murphy, 2000 photo courtesy of Ralph Dormitzer

Downtown Businesses, 1950 and 1998

1950	1998	Address
Social Service League Thrift Shop	Lilac House	76 South Main St.
Red Lion Inn	Red Lion Inn	71 South Main St.
Kerr Motors "Your Friendly Ford Dealer"	Olympic Texaco	55 South Main St.
2-family home owned by William H. McGaw; pharmacist and Norman Card lived there	Cards & Shards	45 South Main St.
	Heads-N-Tails Pet Gooming	41 South Main St.
Cohasset Taxi Service operated from Edith Grassie's living room	Really Great Pizza (RGP)	35 South Main St.
Sydney S. Gates Clothing Store Simeone's Liquor Store	Village Wine & Spirits	27/29 South Main St.
Ruth's Shoppe, ladies' and children's wearing apparel	Hernan Salon	25 South Main St.
Sherman Merrill's Dry Cleaning	Floral Gallery	23 South Main St.
Shoe repair shop	On-Line Cable Services	21A South Main St.
Joe's Coffee Shop	Circa Home Furnishings & Accessories	17 South Main St.
Old St. John house	Hunneman's real estate and Stagecoach Way businesses	11 South Main St. Stagecoach Way
A&P Grocery Store	Fitness First Plus	7 South Main St.
Cohasset Restaurant	The Silver Spoon Cafe	5 South Main St.
Cohasset News Co.	Goodale Company Insurance	3 South Main St.
Call's Drug Store Cohasset Colonial Pharmacy in 1954	Farsh Oriental Rugs	1 South Main St.
Independence Building Police Station	Independence Building	South Main & Elm St.
August Petersen's Real Estate	Lilac House Antiques	26 South Main St.
Cohasset Hardware Co.	Cohasset Hardware Co.	40 South Main St.
Pilgrim Co-operative Bank and Rockland Trust Co.	Pilgrim Co-operative Bank	48 South Main St.
D.S. Campbell, Jeweler	Pilgrim Co-operative Bank	50 South Main St.
First National Grocery Store	Tedeschi Food Shop	52 South Main St.
William Raymond's Cohasset Radio and Television Co. and Sarah Lawrence Beauty Salon, 2d floor above Delory's Delory's Drugstore	Ship Cove Park	56 South Main St.

Downtown Businesses, 1950 and 1998 *(continued)*

1950	1998	Address
Central Market	French Memories Bakery	64 South Main St.
Elizabeth Bristol's Sportswear 1st and 2d floors	Children's Exchange consignment shop Apartments	62 South Main St. .
Dr. William Matteson, dentist 2d floor above Reddy's Reddy's Garage Studebaker, Tydol gasoline	Dependable Cleaners	66 South Main St.
Masonic Hall, 2d floor	Masonic Hall, 2d floor	
Towle Electrical Co.	Nuth'n More Natural	5 Brook St.
Captain John Wilson Historic House	Captain John Wilson Historic House	4 Elm St.
Carlos ("Charlie") Tanger Barber Shop	Donna Green Studio	11 Elm St.
Cohasset Savings Bank	Hingham Institution for Savings	13 Elm St.
The Vanity Box Beauty Salon	Dean & Hamilton Realtors	18 Elm St.
Fleming's Marine Hardware and Gift Shop	Fleming's Gift Shop	24 Elm St.
Post Office Telephone Exchange, 2d floor	Atlantic Valuation Group	9 Depot Court
Bill Poland's Jenney Service Station	D J Nails Dramatic Kitchens & Sunroom Conservatories	22 Depot Court
Lincoln Bros. Coal & Oil	Strawberry Parfait bldg. moved later to 2 Pleasant St.	Entrance to parking lot
Cohasset Lumber Co.	ABB Optical [Target Industries]	1 Pleasant St.
Railroad Station	Bernard's Restaurant	107 Ripley Road
Jason's Color Centre paints and wallpaper	Edward Jones Investments	113 Ripley Road
Hyland & McGaw carpenters and builders	Decision Mortgage Prudential and Hallmark 100 real estate	103 Ripley Road
Clarence Patrolia & Sons builders and plumbers	Carousel Antiques	93 Ripley Road
Fred R. Burnside & Sons upholstery	Fred R. Burnside & Sons	Smith Place

THE HIGHWAY

What no one knew at the time was that Route 3A (Chief Justice Cushing Way) was destined to become the new center of commercial activity, ringing the death knell for many village businesses. Constructed in 1931, Route 3A, at that time a three-lane country road bordered by woods, was the main highway to Cape Cod. The portion that went through Cohasset bisected King Street, creating "two" King streets on both the north and south sides of 3A, although the 3A stretch is still labeled King Street.

Commercial development on Route 3A began near the Scituate line. The first building was Evans's Fish Market, near the corner of what is now Brewster Road and Route 3A, an area then known as Evansville. Next came Mitchell's Gulf Service Station, across from what is now Tedeschi Plaza. Francis L. Mitchell, who built the station with his father in 1946, remembers the time when gasoline cost only 18 cents a gallon and you could count the number of cars that traveled Route 3A to the Cape. Robert Cowdrie had a grocery store where Dwyer & Mullin Real Estate is now located (812A Route 3A), and Cohasset Liquors package store was built in 1949. Between Pond and Sohier streets was Kenneth Souther's Garage (now Peter Cappazoli's Cohasset Imports) and, across the street from the garage, his Konohassett Motel (now gone).

Until water service was extended to the highway around 1949, little development took place, but the pace quickened in the mid-fifties. In 1954 D.S. Kennedy, designers and manufacturers of large radar antennas, moved from 430 South Main Street to Whitney Hill (known more commonly as Scituate Hill or Town Hill) on Route 3A, where they built a 102,000-square-foot plant for administration, engineering, and light manufacturing. They did their heavy manufacturing at the Hingham Shipyard. The company became the world's largest antenna manufacturer and gained a worldwide reputation for radio telescopes and antenna systems designed to detect intercontinental ballistic missiles. Kennedy's radar antennas were deployed in northern Canada in the DEW (distant early warning) line to serve as an early warning system against attack from the Soviet Union.

The town's largest industry, over the years D.S. Kennedy employed more than a thousand people from Cohasset and other local communities. In 1963 it was acquired by another company and moved to California. John M. Seavey, who worked for Kennedy from 1956 to 1963, notes that the firm's pioneering experiments led to the development of improved two-way communications satellites, which enable us to telephone or send faxes anywhere in the world at any time. "Kennedy's great radar antennas still stand in Thule, Greenland; the Aleutian Islands; and England," says Seavey.

Another industrial plant on Route 3A, north of Sohier Street, was Weston and Kennedy, a maker of concrete products, which had been based in Rockland for 44 years and moved to Cohasset in 1959. The only other manufacturing industry in town was Francis W. Hagerty's Cohasset Colonials, at the harbor end of Parker Avenue. Originally a boat-building shop, "Hagerty's" made high-quality reproduction colonial furniture in "knocked-down" kits, which customers could reassemble themselves. The company, under new ownership, moved to Hingham in the early 1990s.

In 1954 the A&P moved from Cohasset village to the new Cushing Plaza at the corner of Beechwood Street and Route 3A, on property owned by Claude L. Rice. The relocation of the A&P marked the beginning of the shift of business away from the village to the highway. Steve Dwyer's Real Estate firm, the M.A. Street Insurance Company, and other stores and business offices soon filled the plaza. Commercial activity on Route 3A then migrated north of Beechwood Street. In 1956 Salvatore Signorelli and his son William opened the Deer Hill Snackery and Fish Market (later renamed Signorelli's Restaurant) on the King Street portion of 3A, where Ko Ko Island Restaurant is now located. Signorelli's remained a family-owned and operated business until 1974. JJ's Dairy Hut opened in 1959 at 140 Chief Justice Cushing Way, where it still stands today, and gas stations sprang up to service the growing number of automobiles.

By the late 1950s, postwar prosperity and cheap gasoline made cars more affordable. Families began to buy second cars. This further accelerated the decline of the village, as housewives could now hop in their cars and drive to Cushing Plaza. Brown's General Store in Beechwood and the small shops in the village slowly declined. Cars competed with the railroad as more commuters drove to work, siphoning customers away from downtown.

DEMISE OF THE RAILROAD

The Old Colony Railroad had taken passengers from Cohasset to Boston and back since 1849. In 1893 Old Colony became part of the New York, New Haven & Hartford Railroad (which went bankrupt in 1968 and was merged with Penn Central, which also declared bankruptcy two years later). In the mid-nineteenth century proximity to the train station was the magnet that attracted business from the Cove to the village. Shops were busiest when trains arrived in the morning and evening. Watching the steam locomotive chug into the station was a favorite pastime for Cohasset schoolboys until the railroads switched to diesel engines in the late 1940s and early 1950s.

We know that steam locomotives ran through Cohasset at least as late as 1949 from a *Boston Herald* account of "the year's oddest accident": One winter morning during a blinding snowstorm, Cohasset fireman Lot E. Bates was driving to work. Just as he was crossing the tracks on Beechwood Street, his car stalled. The next thing he knew, a steam locomotive had crashed into the side of his sedan. Pinned against the steering wheel, Lot was swept up into the train's cowcatcher and carried more than a mile down the tracks. Finally an alert flagwoman at the Smith Place grade crossing saw the wreckage and frantically waved at the engineer to stop. It took the train crew and Cohasset firemen 20 minutes to dig through the snow and ice and pry open the car to free Lot. Fortunately, despite broken bones and other injuries, he survived his harrowing ride.

Louis Eaton, Jr., notes that in the 1950s the train "made for a different kind of life. You could be in Boston by 8:20 a.m. if you took the 7:38 train, which went express from Hingham to South Station. If you made the 5:11 p.m. train back in the evening, you could be home before 6:00, leaving you time for your family. Fathers had more time with their kids that way." He also recalls the private club car at the rear of the train, for which members paid a special fee. The seats were comfortable, and porters served coffee and toast in the morning and cocktails in the evening.

The ride was not always enjoyable. Passengers in the late fifties complained that trains broke down, causing long delays; failed fuse boxes left commuters in darkness; broken air conditioners turned cars into ovens as they sat idle in the hot sun; and windows were so dirty you could not see out of them. The problem was that the Old Colony Line was losing money on its commuter service and could not afford to maintain its cars. George Alpert, president of the railroad, explained: "This is necessarily a deficit operation because it is a peak-hour business requiring crews that are paid on a daily basis for a few hours work and the use of equipment which stands idle 80 percent of the time" (*South Shore Mirror*, 9/19/57). The railroad depended on subsidies, and the state legislature finally refused to continue its support.

In June 1959 the Old Colony ran its last train to Boston. The *South Shore Mirror* described the final farewell from North Scituate. A small crowd gathered at the station to bid adieu to their old friend, and a bugler played taps. "As the train pulled away from North Scituate, the engineer kept the whistle going on the Buddliner [one of the newer single-unit diesel cars designed to improve commuter service] and a conductor waved from the rear platform. A bend in the tracks, and the Old Colony Railroad was no more." Bus service replaced the railroad. The Plymouth & Brockton Street Railway ran buses from Scituate and Cohasset to South Station and Park Square in Boston. David Wadsworth,

Poster courtesy of Hubert van der Lugt

who commuted to work in Boston, notes that many of the buses used at this time were old and not as comfortable or reliable as the trains.

A week before train service ended, the new link of the Southeast Expressway from Boston to South Hingham (Route 3) was opened. Throughout the United States new roads were being built. In 1956 the federal government had authorized construction of 42,500 miles of interstate highways connecting the nation's cities, and shiny new two-tone, chrome-trimmed automobiles with rear fins swept the country. By the end of the decade two of every three American workers drove to work. The car was king.

NEW FACES, NEW HOMES, NEW STREETS

Cars and highways made it possible to live in Cohasset and drive to work in Hingham, Weymouth, Quincy, and Boston as well as at the high-technology companies along Route 128. The commuters moving into Cohasset in the 1950s were part of the new middle class, the first college-educated postwar generation. They were managers, attorneys, engineers, salesmen, executives. Some came from places as distant as New Zealand and the Netherlands, adding diversity to the town. The newcomers, whether from far away or from New England, brought with them new ideas, new energy, and new talent.

Many in the first wave of families bought old summer homes on Atlantic Avenue and Jerusalem Road and winterized them. We can picture these dwellings from this description by John J. Rowlands, who lived on the shore in Cohasset:

> The beach house of the late eighteen hundreds was a comfortable rambling refuge, not only from the heat of the city, but from the formality and exacting demands of winter's social life. It made no pretense of reflecting the taste of its owner nor his culture. Its gloomy dark woodwork and sullen papered walls were usually bare of decoration. Pictures, if any, were prints of the day, such as "Stag at Bay," "Notre Dame Cathedral," "Scottish Highland Cattle," and perhaps some Godey prints.
>
> The old shore houses had many windows and spacious bedrooms, furnished as a rule with the brass-knobbed iron

beds and hard hair mattresses of the era. Here you found old commodes and painted pine bureaus, curtained clothes-closets, and window shades cobwebbed with fantastic patterns of cracks from flapping in the wind.

[From *Spindrift from a House by the Sea*, pp. 49 and 52]

Such homes had been heated on cool September evenings through a grate in the living room floor from a single-pipe wood-burning furnace in the cellar. Now they were updated with oil burners, insulation, and storm windows. Tennis courts and swimming pools were built on some properties. "It was right after the war, and we were all invincible," says Ann K. Whelan, who, with her husband, Jim, and their seven children, bought a former summer home on Atlantic Avenue and installed a new tennis court. "No one ever had a feeling they couldn't have everything they wanted" (*Cohasset Mariner*, 10/24/91).

New houses were also being built in Cohasset. During World War II, home construction had come to a standstill. A serious housing shortage faced returning service men and women. Eager to remedy the situation, developers bought up land outside cities, subdivided it into house lots, and constructed new homes. In Cohasset they bought large old Victorian estates from property owners who could no longer carry the tax burden. The land was subdivided and transformed into residential neighborhoods.

Ernest Howes's estate off Jerusalem Road was bought by Thomas Diab. In the 1950s Diab subdivided the property, converted the original outbuildings into new homes, and added several more on what became Howe Road, Diab Lane, and Tad Lane. The main building, the huge summer "cottage" originally owned by Boston financier Asa Potter (and later by Columbia bicycle and automobile manufacturer Colonel Albert A. Pope), was divided into 10 condominiums and named the Howe Estate. The outbuildings, fashioned in the style of English country houses with thick stone walls, small-paned windows, and gently curving roofs reminiscent of Cotswold thatched roofs, also became new homes. These included the original horse and cow barn, the piggery, the pheasantry, the dog kennels, the duck and chicken house, and the estate manager's house.

The Howe Estate, built for financier Asa Potter, later owned by Col. Albert Pope and Ernest Howes. Now condominiums. Photo from H. Langford Warren's Picturesque and Architectural New England

Competing for grandeur, Grenville Temple Winthrop Braman's estate comprised about a hundred acres between Jerusalem Road and Forest Avenue. Its Victorian stone mansion, originally called the Pool and now Stoneleigh, was designed for Braman by Boston architect Ralph William Emerson and built in 1886. Later bought by William Davidson, president of the A & P

stores in the 1930s, and then by Judge Pappas, owner of Suffolk Downs race track, it still exists at 478 Jerusalem Road as a private home. The casino and stable, with their large Romanesque stone arches, were converted into homes, as was the dog kennel (where music

Stoneleigh at 478 Jerusalem Road, built for G.T.W. Braman in 1886 and still a private home. Photo from H. Langford Warren's Picturesque and Architectural New England

had been piped in to soothe the prize German shepherds), the chicken house (with radiant-heated floors), and the cow barn. The backlands between Forest Avenue and what is now Linden Drive contained a forested deer park enclosed by a 10-foot-high fence, where guests had once hunted deer from carriages.

In 1947 Daniel J. Buckley bought several acres of land off Forest

Avenue and began to build houses. Until he piped water along the street, there had been only two houses in the middle, which utilized well water, and a few houses at the ocean end, which used Hingham water. The land was difficult to develop because of the rocky terrain and the swampy backlands. Despite the challenges, in the 1950s Buckley not only built eight houses on Forest Avenue and two on Forest Notch, but also created Linden Drive, with 27 houses, Linden Circle (4 houses), and Rustic Drive (no houses at that time) from the woodlands of the old Braman estate. Moving vans were a familiar sight as families took possession of the new Ranches, Cape Cod cottages, Garrison Colonial Revivals, and Split Levels.

Twenty-two houses on broadly distributed parts of Jerusalem Road and at least 10 on Nichols Road were also built in the 1950s. Charles Orchard Smith bought estate properties on Nichols Road and built several houses where previously there had been only woodlands, a few large estates, and a handful of smaller homes. He also converted the Caravels, an estate formerly owned by the McCormick family of Chicago, into 11 apartments; in 1987 they were made into 6 luxury condominiums. Joseph Kealey, the developer of Stagecoach Way in downtown Cohasset, also developed Jerusalem Lane. The architect Royal Barry Wills, who had developed Deep Run (the former Bolles estate), designed and built his classic New England Colonials and Capes on Fernway and Jerusalem Road. Donald E. Rust, cofounder of the Rust Craft Greeting Card Company, subdivided his land off Jerusalem Road and created Rust Way.

William E. Poland, owner and operator of the Jenney Gas Station on Depot Court in downtown Cohasset, developed Little Harbor Road on previously open land. With his partner Irwin Golden, a lawyer, he also developed Holly Lane (off Pond Street). Near the present high school on Pond Street, 34 new houses were constructed in the 1950s in what became known as the Pond Hill Veterans Development on Clay Spring, Bayberry, Tupelo, and Arrowwood roads. This area had been part of the former Town Farm on Pond Hill, which the town subdivided in 1947 and sold to returning World War II veterans, who built their own homes there. (The Town Farm lay behind the old Town Home on Pond Street, built in 1906 to shelter the poor. Transients could stay overnight and pay for their bunks by working on the farm the next day. Looking more like a hotel than a poorhouse, the Town Home was expensive to maintain and was torn down in 1943.) Reservoir Road, northeast of the Veterans area, was developed by Charles Howe, who managed Oaks Farm.

Other, smaller streets built up in the fifties include Stanton Road, off South Main Street, developed by Irwin Matthew; Hammond Avenue, off Beechwood Street, subdivided by Forrest ("Pop") E. Hammond; and nearby Locust Road, developed by Clarence Patrolia. Hammond Avenue and Locust Road were developed on what was formerly William Pratt's Homeland Dairy Farm. Some residents of the area still remember the barn, the creamery, and the large field where about 18 cows used to graze.

Many of the new homes in Cohasset were built on impermeable granite ledge or clay or in areas with high groundwater levels. Such sites were unsuitable for septic systems. Unfortunately, it was not until 1959 that the Board of Health adopted regulations on sewage disposal and required developers to meet standards for septic systems, including percolation tests to measure the absorption capacity of the soil, before granting building permits. The permissive building that took place before these regulations were drafted contributed to the sewerage woes that beset the town decades later. From 1960 to 1969 building permits were issued by the Board of Selectmen. Then in 1970 the town published its first building code, (soon to be replaced by the state building code) and appointed its first building inspector.

The breakup of large estates, the winterization of summer homes, and the development of new residential areas, together with the influx of new families, began the transformation of Cohasset from a town of socially cohesive neighborhoods and locally based employment, with a large colony of summer residents, to a broadly integrated, residential bedroom community. Homes in Cohasset could be bought at low prices in the fifties, before the housing market began to skyrocket. In 1957, for example, Edward Goff, a Metropolitan District Commission police officer, bought a two-bedroom Cape-style house on Tupelo Road, in the Pond Hill Veterans area, for $11,000. He later added a second floor and a pool. In 1998 the house was valued at $270,000.

By the end of the 1950s, 600 new dwelling units had sprung up in Cohasset, the population had increased by nearly 60 percent, and the number of children in the Cohasset schools had more than doubled. The influx of young families, their relative affluence, and the high birth rate, as well as the influence of Dr. Spock and other child "experts," made Cohasset, like communities all over the country, increasingly child centered. Attention now focused on children's activities and, in particular, the schools.

NEW SCHOOLS

In 1950 there were only 655 students in the entire school system, and 29 seniors in the graduating class. Signaling the start of the baby boom generation, however, 75 children were enrolled in kindergarten that year. The first six grades were housed at the Ripley Road School (renamed the Joseph Osgood School in 1961). Grades 7 through 12 were at the Osgood School on Elm Street. Built in 1890, the Osgood School was a three-story wooden building featuring a beautiful, wide central staircase. Classes were held on the first two floors and gym on the third. During gym class, Anna Abbruzzese recalls, the whole building would shake. She also remembers the school lunches made by the girls in Helen Welch's home economics class. A specialty was scrambled hamburger in cream sauce. Not surprisingly, many students brought their own lunchbox or brown bag to school, went home for lunch, or walked downtown for a sandwich.

By 1951 the kindergarten class in the Ripley Road School had grown to 90 children, up from 50 just five years earlier. Cohasset was clearly experiencing a population boom, one that would dramatically alter the schools. Parents were concerned that the town was "not offering the caliber of education . . . that makes people say, 'We moved to Cohasset because we wanted our children to go to school there'" (School Study Committee Report, 1951). The School Committee therefore requested the appointment of a School Study Committee to recommend ways to strengthen the educational program. With the direct participation of over 100 residents, the committee, chaired by Walter H. Lillard, delivered a comprehensive report to the School Committee in March 1951. The study touched on a wide range of subjects, from the K-12 curriculum to the schools' relations with the community. It concluded with a mandate for a strong educational program "with no waste." The report served as a long-range guide for the schools, and several of its ideas were implemented.

For many years the Osgood School on Elm Street had been deemed unsafe, inadequate, and uneconomical. So in the late 1940s the town approved the construction of a new school building, and in March 1950 ground was broken on the north side of Pond Street for Cohasset High School. Despite its high elevation, the ground was wet owing to its high clay content. The same was true of the adjacent athletic field. Many did not realize that the field had been constructed on the site of the former Pond Street Cemetery, a paupers' graveyard for the Town Home. The story goes that the water table in the clayey soil was so high that boulders had to be placed on the graves to keep the caskets from rising in the spring rains. Out of respect for the dead, the caskets were removed to Woodside Cemetery.

The Volpe Construction Company had won the bid to build the school. Working with his father on the project was John Volpe, who later became governor of Massachusetts. The wide, flat-roofed brick building with strong horizontal lines was a radical departure from the old-fashioned Osgood School with its turret and steeply pitched roofs. A bargain by today's standards, the total cost of the school, including equipment and landscaping, was $890,000.

At its opening in September 1951, the *South Shore News* raved: "This building is without doubt the most modern and well-equipped high school in the Commonwealth." Elizabeth B. Ripley (the superintendent's daughter-in-law) recalls how exciting it was to be in the new school: "The kids had their own lockers, showers, and a new gym. There were only 175 kids in the high school at the time. You would play basketball on the girls' team and then change your clothes and cheer for the boys' game. You did everything because there weren't enough kids to fill all the spots. You sang, played sports, cheered." In such a small system, an able administrator could play dual roles: William Ripley, Jr., was both school superintendent and high school principal until the two positions were separated in 1954.

By 1956 enrollment in the new school had soared to 370 students. The school had been designed for only 350. "The rapid growth of the school population has forced the school department to put every available space in the building to classroom use. At some periods of the week every room, including the auditorium, gymnasium, and cafeteria, will be in use as a classroom or study hall," said high school principal and math teacher Anthony D'Antuono (*South Shore Mirror*, 8/30/56). In 1959 a new junior high school wing (the north wing) was opened, bringing the capacity of the school to 615 students. The enrollment by then was 525.

The school system was both expanding and improving rapidly. Osborne F. Ingram, chairman of the School Committee from 1954 to 1964, credits Superintendent Ripley and Cohasset resident Henry B. Perry for building up the academic strength of the school. Perry was a teacher placement officer at the Boston University School of Education and, knowing the field, volunteered to scout for new teachers. With his help, Ripley hand-picked good teachers and gave them his full support. Cohasset also competed for teachers by increasing salaries to the levels offered by other towns in the area. Inevitably this led to larger school budgets and higher tax rates, a growing concern for the town.

Ripley is fondly remembered today as a wise and capable administrator who served our system with dedication for 42 years. He was born in Hingham to a family whose ancestors emigrated from Hingham, England, in 1638. After graduating from Brown University in 1926 with a degree in chemistry, he immediately took a job in Cohasset as a science teacher and football and baseball coach. In 1941 he replaced Superintendent James W. Doyle, who left to accept an Army commission. Two years later Ripley earned his master's degree in education at the Harvard Graduate School of Education. As an administrator he was relaxed and unpretentious, a good manager who won the respect and devotion of his staff. "When he called you to his office and asked you to do something," recalls Robert M. Thompson, a high school science teacher, "you'd leave trying to figure out how you could do even more for him."

Ripley's daughter-in-law Elizabeth laughingly tells of the time when a young, new high school teacher was having trouble managing his students. Ripley roared into the room and berated the class for their unruly behavior. When he had finished his diatribe, he wheeled around to leave. But instead of making a grand exit, he unwittingly strode right into a closet.

Robert Ripley remembers how much his father loved his work. "He knew all the kids and went to all their games, but he was also tough. He set high standards and expected people to meet them." Ripley liked working with his staff one-to-one. When the teachers became unionized in the 1960s, he decided to leave the system. Not caring for the idea of negotiating with a representative and losing personal touch with his teachers, he felt he was leaving at the right time. "I was there for the best of it," he told his son. He retired in 1969, after 28 years as superintendent.

With a supportive School Committee, one that represented a cross-section of the town, Ripley was able to develop a first-rate system. In 1955 Cohasset students were the highest scorers in a national mathematics contest in which 23,000 students competed. In that same year the American Field Service, a student foreign exchange program, was introduced into the school. In 1957 Cohasset was one of only 360 schools in the country to offer an Advanced Placement program in mathematics and literature. The first annual science fair in Cohasset was also held in 1957, the year the Soviet Union launched the Sputnik space probe, marking the start of a new era in science, engineering, and education.

The athletic program, particularly football, was also a source of pride. The football team had gone through four consecutive years since 1951 without winning a single game. In 1955 they finally won against Hanover. Then in the fall of 1957 they had an undefeated season. For a small town, the team fielded outstanding athletes such as Frank Carey, Clark Chatterton, Alan Ingram, Greg Koval, Roger Pompeo, Walter Sweeney, and Gary Vanderweil. Walter Sweeney, in particular, became legend in Cohasset. Rated as a "coach's dream" by his coach Everett W. Dorr, he was the top schoolboy football scorer in the 1958 season. After graduating from college, he was drafted by the San Diego Chargers in 1963. From 1964 to 1969 he was named to the AFL All-Star Game, and from 1970 to 1972 to the NFL Pro Bowl. He also played two years for the Washington Red Skins. His career, however, came to a disappointing end in 1975 due to alcohol and drug addiction, as well as physical injury.

At the elementary school on Ripley Road, four new classrooms were added in 1950. Two years later the school was again overcrowded, and the School Committee began to plan a second elementary school, for grades 4 through 6. For the site it chose a 15-acre tract on Deer Hill, next to the Oaks Farm on Sohier Street. Most of the land was owned by Jane Bancroft Steele, who generously donated it to the town. The 12-classroom cinderblock-and-brick building, designed by J. Williams Beal Sons, was constructed on the former tennis court of her estate. Cohasset resident Harry H. Reed, Jr., chairman of the Grade School Facilities Committee, served as volunteer clerk of the works. Completed at a cost of about $587,000, the new Deer Hill School opened in September 1955.

In five short years, between 1950 and 1955, the town had built two new schools and expanded the third. By 1960 a wing had been added to the high school, and the Deer Hill School was filling to near capacity.

CHURCHES

The churches in Cohasset, seven in number, faced the same population pressure as the schools. Newcomers joined church guilds, clubs, and societies, and youth programs flourished. To raise funds for expansion and renovation, parishioners organized suppers, fairs, minstrel shows, balls, and other special events. Churches played a vital role in the community, serving social needs as well as spiritual ones, particularly before cable TV and videos kept people at home in the evening.

First Parish Unitarian Universalist Church

The slender white steeple of the First Parish Meeting House rises high above the trees on Cohasset Common. Built in 1747, the Meeting House on the Common is one of the most cherished historical landmarks in Cohasset. It is the oldest church in town and the seventh oldest Protestant church in the United States. During the fifties and sixties (1951–1968), as well as from 1945 to 1949, the Reverend Roscoe E. Trueblood served as its minister. He was born and raised on an Iowa farm and brought up as a Quaker. Molly Bowditch remembers him as "a gentle man with wonderful humor. He wrote beautiful poetry and was very approachable." First Parish collected his poems and published them in *I Was Alive and Glad: An RET Anthology* (1971). The title reflects the final words of a poem he wrote before his death on June 17, 1969:

Say I Was Glad

If sometime when this hour is memory
Someone makes mention chancewise, of my name,
(Though I should be surprised if such time came,)
This one might ask, "What sort of man was he?
Was he wise or wicked?" (Speaking of *me!!*)
Say as you will; say I was wild or tame,
Rating some praise — and quantities of blame —
But say I spent my days most gratefully.

Yes, one may keep or break the rules and signs
That line the highway where the living ride
And one may draw some punishments and fines
But still find vast rewards on every side —
So tell the world that I was good or bad —
But tell them first, *I was alive — and glad!*

Like other churches, First Parish expanded as the baby boom generation reached school age. The Sunday School population nearly tripled, from 53 children in 1953 to 130 in 1961. To accommodate larger classes and the needs of a growing congregation, the church renovated its Parish House, built in 1722 for Cohasset's first minister, Nehemiah Hobart, and his bride, Lydia Jacobs. A successful capital building and repair campaign, led by Daniel C. Cotton, raised $90,000, well exceeding the goal of $75,000, a lot of money in those days. Several rooms and a new meeting hall were added to the historic Georgian building. In 1961 the hall was dedicated to Rev. Trueblood. Soon it was serving the broader community as well as First Parish. The Cohasset Senior Citizens lunch program began in Trueblood Hall in 1963. It also became a meeting place for Scout troops, the Red Cross bloodmobile, the Cohasset Historical Society, the League of Women Voters, and other town organizations.

Second Congregational Church of Cohasset

The Second Congregational Church was founded in 1824, when the Orthodox congregation split from the Unitarians, who opposed the doctrine of the Trinity. The Congregationalists built their church just a few steps away from First Parish, next to Town Hall. From 1950 to his retirement in 1972, it was led by the Reverend Frank B. Chatterton. Rev. Chatterton grew up in Gloucester, Massachusetts, and was a graduate of Boston University.

In the 1950s "Sunday School was tremendous," says his wife, Frances ("Fran"). Many young couples with three or four children were moving into Cohasset at the time, and "everyone sent their children to Sunday School, even if they didn't attend church themselves." Often the men were transferred here for a limited period by their companies. "It was like losing a congregation but also gaining a new one every three years."

Rev. Chatterton had a special bond with young people, and every Sunday night the Chatterton home would be filled with teenagers. The minister and his wife would chaperone them on field trips, including a special annual trip to the Ice Capades.

Longtime church members warmly remember Rev. Chatterton for his personal touch, for example, going from door to door to see his parishioners each year. That personal call "made it easier for them to discuss what was on their minds," explains Fran.

Several improvements were made to the church during Rev. Chatterton's ministry. Sunday School classrooms were added to the rear of the church (the addition was completed in 1964), a new organ was installed, and the vestry was renovated for use as a fellowship hall. Dedicated in 1963, the hall was named in honor of Samuel B. Bates, choir direc-

Easter Sunday 1955 at Second Congregational Church. In their Easter finery, back row: Clark Chatterton, Jean MacDonald, Carol Blossom, Carolyn Pratt, Keith Megathlon, the Rev. Frank B. Chatterton; front row: Nancy Orr, Heidi Lincoln, Ann Chatterton, Nancy Cooney, Caroline Cooney. Photo courtesy of Ann Pompeo

tor and soloist for 67 years before his death in 1962. In addition to the new hall, the Chattertons also offered the use of their home on Red Gate Lane for deacons' meetings, teas, and open-house receptions. Several weddings were held there too.

The major fundraiser for the Second Congregational Church was its annual June Festival, held on the Common. This communi-

Two young models in one of Elizabeth Bristol's fashion shows at Town Hall, a feature of Second Congregational Church's June Festival. Bristol's downtown shop was known for matching mother-daughter and sister outfits. Photo courtesy of Ann Pompeo

ty fair featured a square dance on the green with professional callers; a Square Dance Queen competition; a trained chimpanzee that did tricks; a miniature ferris wheel borrowed from Scituate; a merry-go-round; boat rides on the Common "lagoon"; pony rides and hay rides; a wishing well from which children drew prizes; and a midway with games of skill like ring toss and golf putting. The ladies put on a fashion show featuring Elizabeth Bristol's "After Five" collection and held an elegant tea at Town Hall, with small tables, crisp linen, and dainty tea sandwiches. The June Festival was "one of those events that made Cohasset special during the fifties and sixties," says Fran Chatterton, but by the seventies it had begun to fade. The other "big event" was the annual Village Fair held just before Christmas at Town Hall. It was organized jointly by the three churches around the Common: First Parish, Second Congregational, and St. Stephen's. The tradition, begun in 1940, still continues today.

Beechwood Congregational Church

The small, white Beechwood Congregational Church on Church Street was built in 1866 for the residents of Beechwood and west Scituate. Its tall steeple, destroyed by lightning in 1948, was replaced by the present cupola, topped by the original weathervane. In 1957 parishioners built a two-story addition to the church, financed in part by the sale of the parsonage at 505 Beechwood Street. Pastors at Beechwood Con-

gregational serve as permanent part-time ministers, preaching every Sunday but working elsewhere during the week. During the 1950s the pastors included the Reverend Fred V. Stanley (1948–1952), followed by Rev. Gordon Goodfellow (1952–1954) and Rev. William G. Sewell (1954–1965). More recently the parish has been served by Rev. Robert Campbell (1965–1985), Rev. Stephen Hall (1985–1994), and as of 1994, Rev. Dr. Branson Roberts.

Beechwood Congregational Church Girls' Youth Choir, 1950. Back row: Joan Sargent, Music Director Dorothy Bates, Frances Andrews; front row: Priscilla Lincoln, Diane Litchfield, Sissy Litchfield, Harriet Lincoln. Photo courtesy of Jeanette C. Somerville

Beechwood Congregational is famous for its church suppers, lawn parties, and fairs. In the fifties the Country Fair, held each July in Billings-Pratt Park, included a doll carriage parade, a baked bean supper, a green thumb table with plants, and the popular turtle races. A continuing tradition is the annual Election Dinner, held shortly before the town election. At the social hour after the meal, everyone has a chance to meet the candidates—no speeches allowed. You can experience the friendliness and simple pleasures of old Cohasset at Beechwood Congregational's suppers and fairs. Many traditions have been preserved. For instance, at the Christmas Fair you can still get small jars of the special beach-glass candy made by the women of the parish. The tiny, multicolored pieces of "glass," highly flavored with peppermint, spearmint, cinnamon, and other spicy essences, delight the eye as well as the palate. And no one has yet been able to surpass Flossie Cogill's perfectly seasoned mashed potatoes and May Merritt's tangy Harvard beets.

Saint Anthony's Roman Catholic Church

In the 1950s St. Anthony's was a small, white, wooden church on South Main Street, directly across from the present Rectory. It had been built in 1875 as a mission church of St. Paul's in Hingham. Roger Leonard and others nostalgically remember it as a lovely building with a spire and gables, a domed rotunda above the altar, and detailed frescoes adorning the ceiling. Monsignor Thomas F. Devlin, appointed to the parish in 1947, was pastor. With Rev. Daniel Lynch, his assistant, Msgr. Devlin served 1,300 parishioners in the fifties.

In the spring of each year, the priests would invite Portuguese and Italian confessors to St. Anthony's to assist first-generation parishioners in making their Easter confession. This dual-language service continued as late as 1957. By that time Cohasset had become culturally more homogeneous, and special assistance was no longer necessary. The priests' duties also included saying Mass at Minot Chapel, a mission church of St. Anthony's built in 1903 for summer residents in Scituate. It was closed in 1962, when North Scituate was separated from St. Anthony's parish.

Parish organizations such as the Holy Name Society, the Ladies Sodality, and the Knights of Columbus enhanced the spiritual mission of the church while supporting it through fund-raising activities. In 1958 the Knights of Columbus presented "Plantation Follies," a minstrel show and musical revue, at Town Hall. Directed by E. Leo Madden of Weymouth, a well-known director of amateur minstrels, it featured over 60 performers from the parish. Roger Leonard, in *We Protect*, his history of the Portuguese in Cohasset, recalls the stellar performance of his father, Robert ("Bing," for his singing) Leonard: "I fondly remember how he dazzled an appreciative audience with his snappy rendition of 'Way Down Yonder in New Orleans' . . . We heard his baritone voice sing the lyrics to 'Sentimental Journey' . . . My mother, not to be upstaged, was one among the fancy complement in the tambourine chorus . . . What a magical night!" In the late 1950s the minstrel show, performed by white actors with blackened faces, died out as an American genre. Blackface had become unacceptable, and the performances were recast as variety shows.

The proceeds from the 1958 show were to go toward constructing a Knights of Columbus hall on land that the Columbans had purchased from Kitty McMahon, a Cohasset schoolteacher, and her sister Genevieve Hill on the corner of Summer and South Main streets. The Columbans, however, generously donated to St. Anthony's Building Fund both the land and the money they had saved. The old church had become crowded and unsafe, and a new building was a priority.

Saint Stephen's Episcopal Church

St. Stephen's commands a lofty site on a high ledge at the southern end of the Common. It was built in 1900 by and for the well-to-do summer residents of Cohasset. It is famous for its magnificent carillon, one of the finest in the world. Most of the 57 bronze bells mounted in the church's Gothic tower were donated in the mid-1920s by Jane W. Bancroft in memory of her mother, Jessie M. Barron.

The Reverend Bradford H. Tite became rector of St. Stephen's after Rev. Charles C. Wilson retired in 1951. John Bishop, a member of the church, presents a frank and perceptive account of St. Stephen's in his 1970 "Historical Profile" of the church, reprinted in *So Worship We God* (ed. David H. Pottenger, 1998). He notes that in the early part of the century, St. Stephen's was "a church for the few." In 1904 the Reverend Howard Key Bartow began a process of reconciliation with the larger community, which the Reverend Charles C. Wilson (1920–1951) "continued and expanded." By 1950 the division that had existed between summer people and natives had "all but disappeared." Nevertheless, tension again appeared, this time between newcomers and oldtimers. New church members felt unaccepted and were frustrated by the reluctance of old-timers, who dominated the organizations, to include them in the activities of the parish.

Within a few years, however, Rev. Tite's decision to construct a greatly needed new wing for the Parish House "joined all members together in a common purpose and a shared accomplishment." Sunday School by that time had become so crowded that the children had to be marched across the street to the Community Center for classes. Other church activities were also hampered by lack of adequate space. Under the leadership of Rev. Tite, members of St. Stephen's worked together in fundraising and planning. The Planning Committee, chaired by Stewart Sanders, hired the firm of Cram and Ferguson to design the building in the same Perpendicular English Gothic style as the main church. In 1957 the beautiful Charles Chase Wilson Parish House was dedicated in a service officiated by the Right Reverend Anson Phelps Stokes, Bishop of the Diocese of Massachusetts.

Vedanta Centre

The Vedanta Centre at 130 Beechwood Street was founded in 1929 as an *ananda ashrama,* a peace retreat modeled after the ancient forest schools of India. In quiet, secluded communities people who sought the Truth lived near their teacher to learn and practice Vedanta, the teachings of the Veda, the sacred Wisdom litera-ture of India.

In 1952 Rev. Mother Gayatri Devi, the spiritual leader of the Vedanta movement in the United States, merged the Boston Vedanta Centre with its Cohasset summer country retreat, making Cohasset the permanent East Coast residence for the community. The western headquarters are at La Crescenta, in southern

California. To celebrate the fiftieth anniversary of the founding of the Vedanta Centre in the United States, members of the Cohasset ashrama built a temple on their wooded grounds from local field-stone and timber milled from oaks felled by the 1954 hurricanes.

The new Temple of the Universal Spirit, dedicated to all religions, was designed by William C. Chin of Boston and constructed by the members themselves, under the direction of Brother Richard. L. Creesy. Opened in October 1959, it features a large, circular stained glass window above the altar, designed by Mother Gayatri and made by Joseph G. Reynolds, a Boston stained-glass master. The window depicts the Indian symbol for God (*Om*, the One Universal Spirit), circled by a many-petaled lotus representing the illumined soul. Ten smaller windows around the temple contain stained glass medallions created by South Shore artist Donna Normand, depicting symbols of Christianity, Judaism, Buddhism, and other major world faiths. Vedanta is a philosophy, not a religion, and its adherents do not proselytize. Those who attend services at the Vedanta Centre often retain their own religious affiliation while seeking spiritual renewal through meditation and prayer.

Pope Memorial Methodist Church

The Pope Memorial Church was built in 1900 to memorialize Charles Linder Pope, the son of summer residents Colonel Albert A. and Abbie Linder Pope. Their home on Jerusalem Road in North Cohasset is now the Howe Estate condominium. Charles drowned in 1898, at age 18, in Straits Pond, not far from the family residence. His parents built the memorial to their son on the shore of the pond, on land that they owned. The church was designed in the Richardsonian Romanesque style, with rounded arches and masonry walls of Quincy granite. The roof tiles were imported from Italy. At the dedication of the church, the Popes placed some gold coins and a portrait of Charles in the cornerstone. Originally non-denominational, Pope Memorial became a Methodist church in 1923.

Very little is known about the church in the 1950s. The pastor from 1949 to 1959 was Rev. J. David Townsend. He was followed by Rev. Franklin E. Blanchard (1959–1961), Rev. John VanDuzer (1961–1964), Rev. Earl Luscombe (1964–1968), and Rev. Max M. Munro (1968–1973). Rev. Munro continued to serve as part-time pastor for a few more years. Since the Methodist congregations in Cohasset and Hull were small, Pope Memorial and the Hull Village Methodist Church were "yoked," the same minister serving both churches. Former parishioners recall that Pope Memorial had an active Sunday School during the fifties, and that the Hull and Cohasset choirs were combined. In 1979 the small Cohasset congregation, no longer able to support the church, merged with the Hull Methodists. The church building was rented to a newly formed group, the Cohasset Community Church of the Nazarene. A year later, in 1980, Pope Memorial was purchased by the South Shore Greek Orthodox community, who converted it to the Nativity-Assumption of the Virgin Mary Greek Orthodox Church.

TOWN ORGANIZATIONS

The newcomers sought inclusion not only in the activities of their churches but also in the elected, appointed, and voluntary organizations of the town. They helped to create new ones as well, such as Little League, the South Shore Art Center, and the Community Garden Club. Parents contributed their time particularly to organizations that provided group activities for their children, such as Little League and Scouts.

Little League

One of the most popular activities for children in Cohasset was, and continues to be, Little League. Originating in Pennsylvania in 1939, Little Leagues sprouted up across the nation after the war, tapping the American passion for baseball, the "national pastime," played by youngsters on a pickup basis in sandlots, city streets, and backyards. It is now a worldwide organization, with teams in 91 countries.

Cohasset formed its Little League program in 1952, under the leadership of George W. McLaughlin, chairman of the board of directors. The *South Shore News* (3/21/52) predicted "a great future for local youth athletics." Enthusiasm was high. For the inaugural spring training session, held at Milliken-Bancroft Field, 112 boys between the ages of 8 and 12 showed up. They were divided into four teams: Red Sox, Braves, Dodgers, and Yankees. Each team had a sponsor, such as restaurateur John Carzis and developer William Poland, who paid for the uniforms, and a manager. Robert Montague, whose family moved to Cohasset in 1943, remembers the thrill of riding to the field on opening day on a fire engine, which led a big parade from the library, complete with high school band, Boy Scout color guard, and members of the Police and Fire departments. The traditional opening day parade continues to this day and is still a major event.

The teams played 18 games during the season. On July 4 the outstanding players on each team competed in an all-star game. Roger Leonard remembers that Rev. Frank Chatterton, official record keeper for the league, came to all the games neatly dressed in a suit. He printed the scores for each game in a "newspaper," which he gave to the eager children that flocked around him the minute he appeared. In 1954 Little League acquired its own ball-field on North Main Street, designed by W. Chester Browne & Associates. It was named after Harold F. Barnes, a strong supporter of youth-oriented activities such as Little League and the Community Center. Assisted by Richard Potter, Barnes built both the bleachers and the fence surrounding the field. The field itself was owned by the town and leased to Little League for one dollar a year. For about 40 years the Little League field remained virtually unchanged. Then, in the mid-1990s, the directors of Little League raised funds to bring it up to modern standards. Sporting new aluminum bleachers, an electronic scoreboard, and on-deck cages near each dugout, the renovated field was opened in 1996.

Scouting

Two other youth organizations that thrived in the fifties (and sixties) were Boy Scouts and Girl Scouts. Both had begun in Cohasset in 1912. Arthur L. Lehr, Jr., served as volunteer Scoutmaster for the Boy Scouts from 1938 to 1968. In 1951 the Cohasset Rotary Club voted to sponsor the Boy Scout movement. "Although the Boy Scouts in Cohasset have had a Troop Committee in the past, this is the first time in recent years that they have been backed by a permanent organization in town," said the Rotary Club representative. "We want to give the Scoutmaster and the boys the enthusiastic and continuing support they need to make Scouting a completely worthwhile youth activity in town" (*South Shore Mirror*, 10/23/51). Lehr had 45 to 50 boys in his troop, divided into five or six patrols. They met at the Ripley Road School hall on Friday nights, all in uniform. Boy Scouts and, for younger boys, Cub Scouts had active programs in the 1950s, strongly supported by parents.

The Girl Scouts in the fifties were led by Dorothy B. Bates, wife of the farmer and town tree warden Howard Bates. Dorothy was credited for her work in building up the Girl Scouts and Brownies in Cohasset and for "promoting one of the best programs in Massachusetts" (*South Shore Mirror*, 3/21/57). By the end of the fifties Cohasset had 16 Girl Scout troops. They were sponsored by the Cohasset Woman's Club, an organization that also awarded an annual scholarship to a Cohasset High School senior who chose to become a nurse. According to Rebecca Bates-McArthur, Dorothy's daughter, the scouting programs were successful in the fifties and sixties partly because "there wasn't a lot else going on for kids, compared to now. It was Scouts, school, church. You made your own fun. There was not much to watch on TV."

Red Cross Water Safety and Other Programs

A popular summer activity for children was the Red Cross Water Safety Program. Established at the Cohasset Yacht Club in 1943, the program moved to Government Island in 1948 and then to Sandy Beach in 1953. Cohasset children, taught by local instructors such as Helen J. Pratt, learned to swim while earning certificates for various levels of proficiency: Beginner, Intermediate, Swimmer, Advanced Swimmer, Junior Life Saver, and Senior Life Saver. In 1957 there were 350 youngsters in the program; in 1959, over 400.

The Cohasset Chapter of the American Red Cross provided other valuable services to the community, including home aid for servicemen, transportation to hospitals and clinics, disaster relief, home nursing courses, nurses' aides, and a blood donor program that continues to this day. Over the years Cohasset has contributed generously to this program. We have three bloodmobiles a year, which is unusual for a town our size, and a cadre of loyal donors recruited from church groups, Rotary, and the Masons. One resident, Louis F. Eaton, Jr., has given blood each year since 1946, donating a total of more than 17 gallons. In 1991 the American Red Cross presented an award to longtime volunteer Alfred G. Odermatt for the outstanding participation of this region in the program.

Cohasset Community Center

The Cohasset Community Center, founded in 1944, was a popular spot for teenagers in the fifties and sixties. One of its organizers, first president, and director for 10 years was Nathaniel M. Hurwitz. A leader in many civic activities, Hurwitz had also directed the Boys Club of Boston for 23 years. One of his aims for the Community Center was to channel the energy of Cohasset youth.

Within a few years the center outgrew its quarters in the Furber estate, at the corner of Sohier and North Main streets. In 1949 it was moved to the Elisha Doane House, an eighteenth-century Georgian mansion and former inn, at the corner of Depot Court and North Main Street. The A&P had wanted to buy the old Doane House and raze it to build a larger store. It was saved from the wrecking ball by summer resident J. Franklin McElwain and his wife, who organized a group of citizens to raise funds to buy the Doane House for the Community Center. The McElwains also donated money to construct a new auditorium and four bowling alleys. Instead of hanging around downtown, youngsters now had somewhere to go for bowling, pool, ping-pong, and dances. Children could watch Saturday matinees at the center for 15 cents, and teenagers had their own movie nights to see favorites such as Hopalong Cassidy and John Wayne.

The Community Center offered many other activities, including a nursery school program, which began in 1953 and is still active today, baton twirling, arts and crafts, exercise classes, dancing,

badminton, French, Spanish, and Russian (taught by Harvard pro-
fessors), bowling leagues, camera club, dramatic club, and square
dancing. "The Community Center is one of the best working models in the area," reported the *South Shore Mirror* (5/14/59).

Town Hall and the Cohasset Dramatic Club

Cohasset Town Hall housed an auditorium with an elevated stage
as well as the town offices. The auditorium served as a center for
a great variety of events. Town historian David H. Wadsworth
describes its sometimes surprising uses:

> By the decade of the 1950s the Cohasset Woman's Club
> was a regular user of the [Town Hall auditorium] for its
> monthly meetings. Bridge and whist parties, High School
> plays, barn dances (one held by a group known as
> "Bundles from Home"), the Parent-Teachers Association,
> the Village Fair, and the Grange all were users of the
> Town Hall, as was the Baptiste School of Dancing.
>
> The Second Congregational Church School and Men's
> Club held events in the auditorium, and the South Shore
> Film Society presented foreign films there. The Cohasset
> Girl Scouts, the Knights of Columbus, the Christian
> Science Church, and the town's Historical Society also are
> on the list of organizations using the hall, along with the
> Republican Town Committee, the Community Center,
> and, in 1954, the Massachusetts Registry of Motor
> Vehicles. The Cohasset Dramatic Club . . . began produc-
> ing three major productions per year on the Town Hall
> stage.   The summers of 1950, 51, and 52 saw the
> Brattle Theater Company occupy the hall for presentation
> of, among other serious dramas, plays of William
> Shakespeare.
>
> [*Cohasset Mariner*, 8/2/84]

The Cohasset Dramatic Club, organized in 1921, continued to
flourish during the 1950s and is today the oldest continuing com-

munity theater in the area. The club was the envy of many other community theaters because it had a permanent home on the Town Hall stage and could use part of the basement to store set pieces and props. Thus relieved of commercial pressures common to other groups and blessed with several good directors, the club was free to tackle more challenging dramas along with the usual comedies and mysteries. It developed a decades-long reputation as a real actors' company. It was also a very sociable group, holding playreadings and cast parties at members' homes. Actors and technical people from surrounding towns flocked to join local thespians.

South Shore Music Circus

While the Town Hall stage was and remains perfect for the local amateur group, the venue grew too small to support professional summer theater, which had been a fixture in town since 1933. It had been run by outside theater professionals under the name of the South Shore Players. After World War II the star system and packaged shows took over the "straw hat" circuit. Well-known, if aging, actors from Hollywood and Broadway commanded prices higher than a 400-seat auditorium could support. Reluctant to relinquish what had become a tradition of professional theater, residents Helen Vosoff, G. Prescott Low, and Dr. Henry Howe formed a group called the South Shore Playhouse Associates to continue it. After two less-than-successful summers at Town Hall, the Associates began to raise money to build a larger venue.

At first they planned to erect a theater building that might also serve as an art center, but the actress Gertrude Lawrence suggested that they consider a theater-in-the-round under canvas like the tent theater established by her husband, Richard Aldrich, in Hyannis in 1950. The Associates were intrigued by the idea and acquired from the Bancroft estate its former horse show grounds on Sohier Street. A shallow amphitheater was dug out and wooden risers were installed around a circular stage. An audience of 800 could sit on canvas director's chairs under the big top. In the 1970s a concrete amphitheater was constructed and topped with permanent seating. The tent now seats 2,200.

The Playhouse Associates dubbed the facility the South Shore Music Circus and hired the Aldrich organization to run it. The first attraction was the hit musical *Show Boat*, which opened in June 1951 with a top ticket price of $3. The remainder of the ten-week season featured then-popular operettas such as *Naughty Marietta*, *Blossom Time*, and *Merry Widow*, along with *Brigadoon*, another Broadway musical. In the early years resident dancing and singing choruses would be hired for the season and rent rooms in town while lead characters—usually Broadway or television celebrities like Jack Cassidy or Faye Emerson—would rotate in and out with the shows. Often they would perform the same show in Hyannis the next week.

Rosemary O'Reilly, starring as Daisy Mae in the 1959 production of Li'l Abner *at the Music Circus, auditions some local muscle men as extras. Photo courtesy of Cohasset Historical Society*

Local young people served as unpaid apprentices. "We'd build sets, handle the props, and get to be extras in the shows," recalls David Wadsworth, who was an apprentice in 1954. "Shows would

The South Shore Music Circus as it appeared in 1951. At that time, even the outbuildings were tents. Photo courtesy of Cohasset Historical Society

Flyer advertising opening performance of the South Shore Music Circus on June 25, 1951.

play for a week, and every Monday a new production would open. I'll never forget the night we apprentices were still building the set at 6:30. People were coming in and we were nailing things together and slapping on a coat of paint."

The resident chorus members provided some exotic color during the summer with their glamorous clothes and makeup. "In the 1950s young people in Cohasset were crew cut and buttoned down. These people really stuck out in their sexy halters and short shorts," says Wadsworth. "I remember Chief Pelletier coming down at the beginning of the season to talk to the company. It seems there had been a problem the summer before with company members skinny-dipping at Sandy Beach."

The 1954 season was cut short when 100-mph winds from Hurricane Carol uprooted and ripped apart the great green tent during the late-summer run of *Paint Your Wagon.* "Our tent man was an old, old former employee of Ringling Bros. He tried to sew the curtain together during the hurricane using one of those sailmakers' palms, but it was no use," says Wadsworth. Now, general manager Vincent Longo says that the tent can be quickly lowered if very high winds are expected.

While the theater's attractions have changed over the years with changing public taste, the tent facility has remained viable. One-night concert stands by singers, musicians, and comics have replaced the Broadway musicals and comedies. Stars like Carol Channing, Angela Lansbury, Zero Mostel, Bob Hope, and Liberace have given way to Tony Bennett, Bill Cosby, Liza Minelli, Kenny Rogers, and the Pointer Sisters. The Music Circus has weathered disgruntled neighbors and zoning battles to stand (along with its sister theater in Hyannis) as one of only a few tent theaters in the country at the end of the century. The South Shore Playhouse Associates remains a nonprofit entity that has distributed more than $1.3 million in proceeds over the years to area arts groups and scholarships.

South Shore Art Center

In 1955 South Shore Playhouse Associates, Inc., provided financial support for the formation of the South Shore Art Center. Thomas J. Lucas, art supervisor at Cohasset High School, was the center's first chairman. According to Lucas, the Art Center actually began in 1952 and was called the Cohasset Workshop. It was located in an old ship's chandlery by the harbor (the same building that became the Maritime Museum after being moved to Elm Street in 1957). The building was owned by Jessie Cox and had been used to store rowboats. Lucas cleaned it up and converted it to an art gallery, gift shop, and art school. In the summer of 1953 Lucas and some friends organized Cohasset's first art festival on the Common to promote the work of local artists. Lacking financial resources, they improvised by displaying paintings on easels fabricated from clotheslines and ladders. It was a great success, and several people volunteered to help Lucas the following year. In 1954 these friends of the arts organized a real festival, this time using tents. The Cohasset Art Festival on the Common has been held every year since then and is now the oldest continuous art festival in the United States.

An outgrowth of the festival was the South Shore Art Center, incorporated in the fall of 1955. Located in the Joy-Stoddard house at 15 Brook Street, the center provided opportunities for both amateur and professional artists to exhibit their work and to give and receive class instruction. The first board of directors included Thomas J. Lucas, chairman; Pauline F. Blanchard, Marjorie E. Cramer, Genevieve G. Good, Marian Keith Harris, Eleanor Marsh, Mercie Nichols, MacIvor Reddie (a well-known landscape and portrait painter), and Sarah A. Stannard.

The center was open to all South Shore residents and by 1956 had nearly 300 members. It offered courses in painting, copper tooling, leather craft, flower arranging, children's art, wood carving, pottery, decorative arts and crafts, music appreciation, ceramic sculpture, decoupage, and block printing. In 1957, when the Joy-Stoddard house was damaged by fire, the Art Center relocated to the Oddfellows Hall above Cohasset Savings Bank. There it remained until 1971, when it moved to the "flatiron building" at 103 Ripley Road.

Community Garden Club

Cohasset had two long-established garden clubs, the Cohasset Garden Club and the Amateur Gardeners of Cohasset. With limited memberships and few openings, they were unable to accept new members, particularly the novices who had recently moved to Cohasset. In 1959 Paula ("Polly") E. Logan, herself a relative newcomer, held a tea open to Cohasset residents to explore interest in forming a new club. Polly and her husband, Edward, lived at the Logan family estate, called The Ridges, at 50 Jerusalem Road. It was a grand estate built on a steep gravel bank deposited by the glacier. On the day of the tea, hundreds of young matrons, all

"The Ridges," built for A. S. Bigelow, home in the 1950s to Polly and Edward Logan. Photo *from H. Langford Warren's* Picturesque and Architectural New England

dressed up in hats and white gloves ("I couldn't believe it!" said Polly), swarmed across the lawn to the front door. The house was spacious, however, and the hostess generous. The lovely setting must have inspired her guests, because by the end of the afternoon, an astonishing 225 members had signed up and paid their dues. The Community Garden Club had burst into full bloom.

Charter members included Eleanor C. Barrie, Barbara R. Blackett, Pauline F. Blanchard, Sarah T. Brewer, Barbara T. Gregg, Mildred ("Tish") P. Grinnell, Virginia F. Leach, Katharine M. Lincoln, Paula E. Logan, Edith Metcalf, Rita Morgan, Penelope G. Place, Claudia H. Sears, Martha Ann Selph, and Lucia R. Woods. At first the new club was affiliated with the Community Center; in 1960 it became a member of the Garden Club Federation of Massachusetts and the National Council of State Garden Clubs. The garden club held the first of its famous Christmas house tours in 1960 to benefit the Community Center, which had donated the use of its hall for club meetings. In 1971 the tours became a biennial event and the major fundraiser for the club's scholarship fund and other causes. Residents of Cohasset generously open their homes so the public can view the beautiful interiors, festively decorated by club members. By the late 1990s the Christmas house tours would regularly attract nearly a thousand visitors.

Social Service League

Women who stayed home in the fifties found an outlet in volunteer activities. Molly Bowditch, a member of the Social Service League, noted that volunteer services were dominated by second-generation Cohasset women, but by the mid-fifties newcomers were at last integrated and given significant positions.

The Social Service League, according to the 1952 Town Report, aimed "to promote the welfare of the town and its people by improving public health, relieving poverty, encouraging thrift, and helping those who are trying to help themselves." In 1953 the league's 75 volunteers were organized into eight committees. The women operated a Thrift Shop at the Lilac House, 76 South Main Street, where they sold donated items to the needy at low prices. In 1953 Jean Cotton, Lydia Ericsson, and other members of the league opened a Consignment Shop at the railroad depot to supplement funding from Red Feather, a volunteer organization that supported many charitable agencies and programs. (Red Feather became the United Way in 1961.) The Consignment Shop, which became a major funding source for the league, moved to larger quarters in the newly built Cushing Plaza on Route 3A in 1955. (In 1999 it moved across the highway to Tedeschi Plaza, to the building vacated by Woolworth's in 1997.)

Every year Cohasset would hold a huge fund-raising drive for Red Feather. More than 200 citizens participated in 1953, topping all the other cities and towns in Massachusetts in the relative size of its organization. Cohasset raised a record amount of pledges and contributions. "This is not only proof of the diligence and devotion of the people who worked on the Red Feather campaign. It is stirring evidence of the exceptional generosity of the people of our town," said chairman Frederick E. Howe (*South Shore News*, 12/4/53).

The Social Service League used its share of the funds to help the needy and, increasingly, to provide health services and public health education. Selectman Helen E. Scripture, chairman of the Cohasset Board of Public Welfare, proudly announced: "Our Social Service League . . . is recognized not only here in the town but also by schools of social service and public health work. Our Well Baby, Well Child, and Pre-School Clinics will care for the health of Cohasset children from the time they return from the hospital after birth until they enter school. We have a record of almost 100% immunization of children in the town, and you won't go to any town where the health of children is taken care of better" (*South Shore News*, 6/26/53). In 1956, during the nationwide polio epidemic, Health Board chairman Nathaniel Hurwitz inaugurated the Social Service League's first polio vaccine clinic for Cohasset schoolchildren.

Fraternal, Business, and Other Organizations

The Konohassett Lodge, A.F. and A.M. (Ancient Free and Accepted Masons), was established in 1865 as a mutual aid society to assist members in need, bury deceased members, and help their widows and orphans. By the 1950s it had become primarily a fraternal and charitable organization. The Masons are the oldest civic organization in town. They built their own hall at 5 Brook Street in 1891. Many town leaders have been Masons. "Worshipful Brother" Norman Card, selectman, was treasurer of the Lodge from 1946 to 1960. Rev. Brother Fred Stanley, minister of the Beechwood Congregational Church in the early 1950s, was its chaplain for 34 years. Other prominent members in the fifties include Moderator Robert James, Board of Health Chairman Nathaniel Hurwitz, and Scoutmaster Arthur L. Lehr, Jr.

Founded in 1941, the Cohasset Rotary Club is an association of business and professional executives. Rotary has long provided college scholarships and student loans to Cohasset High School students. In 1950, as part of its annual fund-raising drive, it produced a blockbuster musical comedy called *March Meeting*. A spoof on Cohasset's town meeting and local "luminaries," the show was created by Isobel Grassie, Gudrun Birch Howe, and Jeanne Toye Gormley. Popular demand brought it back to the stage in

1956. Another successful fundraiser, which continues to this day, is the Rotary Club's Cohasset Telephone Directory and Buyer's Guide, first published in 1963.

Also active in the 1950s, and for the most part still active today, were the Cohasset Historical Society; the Cohasset Woman's Club; the Colonel Thomas Lothrop Chapter of the Daughters of the American Revolution; the Cohasset Garden Club; the Amateur Gardeners of Cohasset; the George H. Mealy Post 118 of the American Legion; the American Legion Auxiliary; Discussion Club; the Cohasset Sportsmen's Association, chartered by the National Rifle Association in 1952; the Junior Cohasset Sportsmen's Club, begun by E. Lawrence Parker and G. Prescott Low in 1951; and the Board of Trade, which evolved into the Chamber of Commerce. The Woman's Club and the Sportsmen's clubs (which used the rifle range installed in the basement of the Ripley Road School in the 1940s) no longer exist.

Golf and Yacht Clubs

Cohasset has two private clubs, the Cohasset Golf Club and the Cohasset Yacht Club, both founded in 1894 by summer residents. The clubs were exclusive at first, admitting mostly well-heeled, established Yankee families. The Golf Club in particular comprised a closely knit group of Cohasset summer residents. Catholics, with some exceptions, and Jews were not welcome. The story of Rose and Joe Kennedy, the wealthy and socially ambitious parents of John F. Kennedy, who became the first Catholic president of the United States in 1961, is well known. Author Laurence Leamer tells the tale of the now legendary snub:

> When it came time for the Kennedys to take their summer vacation, they would not head up to the sunny Catholic ghettos of Nantasket where the Fitzgeralds [Rose's parents] now had a house. Instead they rented a house only a few miles away on the rocky beaches of Cohasset [east side of Sandy Beach] among the Protestant elite.
>   The sight of these Catholic arrivistes tooling up the coast

to Cohasset in a golden Rolls-Royce was enough to set the Brahmin tongues wagging. Rose and Joe didn't seem to understand that the way you impressed the Old New Englanders was by affecting a calculated casualness, and not by ostentatiously displaying one's wealth, the printing hardly dry on one's dollar bills.

Rose and Joe were not merely content to sit on the beach in full view of the Protestants, but in the summer of 1922 applied for membership in the Cohasset Country Club [the Golf Club]. The club had a few Catholic members, including Eddie Moore, Joe's assistant who was living in a gate house attached to the Kennedys' rented home. The women of Cohasset, however, had no intention of sharing their bridge tables and tennis sets with the likes of Rose Fitzgerald, and their husbands were not about to play golf with Joe either . . . The summer gentry said that they had a desire "to see old faces" but Joe didn't quite get the message. June went by, and July, and now it was August, and Joe's application languished, and finally he understood.

[From *The Kennedy Women*, pp. 169-170]

The Depression and World War II, however, took their toll on the Golf Club. The war allowed no leisure time for golf, and membership declined to only 70. After the war the club began to accept people from Hingham and other nearby towns. Later, as Ronald P. Hobson relates in *Cohasset Golf Club: The First 100 Years*, "The guidelines for membership were broadened and a true cross-section of men and women in the community gradually joined the club." (After the clubhouse burned down in 1971, the need to finance its rebuilding opened the membership to many who had previously been denied.) Golf had begun its phenomenal rise in popularity, and tennis was active again. In 1958 the first Southern New England Tennis Championships held on the South Shore took place on the Golf Club courts.

The Cohasset Yacht Club also gained members in the fifties. At this time the club had some of the nation's top sailors. National Class champions competing in International 210s included Philip Benson (1952), F. Gregg Bemis (1954, 1956, and 1957), Richard A. Sullivan (1958), and Edwin A. Hills (1959). In 1956 the Yacht Club hosted the National Women's Sailing Championship. By 1960 the club had 225 members, with 125 children enrolled in sailing and swimming classes. Races were scheduled every weekend for adults and children in International 210s and 110s, Mercuries, Herreshoff 12s, and Rookies. John J. Rowlands, in *Spindrift from a House by the Sea*, appreciated the beauty of these races from the shore: "The breeze freshens and now, strung out in a long line, the Two-Tens head for the turning-marker. As they round the buoy, clouds of color suddenly explode at their bows as the spinnakers, red and green, pale blue, and stripes of white and red, flutter for an instant and fill as the poles are set."

TOWN GOVERNMENT

In the 1950s the general direction and management of the Town of Cohasset was conducted by three selectmen: Ira B. P. Stoughton (elected in 1946), Norman C. Card (1950), and Helen E. Scripture (1952). Their duties included signature authority over the expenditure of money by the town, enforcement of the town bylaws, and appointment of officials in nonelected positions. As if that were not enough, they also served at that time as assessors and public welfare officers.

Town government was simpler, smaller, less fragmented, and much less costly than today. Town departments had fewer employees, and salaries were low. Louis C. Bailey, who became highway surveyor in 1956, notes that his men were paid $1.25 an hour: "In those days, the town received a lot of value for a day's pay." The structure of government was sparer then. In the early 1950s only 14 appointed committees existed; by the late 1990s the town's business would be conducted by more than 50 committees, commissions, and representatives. In the 1950s the voters of Cohasset were content to let the officials they elected run the show. Most townspeople trusted the selectmen to manage the town sensibly.

The Selectmen

Ira Stoughton was a "full-time" selectman, similar to a town manager.
Having lost one arm to cancer, the
former milk truck driver for
Wheelwright's farm devoted himself
to his duties as selectman. He "ran
the town from his kitchen and knew
more about town, state, and federal
laws and grants than anyone," says
longtime resident George E. Buckley.
Louis Eaton, Jr., adds that Stoughton
was a dignified official and did a fine
job as a typical high-quality small-
town politician.

Ira Stoughton, Cohasset's "full-time" selectman during the 1950s, first elected in 1946. Photo courtesy of Ivy Stoughton

Selectman Norman Card, as
mentioned earlier, was the grocery manager for the First National
Store. James Sullivan, who as a teenager had worked for the
Sliding Grocer, describes Card as a "short man with a cocky walk
and the heart and the nerves of a politician (*Hingham Gazette*,
12/19/95). He also notes the synergy that existed among the
Stoughton-Card-Scripture triumvirate, who were elected and
reelected to the Board of Selectmen all during the fifties: "The
essence of this form of cooperation is a freedom felt by the board
members to be themselves in a corporate setting . . . [Everyone
allowed] fellow members the full scope of the powers they were
elected to exercise."

Helen E. Scripture was the first woman selectman in the history of the Commonwealth. Helen and her husband, Ralph, had
moved to Cohasset from Brookline in the early 1920s and became
active in town affairs. Helen was elected to the School Committee,
and Ralph to the Planning Board. For 30 years Helen was also a
volunteer for the Social Service League. When her husband died in
1947, she decided she wanted to do more than volunteer work. "I
think there's a freedom which comes from widowhood," she said to

her daughter, Nancy S. Garrison. In 1952, at age 66, she ran for selectman against the incumbent, Everett W. Wheelwright, and won. Her pledge was that her door would always be open and she would be totally accessible. A vital, intelligent woman, "she was a born manager," says her daughter, "and could grasp the big picture." Helen continued in office until 1970, when at age 84 she was defeated and passed the torch to another woman, Mary Jeanette Murray.

The Young Turks

Until the early 1950s Cohasset, like most small towns, had been insular, conducting its affairs with little regard for how other towns managed theirs. Despite general satisfaction with the way things were run, some relatively recent arrivals and former summer people, for the most part professionals and businessmen, challenged the old patriarchal tradition of town government. These "Young Turks" wanted to modernize the system and bring it up to date. In 1952 Louis Eaton, Jr., a lawyer; William Fitzgerald, president of the Fitz-Inn Auto Parks, Inc.; Edward Bursk, editor of the *Harvard Business Review*; and Richard Sullivan, manager of the MTA (Metropolitan Transit Authority), formed the Cohasset Taxpayers Association. They systematically compared Cohasset's expenditures with those of similar towns. They also researched the selectmen/town-manager form of government, foreshadowing the shape town government would assume in the late 1990s.

In 1956 the Taxpayers Association was successful in changing the appointment of Advisory Committee members. Previously chosen solely by the selectmen, they would now be appointed by a "Troika" comprising the chairman of the Board of Selectmen, the chairman of the Advisory Committee, and the moderator. Further, Advisory Committee members would be limited to two consecutive terms. In 1957 the town appointed a "Baby Hoover" committee, a local version of the postwar Hoover Commissions whose purpose was to find ways to reduce the number of federal government departments and improve their efficiency. One of the committee's recommendations, to combine certain town departments, was met with much resistance. Department heads did not want to be told how to run their bailiwicks. "No one wanted to listen," said Philip N. Bowditch, chairman of the committee.

Yet the town was undergoing an inexorable process of modernization. In 1957 town meeting created a five-member Personnel Committee to study job classifications and salary schedules and to make recommendations to the town for employee pay increases. It was a response to allegations of favoritism or bias by the selectmen in granting pay raises. The committee provided professional expertise, comparing the pay rates and fringe benefits of other towns with ours, factoring in the rise in the cost of living and the town's ability to pay its employees. They also recommended the setting of salary standards, establishing criteria for increases. All of this provided major relief to the selectmen.

In another step toward modernization, the Water Department installed meters on all water services in town in 1957. Previously homeowners were charged a flat rate for water usage based on the number of fixtures in their homes. Now they would pay for the water they actually used. The Water Department also standardized its meter reading and billing procedures. A problem it could not readily solve, however, was the increasing demand on the town's water supplies due to the burgeoning population. Severe water shortages during dry spells in the summer forced department workers to drive around town in their truck with loudspeakers asking residents to conserve water.

The Moderator

Next to the selectmen, the most powerful official in town was the moderator. He presided over town meetings and appointed ad hoc committees authorized to him by town meeting. As of 1956 he was part of the "Troika" that appointed members of the Advisory Committee.

Robert B. James, moderator for 29 years, ran town meetings from 1939 to 1968 with a firm hand. A native of Cohasset, his ancestors were among the earliest settlers in the town. He was born at the family home on King Street in 1905, the next to youngest of 14 children, and was educated in the Cohasset schools. Although he did not have a college education, he rose to become the eastern division manager for Gulf Oil Corporation in Boston. According to his children, Marcia C. Carthaus and Philip M. James, his real passions were sports (he was a college football referee for about 25 years) and the well-being of Cohasset. In particular, he fought to maintain a stable tax rate and to preserve the character of the town. "He gave his life to the town," says his daughter.

A decisive man who was not afraid to say exactly what he thought, Bob James was known on occasion to relinquish his gavel at town meeting in order to speak from the floor as a private citizen. The 1953 Town Report printed a speech he made at town meeting against general salary increases for full-time town employees. After describing the debt for the new high school and the large, probable capital expenditures that faced the town for sewerage, a new grade school, and new fire and police stations, he said:

There my friends are the cold hard facts, [so] obvious that there can be little if any room for difference of interpretation. To me the answer stands out bold and clear. *It's time to stop spending money . . .* it is not an easy task — certainly not a pleasant one — to stand here and take a firm position against the personal finances of many friends of long standing. In doing so, I am motivated only by a sense of duty to the Town of Cohasset and all its citizens which, we must never forget, is bigger and more important than our individual interests or our personal popularity.

Robert B. James, Cohasset's decisive town moderator from 1939 to 1968. Photo courtesy of Philip James

Town meeting went along with the moderator's recommendations. Although the quintessential conservative patriarch, he championed efforts to pass a controversial zoning bylaw. One of the most contentious issues ever raised before town meeting, zoning pitted oldtimers against newcomers.

Zoning

Cohasset was one of the last towns in the Boston metropolitan area to adopt a zoning bylaw. Most residents and, especially, large landowners had been opposed since the idea was first broached in 1937. At the 1953 town meeting Beechwood resident Benjamin LeClair rose to speak on the issue. Benny was a colorful character who had tried to get a bylaw enacted that authorized the levy of a fine on people such as his neighbors who had noisy guinea hens that woke him up each morning. Later he proposed an article to limit the number of lawyers on committees to one. Now he angrily shook a big brown bag. "Do you know what's in this bag?" he demanded. "No, of course you don't. It's like this law—you don't know what you're getting. You're buying a pig in a poke!"

Many (but not all) oldtimers resisted the intrusion of local government into what they saw as their God-given right to do as they pleased with their own land. New residents, however, perceived that the ordinance would preserve the residential character of Cohasset and ensure an orderly pattern of growth by classifying the town into separate districts for residential and business uses, and by setting minimum lot sizes and minimum setback lines for new buildings.

By 1955 newcomers in favor of zoning were joined by residents of North Cohasset. The latter had twice opposed an application for a drive-in movie theater in their neighborhood. Now they feared that without zoning regulations, the theater would become a reality. Moreover, in the Lincoln Hillside area, a couple had recently built a half-house on a lot only 20 feet wide after seeing a plan of New York City row houses. Without zoning restrictions, people envisioned hundreds of little houses springing up all over town. Creeping urbanization, with densely populated neighborhoods and a lack of open space, was a major concern.

In the end, it was probably a concession to landowners on Route 3A that made zoning possible. Previous zoning committees had wanted the highway to remain primarily residential. The only industry there was D. S. Kennedy. Now the committee was willing to allow business and light industry (the latter by permission of the Zoning Board of Appeals) along certain sections of the highway. Landowners saw gold, and others reasoned that commercial and industrial activity would "help the tax rate." In November 1955, at a special town meeting attended by as many as 1,180 voters, the zoning bylaw finally passed after nearly two hours of debate, 665 to 471.

NATURAL DISASTERS

Despite occasional contention at town meeting, life in Cohasset during the 1950s could be described as idyllic. Nature, however, was not always so tranquil. In the summer of 1954 two tropical hurricanes, Carol and Edna, lashed Cohasset, toppling trees and power lines. Lobstermen suffered heartbreaking losses as high wind, heavy seas, and tidal surges drove boats onto the shore and uprooted lobster pots. In Boston, hurricane Carol reached peak gusts of 100 mph. It killed 63 people and injured a thousand. Two million homes were left without power for nearly two weeks, and damage was estimated at $500 million. The toll from Carol was worse than from the infamous 1938 hurricane. Hurricane Edna finished the job of destruction that Carol had begun. In Cohasset streets were blocked by fallen trees and downed power lines. Utility crews came from as far away as the Midwest to repair the damage.

In the mid-fifties Dutch elm disease struck Cohasset. It devastated the beautiful trees that shaded the Common, Elm Street, Depot Court, and part of South Main Street, and those that stood majestically in many front yards. Caused by a fungus carried by the elm bark beetle, the disease had been transmitted from Holland to Ohio in 1919. It reached Massachusetts in 1941 and by 1955 had spread throughout the state. There was no cure; the only recourse was to cut down and burn the afflicted trees. Hundreds of elms in Cohasset were lost over the decade.

WAR AND THE THREAT OF WAR

Far from the peaceful town of Cohasset, conflict loomed on the Korean peninsula. On June 25, 1950, the communist North Koreans invaded South Korea, crossing the 38th parallel, the coordinate of latitude dividing the two Koreas. In March 1947 President Harry S Truman had announced a doctrine of containment of Soviet and communist expansion, promising to defend the free peoples of the world against aggression. Consequently he asked the United Nations Security Council to authorize a "police action" to drive the North Koreans back to the 38th parallel. Of the huge UN ground forces, 302,483 consisted of American Army and Marine troops. It had been just five years since the end of World War II, and the young men of Cohasset were again called to battle.

The North Koreans slashed south across Korea, driving South Korean and American soldiers to the southernmost tip of the penin-sula at Pusan. A daring amphibious landing at Inchon on September 15, 1950, conceived and successfully executed by General Douglas MacArthur, routed the North Koreans and turned the fortune of war. MacArthur pursued the North Koreans across the 38th parallel all the way to the northern border of Korea at the Yalu River. By so doing he envisioned a new objective, namely, to unify Korea and free it from communism. Perceiving a potential threat to themselves, however, the communist Chinese under Mao Zedong came to the aid of North Korea, launching a massive coun-terattack. Human waves of Chinese drove the UN forces back to the 38th parallel. Three years later, in 1953, the war ended in a stalemate, with Korea still partitioned near the 38th parallel, and 33,000 American lives lost.

Several Cohasset men served in the war, among them, Sergeant First Class Nelson C. Pratt, Jr. In 1952, 22-year-old Pratt was drafted into Company A of the 180th Infantry Regiment, 4th Infantry Division. Stationed on Hill 931 in the mountainous terrain of Korea, he arrived when the war was being fought in the trench-es near the 38th parallel. He was just out of communications school. As he was getting himself ready to join the communica-tions group in the trenches, his company was surrounded by

Chinese. During the ensuing combat, five of the six men in his group were wounded. With one hour of seniority over the remaining man, Pratt became the new communications chief.

Pratt's job was to receive orders from commanding officers by radio and transmit them by telephone to soldiers farther down the trenches. For several months he alternated between days fighting in the trenches and relief at the rear, where he could recuperate in the relative comfort of a tent and eat a hot meal instead of subsisting on cold C rations. Then, on the night of July 26, 1953, his company heard that the armistice was signed. All the men shot off their weapons to celebrate. "It was like the Fourth of July," Pratt says.

After the war was over, he wondered what it was all about. "What had we accomplished? It cost the nation 33,000 men over there, and we ended up where we started." Nevertheless, "the war was a maturing experience for me," he reflected. Pratt now appreciated the need to establish goals in life and to make the world a better and safer place for children. Back home he got involved in the Boy Scouts, whose emphasis on character development and citizenship he wholeheartedly endorsed.

In February 1952 town flags were flown at half-staff for Private First Class Clifford David Strout. Cohasset's only fatality during the Korean War, Strout was killed in action near Sungyang-ni, North Korea, on February 6, 1952, while serving in the field with the 279th Infantry Medical Corps. He was born in Brookline and had lived in Arlington and Weston before moving to 352 South Main Street with his family in early 1950. He graduated from Valley Forge Military Academy and studied at Boston University and Skidmore College before entering the Army in November 1950.

Local newspapers from the early 1950s name a few of the other Cohasset men who served in Korea. The *South Shore News* (1/5/51) had this to say about Joseph L. Salvador:

> Staff Sergeant Joseph L. Salvador, a 22-year-old Cohasset airman, was injured in a bomber crash during the Allied evacuation of Hungnam in Northeast Korea. Sergeant Salvador, who has flown more than 100 missions, listed his

injuries in a letter received by his father, Louis E. Salvador
of 41 Pleasant St., Cohasset. Knocked unconscious when
his head hit the radar equipment, he came to in a hospital
in Japan, suffering cuts about the back and face, a twisted
leg, fractured foot, three broken toes, a fractured finger,
and numerous bruises. "Outside of that, I am feeling fine
and enjoying the rest," he said. Four other men were killed
in the crash which injured Sgt. Salvador, who pays special
tribute to the Red Cross for the services which it extends to
the hospitalized men.

Sergeant Salvador was decorated 21 times. His brother Barron, a
gunner on the *USS New Jersey*, was also on active duty in Korea. He
earned the Purple Heart Medal and other awards (*South Shore
News*, 7/24/53)

Unlike World War II, the Korean War ended inconclusively.
Accorded little fanfare at home, it came to be known as the
Forgotten War. It was followed by the cold war, an ideological conflict between the United States and the Soviet Union, and by the
arms race between the two superpowers. Fear of nuclear attack
from the Soviet Union led the U.S. government to deploy a ring of
anti-aircraft Nike missile sites around the Boston metropolitan area
and other cities along the East Coast. One of those sites was in
Cohasset, on Scituate Hill (also known as Town Hill) on the west
side of King Street (Route 3A section). Here, underground in three
bunkers, were stored 48 Nike anti-aircraft missiles. They could be
launched within 15 minutes of sighting an enemy bomber.
Incoming aircraft could be tracked by radar from another Nike
installation on Turkey Hill in Hingham. In later years conventional
missiles at some of these sites were replaced with nuclear war-
heads. Because the Cohasset installation was not converted to
nuclear capability, it was closed in 1964. None of the missiles in
Massachusetts was ever launched. By the mid-1970s the Nike was
obsolete and all the sites were decommissioned.

Meanwhile, in Cohasset a vigorous Civil Defense was organized under the leadership of Colonel Walter H. Lillard. By 1952 he

could state in the Town Report: "We have now . . . a fairly depend-
able organization of Minute men and women who, in the event of
enemy attack, would be supported by all hands—men, women, and
children, as in colonial days. Remembering that Cohasset is designated as a part of a top priority critical target area, we must remain
alert and ready for emergency defense action as long as the storm
clouds threaten." He had assigned 800 people, many of them with
wartime experience, to special duties. Lillard's Minute men and
women included 61 people to handle administrative duties for six
sections of town; 45 regular, special, and auxiliary police officers;
65 regular, call, and auxiliary firemen; 93 medical personnel; 500
people with first-aid training; and other personnel for transportation and rescue, welfare and shelter, and communications, as well
as numerous wardens ready to lead in emergencies. In addition,
the Fire Department sounded more than 40 practice air raid siren
alarms each month at all hours of the day and night.

    Residents were encouraged to prepare fallout shelters in their
cellars and stock them with five-gallon containers of water, canned
goods, Coleman lanterns, and medical supplies. Laniel and Jean
Comstock of 76 Pleasant Street built a shelter of railroad ties in their
backyard and connected it to their house through a four-foot-diam-
eter tube. Public shelters were set up at Town Hall and in the
schools. From government surplus property Cohasset received
equipment for a 200-bed emergency hospital, complete with
stretchers, cots, bed linens, X-ray machine, operating table, ether,
lights, test tubes, and microscopes. These were stored in boxes at
the high school.

    The town also had sirens, radio equipment, and generators.
And most exciting, Cohasset was able to procure an army surplus
duck (DUKW, in army code) — a four-and-a-half-ton amphibious
truck for use on land or water. It looked like a boat on wheels and
could be used to rescue people stranded by floods. The skipper and
chief maintenance mechanic was Clifford Dickson, call firefighter
and steward of the Cohasset Yacht Club. He took delivery of the
duck in Toledo, Ohio, drove it all the way back to Cohasset, and
with the help of Robert Andrews, another mechanically skilled

Cohasseter, rebuilt its engine. Used a few times to rescue people in Hull during exceptionally high tides, it was finally auctioned off along with other civil defense equipment in the 1970s.

Despite Colonel Lillard's best efforts, most people in Cohasset did not take the threat of nuclear attack very seriously. In 1991 Civil Defense was renamed Emergency Management to reflect its post-cold-war duties and responsibilities, namely, to prepare the town to deal with emergencies in the event of hurricanes, floods, blizzards, explosions, spillage of hazardous wastes, and terrorism, an ever-present danger and threat to Cohasset as to the rest of the nation. Arthur L. Lehr, Jr., is the current director of the town's Emergency Management system.

During the 1950s Cohasset changed significantly as it evolved from a rural community, where most of the residents earned their living in the town, to a suburb, where the majority commuted to work. The decade was characterized by rapid population growth and the influx of more-affluent, well-educated people of diverse backgrounds and origins. Generally speaking, the newcomers were conscientious, good citizens who participated in town organizations, formed new ones, and worked to improve the schools and town government. But the nearly 60 percent increase in population also resulted in tension between the established longtime residents and the newcomers, and the pressure to improve town services led to inevitable increases in spending. At one time, according to the *South Shore News* (5/1/53), Cohasset's tax rate had been the lowest on the South Shore. This was no longer the case. Taxes were on the rise, and population growth and development were to continue unabated into the 1960s.

Cohasset in the 1960s:
TWO EXPANSION

The sixties in Cohasset were a decade of expansion. The town continued to grow rapidly, to form new organizations, and to construct new homes and municipal buildings. The decade was also one of "half euphoria, half growing disaster," in the words of Cohasset resident and political scientist Lincoln P. Bloomfield.

If euphoria characterized the early years, it was because in 1960 the United States was enjoying unprecedented prosperity and had just elected John F. Kennedy, the young, vigorous, and glamorous Democratic senator from Massachusetts, as president. Massachusetts voted overwhelmingly for Kennedy—but not Cohasset. Cohasset voters, with an impressive 95 percent turnout, cast their ballots for Republican presidential candidate Richard M. Nixon, 1,886 to 1,257. In 1964 William D. Weeks of Cohasset, also a Republican, was elected to the state Senate. He served for the next six years, representing the Norfolk-Plymouth district. A traditionally Republican town, over time Cohasset would become politically more evenly balanced (by 1994 registered Republicans and Democrats were about equal in number).

In local politics, however, neighborhood identity was more important than party affiliation. Some oldtimers even thought of themselves as living in the divisions of Conohasset laid out in 1670. One resident tells the following story of a friend from Beechwood who appeared one winter day at Town Hall for an important meet-

75

ing. A selectman called over to him saying, "Herbert Marsh, how are you? I haven't seen you in ages. Where have you been keeping yourself?" Herbert replied, somewhat cantankerously, "I've been hibernating in the Third Land Division. I don't get down much to the First Division anymore. You guys from the First Division, you've been ruining the town for the last 200 years, and you're still doing it!"

The Third Division, where Herbert lived, included the entire Beechwood section. Until the mid-1950s you probably could not get elected to town office without the support of the Beechwood bloc. But by the 1960s, church affiliation began to play a role in local politics. As more and more Catholics moved into Cohasset, for example, members of St. Anthony's became politically more powerful. Church membership was an easy way to classify people you did not know well: the activists belong to First Parish; the old Yankee families to Second Congregational and Beechwood Congregational; the social elite to St. Stephen's. Simplistic as that may be, people began to note which church a candidate for office belonged to.

Whether you were a selectman, a School Committee member, or a town board appointee, the immediate challenge you faced was coping with growth. By the end of the sixties the town's population would swell to 6,954, an 87 percent increase in just 20 years from the 1950 level of 3,731. The number of dwelling units would rise 75 percent, from 1,268 to 2,216, and the public school population would almost triple, from 655 students to 1,910. More people and more homes translated into higher taxes to support the addition of teachers and classrooms in the schools and of personnel in the Fire and Police departments. The town also experienced severe water shortages in the summer, flooding and drainage problems during storms, and pollution from poorly designed septic systems. "People at cocktail parties would talk of nothing but the problems with their septic systems, or the water in their basements," recalls Sheila S. Evans, who came to Cohasset in 1956. Clearly the old ad hoc way of dealing with these issues did not work any longer. The selectmen, who had run the town informally, sometimes even from the back office of the First National Store, now had a long-range plan known as the Benjamin Report. Town meeting was asked to vote on new zoning bylaws, and the town imposed new ordinances to address the complaints of a growing population.

While Cohasset was minding its business at home, a militant Soviet Union pursued the cold war in Eastern Europe and Latin America. In August 1961 the Soviets erected the Berlin Wall in Germany, 110 miles of concrete and barbed wire dividing Communist East Berlin from Allied-controlled West Berlin. In the spring and summer of 1962, America and the Soviet Union came to the brink of nuclear war over missile bases that the Soviets had installed in Cuba. On November 22, 1963, President Kennedy was assassinated in Dallas, Texas. In 1964 President Lyndon Baines Johnson announced that the North Vietnamese had attacked American destroyers in the Gulf of Tonkin, and in 1965 the United States began to bomb North Vietnam. In August of that year racial rioting exploded in Watts, a black ghetto of Los Angeles, setting off hundreds of riots in other cities during the next three years. On April 4, 1968, the black civil rights leader Martin Luther King, Jr., was assassinated in Memphis, Tennessee, and on June 5, 1968, Senator Robert F. Kennedy, brother of the slain president, and himself a candidate for president, was assassinated in California. In 1968, during the Democratic National Convention in Chicago, riots erupted between anti Vietnam War demonstrators and Chicago police. Closer to home, in April 1969 student protestors at Harvard violently seized and occupied University Hall, confronting the staff and, among other things, throwing administrator Robert Watson, a Cohasset summer resident, down the stairs. The decade ended with a moderate boost to our spirits when, in July 1969, an American astronaut, Neil Armstrong, became the first man to walk on the moon, fulfilling a goal set by the late President Kennedy in 1961.

Although the threat of nuclear annihilation and the tragic deaths of the Kennedys and Martin Luther King, Jr., profoundly affected people's sense of well-being, day-to-day life in Cohasset continued much the same as before, with Little League games, parades, and interesting new activities. At the end of the decade, however, the turbulence in the rest of the nation came home. In October 1969 the divisions in the town over America's involvement in the Vietnam War flared up after a peace rally held on the Common. Moreover, the particularly troubling problem of alcohol and drug abuse was showing up in the high school. The exuberant optimism of the fifties gave way to uncertainty, turmoil, and polarization.

PRESERVING THE PAST

By the end of the fifties, the old Cohasset seemed to be slipping away. Most of the farms had disappeared, fishermen were adopting modern technology, the vitality of downtown Cohasset began to decline, and old estates were being carved into new developments. As if in response to this imminent loss, the Cohasset Historical Society opened two new museums, the Maritime Museum in 1960 and the Gown Museum in 1963.

The driving force behind the museums was Eleanor Stoddard Marsh, a descendant of the first Hingham settlers and curator of the Historical Society since 1949. She had painstakingly restored the early-nineteenth-century Captain John Wilson House on Elm Street, using furnishings and memorabilia acquired from old Cohasset families. The Wilson House became a repository for local antiques, many of them from the town's maritime past. Soon it was crammed with museum pieces and losing its character as a historic home.

To the rescue came Jessie and William C. Cox. In 1956 they donated to the Society a suitably historic building, the Samuel Bates Ship Chandlery. Built in about 1760 and originally located on Border Street, it had been the headquarters and supply store for the Bates fishing fleet, the largest in Cohasset. On the ground floor you can still see the "counting house," where fishermen were handed their pay over the counter through a window. This room is also believed to have been Cohasset's first bank. The second floor served as a cutting room for small sails and later as John Bates's office. John, who died in 1882, was the last of the family to own the business. Clarence W. Barron, Jessie Cox's grandfather, bought the chandlery from the Bates estate and used it for storage. For a brief time it also housed Cohasset's first art center. In 1957 the building was cut in half and moved in two sections from the Cove to a vacant lot on Elm Street, next to the Captain John Wilson House. Three years later it was opened to the public as the Cohasset Maritime Museum.

Visitors to the museum are brought back in time to the town's fishing and ship-building heyday. Between 1780 and 1885 over 160 fishing and trad-ing vessels were built in shipyards around the Cove. Most were fishing schooners, but 20 barks and brigs and 6 or more full-rigged ships were also made in Cohasset. The museum displays fishing gear from the age of sail, ship models, including a fine one of the *Tecumseh*, commanded by Cohasset captain

The Historical Society's Captain John Wilson House on Elm Street, furnished with antiques and memorabilia from old Cohasset homes. Photo © Lynne Layman

The Maritime Museum was once the Samuel Bates Ship Chandlery on Border Street. It was moved to Elm Street in 1957 and now contains artifacts from the town's seafaring past. Longtime curator David Wadsworth welcomed visitors to the museum for many summers. Photo © Lynne Layman

James Collier, Jr.; portraits of local sea captains; navigational instruments and equipment; scrimshaw and life-saving medals (the first lifeboat station in America was built in Cohasset on White Head shore in 1807); figureheads and quarterboards from Cohasset fishing schooners; ship captains' desks, one of them from the brig *St. John*, an Irish "famine ship" wrecked on treacherous Grampus Ledge in 1849; and models of the first and second (current) Minot's Ledge lighthouses, fashioned by Robert N. Fraser, a descendant of the same Bates family that had owned the chandlery. An expert ship-model maker, a marine artist, and local historian, Fraser was named curator of the Maritime Museum in 1969 upon Eleanor Marsh's retirement.

The grounds of the Maritime Museum and the Wilson House were landscaped by the Cohasset Garden Club and appropriately planted with old-fashioned flowers. The club still maintains these lovely gardens. Adding further interest is an old ship's anchor, over six feet long and more than two centuries old. Fisherman Herbert Jason, who was also a salvage diver, discovered the anchor deep in the ocean off Lodan Ledges in 1960 and donated it to the Historical Society.

The museum has unique charm. Besides maritime treasures, there are farm implements and tools from early local trades; an old printing press; an antique post office "drum" from which people once picked up their mail; children's desks, books, and other articles from the old district schools; and prehistoric Indian artifacts, including dolls and several arrowheads found on Government Island, at Little Harbor, near Cunningham Bridge, and on the marshes along the Gulf River.

Few visitors, however, are aware of the spectral presence that haunted the premises. Here is a true account, as told by David Wadsworth, local historian and curator of the museum since 1982:

Ghost Story

Not long after the Maritime Museum opened to the public, Society Curators began hearing "strange" sounds coming from the upstairs office, formerly used by John Bates to conduct the family's fishing and mercantile business. The sound of footsteps pacing the floor above could be heard, when in fact there was no one at all upstairs. At one time, several small artifacts in the office were found to be out of their proper place. The pacing of feet above was heard frequently when Curators were working downstairs, and it was suspected that the Maritime Museum was . . . being haunted by a ghost. Finally one evening, when the

Historical Society was holding a meeting downstairs, the sounds from upstairs disrupted the meeting and, when sent upstairs to investigate, a Curator reported that no one was there . . .

The Cohasset ghost story came to the attention of a "ghost hunter" named Hans Holzer . . . [He] visited the Maritime Museum [in November 1964], and though he himself did not happen to hear the ghostly footsteps, he deduced that the haunting presence was that of John Bates, last of the family to own the old chandlery, and that he was haunting the building because he was distressed that it had been moved from its rightful location at Cohasset Harbor.

It has been said that the ghost of John Bates departed from the Maritime Museum in 1972. Perhaps he became reconciled to the new location . . . One cannot help but feel, however, that the ghost of the old shipowner John Bates just might be keeping a close if benign eye on events that have transpired since that time in the chandlery that became a museum, ready to resume his haunting should the occasion ever demand.

[David Wadsworth, "Cohasset's Maritime Museum Was Host to a Ghost," Cohasset Historical Society pamphlet]

The ghost upstairs notwithstanding, the Historical Society used the second floor of the museum as an art gallery in 1964. One of the first shows was a special exhibit on Cohasset's "glamorous era" at the end of the nineteenth century. Photographs captured the lifestyle enjoyed by members of the summer colony as they socialized at Cohasset Hunt Club breakfasts, danced at Hunt Club balls, admired thoroughbreds at the horse show grounds on Sohier Street, attended Garden Club lawn parties; and cruised on private steam-powered yachts. Also on display were paintings by famous local artists such as Frank Shapleigh, MacIvor Reddie, and Grace Collier.

Gown Museum
The glamorous era was also memorialized in the Historical Society's superb gown collection, comprising over 600 costumes dating from the 1700s to 1940. In 1963 the society leased the Independence Building from the town and moved the gowns there. The building was only two doors down from the Maritime Museum and a more suitable place to show the collection.

The Independence Building has a colorful history of its own. It was the town's first municipal building, constructed in 1848 to house Cohasset's first fire engine, a horse-drawn hand-pumper called the *Independence*, giving the building its name. In 1913 the fire company moved to the Central Fire Station at the Cove. The Independence Building then became the police headquarters and lockup, with two jail cells on the first floor. It served as the police station for 50 years, from 1913 to 1963, when the Police Department moved to its new headquarters on Elm Street.

For curator Eleanor Marsh the museum was a labor of love. She had collected many of the gowns herself from local families. With the assistance of Marjorie Ladd and Eleanor Clemens, she displayed them in historical settings with costumed mannequins and elegant backdrops furnished with antiques and old paintings. The Richardson Room featured a ballroom scene whose centerpiece was an "exquisite ball gown of ivory satin embroidered with gold thread and accented with gold lace" (*South Shore Mirror*, 7/2/64). The room was named in memory of the Richardson family, one of the first sum-mer residents and ancestors of the farmer-artist Richardson White. Richardson and his wife, Cornelia, donated several gowns that belonged to the family. The Heritage Room displayed "historic hats, wedding bonnets, fans, hair combs, and other whimsies to comple-ment milady's costumes," and the Wedding Room contained beauti-ful wedding gowns, some from the early 1700s.

By 1980, however, support for the Gown Museum was dwin-dling. It was hard to motivate volunteers to create new tableaux every year and plan opening teas, parades, and other special events to promote the museum. Women were returning to work or want-ed to be paid for their time, and the directors of the society, most of

Christina Laney wearing a Victorian dress from the Historical Society's collection in 1964. Photo courtesy of Christina Rifkin

The Historical Society's Gown Museum occupied the Independence Building from 1963 (when the Police department moved out) until the early 1980s when it was determined that the building was too damp for the delicate dresses. The gowns were carefully packed away at that point and remain so. Photo courtesy of Cohasset Mariner

them natives, were not interested in making the effort to recruit newcomers. Then, too, maintenance of the fragile fabrics required expensive drycleaning and storage. In 1983 the museum was closed and the gowns carefully packed and stored. As of 1999 many of the gowns in this priceless collection are still in cartons.

Minot's Light Construction Site

In 1967 a chance discovery of two large circles of stone under a tangle of weeds and grass rekindled interest in Cohasset's maritime heritage. The slabs were exposed by accident when lobstermen Harry Ritter, Charlie Butman, Sheldon Sladen, Charlie Wood, and Joe Figueiredo were clearing some land on Government Island to build lobster cars. Watching them work was Historical Society president Prescott ("Pete") T. Cumner, who identified the slabs as the old templates used to fabricate granite blocks for the second Minot's Ledge Lighthouse.

The first lighthouse, supported on nine thin iron legs, had been destroyed in the fierce "Lighthouse Gale" of 1851. Four years later the Army Corps of Engineers decided to build another one, this time of granite. One thousand and seventy-nine blocks of Quincy granite, weighing in total more than 3,500 tons, were shaped on the two templates and transported by ship to Minot's Ledge. There the precisely cut blocks were dovetailed together to form the 114-foot-high tower topped by a lantern house and copper dome. Completed in 1860, this lighthouse was deemed the engineering marvel of the century. At a cost of $300,000, it was also one of the most expensive lighthouses ever built in the United States. In 1977 the American Society of Civil Engineers declared it a National Historic Civil Engineering Landmark.

Templates for cutting and fitting the stones used in building the second Minot's Ledge Lighthouse, 1855-1860. The templates, which can be seen on Government Island, were uncovered by lobstermen in 1967 and restored by the Historical Society. Photo courtesy of Ralph Dormitzer.

The Cohasset Historical Society restored the original construction site. The benefactors of the the project were Jessie and William Cox, who earlier had donated the Bates Ship Chandlery to the society. Heading the restoration committee was Pete Cumner; other members included George W. Benedict, Charles G. Fink, Jeanne Toye Gormley, Bettina H. Pratt, Burtram J. Pratt, and Martha E. Smith.

COPING WITH GROWTH

Cohasset was losing some of its distinctive qualities. Its days as a fashionable summer colony had faded; shipbuilding had ceased long ago; fishing was no longer a major occupation; and farming had virtually ended. In the 1960s local tradesmen such as carpenters, plumbers, and builders continued to prosper because of the housing boom. For newcomers, however, this was a bedroom community, not a place to earn a living. You educated your chil-

Large Estates and Their Subdivisions from 1950

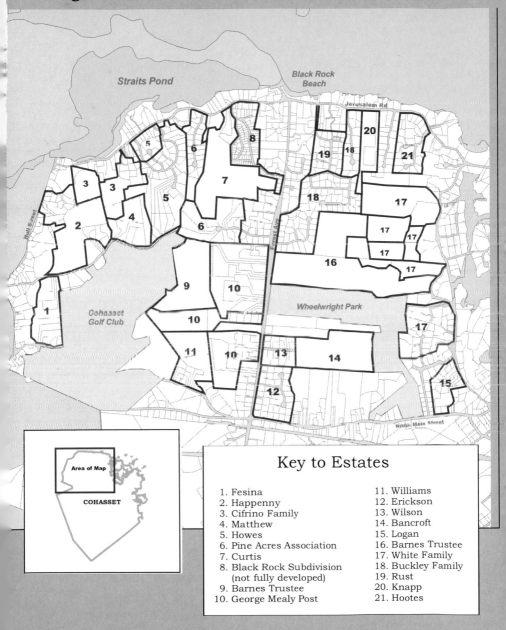

Straits Pond

Black Rock Beach

Jerusalem Rd

Hull Street

Cohasset Golf Club

Wheelwright Park

North Main Street

Area of Map

COHASSET

Key to Estates

1. Fesina
2. Happenny
3. Cifrino Family
4. Matthew
5. Howes
6. Pine Acres Association
7. Curtis
8. Black Rock Subdivision
   (not fully developed)
9. Barnes Trustee
10. George Mealy Post

11. Williams
12. Erickson
13. Wilson
14. Bancroft
15. Logan
16. Barnes Trustee
17. White Family
18. Buckley Family
19. Rust
20. Knapp
21. Hootes

Map of Cohasset 2000

Roads shown in orange are new since 1950.

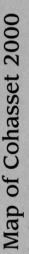

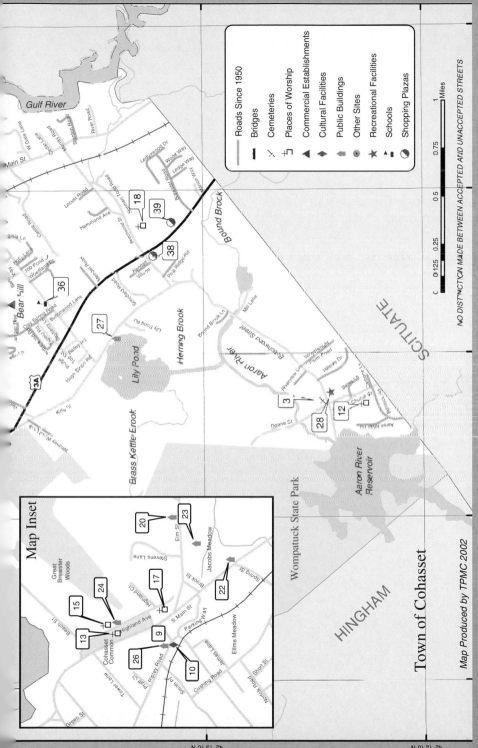

See next page for key to map numbers.

Map Legend for center spread Cohasset map

Bridges ▬

1 Border Street Bridge
2 Cunningham Bridge

Cemeteries ✕

3 Beechwood Cemetery
4 Central Cemetery
5 Woodside Cemetery

Commercial Establishments ▲

6 Atlantica
7 Cohasset Heights Ltd. Landfill
8 Kimball's by the Sea

Cultural Facilities ✦

9 South Shore Community Center
10 South Shore Art Center
11 South Shore Music Circus

Places of Worship ☩

12 Beechwood Congregational Church
13 First Parish Meeting House
14 Panagia Greek Orthodox Church
15 Second Congregational Church
16 St. Anthony's Church
17 St. Stephen's Church
18 Vedanta Centre

Public Buildings ◆

19 DPW Garage
20 Fire / Police Headquarters
21 Joseph Osgood School / New Library
22 Paul Pratt Memorial Library
23 Sewage Treatment Plant
24 Town Hall
25 Town Recycling / Transfer Station
26 U.S. Post Office
27 Water Treatment Plant

Recreational Facilities ★

28 Beechwood Ball Field
29 Cohasset Golf Club
30 Cohasset Sailing Club
31 Cohasset Yacht Club
32 Harold F. Barnes Field
33 Swim Center

Schools ⌐

34 Deer Hill School
35 Joseph Osgood School
36 Middle –High School

Shopping Plazas ◉

37 Cohasset Plaza
38 Shaw's Plaza
39 Tedeschi Plaza

Other Sites ◉

40 Holly Hill Farm
41 Mariners Park
42 Veterans Park

dren in the local schools and enjoyed the recreational amenities of the town, but you worked in Boston or Quincy or on "128." Cohasset was no longer the same quaint little seacoast village it had once been. The rapid subdivision of land for new homes and the commercial development of Route 3A had awakened the town to the need for planning and control. To this end, Cohasset had passed its first zoning bylaw in 1955. Three years later the town engaged consultant Allen Benjamin from Wayland, Massachusetts, to prepare a long-range master plan.

Benjamin Report

Commissioned in 1958 and completed in 1961, the Benjamin Report was to be the Planning Board's Bible. It laid out in detail the steps Cohasset should take to manage growth on the way toward "saturation" (ultimate development). The plans were based on a projected population of between 13,400 and 14,800 by the year 2000. Although criticized in later years for its wildly inflated population projection (actual population in 2000, only 7,261) and its impractical highway scheme to bring Route 3A traffic into downtown Cohasset, it nevertheless gave an accurate account of the town's problems. The report made recommendations on a range of issues, including zoning and traffic patterns; schools, parks, and libraries; fire and police stations; water supply, flood control, and sewage disposal; and the harbor and downtown areas. Several of its ideas were implemented, notably the new fire-police station on Elm Street, the park at the Cove, the acquisition of land for new schools, and the formation of a capital budget committee to schedule capital outlays.

From Parkway to 3A

The state had originally intended all of Route 3A from the Hingham circle south through Cohasset, Scituate, and Marshfield to be a rural parkway, with trees and shrubs on each side. The towns, however, controlled the land adjacent to 3A through local zoning requirements and were free to define acceptable use. In Cohasset village the need for retail space and parking was outgrowing the available space, and 3A was an attractive option for expansion. Moreover, a business on 3A could draw customers from the population of neighboring towns as well as from Cohasset. This pressure resulted in a decision to zone certain sections of the highway for commercial and light-industrial use. The two business zones authorized were 3A north from Sohier Street to about where Frank Williams Landscaping Supplies is located (133 CJC Highway) and 3A south from Beechwood Street to the Scituate line, with the land between Sohier and Beechwood streets reserved for residential use only.

The early businesses attempted to preserve the forested beauty of the "parkway." D.S. Kennedy, for example, was well hidden from the highway by a large buffer of trees. When the company moved from its Whitney Hill site, it was replaced in 1966 by Webb-Norfolk Conveyor Company, maker of motor-driven conveyors such as those used at airports to move luggage. Drivers along Route 3A would never suspect that a manufacturing plant existed nearby. Some businesses that were exposed to the highway strove to maintain a residential appearance; for example, the owners of Cowdrey's Gift Shop in Cushing Plaza surveyed South Shore architecture for homey details to include in the design of their store.

But esthetic preservation was not a priority for car dealerships, gas stations, and shopping centers. They required roadside visibility and large parking areas, and so the woods were bulldozed and the land paved. As early as 1960 neighbors in Scituate were making disparaging remarks about our portion of the highway even while they enjoyed the convenience of shopping there. In response to a proposal to rezone part of Route 3A in Scituate for business, a reader of the *South Shore Mirror* (March 1960) wrote: "One has but to look at the reckless wrecking of its State-owned aisles in the Cohasset section . . . to appreciate how the purposes of this road have been disregarded . . . Let me plead with the abutters of 3A, particularly in the Cohasset section, to curtail their oversized signs and neon lights and with the cooperation of the state recover by planting and laws, as far as possible, the beauty that has been destroyed." Another reader commented: "This is an invitation to repeat Cohasset's pattern of creeping destruction. Don't we all breathe a sigh of relief when we drive out of Cohasset's strip of commercialism into our more attractive town?" (1/12/61).

Well! Commerce in Cohasset had to go somewhere, and better along Route 3A than downtown. The convenience of "one-stop shopping" and plenty of parking had irresistible appeal. In 1962 a new plaza, the Tedeschi Shopping Center, opened southeast of Cushing Plaza and featured "a completely modern supermarket" operated by the Tedeschi Division of Stop & Shop. Other stores, such as Woolworth's in 1962 and Noble's Camera Shop in 1966, also moved in. Nearby was Bergson's Ice Cream Shop, a popular place for a snack or lunch, which opened in 1964. A new skating rink, the Cohasset Winter Garden, opened farther north in 1965. For about 20 years until its closing in 1987, the schools' youth hockey programs were held there. (One of Cohasset's star Pee Wee players of the 1960s, Michael O'Connell, went on to play for the Chicago Blackhawks and, in the 1980s, for the Boston Bruins.) In 1967 Cohasset Knoll, a convalescent home, was built at the Hingham line.

"Old Cohasset Village"

How did downtown Cohasset adjust to the upstart competition from Route 3A? Its first response was to advertise itself as "Old Cohasset Village Shopping Center—Only a Short Distance Off Route 3A" (*South Shore Mirror*, 8/18/60). Then in 1963 merchants got together and formed the Cohasset Village Association, whose aim was to "protect the 'village' flavor of the town center" by painting the shops white and perhaps adding flower boxes (*Boston Sunday Globe*, 5/10/64).

Yet the pace of change in the village accelerated. In the summer of 1960 Cohasset Motors moved to Route 3A, and its Colonial-style showroom on South Main Street was replaced by a new super Texaco service station. In 1964 Delory's Drugstore burned down, leaving an empty lot (now a "pocket park"). A year later the U.S. Post Office moved from its temporary quarters in the old A&P building on South Main Street to a new building on Ripley Road, built over pilings driven into swampland. Colonial Pharmacy relocated from the corner of Depot Court to the former A & P site. Curtis Compact Food Store opened in the old First National building at 52 South Main Street in 1965. In 1966 Cards & Shards moved into a former private residence at 45 South Main Street, and in 1968 Philip Smith Ltd. opened a new sports shop and antiques store in the old post office space at 3 Depot Court.

The turnover of small businesses would continue over the next two or three decades as merchants struggled to find the combination of uniqueness and market presence that would give them long-term viability. The enterprises that have tended to succeed are those that provide local food service or convenience goods, offer unique gifts, or sell antiques.

More New Homes

The settlement pattern of the sixties differed dramatically from that of previous decades. Gone were most of the farms and open fields that gave Cohasset its rural character. Vanished too were many of the estates of the summer people. In their stead were subdivisions and developments, new properties and homes for the families that continued to pour in. Not until 1967 did higher interest rates slow house construction. Between 1960 and 1965, 50 to 75 new houses were built each year. In 1965 alone, the Planning Board approved three subdivisions containing a total of 93 lots; in addition, the board reviewed plans for 30 more houselots that needed no approval. In the Town Report for that year, the Planning Board chairman warned: "This means that the space between houses is growing smaller and that our town is rapidly losing the look of a sprawling country town which is the very thing that makes it so attractive. The need for a properly restrictive zoning bylaw cannot be overstressed."

The town tried to pass a new, more restrictive zoning bylaw and map in 1963. The bylaw would have established a residential zone C in certain areas of town, with a minimum lot requirement of 40,000 square feet. In contrast, the 1955 bylaw required a minimum of 20,000 square feet, and in some areas only 12,000. The new measure failed to win the necessary two-thirds majority vote. It was again proposed at a special town meeting on November 9, 1965. This time a concerted effort was made to bring in supporters but, incredibly, that was the night of the Great Blackout. The power failure kept many people home, and the article failed by two votes. It failed again in 1966, at the second largest town meeting in Cohasset's history. On the fourth try, in 1968, the town finally succeeded in at least amending the zoning bylaw by increasing the minimum frontage for a lot from 20 feet to 50 feet. Still, some residents saw the change as unduly restrictive. Gilbert Tower, a native of Cohasset and a dedicated, if unofficial, town planner, complained to the *South Shore Mirror* (9/11/69): "Will Cohasset want to continue 'snob-zoning' and even enlarge upon it for people with money? Or will the town recognize that there are almost no places in the town where people with not much money can afford to live? In short, it will be money versus people."

One of the largest new developments of the sixties was Fairoaks Lane. It was subdivided and built by Charles T. ("Ted") Patrolia, who bought the land, consisting of open fields, from Robert Pape, manager of Oaks Farm. In the early 1900s the site had been occupied by young Italian immigrants, who built shacks in the fields. Encouraged to come by relatives and attracted by the availability of jobs, they worked at Oaks Farm and other estates in town. Some of the men settled in Cohasset; others returned home and later, in some cases, brought their families back with them. While clearing the land for development, Patrolia's men found some old bottles, historic remnants from "the Camp," a name given to the settlement area on Fairoaks Lane. Soon what had been the Camp was built up with spacious "executive homes" for middle-class families.

On the southern side of Oaks Farm, Bill Poland and Irwin Golden bought a pasture on Bear Hill and subdivided it into house lots. Evelyn and Lloyd Prescott were the first couple to build a house on what was now called Old Pasture Road. This was still a time when you could make your own archaeological discoveries. On the unpaved road beyond their home, one of the Prescotts' daughters found an arrowhead, a relic from the bands of archaic Indians that hunted deer on Deer Hill, wild turkey on Turkey Hill, and bear on Bear Hill. Farmland at the western end of Beechwood Street was also subdivided and developed in the sixties, creating Hillside Drive, Flintlock Ridge Road and, farther east, Bound Brook Lane and Pine Ridge Road.

On the east side of Route 3A near the Scituate line, Walter Winchester developed Brewster Road, starting with three houses in the 1950s. Evans's Fish Market, on the corner of Brewster Road and the highway, supplied crushed lobster shells to form the base for part of the road. Used lumber from dismantled buildings at the old horse show grounds on Sohier Street framed the first new homes.

Still more building took place on Forest Avenue. In the mid-1960s Joseph Kealey developed Cedar Acres Lane near North Main Street. Closer to the ocean, D. J. Buckley cleared the woods and filled the lowlands to create Old Coach Road. Nearby, real estate agent Eleanor Collins and architect Royal Barry Wills built Surrey Drive. Wills also developed Fernway, off Red Gate Lane, and designed and built homes on Windy Hill Road off Jerusalem Road ("Cohasset's newest community of prestige homes . . . Living in Windy Hill has become a symbol of distinction," advertised Eleanor Collins in the *South Shore Mirror*, 4/23/64). Two other developments in this busy era were Sandy Beach Lane off Nichols Road and Lantern Lane off Pond Street.

SEWER SAGA: PART 1

Many newcomers who had moved here from cities were surprised to hear vigorous debate at town meeting on subjects as basic as sewage and sewers. Few had ever had to consider where the water in their homes came from or where it went. Yet sewage had been a perennial issue in the town, the subject of numerous special committees and the preoccupation of the Board of Health for many years.

Even before the twentieth century, pollution had become apparent in James Brook, a creek that flowed from Sanctuary Pond through the center of town and into the Cove. Sewage from failed cesspools along the way drained into the brook, which flooded in the spring and stagnated in the summer, producing high levels of effluent and noxious odors. In 1906 the town appointed a committee to study this problem. After consulting with the state Board of Health, the committee recommended sewering the center of town. Thus began our long sewer saga. The following year, in 1907, the study committee introduced a warrant article at town meeting to authorize the construction of a central sewerage system designed by Boston engineer Leonard Metcalf. It was defeated. At $34,000, the system was considered too costly, and the town opted instead for the installation of "sand filter beds" on individual properties in the vicinity of James Brook, at the homeowner's cost.

This was a stop-gap solution. The pollution of James Brook got worse. In 1934 the town decided to deal with it by banishing at least a portion of James Brook from sight. The offending stream was concealed in a culvert in the center of town. This did nothing, of course, to diminish the problem. In 1948 the state health commissioner ordered the town to "take necessary action" to prevent further pollution. Accordingly, the town hired the engineering firm of Camp, Dresser & McKee to conduct another study. In 1950 the firm presented the town with plans for a sewerage system that would cost $620,000. But again the town took no action.

The conversion of many summer homes into year-round residences made the problem of septage runoff into tidewaters and storm drains a year-round issue. Moreover, the installation of must-have conveniences—dishwashers, washing machines, disposals—in the new homes impaired the effectiveness of their septic systems and accelerated their failure. The Board of Health urged homeowners to improve cesspools and septic tanks that were failing, and many did comply, spending "hundreds and even thousands of dollars," according to the 1957 Town Report. The Cohasset Board of Health, grateful for the cooperation, commended "all these fellow citizens who prevented the expense of a town sewer system [from] being forced on us."

The Board of Health nevertheless was concerned about the

health risks posed by failing systems, and in 1960 a Public Sewerage Study Committee was appointed. The committee, chaired by Richard B. Singer, reconfirmed that James Brook was heavily polluted in the center of town. The high population density, the concentration of old cesspools, and the semipermeable soil made the area unsuitable for on-site sewage disposal. The Board of Health for the first time banned swimming in Cohasset Harbor because of high coliform bacterial counts. Again there was much resistance at town meeting to a central sewage treatment plant, especially from those at the "back of the hall." Residents who had lived in the town all their lives claimed they had never become sick from swimming in the harbor. Lobstermen feared that pumping treated fresh water from an outflow pipe into the harbor would kill the lobsters stored there in lobster cars.

In 1962 the Boston engineering firm of Fay, Spofford & Thorndike, hired by the Public Sewerage Study Committee, also confirmed evidence of extensive pollution of James Brook from failed sewage disposal systems in the center of town. "The downtown area was horrendous," recalls Henry Rattenbury. "The sewage would run right out of the Red Lion Inn down the parking lot to Main Street and into catch basins. When you walked by Central Market in summer, the odor was terrible."

Forty concerned residents formed a grass-roots committee to support the study committee's proposal for town sewerage. In frustration, the committee soon voted itself out of existence. A member wrote: "Cohasset Harbor is so polluted it's a disgrace. It's something that ought to be corrected but the town has done absolutely nothing because it would cost money. We have dissolved the committee because we have done all we can" (*South Shore Mirror*, 12/20/62).

The conflict over the sewer issue fueled a spirited contest for election to the Board of Health in 1963. Robert T. Sceery, a local physician and strong advocate of sewerage, ran for an open position on the board. He recalls that a committee of highly active young mothers led by Polly Logan conducted his campaign. "You would think you were running for president," he says. Sceery won by a margin of a few votes. Opponents included the local merchants, who stood firmly against change and pressured town officials to reject the notion of a municipal sewer: "It wasn't called for," was the laconic comment of Fred Mulcahy, the owner and operator of Central Market (*Boston Sunday Globe,* 5/10/64).

Finally, in March 1965 town meeting voted to accept enabling legislation authorizing the town to construct and operate a sewerage system. After nearly 60 years of surveys and studies and special committees, and no action, the town was ready to accept limited sewerage. What ultimately forced the issue was the need for a new junior high school wing. The state, becoming ever more involved in Cohasset's affairs, would not approve its share of funds for the addition unless the town provided sewerage for the school on Pond Street. The hilltop, with its clayey soil and pockets of swamp, was not suitable for an on-site system.

It was not until 1967, when town meeting approved the new wing, that the town actually voted (530 to 144) to appropriate $344,000 to construct, maintain, and operate a sewage treatment plant and sewerage system. The plant, to be built in Jacob's Meadow (the area south of Elm Street through which James Brook flowed into the harbor), would be capable of servicing the town schools, Pond Street, and the town center. The 1967 town meeting also authorized the Board of Water Commissioners to act as a Board of Sewer Commissioners, charged with constructing and operating the town's treatment facilities. In 1968 the town appropriated an additional $191,000 for construction of the sewerage system. On August 18, 1969, the new Water Pollution Control Facility in Jacob's Meadow began operation, "a milestone in the progress of the Town to eliminate pollution" (1969 Town Report).

OUT WITH THE OLD, IN WITH THE NEW

The treatment plant was one of the more important but less visible changes that took place in the sixties. More obvious to the townspeople were the new landmarks that emerged as old ones disappeared or changed hands. As if marking the end of an era, small neighborhood institutions gave way to larger, more centralized ones.

From Neighborhood to Central Library

In the Beechwood area, the local branch of the Paul Pratt Memorial Library closed in 1961. Located at the back of the BIA Hall, it had served the people of the "Third Division" since 1913. Mary A. Stoddard was its librarian for 44 years, from its opening to her death in 1957. The decline of the library began during World War II, when the U.S. Navy expropriated part of Beechwood for its Ammunition Depot, thereby reducing the library's service area. The circulation of books diminished further during the 1950s, as library users were more inclined to drive their cars to the larger Paul Pratt Library on South Main Street. In 1961 the library trustees decided that operation of the Beechwood library was no longer practical; they closed it and transferred the librarian, Constance Jones, to the central library.

Three years later a new two-story wing was added to the Paul Pratt Library. Funded through the Pratt Estate and gifts and bequests from citizens, the $75,000 wing provided much-needed space for the librarian and staff, for research and study, and for meetings. New services and programs were offered at no cost to the town through the Friends of the Library, organized in 1968. Over the years the Friends have manned the circulation desk, brought books to nursing homes, arranged special programs for adults and children, raised funds for the library, and provided free passes to Boston area museums.

In 1969 the chief librarian, Sarah Heywood, retired after 22 years of service to the town. To replace her the Board of Trustees hired Richard Hayes, an instructor of library science at Northeastern University. Hayes propelled the library into a new era. One of the first things he did was to open the stacks. Now you could browse for books yourself instead of asking the librarian to get one for you. He also challenged the community with unconventional ideas. He gave an eye-opening talk, for example, on the

Richard Hayes, chief librarian of the Paul Pratt Memorial Library, 1969-1997. He not only opened the library's stacks to the public, but also encouraged the use of the facility as a forum for discussion and debate. Photo courtesy of Cohasset Mariner

contemporary black-humor fiction of Kurt Vonnegut, author of *Slaughterhouse-Five*. "Mr. Hayes hopes that there will be continued interest in using the library as a forum for discussion and debate in the community," reported the *South Shore Mirror* (4/24/69). As we shall see, he got what he wished for.

New Fire-Police Headquarters

In 1960 the Police Department was still housed in its small head-quarters in the Independence Building downtown, and the Central Fire Station still operated at the Cove. For years the police and fire chiefs had been complaining about the inadequacy of their head quarters. The Police Department had doubled in number, from the chief, one sergeant, and five patrolmen in 1950 to the chief, two sergeants, and 10 patrolmen in 1960. The Fire Department had grown from the chief, a deputy chief, and 10 drivers in 1950 (aided by many call firefighters) to the chief, a deputy chief, and 15 per manent firefighters in 1960 (also aided by many call firefighters).

The fire station at the Cove, one of three in Cohasset, was an old two-story wooden building that itself was a fire hazard. Renovation was considered expensive and impractical. At the same time, the police headquarters in the Independence Building was overcrowded and, with no garage and parking space, had out-lived its usefulness. Especially inconvenient, the ambulance, which the police, not the firefighters, operated in those days, had to be parked some distance away in the Highway Department Garage behind the Red Lion Inn.

In 1962 town meeting authorized the construction of a new combined fire and police headquarters on Elm Street (at a cost of $225,000). Designed by local architects Eastman Studds and Irwin D. Matthew, it was built on the site of the old Osgood School, demolished 10 years earlier. The "Little Red Schoolhouse" nearby was also razed. Formerly the Central District School, it had stood on Bourne Rock (where St. Stephen's Church is now located) until it was moved in 1921 to Elm Street, next to the Osgood School. The small building served as an industrial arts building and, for a few years, as a nursery school run by the Community Center.

At the Cove, the old fire station was also torn down. The open space thereby created was landscaped after a design by Irwin Matthew. George Jednick, a Cohasset resident and veteran of the Korean War, supervised the transformation of the site into Veterans Memorial Park. The fire station bell from the old building was saved. You can see it now at Government Island, standing next to a retaining wall near the two stone templates. The Independence Building would also have disappeared, but it won a reprieve when the town leased it for use

The Independence Building served as police headquarters from 1913 to 1963 when the new Fire-Police Station was completed. *Photo courtesy of Cohasset Historical Society*

The present Fire-Police Station was built in 1963 on the Elm Street site of the old Osgood School. *Photo courtesy of Ralph Dormitzer*

The old Central Fire Station at the Cove, razed in 1963. Veterans Memorial Park now stands on the site. *Photo from* Massachusetts Selectman, *April 1961, courtesy of Peg Stoughton*

as the Gown Museum. Interestingly, the old *Independence* hand-pumper that gave the building its name still exists. Built in 1847, it had been stored for decades in various outdoor locations, where it slowly deteriorated. In the 1980s Tom Finegan, a Cohasset fire-fighter, rescued it from neglect and has been meticulously restoring it at his own expense.

In 1967 Hector Pelletier, Cohasset's longtime police chief, retired after 40 years of service. Widely admired for his police work and civic activities, Pelletier had risen from the rank of state trooper, with only a seventh-grade education, to chief of the Cohasset Police Department in 1924. He also served as secretary and treasurer of the Massachusetts Chiefs of Police and founded a training academy for police officers at the State Police Headquarters in Framingham. A member of the executive committee for the Jimmy Fund, established in 1948 to support cancer research and treatment for children, he had raised over a million dollars for the charity. At his retirement he was honored at a testimonial dinner attended by more than a thousand people, including state officials, officers of the Federal Bureau of Investigation, executives of the Jimmy Fund Foundation of Boston, and members of the clergy.

Stepping into Pelletier's very large shoes was Randolph A. Feola, a Cohasset police officer since 1946. He had served in the Seventh Armored Division of the U.S. Army during World War II and was awarded four battle stars and the Bronze Star Medal for bravery in the Battle of the Bulge in Belgium, where Allied forces successfully stemmed Hitler's last offensive. As a teenager, Feola had achieved the rank of Eagle Scout, the highest award in Boy Scouts. Gifted with a near-photographic memory, he was the highest scorer in the Civil Service exam for the position of police chief in Cohasset. Considered a diamond in the rough by his friends, he had a gruff voice, used

Program for the testimonial banquet given for Police Chief Hector Pelletier when he retired in 1967 after 40 years of service. Program courtesy of Arlene Orr

Randolph A. Feola, a decorated member of the U.S. Army's Seventh Armored Division during World War II and a Cohasset police officer since 1946, was appointed to succeed Pelletier as police chief in 1967. Photo courtesy of Ruth Ann Feola Semel

salty language, kept a little brown book in which he recorded the acts of local transgressors, and developed a justified reputation as one of the last "characters" in town. Residents still remember him driving around in his cruiser, a lit stogie tucked behind his ear and his tiny chihuahua, Pépé, riding beside him. As we shall see, he and his son, Randy, Jr., also on the Cohasset police force, became the focus of media attention in the 1970s.

New St. Anthony's Church

In 1960 the Reverend Joseph T. Brennan was appointed pastor of St. Anthony's Church, after the death of Monsignor Thomas F. Devlin. He inherited a parish that had outgrown its old wooden church on South Main Street and could no longer accommodate the congregation, which by 1958 included more than 600 families, twice the number the church had been designed for. Embarking on a program to design, fund, and build a new church, Father Brennan trav-

The first St. Anthony's Roman Catholic Church, which was outgrown by the 1960s. Built in 1875, the old wooden church was razed in 1979. Postcard courtesy of Ann Pompeo

Richard Cardinal Cushing blessing the cornerstone of the new, brick St. Anthony's Church in 1964. Photo courtesy of Glenn Pratt

eled around New England seeking just the right model for St. Anthony's. He found it in New Hampshire, in the form of a Congregational church, and replicated the style in Cohasset.

In 1963 ground was broken on the corner of South Main and Summer streets, on land donated by the Knights of Columbus and parishioner Dr. Frederick O'Brien. The architect for the new church was also a parishioner, W. Chester Browne. Completed in 1964, at a cost of about $500,000, the Bulfinch-style red brick building with white trim could seat 850 people, the largest capacity of any church in Cohasset. On July 11, 1965, the cornerstone was blessed by Richard Cardinal Cushing, Archbishop of Boston. Assisting him at the dedication ceremonies were Rev. Richard Brady, former curate of the parish, and two Cohasset men who had been ordained to the priesthood, Rev. Hubert Desmond and Rev. Ralph Enos.

A departure from the traditional Roman Catholic church, the new building's simple Colonial-style interior had white walls, white pews, plain windows, and large brass chandeliers. It was adorned only by a crucifix behind the altar, a statue of St. Anthony of Padua on one side altar and Our Lady of the Immaculate Conception on the other, and Stations of the Cross along the walls of the nave. All were made of mahogany and hand carved in Italy.

A special niche was reserved for the small, primitive wooden statue of Saint Anthony brought from the Azores to Cohasset by Ignatia Concepcion Fratcs in 1875. Local folklore relates that on the voyage to America, the little statue became separated from Ignatia's luggage. It is reported that she was not concerned. After all, Saint Anthony was the patron saint of lost articles and, she said, "Saint Anthony cannot become lost." Two weeks later, he was miraculously found. The first Roman Catholic church in Cohasset was under construction at the time, and it seemed appropriate to name it after St. Anthony. The Irish, however, wanted to name the church after Saint Patrick. The issue was decided by a flip of a coin, and St. Anthony won.

The old church continued in use as a place for occasional meetings, held in the basement, and for religious education classes. Considered a fire hazard, it was torn down in August 1979.

Black Rock House
In the summer of 1968 a famous Cohasset landmark, the old Black Rock House on Jerusalem Road, was demolished. Located at the southeast end of Strait's Pond high up on a ledge overlooking the pond, Black Rock Beach, and the ocean, it was the last of three hotels of the same name built to accommodate summer visitors. The first Black Rock House had been the home of Captain Nathaniel Nichols. Constructed in 1757 on ledge at Black Rock Beach, near what is now 475 Jerusalem Road, it was later opened to the public as an inn. It was used in the 1830s mainly by those who came to our shores to fish and shoot migratory waterfowl known as "coot."

By 1850 the small inn had been enlarged to a substantial boardinghouse, the "second" Black Rock House. Summer guests would spend several weeks there, enjoying the ocean, the rocky coastline, the fresh sea air, and the shaded woods. In 1903 a family who had built a summer estate on the inland side of Jerusalem Road complained that the boardinghouse spoiled their view. They bought the place from its owner, Sarah R. Smith, and tore it down. One section, however, was moved over the beach to Hull and became a private residence, which still exists, on the shore of Strait's Pond across from Green Hill.

In 1904 Sarah Smith decided to build a much grander, third Black Rock House on Jerusalem Road west of Forest Avenue, on a steep ledge overlooking Strait's Pond and the ocean. She modeled it after a medieval English castle, complete with towers, turrets, and balconies. A huge shingled edifice, it eventually contained 60 guest rooms, lounges, a dining room, and rooms for 45 employees, including orchestra players. It became world famous for its elegant decor, fine service, and continental cuisine. Guests included visitors from Europe and Asia as well as New York and the Midwest. Celebrities performing with the South Shore Players at Town Hall stayed there frequently. In the 1930s playwright Thornton Wilder, who performed in his play *Our Town* at Town Hall, wrote notes for some of his works in an octagonal tower room at the hotel. He was also a frequent summer visitor at the Higginson home in Sandy Cove.

The third Black Rock House, built in 1904, was a world-famous hostelry until World War II, when business began a steep decline that continued into the 1960s. The building was razed in 1968. Photo courtesy of Glenn Pratt

In 1926 Albert Golden, the father of local developer and lawyer Irwin Golden, bought the building. For nearly 40 years he operated it from June to September. During World War II, however, business evaporated. It never fully recovered, and by the early 1960s only a few rooms were occupied. The Ship's Bar, the only remaining center of activity, closed in 1964. Declared by the Fire Department to be the largest single fire hazard in town, the building was razed in 1968. With it went fond memories of oldtime Cohasset and a significant slice of its history as a summer playground for the elite.

YOUTH DAYS, SAILING CLUB, AND MORE

For many in Cohasset there was no memory of this history, and most people were too busy to note its passing. They were creating a new history of community activities for children and adults, among them the Sailing Club, Swim Team, and the Cohasset League of Women Voters. The recreational programs for youngsters were extensive for a small town, making Cohasset an even more powerful magnet for new families. The proliferation of activities was not uniformly perceived as a benefit, however. "The town is certainly overorganized," said Reverend F. Lee Richards, rector of St. Stephen's Church. "Parents don't have time for their children, and too many of them get into trouble as a result" (*Boston Globe*, 5/10/64). Yet few towns could have made a greater effort to keep their youth occupied and out of trouble.

CYAA and Youth Days

In 1960 a citizens' group formed the Cohasset Youth Athletic Association. The CYAA was an outgrowth of earlier organized activities for children such as Little League, but was a response to the needs of the now teenaged baby boomers. Its first president was Nathaniel Hurwitz, a founder of Little League. The association set up a Pony League for teenaged boys and organized a Field Day at Milliken-Bancroft Field, held annually for several years. The CYAA would become the umbrella organization for both Little League and Pony League, merged under the same board of directors.

In 1962 the sports program included a football team, the Cohasset Midgets, which played in the Old Colony Football League and won the 1963 league championship. A year later the CYAA organized a girls softball league for 8-to-12-year-olds. But its most remarkable program was Youth Days, organized in 1961 by Philip Murray, Nate Hurwitz's son-in-law. Under his leadership it flourished for many years.

The Youth Days Program began with a spectacular parade led by fire engines and followed by an MDC mounted-police unit, a color guard, marching bands, colorful floats, military units, drill teams, town officials, and town organizations. A star attraction was Hanscom Airforce Base's Jody Drill Team, whose spirited routine thrilled the spectators. As described by the *South Shore Mirror* (4/28/66), "the Jodys, at the command 'Think now—Jodys—hit it!' begin a demonstration of precision marching, jazz 'scat singing,' and circus ring humor which is fast becoming a national trademark . . . The Jody Drill team has thrown the book away. Instead of half step, double time, and cadence count, the Jodys have substituted the stockade shuffle, the razzle dazzle, the wine bowl, and the ducky step."

Youth Days festivities also included a Midway on the Common, a "Horribles Parade" with children and adults dressed in "weird and fantastic costumes," award ceremonies for the best costumes and floats, a dance for teenagers at Town Hall, and the crowning of the winner of the "Miss Cohasset" contest. The Teenage Queen, chosen on the basis of poise, appearance, and person-ality, rode with her court (the two runners-up) on a flowerbedecked float in the parade. All were "showered with gifts donated by village

Candidates for Miss Cohasset pose during the 1969 Youth Days celebration. Starting with the front row, contestants were: Donna Green, Mary Oldfield, Maribeth Ahearn, Cathy Oliver, Suzy Marsh, Vicki Watkins, Barbara Joseph, Sheila Sullivan, Hilja Rautiala, Nancy Antoine, Mary Grayken, and Rita White.
Newspaper clip from South Shore Mirror, courtesy of Polly Logan

merchants" (*South Shore News*, 7/8/65) The Youth Days Program had such crowd appeal that in 1966, an election year, political can-didates for major state offices marched in the parade, led by Governor John A. Volpe, and were cheered by 5,000 spectators.

In 1966 the CYAA sponsored yet another athletic program, the Cohasset Swim Team. Organized with the help of Cohasset Red Cross swimming instructor Helen Pratt, the team included boys and girls aged 8 to 16. The youngsters competed in swim meets with teams and clubs from neighboring towns. Because Cohasset had no municipal pool at the time, instructors planned to hold training practice in the chilly ocean waters off Sandy Beach. But when 150 children signed up for the new program, far exceeding the expect-ed number, Cohasset residents volunteered the use of their pools for both practice and swim meets.

Boosters Club and Hot Sullivan Day

Sports for youth were a priority in the sixties. Over half (60 percent) of all households in Cohasset had children under the age of 18 in 1960 (compared with only one-third in 1990), and the first of the baby boomers were just reaching junior-senior high school age. To promote school sports and to recognize the achievements of high school athletes, a group of parents formed a Boosters Club, led by Lawrence ("Chick") S. Gates, in 1964.

The Boosters sponsored Hot Sullivan Day on October 3, 1964, to honor Michael Joseph ("Hot") Sullivan, caretaker of Milliken-Bancroft Field for 45 years and a devoted supporter of Cohasset youth and high school sports: "He has been Cohasset's number one fan for as long as most people can remember," reported the *Patriot Ledger* (10/1/64). "He attends as many football, baseball, basketball games, track meets, and high school graduations as he possibly can." The owner of seven champion hunting dogs, Hot was also a noted fox hunter in his younger days, winning more than 125 awards and trophies. When asked how he got his nickname, he told the following story:

> I've had the name since I was about 12 years old [in 1905]. I had just gotten a job helping Jim St. John deliver groceries [to Cohasset homes from his wagon], and I didn't want to do anything wrong. The first day was freezing cold and Jim was taking orders into the houses, chatting for four or five minutes and then coming out. Each time he'd ask me if I was cold, and I'd say no. This went on all afternoon long. I kept on denying that I was cold, and finally I went so far as to say, "No, I'm hot!"

Word got around, and he was called Hot ever since. His son, Ernest, and his grandson were also nicknamed Hot.

Sailing Club

Sailing had been the sport of the elite. For most youngsters in Cohasset, it could only be a spectator sport, unless they were fortunate enough to have parents who belonged to the Yacht Club and owned a boat. This did not seem right to Herbert R. Towle: "If a child was raised on a ranch, you would expect him to learn how to ride . . . But how many children in Cohasset have a chance to learn about sailing?" Towle grew up on Border Street across from the harbor and learned to sail by cruising with Yacht Club members. He realized that he was one of the few natives of the town lucky enough to have been exposed to sailing.

On a Yacht Club cruise in the 1950s, he happened to meet Joseph Lee, who had founded Community Boating on the Charles River in Boston in 1937. He inspired Towle to do something similar for Cohasset. Thus was born the Cohasset Sailing Club, where any youngster with an interest could learn to sail on boats provided by the club. With legal help from Cohasset lawyer Roger Coulter and site plans drawn by town civil engineer Edwin Young, Towle developed bylaws and a layout for a public sailing club. He presented his proposal at town meeting in 1960 and asked for the use of town-owned land on Government Island. The town granted him his request, on condition that he raise funds for the club through public donations. That he did, with particularly generous support from Yacht Club members.

In the summer of 1960 the Cohasset Sailing Club was launched, the first of its kind on the South Shore. The executive committee included Herbert R. Towle, chairman; Thomas E. Burke, Roger Coulter, and Gerard Stanton. Herb Towle's dream had become a reality. Now any child in Cohasset had an opportunity to develop navigational skills and self-reliance. "They learn to respect nature, must think and act independently, and when a puff of wind comes, they must react," explained Towle. The club was open to all residents upon payment of a modest fee. Adults could learn to sail too, but the focus was on children aged 10 through 15. The club instructor was J. Edward Younie, assisted by two Cohasset teenagers, Samuel Wakeman and Peter Hagerty.

By the end of the first summer, 128 boys and girls had learned to sail. That number would double by 1997, and the fleet would triple in size, from 7 to 21 boats. Over the years some graduates of the program have gone on to careers at sea; in the 1990s, for example, one became captain of a schooner in Marblehead and two were instructors at the Naval Academy in Annapolis. Even more important than the practical training is the community spirit the club fosters by allowing all citizens to enjoy what was once the preserve of only a few.

Tennis, Anyone?

Tennis was another sport that had been inaccessible to many residents. You played either on private courts or at the Golf Club. The first public courts in Cohasset were built in 1959 at Milliken-Bancroft Field by the newly appointed town Recreation Commission, under the chairmanship of the energetic Herbert Towle.

The following summer the first annual Children's Hospital Benefit Tennis Tournament was held in Cohasset. Jessie Cox was the inspiration behind this tradition. From the porch of her home overlooking the harbor, she had observed several youths at the Yacht Club tossing buckets of water at each other. Then and there she decided they needed to do something for others. She proceeded to organize the tournament as a charitable event to benefit Children's Hospital in Boston, and she invited Cohasset teenagers to run the event. The matches were played on private courts, ending at the Cox estate. Jessie Cox, always generous, donated all the tennis balls, cash for the cash boxes, and prizes for the finalists. During the 1970s, however, interest in the tournament waned. Then in 1989 Annie Abbruzzese, Joy Pratt, and Robert Whelan, who as children had chased balls for the players, revived the tradition. The mixed-doubles contest, played on 21 of Cohasset's most beautiful private courts, now attracts both local players and out-of-town "super pros." In 2001 the tournament, together with a silent auction, raised more than $16,000 for Children's Hospital.

In 1961 still more tennis became available with the founding of the Cohasset Tennis and Squash Club. The idea for the club began with J. Blake Thaxter, his wife, Jayne, and his tennis partners, all of whom wanted to play year round. At that time the only indoor tennis club in New England was the Badminton and Tennis Club in Boston. Not wishing to make the long trip into town, they decided to form their own local club. The first board of directors included Blake Thaxter, president; Joseph H. Bacheller, Jr., of Hingham,

Samuel Baugh, H. Whitin Brewer, George H. Cavanaugh of Scituate, John J. Hayes, Jr., William M. Hunt, Newell W. Rogers, and Edward Rowe Snow of Marshfield. (Snow was not only a tennis player but also a noted author on maritime subjects.) The board sent out notices of their intent to see how many might be interested in joining an indoor club. Much to their surprise, 125 people sent in deposits toward family memberships. Among those who first played on the covered courts was young Heidi Lincoln of Cohasset, daughter of the popular Cohasset Golf Club pro Richard Lincoln, and national indoors doubles tennis champion in the under-18-year-old category.

The new club, located on a two-acre site on Cedar Street, was the first permanent, all-metal construction, indoor tennis club on the South Shore. To finance the building, the directors raised $45,000 by selling shares at $100 apiece, obtained a mortgage for another $45,000, and collected $10,000 from initiation fees. The $100,000 enabled them to erect a building manufactured by Butler Building that included two tennis courts (a third was added in 1976) and a prefabricated squash court, as well as locker rooms, a spectator viewing lounge, and a pro shop. The club opened on Thanksgiving Day, 1961. It was so successful that tennis players from as far as Maine and Connecticut asked for advice on how to build similar clubs in their areas.

White Water Slalom

For more intrepid athletes, the annual White Water Slalom in the reversing rapids under the Border Street Bridge was still another Cohasset summer attraction that began in the sixties. Sponsored by the Boston Canoe and Kayak Club in 1963, it was a challenging event to enter, and thrilling to watch: "Fifty kayak and canoe racers participated in this unusual sport held each year at Cohasset Narrows, where at ebb tide the [Gulf] River rushes over the rocks and ledges under Mill Bridge into Cohasset Harbor. Hundreds lined the shores and Border Street . . . to watch the racers control their flimsy skiffs over the rapids and through the slalom course, trying not to touch the poles of the [sixteen] gates in the tricky cross currents" (*South Shore News*, 9/30/65). The object was to complete the course in the shortest time with a minimum of penalty points. All contestants had to perform three Eskimo rolls. Among the winners in the 1965 competition was 11-year-old Billy Burbridge of Cohasset, who won first place in the junior division. The Border Street Bridge is still the place to kayak in Cohasset.

Kayaking under the Border Street Bridge. It's still a popular pastime. Photo © Lynne Layman

Bridge jumping, the other perennial, if unlawful, pastime at the Border Street Bridge. Photo courtesy of Cohasset Mariner

Cohasset League of Women Voters

Although sports and outdoor activities were important, particularly to young people, many women in Cohasset yearned for more intellectual stimulation and civic involvement. They found a satisfying outlet in the League of Women Voters. Founded in 1920, the National League of Women Voters was an outgrowth of the National American Woman Suffrage Association. Its original purpose was to encourage women to exercise their newly won right to vote. It developed into a nonpartisan political organization dedicated to promoting intelligent and active citizen participation in government. It also aimed to influence public policy through education and advocacy. Cohasset women formed their own chapter of the league in 1962.

"The league started off with a bang," recalls Ann Whelan, a member of the first board of directors. "People were very interested." It was a time of hope, she points out, with the recent election of President John F. Kennedy, who at his inauguration in 1961 urged citizens to devote themselves to patriotism and service with the memorable words: "Ask not what your cou', v' can do for you. Ask what you can do for your country."

The provisional Cohasset league wa .rganized on January 25, 1962. The following year the Cohasse' rhapter became a fully accredited member of the National League of Women Voters, with Jean Cotton serving as president. The league's first project was to conduct a Know Your Town study on Cohasset. The hard-working members published their findings in a booklet titled *Cohasset Through the Spyglass*, an informative and clearly written survey of town government. Every voter in town received a copy before the 1963 annual town meeting. Impressed by this "outstanding public service," an anonymous citizen volunteered to fund the publication.

For nearly 30 years members of the Cohasset league studied local, state, and national issues. In 1967 they prepared a useful survey on soils and drainage in Cohasset. The league took a stand on problems such as sewage treatment, water pollution, and land use and lobbied the town for solutions. They were strong advocates, for example, for the expansion of the high school in 1967 and for connecting the high school to a sewerage system. The league also held an annual Town Affairs Night before election day to allow voters to hear candidates speak on their qualifications for town office, the problems that confronted the office they sought, and the solutions they would propose.

For many women the league was a stimulating and even life-changing activity. Young mothers joined to keep their minds active when their lives were largely consumed with child care and housekeeping. Particularly after 1963, when Betty Friedan's *Feminine Mystique* was published, many had begun to question the conventional ideal of domesticity and longed to get out into the world. As their children grew older, some of them did just that. Through league work they gained self-confidence, knowledge, and contacts, and they could leverage this experience into careers. Roberta K. Leary, for example, had conducted a thorough study on land-use planning for the league; she subsequently enrolled at M.I.T. and became a professional urban planner. Margaret Lynch, a president of the Cohasset league, headed the Massachusetts league in 1971. She later earned her law degree and became an attorney for the state.

Gradually, however, interest in the league began to wane. Women were entering the workforce in ever larger numbers, and they no longer had the time. Those at home with school-aged children became less willing to spend time on league work and other volunteer services. It became hard to find anyone to serve as president. Lack of leadership and loss of commitment took their toll; by 1991 the Cohasset League of Women Voters had dissolved, and those still interested joined the Hingham league.

Scituate-Cohasset Newcomers Club

If you were new to Cohasset in the fifties and early sixties, you integrated yourself into the community by taking courses at the Art Center, joining the Community Garden Club and church groups, and volunteering in town organizations. You established your circle of friends among other parents of school-aged children. Yet the first few months were often difficult. The Scituate-Cohasset Newcomers Club was formed in 1964 to help families adjust to their new homes, new neighbors, and new town. The club provided a friendly introduction to other newcomers through meetings and special events. Its sponsor, Welcome Wagon, called on families and offered them baskets of samples and coupons from local merchants.

The basket also included a booklet titled *Fallout Protection: What to Know and Do about Nuclear Attack*, published by the Department of Defense in 1961. In that cold war era, it was a grim reminder of the threat of nuclear attack. "In a major attack upon our country," it warned, "millions of people would be killed. There appears to be no practical program that would avoid large-scale loss of life. But an effective program of civil defense could save the lives of millions who would not otherwise survive. Fallout shelters and related preparations, for example, could greatly reduce the number of casualties . . ." Although the booklets continued to be distributed throughout the sixties, the risk of nuclear attack diminished in 1963 with the signing of a nuclear-test-ban treaty between the United States and the Soviet Union. We know of only two backyard fallout shelters that were built in Cohasset: one on Pleasant Street and another near Sandy Beach. Both were eventually removed.

Lions and Goats

The Cohasset Lions Club, a chapter of the International Association of Lions Clubs, was organized in February 1965 by James E. Carroll and Louis Simeone. A nonpolitical, nonsectarian charitable organization, the Lions are dedicated to the betterment of the community and the world at large. Ever since Helen Keller addressed the International Convention of Lions Clubs in 1925 and challenged them to "become knights of the blind in the crusade against darkness," one of their major causes has been the prevention of eye disease.

In their first annual Light Bulb Campaign in 1965, the Cohasset Lions raised $2,400 for a glaucoma detection clinic for town residents and eyeglasses for needy children. It also started a scholarship fund for worthy Cohasset High School students and gave an annual award to the school's most outstanding athlete. In 1966 the Lions donated eye-testing equipment to the Cohasset School Department. By the end of the sixties, competition from sales of new so-called five-year bulbs had dimmed their campaign. Another, more innovative fund-raising opportunity came in 1977. The Lions raised $9,500 in "Flights for Sight" by selling one-hour flights on a 707 jet donated by Pan American Airlines. By the end of the seventies, however, the Cohasset Lions decided to merge with the larger and more viable Hull chapter.

A fraternal organization for retired men called the Old Goats Club was formed in 1966 by Robert Arndt, George Benedict, Paul

Blackmur, Prescott Cumner, Herbert Sherbrooke, and Roscoe Sherbrooke. It is still going strong today. In fact it is so popular that there is a waiting list for membership. To qualify, you must be a fully retired Cohasset male — no part-time workers (and no women!) allowed. The Old Goats get together once a month for lunch at a restaurant and often invite a guest speaker. Speeches are limited to 15 minutes so as not exceed anyone's attention span. The fellowship is warm and genuine, the key to the club's longevity.

The Old Goats at a picnic on the Gulf River in 1978. This shot was taken 12 years after the founding of the club and the Goats are going strong to this day.

Front: *Drex Gibson, Ray Remick, Bob James, Osborne Ingram, Arnold Weeks.*

Seated: *Paul Ffield, Gilbert Tower, Roger Coulter, Carl Ferguson, Lyman Gutterson, Tom Johnson, Rollie Crampton, Amby Cray, Dick Parsons, Pete Cumner.*

Standing: *Paul Blackmur, Werk Cook, Bill Ripley, Jack Wilson, Ed Otis, Karl Pfaffman, Arthur Nisula, Bob Knowles, Dan Campbell, Al Hunt, Lou Walinsky, Arthur Nillson, Ed Tower, Jack Bishop, Fred Howe.* Photo courtesy of Osborne Ingram

CHANGES IN TOWN GOVERNMENT

The fifties had been a decade of continuity in town government. The same three people—Helen Scripture, Norman Card, and Ira Stoughton—served as selectmen, assessors, and public welfare officers for eight years. Ira Stoughton was the full-time selectman, with administrative responsibilities. He and Charles J. Fox, a member of the Advisory Committee, ran the town, recalls Richard Leggat, who joined the committee in 1960. Fox was appointed in 1956 and brought to the Advisory Committee valuable expertise from his work as a fiscal advisor for the city of Boston. He transformed the committee into an effective arm of town government. "He knew how to get things done, how to analyze budgets, and so on," says Louis Eaton, Advisory Committee chairman in the mid-1950s. Fox's death in 1962 was a great loss for the town, but the higher standards he had set into motion endured for many years.

New Selectmen

Norman Card's death in December 1960 resulted in an interim elec tion to fill his unexpired term. Two of the candidates were Nathaniel ("Nate") Hurwitz and George W. McLaughlin. Hurwitz was a long-time resident, having moved to Cohasset in 1921, while McLaughlin, a lawyer, had moved here in the fifties. Reflecting the demographic changes in the town, neither was a native and neither was Protestant. Hurwitz was Jewish and married to a Catholic, Lillian R. Daley, and McLaughlin was Catholic. McLaughlin won the 1961 election. Hurwitz ran again in 1962, now for Ira Stoughton's unexpired term (Stoughton had died in

The Cohasset Board of Selectmen in 1961: longtime member Ira Stoughton, newly elected member George W. McLaughlin, and chairman Helen Scripture, another multiterm member and the first woman in the state to be elected selectman. Photo from Massachusetts Selectman, April 1961, courtesy of Peg Stoughton

January 1962). In his contest against Thomas C. Churchill, the vote was a tie, 697-697, but a recount gave Churchill the victory by three votes. Unbowed, Hurwitz ran again the next year, for a full three-year term. This time his campaign was well organized, with coffee hours and committees and check-off lists, the beginning of more intensive political campaigning in Cohasset. The effort paid off. He beat Churchill, and no recount was required.

Nate Hurwitz had a long and distinguished record of leadership. Born in Roxbury and educated in Boston, he was a professional basketball player. As captain of Cohasset's semiprofessional basketball team from 1920 to 1922, Nate led his men to 44 straight victories, making them New England Champions. In 1950 he was elected to the New England Basketball Hall of Fame. His civic service began in 1930, when he was appointed to the Cohasset Advisory Committee. A year later he was elected to the Board of Health and served as chairman for 25 years. During that period he was also elected to the state legislature, representing the towns of Cohasset, Hingham, Hull, and Norwell from 1943 to 1955. From 1955 to 1957 he was state commissioner of veterans services. In Cohasset he chaired the March of Dimes Campaign for 20 years. He was the first president and one of the founders of the Cohasset Community Center, vice president and a founder of Little League, and president and founder of the Cohasset Youth Athletic Association. He was also commander of the Cohasset American Legion and the Veterans of Foreign Wars, having served in France during World War I. And finally, he was selectman from 1963 to his death in 1966, at the age of 73.

A. J. Antoine driving Harold Barnes and Nate Hurwitz in a Little League parade in the early 1960s. Hurwitz, a former professional basketball player, had a long career in public service at both the town and state level.

Photo courtesy of A. J. Antoine

His greatest legacy, however, was not his public career, but his work with underprivileged children. As athletic director of the Bunkerhill Boys Club in Charlestown for 23 years, he provided advice to hundreds of boys, helping them to avoid delinquency, develop character, and go on to college. As a result, many became leaders in their own communities. At Nate's funeral a captain of the Boston Police Department said, "If it weren't for the man in that casket, I'd probably be in jail, just like my brother."

Arthur Clark succeeded Nate as selectman in 1967. Arthur was a native of Cohasset. He and his wife, Eunice, lived in the same house on Hull Street in which he was born in 1908. The owner of a plumbing and heating business, Clark had also served as water commissioner in Cohasset from 1964 to 1967. He was to hold office as selectman for 14 years (chairman for 12), until his retirement from town government in 1981. David Place, who became moderator in 1969, took particular note of Clark's efforts as a peacemaker during the turbulent 1970s, a period of "anger and hate in the world, and even in Cohasset" (*Patriot Ledger*, 5/29/81).

In 1968 the public welfare and assessing functions of the town were separated from the office of selectman. The state took over public welfare, significantly expanding social services under the initiatives created by President Lyndon Johnson's Great Society programs. The town also voted to prohibit assessors from holding other elected offices, including that of selectman. Many citizens believed that the bases for property assessments were inconsistent and possibly subject to political influence.

The sale of undervalued land by selectmen triggered a controversy that came to public attention when the *South Shore Mirror* (1/11/68) reported on a transaction involving 40 acres of town-owned land off Beach Street behind Town Hall. The land had been acquired by the town through foreclosure of a tax title for nonpayment of taxes. In 1953 the Board of Selectmen sold 20 acres of the allegedly unbuildable property for $1,400 to Bruce McLean, the son of selectman Helen Scripture. In 1959 another 18 acres of the property were sold under market price to the Greater Brewster Corporation. In 1967, when McLean attempted to buy the remaining strip of land along Beach Street for access to his 20-acre parcel, selectman George McLaughlin, himself a director of the Greater Brewster Corporation, raised the issue of a possible conflict of interest. At that time the estimated value of the two parcels of land purchased for less than $2,800 had increased to $420,000. McLaughlin referred the issue to the Planning Board for action. Subsequently an article was inserted in the warrant for the 1968 town meeting proposing that the Board of Selectmen hold public hearings before disposing of land under their control. At the meeting the article was indefinitely postponed. Nearly 20 years later, in 1985, the Greater Brewster Corporation donated their 18-acre parcel to the Conservation Trust. Now known as Great Brewster Woods, it is a public park featuring a beautiful nature trail through woods, salt marsh, and granite ledges. The other parcel was sold in 1977 to Cohasset resident Patrick Morrissey and, at the time of this writing, the question of its development remains a matter of controversy.

Conservation

Recognizing the growing need to protect the town's land and resources, town meeting voted in 1961 to establish a five-member Conservation Commission. The charge of the commission was to prepare a survey of the town's open spaces and natural resources, and to develop a program to preserve them and protect wetlands and watersheds. Further, the commission was authorized to accept gifts of land, funds, or buildings on behalf of the town and to manage the properties.

The first concern of the commission was the potential development of Cohasset's portion of the Naval Ammunition Depot to the west of Beechwood Street. About 75 percent of the town's water supply came from this area, which included the watersheds of the Aaron River and Brass Kettle Brook, and feeder streams into Lily Pond (the town's main water supply) and the Bound Brook wetlands. In 1958 the U.S. Navy had announced that it would close the Ammunition Depot and dispose of the property. The town feared that a large-scale developer would purchase Cohasset's 1,051-acre portion, subdivide it, and build 1,500 to 1,600 new houses, nearly doubling the number of homes in the town.

In 1964 the National Aeronautics and Space Agency (NASA) considered locating a new $50-million space center on the land, but the town did not favor that idea either. The *Boston Sunday*

Globe (5/10/64) reported: "In the view of the generally affluent Cohasset residents, income derived from having the Federal installation nearby would not be worth it. The town needs its share of the 2,991-acre ammunition annex for a watershed, they claim. Besides, they hope to see the land transferred to the state for a wildlife preserve, even if it brings not one penny of tax revenue or other income." Fortunately for the town and its water supply, NASA chose Houston, Texas, for its space center, and in 1966 the Commonwealth acquired the annex as a wildlife management area. We now enjoy the land as part of Wompatuck State Park.

The Conservation Commission next turned its attention to preserving wetlands within the town. In 1964 it successfully sponsored an article that required special permits to excavate or fill marshland, bogs, ponds, or brooks anywhere in town. (A 1963 state law mandated permits only for filling wetlands bordering coastal waters, a less stringent requirement.) The commission also made its first acquisition for the benefit of the town, a grant of perpetual easement for Treat's Pond and surrounding marshes from Dr. Henry Bigelow and his wife. This gift would protect the natural beauty of Treat's Pond from any future development. In 1967 Mrs. Theodore Little also gave the commission an easement to preserve the scenic coastal property she owned on Atlantic Avenue, as well as a large tract of marsh and upland on the opposite side of the road.

With somewhat broader aims than those of the Conservation Commission, but in a continuing effort to preserve the town's natural and historical assets, a group of citizens founded the Cohasset Conservation Trust in 1967. Its first trustees included Edward B. Long, chairman; John F. Hubbard, Osborne F. Ingram, Richard D. Leggat, and Hatherly L. Souther. The trust is a private foundation composed of volunteers who work together to fund the acquisition of sites of unique natural beauty or of historic interest to the town, and to preserve them.

The Conservation Trust's first acquisition was Bassing Beach. Consisting of a long spit of unspoiled beach and marsh on Cohasset Harbor, and once used as a site for bass fishing, it is separated from

Bassing Beach on Cohasset Harbor, the first acquisition made by the newly formed Cohasset Conservation Trust in 1968. Photo © Lynne Layman

the shore by Bailey's Creek. The trust bought a 12 1/2 -acre parcel of the beach from Parker F. Schofield of Bailey Island, Scituate, in 1968 for $7,500, raised from dues and contributions. Jessie Cox donated the strip of land along the harbor owned by her grandfather Clarence W. Barron, whose estate on Margin Street faced Bassing Beach. Although on Cohasset Harbor, Bassing Beach is actually within the boundaries of Scituate, owing to the settlement of a dispute in the 1630s between the Massachusetts Bay and Plymouth colonies over the salt marsh, then being utilized for grazing. The Conservation Trust agreed to maintain the property in its natural state and to allow both Cohasset and Scituate residents to use it for recreation and relaxation. The two cottages that came with the land were preserved and continue to be rented during the summer. In 1972 Parker Schofield donated more parcels to the trust, which now owns about half the barrier beach.

End-of-the-Decade Business

In 1968 the town created the position of full-time harbormaster and appointed Harry Ritter to the post. The bylaw charged him with regulation of the harbor: He was to determine the placement of anchorages for boats and issue mooring permits. Boat sales had risen 150 percent during the sixties, and by 1973, 449 boats, including 28 lobster boats, were moored in the increasingly crowded harbor. Before 1968 boatowners had bought and placed their own moorings. Now the harbormaster would carefully monitor their placement and limit their number. Further, the town imposed an annual fee for mooring permits and established a first-come, first-served priority list. In 1968, the first year of the new bylaw, 90 boats were on the waiting list for precious harbor space. Within five years that number would triple; by 2000 the waiting list would grow to over 400 names.

Harry Ritter, first full-time harbormaster. Ritter was appointed in 1968 and served until the late 1980s. Photo courtesy of Cohasset Mariner

The harbor and other amenities continued to draw young families to Cohasset. Meanwhile, an aging population had needs of its own to be met. In 1969 Cornelia H. White and other members of the Sixty-Plus Club, an informal senior citizens group with roots in the fifties, asked the selectmen to establish a council for the aging. With the approval of town meeting, the selectmen appointed a nine-member board to serve the town's elderly. The new Council on Aging created a drop-in center at the Unitarian Parish House, where people could meet and play cards or watch television. It provided information on available services and referrals to other agencies. And it kept in touch with the town's 900 seniors through a monthly newsletter. While the Council on Aging addressed the social needs of the elderly, the Social Service League, as of 1971, began to deliver nutritious hot lunches to the home-bound through its Meals on Wheels program. Services for the elderly would continue to expand, and Cohasset found itself juggling the sometimes conflicting demands of the old and the young.

CHANGES IN THE SCHOOLS

In the 1960 Town Report, the School Committee admitted to being overwhelmed by the avalanche of baby boomers hitting the schools. Chairman Osborne Ingram complained of "the ever-increasing school population, the ever-increasing academic performance expected of our schools, and the ever-increasing cost of everything connected with the schools." A record-breaking 153 pupils enrolled in first grade at the Joseph Osgood School in 1961. The Deer Hill School had already reached capacity by then. And the high school senior class would reach a new high of 117 students by 1965.

Recognizing the dire need for long-range planning, the School Committee created a permanent School Facilities Committee in 1960, headed by Harry H. Reed, Jr. New school construction was the order of the day. In 1962 six classrooms were added to the Deer Hill School, at a cost of about $294,000. In 1967-68 the high school underwent major expansion and renovation. A separate junior high wing (the west wing) was built, containing 11 classrooms and 3 science laboratories, a chorus room, a band room, a home economics suite, and administrative offices. In the original building a second gymnasium, a new library, and a chemistry lab were added. Four new tennis courts were also constructed on school property. The additions and renovations were completed by fall 1968, at a cost of $2,100,000.

When the proposal to renovate the Osgood School came before town meeting, however, the Advisory Committee drew the line, recommending against further renovations. Children in grades K-3 would have to make do with the existing facilities, now filled to overcapacity. In 1969 the Osgood School, with a capacity of 425, had an enrollment of 481. To accommodate all the children, the cafeteria, library, art room, and music room were converted to classrooms, and half the third grade was moved to Deer Hill. Pupils ate lunch at their desks, and teachers improvised with programs such as "Art on a Cart."

Projecting an "ultimate" school enrollment of between 2,850 and 3,300 students in grades K-12, the Benjamin Report had recommended that the town purchase three new school sites in the Forest Avenue, Pond Street, and Beechwood Street areas. In 1969 the School Facilities Committee followed through, at least in part, by deciding to purchase 71 acres of land on the south side of Sohier Street. With an appropriation of $135,000, the committee bought 9 acres adjoining the Music Circus property from the South Shore Playhouse Associates, and took the rest by eminent domain. Cohasset now had sufficient space for a campus arrangement of school buildings. It would take another 30 years, however, to build a new school on the Sohier Street site (the Osgood School, opened in 1999).

In 1962 the South Shore Vocational High School, an alternative to the traditional school system, opened in Hanover. This regional school served Abington, Cohasset, Hanover, Rockland, Norwell, and Scituate. It provided valuable practical training and excellent job opportunities for youths who might otherwise drop out of school. The curriculum included automotive repair, auto body repair, electricity, sheet metal work, metal fabrication, machine drafting, machine shop, mill and house carpentry, and basic electronics. Few students from Cohasset took advantage of "Vo-Tech."

In less than two decades, student life in Cohasset had changed drastically. Back in 1950, the 29 students in the senior class knew each other well and at least tolerated the less popular members. Because the class was so small, everyone participated in school activities. But by 1965, when the senior class had grown to 117, it was harder to know everyone. Students were grouped by ability and cliques had formed. For example, there were the sports-minded "jocks" and the "greasers" or "motorheads," interested mainly in cars. A pecking order emerged, and the friendly teasing of the fifties turned into the malicious ranking of the sixties.

Ranking was a nasty form of teasing that became a problem

around 1964-65. It consisted of picking on and taunting someone from outside the clique. The problem became so severe that Dr. Robert Sceery, the school physician, began to refer victims to Massachusetts General Hospital for psychiatric treatment, and the news was picked up by the *Boston Traveler* (6/11/64). In an attempt to deal with the vicious behavior, senior William ("Rusty") Park, president of the Student Council, organized a special "ranking court" to deal with the offenders. No one, however, was willing to come forward and inform on fellow students. Eventually the cruelty ended on its own.

Young people in the sixties were testing the rules of behavior that had guided an earlier generation. The issue of school dress in particular pitted students against administration. Frank J. Giuliano, Jr., who succeeded Anthony D'Antuono as high school principal in 1964, set the rules: "The school reserves the right to send students home if it is determined that their appearance does not reflect good taste and cleanliness and/or will be a distracting or disturbing element in the classroom. Specific restrictions are on fad haircuts or styles, boots, tight fitting pants and turtle neck sweaters for boys, and on curlers, slacks, shorts, or cullottes for girls. Boys should wear sport or dress shirts, tucked into the trousers, and girls' skirts and dresses must be knee-length" (*South Shore News*, 9/2/65). For a time students grudgingly complied. Otherwise, girls were sent home if their skirts were too short, and boys if their hair was too long. Tensions over the dress code would erupt into a legal battle in 1970.

Cohasset teenagers, like all American youths, were influenced by the popular culture expressed in movies and records (no CDs then) and in particular by what they saw on television. The "Ed Sullivan Show," which had introduced Elvis ("the Pelvis") Presley and rock 'n roll music in the mid-fifties, featured a new British band in 1964, the Beatles, whose irreverent lyrics and innovative sounds captivated their audiences. The Rolling Stones and other rock groups popularized and legitimized (for young people) the drug culture. "Hippies," with their long, scraggly hair and ragged jeans, tie-dyed T-shirts, and beads, made a mockery of the con-

Cohasset teen life just before the hippie era hit...

Here William "Rusty" Park poses with his family and date before the 1965 Cohasset High School prom. *Photo courtesy of William W. Park*

Future police chief Brian Noonan, 17, on motorcycle with station owner Paul St. John and friends Pat Casey and Paul McNeil in 1963. "I worked for Paul, but all the kids hung out there because he's always been such a great guy. We called him Father Flanagan," said Noonan. Photo courtesy of Paul St. John

servative dress and behavior of the adult generation.

By 1968 Cohasset High School students who were "with it" listened to what was then considered radical, countercultural music on radio station WBCN. Girls who had previously dressed in skirts and sweaters, with pearls, and wore their hair short and curly now donned wooden beads and long denim skirts embroidered with flowers, kept their hair long and straight, and used no makeup, preferring the "natural" look. "We enjoyed being thought of as hippies," says Marilyn C. Previte, a member of the Class of 1969. Boys grew sideburns and combed their hair over their foreheads, a deliberate departure from the clean-cut look of the fifties. Some also experimented with drugs; by the mid-sixties the use of marijuana became more obvious among high school students. Concerned about this growing problem, the Cohasset PTA (Parent-Teachers

Association) presented a program in 1968 on "Drugs and YOUR Child." The Cohasset police also sponsored a film on "Narcotics and the Teenager," inviting parents to attend with their children.

Yet the classes of the sixties were also high achievers. The Class of 1965 boasted five National Merit Scholars, and two students won Naval ROTC scholarships to college. That class also put on a highly successful musical production: "With a cast of 32, an orchestra, and two choruses, the CHS Senior Class will present the 1960 Broadway hit 'Bye-Bye Birdie' . . The musical comedy . . . is an exceptional undertaking for a small school with only 104 [sic] members in the class of 1965. Producing a full-length musical show instead of the usual 3-act drama has been the ambition of the show's student director, Greg Brown, since he was in 7th grade. Greg and Sammis McLean, who have both been apprentices with the Music Circus for several summers, were convinced that their classmates had the talent and the skill to handle such an ambitious project" (*South Shore News*, 2/18/65).

For those who were experiencing difficulty in school, help was now available through public funding. In 1965 the federal government passed the Elementary and Secondary Education Act to establish programs for "educationally deprived" children. Under the act Superintendent William Ripley obtained a federal grant of $9,216 to hire a guidance counselor for the schools. Forty-two students in Cohasset qualified for the counseling program because their families were receiving welfare aid.

The Elementary and Secondary Education Act of 1965 also funded the Metropolitan Council for Educational Opportunity (Metco). This was a voluntary desegregation program established in 1966 to "coordinate the busing of Negro students from Boston daily in order to eliminate racial imbalance in a majority of the Boston schools" (*South Shore Mirror*, 4/13/67). In 1968 Cohasset welcomed 9 Metco students from Boston. From this small beginning the program would grow to 49 students by 1999. "Everyone was in favor of Metco," says Louis Eaton. Cohasset residents felt that they were doing the right thing by introducing racial diversity into the schools, benefiting all students in a town with very few blacks (in 1970 the U.S. Census reported only 11 blacks in Cohasset, or 0.2 percent of the population; even by 1990 there would be only 22 blacks, 0.3 percent). A Cohasset Metco Committee was formed to arrange host families for each of the Boston students. These families opened their homes to the students, "providing a place to stay in if they become ill, and providing transportation in an emergency or special occasion, as well as being a friendly place to visit" (*South Shore Mirror*, 8/29/68).

A new state law, Chaper 763 of the Acts of 1965, introduced a more far-reaching change into the schools. It allowed teachers and other municipal employees to bargain collectively on wages, hours, and other conditions of work. The official bargaining agent for the teachers was the newly organized Cohasset Teachers Association (CTA), a union affiliated with the Massachusetts Teachers Association and the National Education Association. More than 90 percent of Cohasset teachers joined the union, and collective bargaining in negotiations with the School Committee began in 1968.

The changed character of the relationship between teachers and administration became apparent in 1969. After two months of continual negotiations, salary talks between the School Committee and the CTA reached an impasse. Before collective bargaining, their differences would have been resolved through personal discussion between Superintendent Ripley and the teachers. Now the process had become impersonal, and the union applied to the State Board of Arbitration and Conciliation for a mediator. In March, after the school budget had already been approved by the annual town meeting, the teachers won an increase in minimum salary, from $6,200 to $6,800. To stay within the budget, the administration made the necessary cuts.

In July 1969 William Ripley stepped down after 29 years as head of the schools. He had seen the construction of two new schools, skyrocketing costs, increasing government involvement, and the unionization of teachers. Appointed to replace him in this new era was Nelson J. Megna, from Northfield, Vermont. A graduate of Keene State College in New Hampshire, with a master's degree in educational administration from the University of

Massachusetts, he came
with 10 years of experience
in the Vermont school system. The Cohasset School
Committee hired him in
July 1969, noting that "in
these days of rapid change
and turbulence in educa-
tion, Mr. Megna had
demonstrated wisdom far
beyond his years in han-
dling difficult problems." The years to follow would test the
mettle of even the most experienced superintendent.

Superintendent William Ripley and his wife, Alice, at Bill's 1969 retirement party after 29 years as head of the Cohasset schools. Photo courtesy of Elizabeth Ripley

"THE SIXTIES" IN COHASSET

The sixties were a tumultuous decade in the nation, a decade that
began with the optimism generated by John F. Kennedy's election.
We were chastened by the failure of the Bay of Pigs invasion in
Cuba and frightened by the nuclear missile crisis with the Soviet
Union; then grieved over the death of "Camelot"—the assassina-
tions of John Kennedy and Robert Kennedy; and profoundly
changed by the civil rights movement, the assassination of Martin
Luther King, Jr., the growing tragedy of the Vietnam War, and finally the civil unrest in the nation. Cohasset was not spared. In small
ways and with increasing awareness, the town experienced the
joys, the fears, and the sorrows of the rest of the nation.

Cohasset's growing activism began with the churches. In 1963
St. Anthony's Church sponsored a talk organized by parishioner
Donald J. Evans on "The Ecumenical Movement and Vatican II."
Vatican II was a council of Catholic bishops convened from 1962 to
1965 by Pope John the 23rd to promote renewal within the Church
and, among other things, to foster ecumenism. Leaders of each
denomination in Cohasset were sent a personal invitation to hear
the talk by Rev. Charles L. Palm, a Jesuit priest, and all residents
were invited to attend. Prelecture dinner parties were held in private homes throughout the town. The clergy were invited to a din-

ner in honor of Father Palm at the estate of Polly and Edward Logan. This was the first time that many of the pastors in Cohasset had ever met each other.

The gathering was a great success and initiated a spirit of ecumenism that was kept alive by other programs. St. Stephen's Church sponsored a lecture series on "Dialogues in Unity" in 1964. Pope Memorial Methodist Church held the first annual Thanksgiving ecumenical service in 1966. Taking ecumenism into the home, in 1967 St. Stephen's organized Living Room Dialogues, based on a book by the same name. Members of the various churches met in small groups in private homes to discuss issues such as the Role of the Church in the Modern World, the Generation Gap, the North-South Dilemma, and the New Morality (situation ethics). In addition to fostering ecumenism, these events were the source of many lasting friendships.

The churches played a major role in getting the people of Cohasset involved in issues that dominated the sixties. The town was insulated from the racial riots that erupted in northern cities from 1964 to 1968. An almost totally white, middle-class suburb about 20 miles from Boston, Cohasset was removed from problems of racism and poverty. Nonetheless, many residents shared the nation's concern over the widening gulf between the two "Americas": a white suburban society and an urban society of blacks and other minorities. In 1965 the Osgood Club of First Parish held two meetings on "Race Relations and the White Suburban Community." Three hundred people attended the first session. An outgrowth of these seminars was the formation of the Committee on Human Concern by a large group of Cohasset clergy and residents.

The president of the Committee on Human Concern was Rev. F. Lee Richards, rector of St. Stephen's Church. He was called to St. Stephen's in 1960, when Rev. Bradford H. Tite left to become archdeacon of the Diocese of Central New York. Born in Philadelphia, Rev. Richards graduated from Lehigh University and had degrees in theology from Episcopal Theological Seminary in Alexandria, Virginia, and Temple University. During World War II he served as an airplane mechanic for the Army Air Force and as a chaplain's assistant on Iwo Jima.

The Committee on Human Concern invited all residents of Cohasset to join their endeavor to improve race relations and further the cause of social justice. In August 1965 the committee sponsored a luncheon-theater party for 120 senior citizens from churches in Roxbury and Cohasset. The group shared lunch together at St. Stephen's and enjoyed a matinee performance of *South Pacific* at the Music Circus. Rev. Richards, Rev. Roscoe Trueblood of First Parish, and Rev. William H. Mullin, the newly appointed curate of St. Anthony's, helped organize this ecumenical outreach event. A strong supporter of the civil rights movement, Father Mullin had joined Martin Luther King's historic March on Washington in 1963 and was an outspoken advocate for the Metco program in the schools.

In a somewhat bolder step, the Committee on Human Concern began its sponsorship of two-week visits in Cohasset homes for black children from St. James Church in Roxbury. Despite some skepticism on the part of a few residents, eight children between the ages of 5 and 14 arrived in July 1965 for their vacation visit. Not too surprisingly, after just one week many of them were homesick and went home. The next year, however, they came back to the same families. Now feeling less strange in Cohasset, they enjoyed the entire two-week stay. By 1968, 39 children from Roxbury were visiting 36 families here.

Corinne H. and John M. Cahill were one of the couples who hosted the children. Corinne recalls how surprised her young guests were to see that a child could have a room all to himself. At the Osgood School playground, the Roxbury children were also amazed by all the space around the building. The visit gave her children and their guests a chance to experience diversity up close. One day, while driving her five-year-old son Stewart and five-year-old guest Carl home from Sandy Beach, she noticed that they were very quiet. She turned around to see what they were up to. The two little boys had their hands on each other's heads. "What are you doing?" she asked. "His hair feels so silky!" said Carl. "His hair feels so funny!" said Stewart. Later her older son Chris was invited by one of the boys to spend a few days at his home in a Boston housing development. He went and had a good time in an environment as unfamiliar to Cohasset children as Cohasset had been to Roxbury children.

The clergy of Cohasset, particularly Father Mullin and Rev. Richards, were also strong supporters of FISH, another new organization formed in the sixties. The name was derived from an ancient symbol for Christianity. Originating in Oxford, England, in 1961, FISH was a group of church volunteers dedicated to helping neighbors in need. The idea of providing emergency services free of charge spread to the United States in 1964

Town resident Andrea Parker introduced FISH to Cohasset in June 1967. Warmly endorsing the new organization, Rev. Richards stated: "As a movement, FISH is as old as the Judeo-Christian tradition. It is based on the ancient ethic of caring for one's neighbor. FISH is a valid expression of the Church in the world, reaching out and touching the lives of people. FISH is an attempt to make personal a world which has de-humanized and de-personalized man" (*South Shore Mirror*, 6/1/67). Thirty years later FISH volunteers in Cohasset still babysit, drive people to doctors or hospitals, and supply other services in an emergency to anyone in need.

While adults in the sixties were involved in numerous organizations and good causes, some Cohasset teenagers were engaged in less wholesome activities. For the first time teenage drinking was publicly acknowledged as a problem. In January 1964 Rev. Richards invited youth groups from all the churches, as well as those unaffiliated with a church, to attend a series of three programs on "Alcohol and the Teenager." He attributed the drinking to the fact that parents were too busy to pay attention to their children. More than 200 youths showed up for the first session. Although alcohol was the more common problem, the schools were also becoming alarmed over the spreading use of drugs.

In a different approach to the problems of youth, the Vedanta Centre welcomed the "hippies" of the sixties. Many of these young people had experimented with drugs and believed they had discovered a new kind of consciousness or spirituality. Attracted by eastern philosophies, meditation, and the monastic life, they came with their long hair, torn jeans, love beads, sandals, and guitars to Reverend Mother Gayatri Devi. She taught her hippie congregation that the way to spirituality was not through drugs but through self-discipline and the age-old ways of meditation, harmlessness, honesty, and purity. Several Cohasset High School students in the late sixties were drawn to the ashrama. Lynn Previte recalls that during summer vacation some of her classmates made a pilgrimage to the center in La Crescenta, California. Mother Gayatri guided young people through the turmoil of the Vietnam era. Some of these "flower children" became monastics and stayed with the center for many years.

Unlike many cities and university towns, however, Cohasset passed through the sixties in relative tranquillity. It was definitely too quiet for the younger, more idealistic clergy who were fired up by Vatican II's call for spiritual renewal and social justice. In October 1968, after three years at St. Anthony's, Father Mullin left, preferring to serve the inner-city parish of St. Mary of the Angels in Roxbury. Likewise, his replacement, Rev. Thomas D. Corrigan, left after six months to return to his former inner-city parish, All Saints in Roxbury.

As the sixties drew to a close, many longtime Cohasset officials retired from their posts, breaking the continuity and stability that had lasted for more than a generation. Hector Pelletier retired after 40 years as police chief; William Ripley after 29 years as school superintendent; Robert James after 29 years as moderator; and Sarah Heywood after 22 years as chief librarian. In June 1968 Rev. Trueblood retired from First Parish. He had served his parish and community with dedication for 23 years.

The Reverend Edward T. Atkinson was installed as the fifteenth minister of First Parish in January 1969. A graduate of M.I.T. and Tufts University, he had been ordained at the Arlington Street Church in Boston. By the time he assumed his new ministry in Cohasset, America's involvement in the Vietnam War was becoming a divisive issue. On October 15, 1969, the newly formed

Cohasset Peace Action Committee organized a Vietnam Peace Day demonstration on the Common. That is when the "sixties" really began in Cohasset.

A TOWN DIVIDED

For the United States the conflict in Vietnam started in 1954, when France was defeated by Vietnamese nationalists at Dien Bien Phu. Forced to withdraw from its former colony, France left the country divided into two temporary administrative districts, north and south. To maintain European and American influence in Southeast Asia, the United States supported South Vietnam with economic and political assistance as well as with military advisers. The communist-led North's initial political efforts to reunify the country turned into armed violence in 1960. Concerned that if South Vietnam fell to the communists, all of Southeast Asia would fall, the United States was inexorably drawn into the conflict. In 1965, after North Vietnamese torpedo boats reportedly fired on American ships in the Gulf of Tonkin, the U.S. escalated its involvement by launching direct bombing attacks into North Vietnam and committing American ground forces to the conflict. What had been intended as limited warfare now intensified into full-scale war with heavy U.S. casualties. By April 1969 the number of American dead, 33,641, exceeded the toll of the Korean War. The accumulating casualty figures, the absence of clear military success, and the apparently endless fighting eroded public support for the war.

The Vietnam conflict was the first war that Americans could watch live on television. From their living rooms they witnessed dreadful scenes of violence that in previous wars had only been seen on movie newsreels. Media coverage of the brutality of the war, the corruption of the regime of Nguyen Van Thieu, who became president of South Vietnam in 1967, and the U.S. bombing raids on Cambodia in March 1969 turned many prowar "hawks" into antiwar "doves." The antiwar movement that started on college campuses spread throughout the United States and eventually reached Cohasset.

In October 1969 the Cohasset Peace Action Committee met at

St. Stephen's Church to organize a peace rally on the Common. As in other South Shore communities, the selectmen agreed to set aside October 15 as Vietnam Peace Day. Five hundred residents of Cohasset showed up for the rally. The *South Shore Mirror* (10/23/69) described the event:

> During the day approximately 425 signatures were signed on petitions to be sent to President Nixon asking that he "withdraw American troops from Vietnam because of the corrupting influence the war has on every aspect of American life." Peace Day began with a special Peace Mass at St. Anthony's Church and the service of Holy Communion observed at St. Stephen's. The First Parish Church, the Second Congregational, the Vedanta Centre, Beechwood Congregational, and Pope Memorial United Methodist Churches as well as St. Anthony's and St. Stephen's were open all day for prayer and meditation.
>
> Early in the evening whole families, young children, young adults, and many elderly citizens began to gather near the Duck Pond on Cohasset Common. Their spirit and determination was shown in the solemnity with which young and old and in-between each lit a candle sheltered from the wind by paper cups and listened to the bells of St. Stephen's toll sonorously at 7 p.m.
>
> Edward T. Atkinson, minister of the First Parish Church, read the Beatitudes . . . The Rev. F. Lee Richards of St. Stephen's Church gave the benediction and the group was then led in singing the great Peace song of the young people, "Where Have All the Flowers Gone." It was then that the candlelit group proceeded solemnly to march around the Common . . . Late in the evening people were still coming to sign the petition to be sent to Washington and a group was continuing to sing folk songs of peace accompanied by young guitarists.

Those opposed to the rally interrupted with catcalls and shouting, reinforced by prolonged blasts of the horn from the Elm Street fire station. Police officers had to monitor the crowd to maintain order.

Many townspeople did not support the antiwar movement. They believed that our involvement in Vietnam was the price we had to pay to preserve peace in Asia. The fear was that withdrawal of our forces would allow Communist China to take over Southeast Asia and expand into the Philippines, creating a "domino effect" of countries falling under communist domination. Veterans groups in particular were offended by the protest movement. One veteran of World War II drove around the Common during a "peace sermon" at First Parish with his hand on the horn of his car to blast out what he considered subversive talk.

The new minister at First Parish, Edward Atkinson, who along with Lee Richards of St. Stephen's strongly supported the peace rally, had to concede publicly that his views did not necessarily reflect those of all his parish. Writing in a Letter to the Editor (*South Shore Mirror*, 11/13/69), he stated: "The fine coverage which your paper has given the activities of the Cohasset Committee for Peace in Vietnam is deeply appreciated. I would like to make it absolutely clear to your readers, however, that the members of the First Parish in Cohasset hold a wide diversity of views regarding the best course of action for our nation to follow in

The Rev. Edward Atkinson, minister at First Parish, 1969-1995. Ed's antiwar views, along with those of other clergymen, stirred up debate in Cohasset during the volatile Vietnam War period. Photo courtesy of Cohasset Mariner

Vietnam, and that my participation in the Committee for Peace in Vietnam represents only an individual commitment and not an official action on the part of our church."

The Paul Pratt Memorial Library also felt the heat of criticism. On November 14 the library allowed the Peace Action Committee to show an antiwar documentary film, "Vietnam: How Did We

Get In?" every hour on the hour. The committee also displayed an exhibit on Vietnam at the library and distributed leaflets with questions and answers about U.S. involvement in the war. Many residents protested this one-sided presentation. According to Richard Hayes, the new chief librarian, "arguments over the war and over dissent flared up and terms such as 'communist,' 'dupe,' and 'unAmerican' were used in an attempt to discredit the film and the sponsoring group and to pressure library officials into denying the use of library facilities" (*South Shore Mirror*, 11/20/69).

Library officials were quick to issue a statement disclaiming support for any one group: "The library grants the use of its meeting room to groups of citizens on equal terms regardless of the beliefs and affiliations of their members. Such use of the meeting room does not imply library or town endorsement of the views expressed . . . One of the principal purposes of the library is to promote discussion of current public questions. We welcome any group which wishes to use the library's meeting room for this purpose" (*South Shore Mirror*, 11/20/69). Those supporting the war effort subsequently put up their own exhibits, thereby balancing the "debate."

Cohasset was left badly divided over the protest movement. In December 1969 Lee Richards announced that he would resign from St. Stephen's. After he left in February 1970 to serve in an inner city parish in his native Philadephia, writer John Bishop made the following observations, which could well be applied to Cohasset as a whole: "The tensions and conflicts within the American society have not left St. Stephen's unscathed. There has been some falling away of attendance and support. A few members of conservative view have been alienated by actions of church leaders and decisions of the Church in Convention [a meeting of Episcopal bishops comparable to Vatican II]. Even among those who are not alienated, the polarization of viewpoints, though muted in expression, is an uneasy fact of the parish temper. Lee Richards's successor will find in his new parish in some degree the same need for reconciliation that challenges America" ("Saint Stephen's Church," pp. 78-79).

IN MEMORIAM

After the loss of more than 58,000 American lives, the Vietnam War ended inconclusively in 1973 with the withdrawal of American forces in exchange for the return of American prisoners of war. Because of the ambiguities of U.S. involvement, returning soldiers were not given the respect accorded veterans of World Wars I and II. It was not until 1982, when the starkly beautiful Vietnam Veterans Memorial Wall was dedicated in Washington, D.C., that the process of national reconciliation began. In Cohasset, however, special Memorial Day ceremonies were organized in 1970 at the new Memorial Park at the Cove. Glenn A. Pratt headed a committee that planned the construction of a fieldstone memorial wall at the park, with four bronze tablets honoring Cohasset veterans who lost their lives in Vietnam as well as in the two world wars and Korea. Another tablet was placed on a boulder in front of the wall dedicating the park to all Cohasset men and women who served in the armed forces.

Again, on Veterans Day, November 10, 1996, Cohasset honored its Vietnam dead in dedication ceremonies organized by Pratt. Town sites were dedicated to the six young Cohasset servicemen, named below, who lost their lives in combat in Vietnam and the two who died in noncombat accidents. In addition, the square at Jerusalem Road and Red Gate Lane was dedicated to C. David Strout, the only Cohasset serviceman killed in the Korean War. Each site was marked with a memorial plaque commemorating one of those who had given their lives in service to their country.

Accompanied by an honor guard, with music from the Brockton Cosmos Legion's volunteer band, crowds gathered for the solemn ceremonies that highlighted the disproportionate sacrifice made by the small town of Cohasset. In 1969 alone, we lost four of our young men in combat. Before the unveiling of each memorial plaque, local clergy gave a benediction, and friends or relatives spoke briefly about the serviceman to whom the site was dedicated. It was clear from their remarks that Cohasset was a wonderful town to grow up in during the fifties and sixties. The recollections were of a happy childhood, with summers spent at Sandy Beach and pick-up games on the Common. As Glenn Pratt observed, in a small community like Cohasset "everyone knew everyone else. I knew those guys' families, or was in high school classes or Little League or the Boy Scouts with them" (*Patriot Ledger*, 11/11/96). The close relationships made their deaths especially hard for the town to bear. This book is dedicated to those valiant young men, and our account of the 1960s closes in proud and loving tribute to them.

Corporal William C. Laidlaw died on August 18, 1965, at the age of 22. He moved to Cohasset with his family in 1959 and left high school to enlist in the Marines. Serving as a tank commander on his second tour of duty, he was killed in a mortar attack by the Vietcong against his outnumbered crew near the American base at Danang, South Vietnam. For his bravery he was awarded a Bronze Star Medal with V for Valor and a Purple Heart Medal. He also received the National Defense Medal, the Vietnam Service Medal, and the Vietnam Campaign Medal, among other campaign and unit awards. The William C. Laidlaw Square is at Beechwood Street and Norman Todd Road.

Private First Class Peter Cogill died on February 27, 1967, at the age of 20. He was a member of the Class of 1966 at Cohasset High School, and enlisted in the Army soon after graduation. A parachutist, he served in South Vietnam with Able Company 326 Engineering Battalion, 101st Airborne Division. On patrol against hostile enemy forces in Binh Thuan Province, he was killed in action while attempting to defuse a land mine. For his courage he was awarded a Bronze Star Medal with V for Valor, a Purple Heart Medal, a National Defense Medal, a Vietnam Service Medal, a Vietnam Military Merit Medal, a Vietnam Gallantry Cross, a Vietnam Campaign Medal, a Combat Infantry Badge, a Parachutist Badge, and other campaign and unit awards. The Peter Cogill Square is at Doane Street and Church Street.

Captain John Paul Lyon died on April 18, 1969, at the age of 25. A 1962 graduate of Cohasset High School, he was voted the Most Talented by his class. At Norwich University, from which he graduated in 1966, he distinguished himself as an artist, an athlete, and an honor student. A career Army officer with the First Air Cavalry, he was killed on a search-and-destroy mission when his helicopter landed on a buried mine in Kan Throng Province, near the Cambodian border. For his heroism in ground combat he was awarded a Bronze Star Medal with V for Valor, two Bronze Star Medals with Oak Leaf Cluster, a Purple Heart Medal, an Air Medal for Meritorious Achievement in Aerial Flight, a National Defense Medal, a Vietnam Service Medal, and a Vietnam Campaign Medal. The John Paul Lyon Square is at North Main Street and Joy Place.

Private First Class Craig Michael Simeone died on May 30, 1969, at the age of 21. He graduated from Cohasset High School in 1966 and was drafted into the Army. Serving as a grenadier with the Second Battalion (101st Airborne Division), 501st Infantry, he was killed during an ambush in the A Shau Valley, South Vietnam, while crawling forward under enemy fire to rescue wounded comrades. For his personal bravery and devotion to duty he was awarded a Bronze Star Medal with V for Valor, as well as a Bronze Star Medal with Oak Leaf Cluster, a Purple Heart Medal, an Army Good Conduct Medal, a National Defense Medal, a Vietnam Service Medal, a Vietnam Campaign Medal, a Combat Infantry Badge, a Parachutist's Badge, and other campaign and unit awards. The Craig M. Simeone Square is at Pond Street and Lantern Lane.

Boiler Technician First Class R. Edward Maree died on July 11, 1969, at the age of 20. A student at Cohasset High School, he left in September 1965 to join the U.S. Navy. He served two tours of duty in Vietnam, including shore duty in My Tho and service as a boiler tender on the USS *John King* in the Gulf of Tonkin. He was killed in an accident at the Navy Yard in Norfolk, Virginia. The R. Edward Maree Landing is at the Parker Avenue boat ramp.

Specialist Fourth Class Allen Francis Keating died on October 19, 1969, at the age of 21. A 1966 graduate of Cohasset High School, he was captain of the baseball team, a quarterback on the football team, a member of the *Patriot Ledger* All-Scholastic Team, and active in many school and community organizations. Before entering the Army he attended Arizona Western College. He went to Vietnam in January 1969 with the 4th Infantry Division. While on leave in Hawaii after nine months of duty, he married his high school sweetheart, Anne Noonan. Shortly after he returned to his unit, he was killed in ambush while leading his squad and its armored personnel carrier near Pleiku in the Central Highlands of South Vietnam. He was cited for conspicuous valor and awarded the Silver Star, the third highest decoration the United States can bestow, as well as two Purple Heart Medals, a National Defense Medal, a Vietnam Service Medal, a Vietnam Campaign Medal, and other campaign and unit awards. The Allen F. Keating Square is at Summer Street and Blackhorse Lane.

First Lieutenant Dennis Joseph Reardon died on November 29, 1969, at the age of 24. A 1963 graduate of Cohasset High School, he was co-captain of the football team and co-captain of the Mayshore League Team. He was also selected as a member of the *Patriot Ledger* All-Scholastic Team. After graduating from Boston College in 1967 he volunteered for service in the U.S. Marine Corps. He earned his wings as a naval aviator in April 1969 and served as commander of a helicopter squadron at Marble Mountain, Vietnam. While flying on a med-evac mission to evacuate combat casualties from the Que San Mountains near Da Nang, his CH-46 helicopter exploded in flight, killing Dennis and his entire crew. For his heroism he was awarded a Bronze Star Medal with Combat V, a Purple Heart Medal, an Air Medal with Numeral 7, a National Defense Medal, a Vietnam Service Medal, a Vietnam Campaign Medal, a Vietnam Honor Medal, and other campaign and unit awards. The Dennis J. Reardon Square is at Elm Street and Highland Avenue.

Sergeant Peter J. Albiani, Jr., died on February 7, 1970, at the age of 21. He was a member of the Class of 1967 at Old Farms High School in Avon, Connecticut. In May 1967 he enlisted in the U.S. Air Force and a year later graduated from the Eastern European Language School at Syracuse University. In July 1969 he was assigned to the U.S. Logistics Group, Detachment 204, of the U.S. Air Force Security Service. He died in an accident when a landslide buried his radar listening post in Turkey. The Peter J. Albiani Jr. Square is at Jerusalem Road and Gammons Road.

Cohasset in the 1970s:
CONFLICT AND
CELEBRATION

"The 70s were when the 60s hit home," noted *Time* magazine (3/9/98). On May 4, 1970, Ohio national guardsmen shot and killed four students at an antiwar protest at Kent State University, turning public opinion against the war effort. Two years later the burglary of the Democratic National Committee headquarters by officials of the Nixon administration triggered the Watergate political scandals, ending in the resignation of President Nixon in disgrace in 1974. On college campuses, posters exhorted young people to Question Authority. Meanwhile, spending on guns and butter (military spending for the Vietnam War and domestic spending on President Johnson's Great Society), together with the quadrupling of oil prices by the Middle East oil cartel, pushed the rate of inflation in the United States from 4.4 percent in 1971 up to 13.5 percent by 1980. We entered a recession. Production declined and unemployment rose.

The deep recession of the mid-1970s ended the building boom in Cohasset. Families worried about just making ends meet. Companies cut back and the rate of unemployment rose from about 4 percent at the beginning of the decade to 10 percent at the end. We had lost our confidence in the American Dream:

Thousands of suburbanites who thought they had job security found the good life was suddenly gone. More than a quarter million persons are out of work in Massachusetts.

The unemployment rate is creeping over 10 percent in what some economists see as the country's worst plight since the Great Depression, and which few see as easing in the near future. The suburbanite, for whom employ-ment is the means to support the two-car family, has been hit hard financially and psychologically by the economic crunch that has forced even firms with longstanding repu-tations for weathering such storms to begin cutbacks . . . the problem is not just that of being jobless and short of money. It's also to be measured by the frustration of being without work, perhaps for the first time in one's adult life, and living the crisis of confidence.

[*Patriot Ledger*, 2/18/75]

The growth of the town's population slowed to a mere 3 percent between 1970 and 1980. As more women went to work and fam-ilies had fewer children, the number of students in the Cohasset schools dropped dramatically from a peak of 1,992 students in 1972 to 1,545 in 1980, a loss of 22 percent.

The baby boom generation was in its teens and early twenties in 1970. It was an alienated generation, reveling in anti-authori-tarian behavior and aggravating the adults around them. Residents of Cohasset recall that teenagers would not even acknowledge your presence when you walked by them. A "Sad Mother" com-plained to the *Patriot Ledger* (6/11/74): "When I was that age and lived at home, I owed my parents respect . . . Today I find this age group immoral and arrogant, and they have an aggressive approach to any opinion their parents may have. They have 'love affairs' while living at home. They call it doing their own thing. If they marry and if they don't find it lives up to their expectations, they get a divorce. Some stay married and have an affair on the side."

Genevieve G. Good, a longtime Cohasset resident, echoed that woman's dismay: "It seemed to me as if the children of that era had lost all sense of responsibility, of family values. They all wanted to leave school and go elsewhere. You went off for a year from col-lege to find yourself. High school kids wanted to model themselves after those who were trying to destroy civilization. This was frightening for parents who were brought up with the idea that you obeyed authority, you respected the police, you tried to emulate your parents, because parents were good people. We were all so appalled at what was happening that we just didn't know what to do."

For adults as well as young people, traditional sources of authority were suspect. Cohasset's police chief and members of his force were lampooned in a humiliating *Boston* magazine article. Parents of schoolchildren contested the judgment of both the school administration and the teachers' union over the firing of a popular high school principal. Citizens criticized the selectmen and other town officials for allowing the construction of a new motel at the harbor and failing to control noise from the Music Circus. Questioning authority, Cohasseters took a cue from the civil rights movement and formed groups to protest infringements on their rights. Civil discourse gave way to confrontation.

The decade had its diversions and accomplishments nevertheless. It began with a year-long celebration of the town's 200th birthday, followed in 1976 by the nation's Bicentennial. The Swim Center was built in 1974; the Paul Pratt Memorial Library was renovated in 1977; and a generous citizen anonymously donated a new clubhouse for the Sailing Club in 1979. The Aaron River Reservoir project was completed in 1978, ending Cohasset's perennial water shortages. But in the final insult of this era, mother nature delivered the Great Blizzard of '78, her parting blow to a turbulent decade.

CELEBRATING THE PAST

Divisive issues were set aside as townspeople came together in 1970 to celebrate Cohasset's birth as a town. Pride in our heritage was reinforced six years later during the national Bicentennial. The historical programs and projects of the seventies delighted both children and adults, bringing to life the people and events of a long-vanished past.

Cohasset's Bicentennial

On a clear, crisp New Year's Day 1970, church bells pealed and a blue and white flag was ceremoniously raised high over the Common, heralding the start of the Bicentennial Year. Two hundred years earlier the precinct of Cohasset, formerly known as Little Hingham, had separated from its parent and become the district of Cohasset (officially called a town in 1786). Emblazoned on the new flag was the Town Seal depicting the First Parish Meeting House, the original Joseph Osgood School, and Town Hall, symbols of Cohasset's religious, educational, and municipal life. At its center stretched the long rocky coastline that gave Cohasset its earliest name, Quonahassit, with Minot's Ledge Lighthouse in the distance.

The crowd on the Common gathered to hear the Bicentennial Committee's prologue to the celebration that lay ahead: "1970 promises to be a gala year in Cohasset's long history, with enjoyment the watchword—enjoyment made deeper by the love we all hold for Cohasset and by the pride we feel in her. It is a time of rededication too; to the spirit, the ideals and the values that have made Cohasset what it is today. The Bicentennial celebration provides an opportunity for all who love Cohasset—today's citizens and former residents—to gather together and let their pride in Cohasset show . . . freely and in full measure."

Leading the Bicentennial Committee was Burtram J. Pratt, author of volume II of the *Narrative History of Cohasset.* A descendant of one of the first families in Cohasset, Pratt cared deeply about the town and its history. The Bicentennial gave him an opportunity to share his knowledge and enthusiasm with others. Assisting him on the committee in planning a year of exciting events were Paul Blackmur, vice chairman; Mary Jane E. McArthur, secretary; Prescott T. Cumner, treasurer; and directors A. J. Antoine, Jr., Sheldon N. Ripley, and Arthur Taft Mahoney, with many other citizens serving on subcommittees. To set the stage, the committee published an article highlighting important facts about the town:

> This year the town of Cohasset is celebrating its 200th Birthday as an incorporated town in 1770. Prior to that, it was a precinct of Hingham.

Cohasset's history began in 1614 when Captain John Smith, "President of Virginia and Admiral of New England," landed in the harbor and declared the area to be "the paradise of all these parts." Originally called "Quonahassit" (the long rocky place) by the Indians, it was later named "London" by Prince Charles of England and finally "Cohasset." Its heritage is rich in Colonial background and the "Great Hundred Years of Sail."

Many shipyards lined the shore of the harbor, and ships built in Cohasset carried on commerce throughout the world under the command of "resident" master mariners. Here the first lifeboat station in America was established under the auspices of the Massachusetts Humane Society. Minot's Light House, just outside the harbor, has flashed its famous "- ---- --- " (I LOVE YOU) beam since 1864 [the 1 4 3 signal was assigned to Minot's Light in about 1890, ed.], or for over one hundred years. The granite structure, 114-foot light, replaced an original structure on iron stilts.

Cohasset is proud of the fact that the ancestors of President Abraham Lincoln, beginning with his great-great-grandfather Mordecai Lincoln, who operated three mills on Bound Brook, lived here.

The first boundary line in America established by private citizens without government intervention is designated by an historical sign [on South Main Street] at the border between the now Plymouth and Norfolk counties. The year was 1640.

Old houses, dating from 1695, still stand. The Cohasset Common is acknowledged to be among the most charming in New England. Residents may hear the [51]-bell carillon of St. Stephen's Episcopal Church as they stroll or recline on the grass on summer Sunday afternoons. This carillon, forged in England, is among America's finest . . .

Cohasset became popular as a summer resort for the "elite" during the late 1800s. Lovely and large residences were built, especially on the ocean front of Atlantic Avenue and Jerusalem Road, which provided a spectacular view of the sea from its rock-bound shoreline. At night time, the lights of Boston Lightship and the lighthouses of Boston Harbor dot the horizon. Sandy Beach offers delightful bathing for residents as waves purl at the edge and breezes from the open sea (nearest land east — Spain) caress the land.

Program for a play written by Helen Ketcham as a semihistorical reenactment of the town's first town meeting during the Bicentennial celebration. Program courtesy of Cohasset Historical Society

In May the Cohasset Dramatic Club produced a humorous reenactment of Cohasset's first moments as a town in *Town Meeting 1770*. The club asked Helen Ketcham to author the work and Arthur Mahoney to produce and direct it. As no record of the first town meeting could be found, the play combined fact and fiction. (In fact, however, the record is stored in the Town Hall vault.) Each character in the play was known to have participated in the meeting, and in some cases direct descendants played the roles. David E. Place, elected town moderator in 1970, acted the part of Deacon Isaac Lincoln, the first moderator, appointed by Thomas Hutchinson, lieutenant governor of the Commonwealth. The play was presented to standing-room-only audiences at the First Parish Meeting House, the same building where the first town meeting was held.

In the opening scene Moderator Lincoln tries to maintain order among the somewhat unruly group of farmers and fishermen who were Cohasset's first citizens. All were pleased that they no longer had to make the long, rugged trip

to Hingham to attend town meeting, but at least one Beechwood
resident opposed separation from
the parent town. "This parish is
small," said Joseph Souther. "Too
small to stand on its own."
Determined to prove him wrong,
the citizenry (men only—women
were not allowed to attend the
meeting, let alone vote) elected
their first town officers: a town
clerk, three selectmen/assessors,
a surveyor of highways, and a
town treasurer. With much ban-
ter and occasional interruption
from family members, they also
appointed people to oversee the
important functions of the little
community, such as culler of fish

*David E. Place, town moderator in
1970, in costume as Cohasset's first
town moderator, Deacon Isaac Lincoln.*

and packer of mackerel, and hog reeve (enforcer of regulations).

In the second, closing scene the narrator tells the audience that
later in 1770 voters at town meeting raised money to pay the school
master and declared that each child must bring wood to school or
money for the school master to buy wood. They also decreed that
hogs could run free for the rest of the year (giving the reeve
a break). The narrator then skips to 1774, when Isaac Lincoln is
appointed to represent Cohasset at a provincial congress held in
Concord. Cohasset voters approve the formation of colonial asso-
ciations to provide "common protection against a possible invasion
by the king." The action of the play resumes at town meeting on
April 28, 1776. The business of the meeting is to decide whether to
join fellow patriots against the "parent enemy." They first agree to
stockpile corn, gunpowder, and flint. One disgruntled citizen, Laz
Beal, objects to all this "hysterical nonsense"and strides angrily out
of the room. The moderator then asks for a vote to "support the
colonies in their fight for freedom." To a man, the crowd votes Aye,

and all pick up a shovel or other implement and walk purposefully out of the room to a drumroll beat. The audience thoroughly enjoyed its glimpse into the formation of colonial Cohasset.

In July the town was treated to two weeks of festivities during Homecoming Days, when "all who lived here or ever loved the place [were] invited to come back and help celebrate the town's birthday" (*South Shore Mirror*, 6/25/70). The first weekend began with an antique auto rally. A special prize for the oldest car to finish the designated route went to John Hagerty of Cohasset, who drove a 1911 Marmon. The rally was followed by a street parade of 16 hand-tubs (hand-pumped fire engines, built before 1882) that came from all over New England. After the parade the hand-tubs gathered at Milliken-Bancroft Field for an old-fashioned firemen's muster, where the object was to see which engine could build up enough pressure to send a stream of water the farthest. Some brawny fire buffs pumped the old engines with such energy that they managed to shoot water from narrow hoses a distance of several hundred feet.

Also on the agenda was a tour of historic homes and buildings. Prescott Cumner had led a committee that spent two years researching and cataloguing 94 Cohasset homes built before 1811. These homes were marked by wooden boards giving their Heritage Trail number and identified on a special map that visitors could follow. The oldest was a center-chimney Cape Cod Colonial at 179 South Main Street. Built in 1695 by Joshua Bates, the red-shingled house faces south instead of toward the street, to take advantage of the sun's warmth during cold New England winters. It remained in the Bates family for 200 years. Another Colonial house, at 45 North Main Street, was built in 1802 by Captain Abraham Tower, one of the "Indians" at the Boston Tea Party and a member of the militia during the Revolutionary War. Still another historic residence was the old Lothrop House at 159 Atlantic Avenue. It is believed to have served as Cohasset's first seaside inn in the early 1800s. It was built in the early 1700s by William Bailey and rebuilt by William Whittington in about 1795.

The historic tour included other venerable old buildings,

among them the Unitarian Parish House, built in 1722 by the Reverend Nehemiah Hobart. Behind it is a small workshop erected in 1803 by Samuel Brown, Cohasset's first postmaster. This building, which still exists, also served as the town's first post office. The First Parish Meeting House, across the street on the Common, was built in 1747 as a place for worship and public assembly; it is believed that ammunition used during the Revolutionary War was concealed in the carved pulpit. A steeple was added to the church in 1799, and a Town Clock installed there in 1860. (In the early 1980s the selectmen named Noel Ripley official Keeper of the Clock after he and the Historical Commission repaired the original mechanism and restored it to working order.)

The second weekend of Homecoming Days featured Cohasset Youth Days, with a three-day carnival on the Common and a colorful Bicentennial Parade directed by Philip Murray. The highlight of the parade was a Historical Pageant of Floats dramatizing important events in Cohasset's history. Organized by A. J. Antoine, Marjorie F. Ritter, and Jean M. Salvador, the gaily decorated floats depicted scenes such as Captain John Smith's Landing in 1614, the Revolutionary War, the Wreck of the *Gertrude Maria* in 1793 (when the King of Denmark awarded four Cohasset residents gold lifesav-

This float, portraying Captain John Smith discovering Cohasset, won first prize in the town's Bicentennial parade in 1970. The parade featured 29 floats and bands from all military branches. Photo courtesy of Patriot Ledger

ing medals for their heroism in rescuing the Danish ship's crew), and Minot's Ledge Lighthouse. The Bicentennial Parade was the last of the Cohasset Youth Days parades, a symbolic end to the exuberant sixties.

Rev. John Fitzgerald, Rev. Frank B. Chatterton, and Rev. Joseph Brennan prepare to bless the local fleet during the 1970 Bicentennial.
Photo courtesy of Ann Pompeo

Fisherman Lawrence A. Figueiredo demonstrates the construction of a lobster pot during Bicentennial festivities.
Photo © Lynne Layman

The grand finale of the Bicentennial summer was the Blessing of the Fishing Fleet, whose gala atmosphere was captured in this *Patriot Ledger* report (8/10/70):

Under cloudless blue skies and bright sunshine, more than 30 fishing boats took part in a blessing of the fishing fleet at Cohasset Harbor. It was the first such event in the town's 200-year history. Dozens of spectator boats of all sizes moored along either side of the harbor channel to watch the spectacle . . . The fishing boats were decorated from bow to stern with colorful flags and balloons. There was even "King Neptune" in white robes seated on the bow of a boat. Bright signal flags also flew from the shrouds of most of the larger spectator boats. Four local clergymen aboard the 50-foot excursion boat, the *Nancy J*, flying the church pennant, took part in the ecumenical blessing ceremonies: Rev. Frank B. Chatterton of the Second Congregational Church, the Rev. Paul Clark of St. Stephen's, and the Rev. Joseph Brennan and the Rev. John Fitzgerald, both of St. Anthony's. The captain's daughter, Maria Jason, 14, sculled out to meet the *Nancy J* in a small boat which she had decorated with yellow flowers. At Government Island fisherman Charles R. Wood demonstrated the art of rope splicing, while Lawrence A. Figueiredo showed the building of a lobster pot. In the water, just prior to the ceremonies, Herbert R. Towle, in oil-skins, rowed a fisherman's dory and pulled lobster pots from the harbor, in the manner of the old-time lobstermen, before the days of motor.

Several town organizations helped to make the Bicentennial a standout. Merchants, Scout troops, sports teams, and neighborhood groups created floats for the parade. The Community Garden Club planted a new flower garden along Depot Court outside the Community Center fence. The Cohasset Garden Club paved, painted, and landscaped the bus waiting station on the Common. Members of a special History Committee wrote a 64-page brochure on Cohasset from the Ice Age to 1970. Their illustrated *Cohasset USA—200 Years*, edited by Robert N. D. Arndt, was lavishly produced with photographs and with maps hand-drawn by Dorothy Wadsworth. The booklets were sold to the public and later given to students in the Cohasset schools. Bicentennial souvenirs included commemorative silver and bronze coins and small replicas of the town flag. The Bicentennial Year ended in the winter of 1970 with a festive ball at the Surf Ballroom in Nantasket and a Harvard Glee Club concert at the high school auditorium.

Cohasset's Historical Assets

The Bicentennial celebration generated a renewed interest in the history of Cohasset. In 1973 town meeting voted to establish a Historical Commission whose duty was to create an inventory of the town's historical assets — its earliest and most important buildings, structures, and sites. Noel Ripley was appointed chairman. The historical survey now includes more recent buildings of architectural significance. David Wadsworth, a longtime member of the commission and curator of the Cohasset Historical Society, has painstakingly researched, photographed, and documented most of the items in the survey, a now voluminous collection of priceless value to the community. As a result of his work, several of Cohasset's properties have been listed in the National Register of Historic Places. These historically important sites include the unique Lighthouse Reservation on Government Island, the site of the former U.S. Lighthouse Service Shore Station for Minot's Ledge Lighthouse; the Cohasset Common, an original New England town common that was part of the "undivided lands" of the early town of Hingham; and the Josephine Hagerty House on Atlantic Avenue, designed by the internationally famous architect Walter A. Gropius. It was built in 1938 as a summer home and was the first house Gropius designed on commission in the United States. As of June 2001, two other National Register nominations are in process: Central Cemetery and the Captain John Wilson House – Bates Ship Chandlery. Noel Ripley was responsible for the listing of the Caleb Lothrop House in the National Register.

Caleb Lothrop House

The Caleb Lothrop House at 14 Summer Street became the Historical Society's new headquarters in 1975. The society had outgrown its meeting room in the Maritime Museum and needed more space to store its expanding archive and library collection. Built in 1821 and originally the home of Caleb Lothrop, a ship chandler who owned a wharf at the harbor and several fishing schooners, the house is the only early Federal-style "brick-end" building in Cohasset. It remained in the Lothrop family until the Archdiocese of Boston bought the property in the early 1960s. Unoccupied or rented out for several years, the house was not in good condition, but Constance Parker, president of the Historical Society, saw great possibilities for it. Under her leadership the society launched a successful townwide drive to raise $18,000 for a down payment.

By 1979 the old Lothrop homestead was nearly restored. The society decorated it with furnishings typical of the nineteenth century, and the Commu-nity Garden Club land-scaped the grounds. (The club continues to maintain the gardens.) The building now houses a fine collec-tion of paintings related to Cohasset's history; an extensive archive on Cohasset history with fold-ers on 2,000 different top-ics; a nearly complete set of Town Reports, which began in 1849; a library of local and regional history books; and some early Cohasset schoolbooks and hymnals. Among the most treasured items is a set of eight historical maps of

The Federal style Caleb Lothrop House at 14 Summer Street, built in 1821, is now the head-quarters of the Cohasset Historical Society. *Photo courtesy of* Cohasset Mariner/Alan Chapman

Cohasset drawn and annotated by Gilbert Tower, a native of the town whose roots reached back to Ibrook Tower, one of the first settlers in Cohasset. Gilbert was not only a local historian and car-tographer, but a naval architect, a naval officer in World War I, and a mechanical engineer. He had been employed as an engineer at the building of the Panama Canal. A prolific writer and frequent speaker at town meeting on planning and zoning issues, he was named Honorary Town Engineer by the selectmen in 1970, a title he held proudly until his death in 1984, at age 99.

The Lothrop House also contains an impressive archive related to Cohasset's long tradition of theater and drama. Called the Helen Howes Vosoff Archive after a prominent patron of the arts in Cohasset, the collection was developed and maintained by the Cohasset Historic Trust, an outgrowth of the Bicentennial Committee. The theater archive contains documents and memorabilia from the Hanlon Brothers, the internationally famous family of acrobats, performers, and artists whose practice studio was a seven-story building at 93 Ripley Road, where Carousel Antiques now stands (the studio was demolished in 1915).

Gilbert Tower (1885-1984), local historian and cartographer as well as a naval officer in World War I, was named Honorary Town Engineer in 1970. Photo courtesy of Cohasset Mariner

The archive also includes programs and records from the South Shore Players, a professional troupe of actors who performed at Town Hall from the early 1930s to 1950; material from the Music Circus and the Cohasset Dramatic Club; and a major collection of books on the theater and history donated by Arthur T. Mahoney.

National Bicentennial

The nation's Bicentennial gave Cohasset another opportunity to celebrate its past. Now an expert organizer of historical celebrations, Burt Pratt was named chairman of the 1976 Bicentennial Commission. He secured the National Bicentennial Community designation for Cohasset, receiving a certificate signed by President Gerald Ford as well as an American Revolutionary Bicentennial flag.

Cohasset resident Francis W. Hagerty initiated and directed the School Bicentennial Project, an extracurricular schoolwide study of the life and times of Cohasset people during the American Revolution. In the course of their research, however, students were disappointed to find little information available on Cohasset in the last half of the eighteenth century. The project regrouped around Cohasset's shipbuilding past when the students discovered that the revenue cutter *Massachusetts 2*, a forerunner of the U.S. Coast Guard fleet, had been built in Cohasset. The shipwright is believed to be Adna Bates, owner of the largest shipyard in Cohasset. For the Bicentennial celebration, high school students built a replica of Bates's shipbuilding shop. Under the direction of their manual arts teacher Patrick Plante, they assembled all the equipment that an eighteenth century shipwright might need, including the actual tools believed to have been made by Mordecai Lincoln. Cohasset, said Fran Hagerty, "was built by the sweat of individuals like Adna Bates . . . and Mordecai Lincoln, an iron master, who were born in a far less complex period of history, when individualism and accomplishment were not only tolerated but cherished. They epitomized a period in which 'Yankee ingenuity' substituted for schooling" (*Patriot Ledger*, 6/19/76).

The shipbuilding shop was displayed on the Common, as well as a reproduction of the living room of Nathaniel Nichols, a Cohasset sailor and navigator who served in the Revolutionary War. Students also gave live demonstrations of eighteenth-century cooking. A unique event was the wool-spinning bee. This competition attracted spinners from all over New England, who endeavored to spin the longest yarn in a given period of time. The spinning bee commemorated the 300 colonial women who had gathered on Boston Common in 1753 to spin wool and sing hymns in protest against British laws prohibiting colonists from importing sheep. The Bicentennial celebration also featured the twenty-first annual South Shore Art Festival on the Common, as well as concerts, roving troubadours, Girl Scout folk dancing and Morris dancing, and dramatic presentations.

The most spectacular regional event of the 1976 Bicentennial was the Parade of Tall Ships that sailed to Boston Harbor on July 11. The tallest of the ships could even be seen from vantage points on Jerusalem Road. The chairman of Boston's "Operation Sail" was Cohasset resident Henry Dormitzer, then treasurer of Boston Yacht Club. The parade route was a sea of spectator boats. Crowds of more than 600,000 people watched the procession of 72 schooners, barks, sloops, ketches, yawls, brigantines, cutters, and majestic square riggers. As one woman marveled over and over again, "This is one of the best things that ever happened in Boston!" (*Patriot Ledger*, 7/12/76).

Town Archives

When the 1970 and 1976 Bicentennial committees were researching Cohasset history, they were hampered by the scattered location of town records around Town Hall. Belatedly, in 1977 the selectmen proposed and town meeting approved the construction of a storage vault at the high school for the consolidation and preservation of our permanent records. These include historic documents and books as well as modern records that the state requires towns to keep. When the new wing of Town Hall was completed in 1989, the records were returned to a secure, controlled-environment vault that meets the state's stringent requirements.

David Wadsworth, appointed town archivist in 1979, has organized a treasure trove of historic documents now safely stored in the vault. The oldest are the "Three-Score Acre" records of the mid-1650s, which pertain to a dispute between Plymouth and Massachusetts Bay colonies over the boundary line between Scituate and Hingham at the mouth of the harbor. The first public records of Cohasset precinct and parish meetings, dating from 1717, are also preserved, together with a complete collection of town meeting records. The early documents are difficult to decipher, as they were written in a fine, old-fashioned script, some of it faded, but they are nevertheless an invaluable original resource for historians. Other important papers include the record of land grants in Cohasset given to Hingham settlers in the seventeenth century; the founding document of April 26, 1770, incorporating Cohasset as a district separate from Hingham; records of the births, deaths, and marriages of the early settlers; and many books, letters, reports, maps, and plans from the mid-1800s to the early 1900s concerning topics ranging from Cohasset's maritime activities to road and bridge construction. Wadsworth's carefully organized and preserved public documents, as well as his survey of the town's historical assets, have made the past accessible to those interested in early Cohasset.

FACING THE PRESENT

Whether it was separation from Hingham in 1770 or taking up arms against King George III in 1775, from the earliest times citizens have disagreed, sometimes bitterly, on important issues of the day. The issues that divided the town 200 years later may seem less significant by comparison. Yet the 1970s were a difficult time for those caught up in the conflicts. The schools were the first arena of controversy. A new superintendent, Nelson Megna, had been hired following William Ripley's retirement. Ripley had provided firm, steady leadership for three decades. When he left, notes former School Committee member John P. Reardon, Jr., "the stopper flew out of the bottle."

Claus's Beard

In the 1960s Cohasset High School had a dress code that insisted on "good taste and cleanliness" and prohibited "disturbing or distracting" elements in the classroom. Enforced by Principal Frank Giuliano (nicknamed "The Bear"), the policy seemed unduly restrictive to students, given the loosening of social mores around them. Giuliano sent girls home if their skirts were more than an inch or two above the knee, and boys if they wore torn jeans or trendy combat boots. Mustaches and beards were forbidden. In 1969, however, Claus Guggenberger, a foreign exchange student from Germany, defiantly crossed the line: over Christmas vacation he grew a sparse beard and in January returned to school unshaven. Giuliano, citing the rules and threatening suspension, told him to shave it off. Claus refused, claiming he had a constitutional right to express himself freely by wearing a beard.

The conflict posed a dilemma for his host family, Francis and Margaret Charles. They resolved it by treating Claus as if he were their son. They allowed him to make his own decision, and stood by him. Claus decided to keep his beard and to appeal his suspension to the Dress Code Committee and the School Committee. Both upheld the principal's action: rules were rules, and Claus had to comply. Enter the high school Student Council. In an assertive spirit, they wrote a letter to the School Committee urging them to abandon the dress code altogether and allow students to freely express their individuality. The School Committee declined to do so. With support from the Student Council, Claus pursued his case at the U.S. District Court in Boston. Agreeing with the arguments of Claus's attorney (Cohasset resident Daniel F. Featherston), the judge barred school officials from suspending the youth.

The matter became a cause célèbre, and adults in the community took sides. Some were appalled by Claus's flouting of the rules; others objected to the school's arbitrary approach. In a pattern often repeated in the seventies, those who supported Claus's rights formed a committee. The newly organized Education Discussion Group met at the Paul Pratt Memorial Library and invited speakers to debate the issue, most of them highly critical of the school's "obsession" with rules. Amid these tensions, Claus finished his year in Cohasset and returned to Germany, still sporting a beard (although it was rumored that he planned to shave it off, as it would not be tolerated at home).

After this incident, the school never officially changed the rules, but the administration no longer enforced the dress code. By the end of the seventies everyone wore jeans to school, and you could even spot an occasional beard or two. In fact sometimes there was no dress whatsoever. In March 1974 six teenaged boys were caught "streaking" in the buff across the school parking lot. Gino DiGirolamo, who was high school principal at the time, cuttingly remarked, "You have *nothing* to be proud of!"

Student Walkout

The furor over Claus's beard was but a prelude to more momentous confrontations. Both students and teachers were now demanding a role in decisions that affected them. In the fall of 1970, high school students were pleased to see that their new principal, Richard T. Streeter, was a good listener and open to their concerns.

Peter J. Pratt, a sophomore at the time, recalls that Streeter was a "breath of fresh air," a quiet, easy-going man who was in touch with the concerns of young people and respected their opinions.

The School Committee had other priorities. When Nelson Megna resigned as superintendent in 1972, they searched for a replacement who would introduce modern teaching techniques, update the curriculum, and control the skyrocketing costs of education. They thought they had found just the right person in James F. Gray, an administrator with advanced degrees from Boston University and Harvard School of Education, who had taught education at the University of Pittsburgh.

From the very beginning of the 1972 school year, however, Gray locked horns with the Cohasset Teachers Association (CTA), which was becoming increasingly militant. His first act as superintendent was to establish a new teacher evaluation policy, one that called for written instead of informal evaluations. He did this without first discussing the new procedure with the teachers. In protest, the CTA filed a complaint against the School Committee, charging it with illegal practices by unilaterally imposing the evaluation program. The union's complaint was later dismissed by the state Labor Relations Committee. Undeterred, the CTA filed 11 more grievances during 1973.

As School Committee Chairman John Reardon later described it, the committee was "locked in a power struggle with the teachers over who was going to operate the schools" (*Patriot Ledger*, 4/30/74). Determined to resist pressure from the union and to run the schools as they saw fit, the committee took a fateful step. Richard Streeter's contract was up for renewal in the spring of 1973. Under Massachusetts law at the time, he would automatically go on tenure the following year, his fourth in Cohasset. He could then continue to be principal until he retired. Unprepared to make this long-term commitment, a majority of the School Committee decided to deny Streeter tenure by not renewing his contract; that is, they fired him. When the news broke, the students and teachers were in an uproar. On the morning of April 4, 1973, in a move unprecedented in Cohasset, nearly all 900 students in the high school walked out of the building. The teachers remained in their class-rooms but released a statement saying: "We feel the walkout has simply highlighted many of the problems that have plagued our system since the change in administration. The teachers and students are 100 percent behind Mr. Streeter" (*Patriot Ledger*, 4/4/73).

Parents and newspaper reporters gathered on the school grounds immediately after the walkout. Among those present was Selectman Mary Jeanette Murray, who said that as a mother and a taxpayer she applauded the students' action. According to Peter Pratt, a student spokesman for the well-organized walkout, the stu-

Students milling around outside Cohasset High School after walking out in support of Principal Richard Streeter, whose contract was not renewed. Student organizer Kevin Fox discusses the situation with resident Nancy O'Toole. Photo courtesy of Patriot Ledger/Everett Tatreau

dents had felt that "their interests had been overlooked in the matter and that their petition in favor of granting the principal tenure and their requests to meet with the School Committee in executive session had been overlooked."

Shocked by the violent reaction to their decision, the School Committee agreed to give people an opportunity to voice their opinions at an open meeting in the high school gymnasium. It became a media event. Attended by TV cameras and reporters, an estimated 1,300 people crowded into the room, the largest number ever to convene in Cohasset. After two hours of heated discussion, with Streeter's supporters urging the committee to reverse their decision and others complaining about the chaos that now reigned in the schools, the committee voted again, 4 to 2, not to rehire the principal.

The tension escalated. On April 10 about 200 parents and teachers met outside the school to consider how they might oust incumbent committee members and the superintendent. In a complete breakdown of civility, they formed a gauntlet as the committee and Jim Gray entered the building, and they proceeded to catcall, hoo, and shake their fists at those who voted against Streeter. The crowd, already furious at cuts in the school budget, demanded to know why the popular principal had been fired. A few days later the superintendent sent Streeter a letter giving those reasons—essentially, that his management and educational leadership qualities did not meet expected standards. When interviewed by a *Patriot Ledger* reporter, Streeter dispassionately commented that "the situation which appears to have divided the town is not unique in Cohasset but seems to be happening nationwide." He noted that "teachers are becoming more powerful with the unions and are demanding more say in school programs and even the students of today want more say in school policies."

The teachers' union was not so philosophical. In May 1973 Bruce Burgess, a Massachusetts Teachers Association (MTA) negotiator, wrote Rand McNally publishers, the employer of Cohasset School Committee member Douglas James. Burgess attached an unsigned letter, which he said was written by the Cohasset teachers' union, threatening Rand McNally with a possible boycott of its products by the 50,000 members of the MTA unless James "begins to cease and desist from taking positions that affect our security and well-being." The letter specifically referred to recent Cohasset School Committee decisions to reduce some teaching positions and reorganize some programs. (Later Margaret Maeder, president of the Cohasset union, said that the CTA did not sanction or send the letter.) In response to James's understandable outrage at this "blatant attempt at legalized blackmail," Joseph Durkin, another MTA official, stated disingenuously: "Bringing pressure to bear in a democracy to persuade a member of the school committee to change his mind is legitimate" (*Patriot Ledger*, 6/28/73).

The situation turned even uglier. In May 1974 vandals broke into Gray's office and spray-painted his walls in black paint with messages demanding that he, the assistant superintendent, and two School Committee members go. They dumped his books and papers into the middle of the room, and smashed his belongings. Later mayhem included the destruction of school lavatories, the smashing of doors and windows, damage to school buses, and theft and destruction of personal property.

Finally, unable to deal effectively with the union or to mitigate the animosity toward Gray, in November 1974 the School Committee voted, 4 to 2, not to rehire the superintendent.   In a public statement Douglas James said, "Almost from the beginning Mr. Gray had been the victim of shocking political intrigue and hostile acts involving various town officials, certain leaders of both the local and state teachers unions, and a number of citizens . . . it is a measure of Mr. Gray's unusual capabilities and qualities that he was able to accomplish so much in the face of such overwhelming odds" (*Patriot Ledger*, 11/26/74).

The beleaguered superintendent had indeed accomplished much. He had brought the school budget under control, updated the educational program, and begun to work on a much needed policy manual. His supporters commended him on his choice of principals, his innovative programs, and his focus on individualized learning. Yet his aloofness (students complained that he was mostly invisible) and his manner of imposing changes without input from teachers or students alienated him from many people. Some also held against him the fact that he had lived in his office during his first six months at the school while he looked for a house. In the end, Gray lost and Streeter won. In March 1975 the American Arbitration Association reinstated the principal on a technicality: the arbitrator ruled that the failure of the School Committee and superintendent to discuss the evaluation of his performance with him violated his contract. In July 1975 John F. Maloney became Cohasset's third superintendent in six years. Peace and harmony returned to the high school.

Other Changes in the Schools

The school population was at its peak in the early seventies. The elementary schools were so crowded in 1970 that the kindergarten class of 138 pupils had to be housed at Trueblood Hall and the Carriage House at First Parish. Portable classrooms were proposed for Deer Hill, and town meeting debated the wisdom of building a new elementary school. But the baby boom was already over. The birth rate had dropped sharply as a result of the changes in family life that swept the nation during the sixties. Contributing to the decline were the introduction of the birth control pill in 1960, the doubling of the divorce rate between 1966 and 1976, and the increase in "child-free" marriages and unmarried couples. By 1977 the kindergarten class had only 70 children. Now the challenge was how to deal with a smaller population.

Fewer students meant fewer classroom teachers. In addition to providing a basic education, however, schools increasingly had to cope with the problems of children from dysfunctional families. Hence the reduction in teaching staff was offset by the hiring of specialists in a variety of fields such as health education, drug education, and learning disabilities. Cohasset, like other schools, hired counselors to help children with psychological problems, as well as a host of specialists to implement the new Chapter 766 Special Education Law. Enacted in 1974, this law guaranteed to each special-needs child between the ages of 3 and 21 the right to an appropriate and individualized educational program.

Another law, Chapter 753, required schools to teach courses in health education. Further, Title IX of Federal Law 622 made it illegal for schools receiving federal aid to discriminate against women in physical education or athletic competition. "The involvement of girls in the athletic program is the biggest change I've seen since I was a student teacher," reflected Cohasset High School Athletic Director Clark Chatterton in 1998. "The participation of girls in sports is up ninefold from the early seventies. Girls' tennis, lacrosse, soccer, track, swimming, sailing, and skiing are all girls' sports that have started since Title IX." Girls also began to play baseball with boys in Little League. In 1978, 12-year-old Gia

Baressi became the first girl to play on the Cohasset Little League All-Star team.

In spite of the changes and tumult of the seventies, there were many examples of excellent performance by Cohasset students. In 1976 two seniors earned perfect scores on their math college boards. In 1978 Michael Christopher Gurnis was named one of the 40 most gifted young scientists in the nation. He had conceived a new statistical system for counting the craters on the moon. The Cohasset High School Drama Workshop, directed by drama coach Ron Emmons, won the 1979 Massachusetts Drama Festival with its performance of *Story Theatre*, a contemporary adaptation of Grimm's fairy tales and Aesop's fables. Also in 1979, the Cohasset basketball team, under the direction of coach John LeVangie, had its best year ever, reaching the semifinals of the Division III South tournament. And the Cohasset High School Jazz Rock Ensemble, led by music director Anthony Hyde, won first place in the Norwood Jazz Classic Festival, its second First Place trophy in two consecutive years.

By the end of the decade the school system had healed and was confidently looking forward to the future. Superintendent Maloney noted in the Town Report the increase in the number of students enrolling in the high school computer science program. He perceptively stated, "The importance of computers in the future cannot be underestimated. We are on the threshold of another technological explosion which will occur during the decade of the 1980s."

Confrontation at the Cove

In the meantime, a crisis was brewing down at the Cove. In March 1972 Cohasset resident and restaurateur John Carzis obtained a special permit from the Zoning Board of Appeals to build a two-story, 62-unit motel at the foot of Elm Street on the harbor. The site was occupied by the old Kimball's Lobster Shop, closed since 1968, and Marks's Service Station. Carzis owned the entire property, including nearby Hugo's Shack. He planned to demolish Kimball's and Marks's to build the motel, and to retain the Shack as its restaurant.

There had long been talk of building a public park on that site. As early as 1910 a town harbor committee recommended the pur-

The Cove and Harbor at the beginning of the 1970s showing Marks's Service Station, Kimball's Lobster Shop and Hugo's Shack at the head of the Cove. *Photo courtesy of Bill Stone*

Contemporary view of Cohasset Harbor and the Cove, showing Kimball's-by-the-Sea Motor Inn at the head of the Cove. *Photo © Margot Cheel*

chase of all the land around the harbor for use as a park. Interestingly, at that time a carriage factory stood at the site of what is now Kimball's-by-the-Sea Motor Inn. Because the town was unable to acquire that factory, town meeting rejected the entire proposal. In 1925 the town again tried to purchase the property, but a frugal town meeting voted it down. Then in 1961 the Benjamin Report envisioned a small park and a "James Brook Reservation" at the west end of the Cove. On that recommendation, Memorial Park was created at the old Central Fire Station site.

To expand the open space, the town would have to acquire Carzis's land and raze the Shack and other buildings—an unlikely prospect. But four years later this notion did not seem so far-fetched. In 1965 Carzis applied for a liquor license for the Shack. The application was opposed at a public hearing. Discouraged by this reaction, Carzis offered to "sacrifice the place at half price if enough Cohasset citizens were interested in [obtaining] the property for the good of the town" (*South Shore News*, 3/4/65). However, nobody took him up on his offer. In July 1971 the elderly restaurateur, nearing the end of his life, decided to build a "beautiful" motel on the harbor as his legacy to the town he had loved ever since moving here in 1948. Jessie Cox, whose estate ("The Oaks") was in close proximity to the proposed motel, offered to buy the property for $500,000, but she was too late. Carzis had already made a financial commitment to proceed with his plans.

Some people liked the idea of a new motel. They felt that the town needed more income-producing properties to broaden the tax base. The motel would bring in more tax dollars while providing jobs for local people and a place for visitors to stay. In a letter to the Zoning Board of Appeals (7/22/71), W. Chester Browne, the architect for the motel, argued: "The town is up to its ears in parks, open land, ocean views and sentimentality . . . Progress and a recognition of reality must come—even to Cohasset." He and other advocates believed that Carzis was a man of vision and courage. Indeed, those who knew the story of his life could not help but admire him.

John Carzis had immigrated from Greece to Boston in 1914, at the age of 15. As related in the *Cohasset Mariner* (1/12/78), Carzis was a real-life Horatio Alger hero who had risen from rags to riches by working two jobs, 16 hours a day, six days a week. At the age of 18 he opened his first restaurant in the North End. By the late 1920s he was running a chain of restaurants. Taking pity on the poor who rummaged for scraps from his kitchen, he opened his door to the needy. In 1928 he began a tradition of providing free Christmas dinners for the down and out. The number of guests grew until one Christmas Day he served 6,000 people. For such generosity he was sometimes called the Saint, or the Savior of the Poor.

In 1948 Carzis moved to Cohasset and bought Hugo Ormo's three restaurants: Hugo's Lighthouse, Kimball's Lobster Shop, and the Shack. He transformed Hugo's Lighthouse into an award-winning restaurant, and in 1960 *Holiday* magazine ranked it as one of the 100 greatest restaurants in the United States. In 1972 he

Hugo's Lighthouse Restaurant during John Carzis's ownership. In 1960 Holiday *magazine ranked the restaurant as one of the 100 greatest in the U.S.* Photo courtesy of Cohasset Mariner

renewed his tradition of free Christmas dinners. Five hundred senior citizens were transported from Boston to Cohasset in eleven busloads through the auspices of Catholic Charities. One hundred and twenty Cohasset residents helped prepare and serve the feast. Many of these volunteers continued this work each year until Carzis's death in 1979.

"A special occasion
for a very special person"

A Tribute to
JOHN G. CARZIS

September 22, 1975
Hugo's Lighthouse
Cohasset, Massachusetts

John W. McCormack, former Speaker of the U.S. House of Representatives, greets Hugo's owner John Carzis at a well-attended tribute to Carzis for his many good works. The event was chaired by Doris Golden, center. Photo and program courtesy of Doris Golden

Jessie Cox confronting John Carzis during a demonstration against the construction of his new motel at the Cove. Photo courtesy of Patriot Ledger/Richard Green

His good works, however, were irrelevant to those who had serious concerns about the motel. Over the vehement objections of neighbors and other townspeople, construction began in July 1974. The site had already been leveled by two fires, both apparently set by vandals: Kimball's was destroyed in August 1972 and the Shack in February 1973. As the new motel went up, people were appalled by what they saw. A forbidding, five-foot-high, charcoal-gray stone wall emerged in front of the motel, abutting the pavement and encroaching on narrow Margin Street. The motel itself grew to completely block the view from Elm Street to the harbor. An added insult was a high roof over the "attic," creating in effect head room for a third story. This design would raise the potential capacity to

96 units, far exceeding the number of parking spaces permitted. Neighbors and concerned townspeople gathered outside the motel carrying signs that read: "Kimball's-in-the-Road," "Cohasset's Folly," "Is This Planning?"

One of the most prominent of the demonstrators was Jessie Cox. Newspaper photographs show her shaking her finger at Carzis—two strong-minded people from two very different backgrounds. In many ways Jessie's life story was the direct opposite of Carzis's. Born to wealth, she was a granddaughter of Clarence W. Barron, who, as mentioned earlier, had founded *Barron's Financial Weekly* and owned Dow Jones, publisher of the *Wall Street Journal*. She was loved for her sense of humor, her energetic, outspoken, fun-loving nature, and her extraordinary generosity. As a child she had spent her summers in Cohasset with her mother, Jane W. Bancroft, her two sisters, and a brother in the Bancroft home on Sohier Street across from Barron's Oaks Farm. An accomplished horsewoman, Jessie kept her beloved Hackney ponies at the Oaks Farm stables on the site of the present Deer Hill School. She judged competitions all around the United States and showed and drove her own horses. In 1936 she became the first American woman invited to judge a Hackney horse competition in England.

In the 1930s Jessie and her husband, William, moved to her grandfather's estate on the harbor, where they built their magnificent brick home. Jessie was a director and major stockholder of Dow Jones. One of the wealthiest women in the United States, she, and her sister Jane, contributed to many causes. In 1970 she gave millions of dollars to Massachusetts General Hospital for the construction of a new building, named the William C. Cox Cancer Management Center in memory of her husband. She also donated a library at Milton Academy and was a major supporter of the Children's Hospital Medical Center, the Boston Symphony, Tufts University, and other institutions.

In Cohasset she was always ready to help when she saw a need. She gave the Bates Ship Chandlery (Maritime Museum building) to the Historical Society, founded and supported the Children's Hospital Benefit Tennis Tournament, financed the restoration of the

Minot's Light Construction Site, and donated land to the Conservation Trust. Now Jessie found that the town she had so liberally aided could do nothing to save her and her neighbors from the "hideous" building at the foot of Elm Street.

Taking independent action, the neighbors mobilized and formed a Cohasset Cove Committee. In May 1975, with financial support from 150 other residents, the committee filed suit in Norfolk Superior Court to block the motel. Hoping to have at least the portion abutting Margin Street removed, they claimed that the town building inspector and the Board of Appeals had violated town bylaws; the suit also named the selectmen and John Carzis. As it turned out in discovery, however, Carzis's property line extended nearly halfway into Margin Street. He had granted an easement to the town to pave his half of the road; hence his motel fell within the allowed setback from the property line, even though it narrowed the already tight roadway. In March 1977 the plaintiffs withdrew the suit, and the case was dismissed.

Many residents felt that town officials were failing to act in the best interests of the town. Not only was the view of the harbor from Elm Street completely obstructed by the motel, but Elm Street itself had been widened and "improved." Formerly shaded by elm trees rising from a long, broad ribbon of lawn, the street had lost much of its charm. The Elm Street project took residents by surprise in 1973. "As we watched helplessly," Francis Hagerty wrote in a letter to the *Patriot Ledger* (1/23/74), "Elm Street was widened, property frontages taken, elms cut, and granite curbings installed. How could this have happened? . . . When we voted to use Chapter 90 funds for work on Elm Street, most of us had in mind similar state-aided work done in Cohasset in the past where no widening of the road was undertaken . . . [A] likely explanation is that the planners were convinced that in the future Cohasset might well have a parking problem in the cove area, and this was the time to prepare for it. The end results of all this work may not necessarily be good planning for the future of Cohasset."

No one seemed accountable for such decisions. The selectmen disclaimed any responsibility for what had happened at the Cove.

Their apparent lack of power reinforced the determination of some citizens to change the structure of town government.

The Fight for a Town Charter

By the early 1970s the operation of the town had become both more complex and more expensive than a decade earlier. In the 1972 Town Report, L. Emmet ("Bim") Holt, chairman of the Advisory Committee, pointed out that between 1966 and 1970 the total expenditures of the town had nearly doubled, from $3.6 million to $6.3 million, and the tax rate followed suit. Compared with other towns of the same size in the Commonwealth, Cohasset was rated by the Massachusetts Finance Committee Association as one of the most costly on a per capita basis.

Moreover, the burden on the three-member Board of Selectmen had become overwhelming. In 1973 chairman Arthur Clark reported that the board had "convened in 50 regular and special meetings . . . and its members spent countless hours on the day-to-day operation of the Department. They also attended various hearings and meetings of other Town boards and committees in addition to regional, County, and State meetings of concern to the Town."

As early as 1957 the town, recognizing the need for greater efficiency, had appointed a Baby Hoover Committee to consider ways to improve town government. No action came of their efforts. Then in 1966 the Commonwealth passed a Home Rule amendment to the state constitution that allowed towns to elect charter commissions. The role of a charter commission was to draw up a document, or charter, establishing a framework for local government. The commission could recommend far-reaching changes in its charter. A town could, for example, choose to eliminate the selectmen/town-meeting form of government in favor of a mayor/town-council structure.

In March 1973 town meeting voted to create a charter commission for Cohasset. "The members represented a good cross-section of people with the best interests of the town in mind," recalls Richard D. Leggat, chairman of the commission. Other members included Henry Dormitzer, vice chairman; David L. Trainor, secretary; Helen Barrow, Paul Blackmur, Philip N. Bowditch, Arthur Taft Mahoney, Joseph Perroncello, and Michael E. Savage.

The efficacy of Cohasset government, as the commission saw it, was hampered by the decentralization of responsibility and authority. The town's various department heads were accountable only to the voters on election day, not to the selectmen charged with running the town. No one had the authority to coordinate town functions and budgets. The result was wasteful duplication of effort, overlap, and other inefficiencies. Instead of sharing personnel among departments, for example, a department that needed extra help would hire part-time employees or incur overtime expenses. Moreover, the selectmen were so burdened with operational tasks that they had little time to consider the important policy decisions that would affect Cohasset's future. A prolific Congress and state legislature were writing new laws and regulations and making grants available for projects that met specific criteria, all with Byzantine rules that required the selectmen's oversight. The commission concluded that the selectmen clearly needed full-time professional help and guidance to carry out their responsibilities.

The Charter Commission, after nearly a year of public hearings, drafted a Home Rule charter addressing these issues. They proposed to retain the selectmen/town-meeting form of government, but to increase the number of selectmen from three to five. The objective was to broaden representation, spread the workload, and increase the diversity of views on the board. Second, and more important, the commission proposed creating the position of executive secretary to the Board of Selectmen. Running town government was no longer a part-time, do-it-yourself activity, they said. The third major proposal was to make most town offices appointive rather than elective. The only elected officials would be the selectmen, the moderator, and, as required by law, the School Committee. All other town officials, such as the building inspector, the highway surveyor, and the assessors, would be answerable to the selectmen. If they did not perform their duties as required, the selectmen would have the authority to take appropriate action. Hence the Board of Selectmen, assisted by an executive secretary, would have more responsibility and authority than ever before. The commission hoped that these changes would induce a larger number of well-qualified people to run for the office.

The newest selectman, Henry Ainslie, elected in 1971, was amenable to the changes. But Arthur Clark and Mary Jeanette Murray (elected in 1970) were adamantly opposed. They believed that the town had functioned well with three selectmen. Instead of saving the town money, they said, an executive secretary would merely add another layer to government and another salary. The town had already saved money by combining the position of treasurer and collector in 1972. It was also looking into the purchase of the town's first minicomputer to streamline accounting functions. Moreover, department budgets were under the careful scrutiny of the Advisory Committee, and the town had no control over the autonomous School Department, which at that time accounted for 65 percent of the town budget. The other two "big spenders," the Fire and Police departments, were under the control of their chiefs, whose jobs were protected by Civil Service. Finally, they asked, how could government by appointment be more responsive to the people than government by the democratic process of election?

The battle over the charter was about to begin. Selectmen Clark and Murray and others opposed to the charter organized the Committee for Responsive and Accountable Government in Cohasset. Picking up the gauntlet, proponents mobilized and formed the Friends of the Charter. Both camps fired a barrage of literature across Cohasset. Letters to the editor appeared in local papers. Each group accused the other of distortion. In the first round on election day in May 1974, the Friends of the Charter went down to defeat, 1,483 to 1,161.

A year of hard work had come to nought. The commissioners were discouraged, but their supporters decided to try again. The Friends of the Charter circulated a petition to place the charter on the 1975 ballot. This was their last chance. The town had only until

1976 to accept the charter; otherwise the existing bylaws would become the framework for town government. (Anticipating this outcome, the selectmen had established a Bylaw Review Committee in August 1974 to propose amendments updating the town's bylaws. They strictly enjoined the committee not to involve themselves with reorganization of town government.)

Proponents of the charter worked zealously to gather the required number of signatures on their petition and submit it to the selectmen within the 30-day deadline required by the state. They made it, with 13 days to spare. Yet the selectmen, determined to stop the charter, tried to persuade Norfolk Superior Court to rule the action illegal. They claimed that the state's 30-day deadline applied only to the original submission of the charter. The state did not specify the number of days for *re*submission; therefore the longer, 60-day deadline required by the town for ballot articles should prevail, and the petitioners were too late. This tactic did not work. Town counsel ruled that the selectmen had no standing to seek a court judgment determining the legality of placing the charter resolution on the 1975 ballot.

Seventy-two percent of the town's registered voters turned out to vote once again on the charter. The Friends of the Charter saw the proposal go down to final defeat, 1,698 to 1,387. At least half the town wanted no change. In retrospect a piecemeal approach might have been more successful. Over time, most of the Charter Commission's proposals were in fact implemented. In 1981 the selectmen hired their first executive secretary; in 1983 the number of selectmen was increased from three to five; and in 1997 many elected positions became appointive. Cohasset, like Rome, was not built in one day.

Citizens v. Music Circus

Selectmen Murray, Clark, and Ainslie confronted a number of difficult issues. One of the thorniest involved the Music Circus. Competition had forced it to shift from traditional "straw hat" productions to the "star" system. Instead of popular plays and musicals, it now featured celebrity singers, rock bands, and Las Vegas-

Ron Rawson, executive director of the Music Circus, 1968-1988. The tent theater came under fire from neighbors in the 1970s despite drawing big-time acts like Bob Hope. *Photo courtesy of Cohasset Mariner/Alan Chapman*

The South Shore Music Circus in the 1970s. *Post card courtesy of Herb Towle*

Clark Chatterton, who ran the concessions at the Music Circus from the 1960s until his death in 2000. During the late 1970s, his staff included daughters Joanine and Kim (left) and Beth Salvador (right). *Photo courtesy of Ann Pompeo*

style entertainers. The number of seats had multiplied from 800 to 2,200, and the number of performances from 48 to 120. The Music Circus was big business, and the neighbors began to complain. If you lived on Sohier Street, amplified sound blaring from the tent kept you awake at night, and endless lines of cars trapped you in your driveway.

The noise and traffic became so unbearable that in 1977 a group of Sohier Street residents appealed to the Board of Selectmen. They claimed that the Music Circus was a liability and a public nuisance. Moreover, it raked in money but enjoyed non-profit status and gave very little to the town. Nothing came of the hearing, except to antagonize the directors. The neighbors then turned to the building inspector (the town's zoning officer) and claimed that the Circus had violated zoning bylaws by detrimentally expanding its operation far beyond the original use. The building inspector ruled that the Circus was in compliance with the law.

Finally the group appealed to the Zoning Board of Appeals, but the board upheld the building inspector's decision.

In frustration, Sohier Street resident Ruth S. Payne wrote to the *Patriot Ledger* (9/10/77): "Many of us wonder why our interests are continually subordinated to the interests of the Circus. Its taxes are a fraction of ours, and our trade is year-round and equally beneficial to Cohasset. We adamantly maintain there is no legal or financial justification for the Circus to profit at our expense. If compliance with the zoning laws and noise pollution guidelines makes the Circus unprofitable, then the directors should consider a move to an area where the operation is legal and welcome."

The 1977 season was the best ever for the Music Circus, with comedian Bob Hope drawing the largest audience in its 27-year history. The Circus was not about to accede to the complaints of a few malcontents. The neighbors decided to appeal the zoning decision and take the Circus to court. They formed a Concerned Cohasset Citizens Committee and in March 1978 filed suit in Norfolk Superior Court. Named in the suit were the building inspector, the South Shore Playhouse Associates, who owned the Music Circus, and the Zoning Board of Appeals. The Music Circus countersued with a $350,000 damage suit on each one of the 29 Concerned Citizens. The Circus claimed that it had "sustained slander and substantial diminution of its public image as a result of alleged reckless and incorrect accusations" (*Patriot Ledger*, 7/3/78).

After four years of legal maneuvering, the two parties finally reached an out-of-court settlement. In July 1982 each agreed to drop its suit in return for mutual concessions. The Music Circus installed a new system that more effectively contained the sound (or noise) in the tent, and the Citizens agreed to refrain from making derogatory comments. This gag rule lasted until the 1990s, when the Music Circus signed a legal document that restored the neighbors' freedom of speech.

Barnyard Bedlam

Not far from Sohier Street, cacophony of another sort ruffled the feathers of neighbors. The offender in this case was a flock of 100 roosters owned by a Pleasant Street resident. The birds created a horrible ruckus by crowing every two to five seconds at what neighbors claimed were abnormal hours. In July 1977 an irate delegation petitioned the selectmen for relief from their mental and physical distress. To prove the point, the group's spokesman, Lester Hiltz, played a tape of the birds so that the selectmen could judge for themselves. Rocco Laugelle, who owned the property where the birds were kept, objected that roosters normally do not crow at all hours. "I know," said a petitioner, "but these must be frustrated or insane roosters." Laugelle assured the group that their problems would disappear as soon as the birds' owner received delivery of a freezer in which to store them. That would not be soon enough, replied Hiltz. "The neighbors have offered to buy the roosters," he said. "Even at ten dollars apiece, they would enjoy wringing their necks!" (*Patriot Ledger*, 7/7/77). The matter was resolved once and for all in 1978 with a bylaw amendment that restricted the raising of farm animals to light industrial zones, and by special permit only.

Law and Disorder

In June 1977 Cohasset received some unwelcomed publicity. On the cover of *Boston* magazine was a full-face caricature of our chief of police, Randy Feola, staring out through dark glasses, a stogie clamped in his mouth. He was the icon for a feature article titled "The Gang That Couldn't Shoot Straight: Suburbia's Cops Are Armed and Dangerous."

The magazine portrayed the Cohasset police as a ragtag group lacking training and experience. As in other small towns, staffing and equipment were inadequate. But Cohasset was somewhat unusual. Most of the men bought their own pistols, typically .38 specials. The chief's son, Randy Jr., also a member of the Cohasset police force, favored a .44 magnum with a solid gold sight and "enough power to drive a bullet through several cars parked side by side." The article told tales on Randy Jr., such as when he drove into Hingham with shotguns in his car, wearing two bullet belts across his chest like a Mexican bandito. And then there was the hot summer evening when Junior "cooled off by taking a spin on his Harley wearing just a pair of boots."

Despite appearances to the contrary, Chief Feola was in control. He kept a "little brown book" prominently on his desk in which he recorded the infractions and peccadilloes of his men, and of other people as well. Some might call that intimidation. Traditional discipline on the force was a problem, particularly when it came to the chief's son. On duty, Randy Jr. was considered a good policeman, with more "street smarts" than most, but off duty he got into trouble, primarily for allegedly driving under the influence of alcohol. He was not the only one, however. Between 1977 and 1979 two Cohasset officers were dismissed because of assaults with guns, driving under the influence, and other misconduct.

Police Chief Randy Feola (center) expounds to George Jednick (left) and Ralph Perroncello (right) during breakfast at the Log 'n Line Restaurant. Photo courtesy of Marie Feola

Chief Feola retired in July 1980, on his sixty-fifth birthday, and moved to Florida a few years later. He died in 1999 and is now remembered as a genuine one-of-a-kind character, a man who used colorful language and ruled his men by fear but had a "good way with kids" (*Cohasset Mariner*, 11/11/99). Randy Jr. continued to have problems. He eventually resigned from the police force and followed his father to Florida.

Police work was a challenge in the seventies. Incidents of burglary in the Northeast increased 50 percent between 1971 and 1978, and vandalism was a persistent problem. Cohasset experienced several cases of malicious destruction. In December 1970 a

gang of youths destroyed the old Sandy Beach bathhouse, a landmark for 53 years. The long white-clapboard building had been a
favorite meeting place for beachgoers. Children loved to trek from
the beach to the candy
stand, and sun-worship-
pers found refuge under
the shady bathhouse
pavilion and its classical
portico. The building was
replaced with a damage-
resistant, characterless
concrete structure. In
other incidents school

*The beloved old bathhouse at Sandy Beach before
it was destroyed by vandals in December 1970.
Photo courtesy of Patriot Ledger/Everett Tatreau*

buses were vandalized, the high school building defaced, and new
floodlights at the Milliken Field tennis courts broken twice in
the first week. In May 1975 the Boy Scout camp in Wheelwright
Park was burned to the ground.

Besides vandalism, there was burglary. The problem was so
widespread that the Community Center hosted a public meeting in
June 1974 with Chief Feola and David Trainor, the assistant district
attorney for Norfolk County. Trainor, a Cohasset resident, attributed the crimes to drug use and the need for money to support the
habit. Generally there was no confrontation between criminal and
victim, but in 1977 masked robbers broke into a Beach Street home,
tied up the homeowners and their daughter, and fled with the family valuables.

The most sensational burglary was the Herrington art theft. In
August 1978 robbers broke into the Arthur C. Herrington estate on
White Head Road while the family was asleep upstairs and stole
two million dollars' worth of art treasures, including oil paintings by
Rembrandt, El Greco, and Breughel and two 600-year-old Ming
vases. The following year a 25-year-old Suffolk University student
from Boston was found in possession of the goods. He claimed that
he had received the artwork from someone else, although he later
pled guilty to the crime.

One of the worst crimes ever committed in Cohasset occurred

the evening of May 30, 1978. Early that Memorial Day, a frightened woman had phoned the police from a neighbor's home on Forest Notch and told them that her husband, a captain in the Merchant Marine, had beaten her during a quarrel. The police advised her to file a complaint in Quincy District Court through an attorney, and then offered to accompany her home and speak to her husband. She declined the offer. That evening at supper her husband apparently went berserk. He shot his wife and three young children, aged eight, six, and three, killing her and badly injuring them. Then he shot and killed himself. Discovered by the neighbors, the children were rushed into surgery at South Shore Hospital, where they ultimately recovered from their wounds. Friends and neighbors came to the children's aid with an outpouring of support and offers of help, but all the goodwill in the world could never erase the horror of that Memorial Day evening in Cohasset.

The case was broadly publicized in the Boston newspapers. It was particularly disturbing to readers, because if such violence could happen within a middle-class family in a "beautiful little Cape Cod-type of town" (*Boston Globe*, 9/24/89), then it could happen anywhere. As a result of this case, Norfolk District Attorney William D. Delahunt created the first domestic violence unit in Massachusetts, and a month after the shootings the 1978 Abuse Prevention Act was signed into law. The act provided that a woman could obtain a restraining order against her husband with a simple, direct plea to the court; moreover, if police had reason to suspect abuse on the part of her husband, they could arrest him immediately.

LIFE GOES ON

Despite all the turmoil, life in Cohasset went on. The town continued to evolve, though more slowly than before. In 1972 Peter and Judy Kulturides opened the Log 'n Line Restaurant in the former railroad station on Ripley Road. The name derived from the logline, a nautical tool used to measure the depth of the ocean. The restaurant became Cohasset's "second Town Hall," where local issues were debated over cups of coffee. Selectman Arthur Clark was among the regulars. If you were running for office, you would show up too. Part of the ritual of town politics required that you solicit votes from patrons of the Log 'n Line.

Around the corner on Pleasant Street stood the old Cohasset Lumber Company and Frank Wheelwright's Lincoln Coal Company office. These relics of a bygone era were converted to new uses. In 1976 Target Industries, a wholesale assembler of eyeglass frames, moved into the Lumber Co. building behind the Log 'n Line. Target's founders, Michael Abbruzzese and Roger Porter, built their success on the then innovative technique of telemarketing. Across Pleasant Street, Martha and Richard Conley transformed the tiny Lincoln Coal office into the

Strawberry Parfait, one of the most popular spots in town. First opened in 1978, it is still where you go for an ice cream cone on a hot summer day or a fried-clam plate take-out supper.

Small buildings were easily recycled. More problematic were the grand old man-

The Log 'n Line Restaurant, Cohasset's "second Town Hall" during the 1970s and 1980s. Photo courtesy of Cohasset Mariner/Greg Derr

sions that had become a burden to maintain. A Cohasset landmark that vanished in the seventies was The Ridges, the magnificent 40-room home on Jerusalem Road owned by Polly and Edward Logan. The house, with its 12 bedroom suites, 13 fireplaces, and four chimneys, had been built in 1870 as a "country seat" for Albert S. Bigelow. Clad in fieldstone and shingles, The Ridges was graced with a long front porch and a balcony supported by 14 white columns. The grounds were designed by Frederick Law Olmsted, the renowned architect of New York's Central Park and Boston's "Emerald Necklace."

The Logan family purchased The Ridges in the 1920s as a summer home. During the winter when the family was gone, towns-people would stroll around the 11-acre estate and peer into the windows to admire the elegantly furnished rooms. In the 1930s it became a year-round home. Polly and Edward, who moved there in the fifties, opened it to the community. "We held receptions for First Communion and Confirmation classes; entertained Cardinal Cushing and Cardinal Madeiros; held religious education classes every week in the billiard room, the library, the music room, the rotunda, and the upstairs living room; and hosted many jazz bene-fits with the Black Eagle Jazz Band," recalls Polly. "Guests sat on the great stairway." The Community Garden Club held flower shows and farmers' markets at The Ridges, keeping flowers and produce fresh in the huge walk-in refrigerator.

The Logans also hosted statewide flower shows; picnics and outings for Scouts, school groups, and senior citizens; political events and fundraisers; and military parties for the U.S. Army and Navy. (Edward was the commanding officer of the 26th Yankee

Edward and Polly Logan (right) host a party for the Navy at The Ridges, their Jerusalem Road estate—just one of hundreds of events the couple hosted over the years. Photo courtesy of Polly Logan

The ever-ebullient Polly Logan in 1996. Polly served as Republican National Committeewoman from Massachusetts, supported and men-tored many public figures and, in 2000, established a fund at the University of Massachusetts for the Center for Women and Politics and Public Policy. Photo courtesy of Tiny Town Gazette

Division of the Massachu-setts National Guard. Polly served as Republican National Committeewoman for Massachusetts, was a founder of the Massachusetts Women's Political Caucus in 1974, and has supported and mentored many public figures. To promote the role of women in public careers, in 2000 she established the Polly Logan Fund for the Center for Women and Politics and Public Policy at the University of Massachusetts.) The 80-foot-high flagpole on their great sweep of lawn was a landmark for airplanes. It was not unusual to see a helicopter land on the grounds to pick up United Way funds or to whisk newlyweds away on their honeymoon. But in the mid-seventies the financial burden on the Logans became too great. It was a period of exceptionally high energy costs and inflation, and the big house was expensive to heat and maintain. In 1975 the Logans sold their property to Cohasset developers John Murphy and John Riley. The mansion was demolished. You can still imagine the grandeur of the old estate from the extensive lawn that was preserved around the attractive single-family homes built at The Ridges.

As land values rose, developers found it more profitable to squeeze housing for several families into a relatively small area. Taking this concept to an extreme, in 1971 Paul F. Igo proposed to build a 126-unit, 11-story highrise on the site of the former Black Rock House on the shore at Jerusalem Road. The highrise proposal did not comply with current zoning regulations (or with the wishes of neighbors), however, and the building inspector refused to issue a permit. Igo appealed to the Zoning Board for a variance, but to no avail. He then took his case to court. The judge upheld the town's decision, and the matter was laid to rest. In 1976 a single-family dwelling was built on the site.

In 1973 a 64-unit apartment complex was constructed at 60 Elm Street, behind the police and fire headquarters. Called Harborview (although it had no view of the harbor), the complex was the first and is still (as of 2000) the only "affordable" housing for senior citizens in Cohasset. In the late sixties the state had begun to pressure towns to provide low-income housing. Accordingly, in 1969 voters at town meeting established the Cohasset Housing Authority, a public agency whose mission was to evaluate the needs of low-income families. The first board of commissioners included W. Chester Browne, chairman, James R.

Harborview, the 64-unit senior citizen residential complex on Elm Street, was built in 1973. Photo ©Lynne Layman

DiGiacomo, Samuel Hassan, Margaret A. Lynch, and Mary Jeanette Murray (appointed by Governor Francis Sargent). The Housing Authority oversaw the construction of Harborview and managed its operation. Harborview now houses both elderly and disabled persons and is subsidized by the Massachusetts Department of Housing and Community Development. To qualify for the housing, you have to be at least 60 years old and your annual income must not exceed $32,100. In 1990 the Housing Authority added eight units of housing for the mentally impaired at 72 Elm Street, subsidized by the state Executive Office of Communities and Development.

The development of open land became increasingly controversial in the seventies. An 80-acre parcel on Forest Avenue, known as the Legion Land, was the subject of intense debate. Thickly wooded with hickory, maple, birch, and hemlock, the area was hospitable to foxes, chipmunks, pheasants, owls, and other small wildlife. Much of it was wetland, but it also featured some of the steep granite ledges so unique to Cohasset. August Petersen, a Cohasset realtor who had emigrated from Denmark, bequeathed the land in 1942 to the George H. Mealy Post of the American Legion. He recommended, but did not require, that some or all of the land be used as a park for the recuperation of war veterans; a portion might also be divided into half-acre lots for permanent "domiciles" or temporary camping for rest and recreation. The Legion did nothing with the land for over 30 years. Then in 1977 they decided to sell it. Members of the Conservation Commission, among others, thought the town should purchase it for use as a park.

At the March 1977 town meeting, the Legion Post offered to sell the land to the town for $100,000; state and federal funds would cover half the cost. The Conservation Commission voted 4 to 2 to support the proposal. The two members opposed argued that the town already had plenty of open space. Wheelwright Park, for example, just across Forest Avenue from the Legion Land, was a beautiful recreational resource that was, and still is, underutilized. They believed the Legion Land could not be developed anyway, because it would not "perk." The Advisory Committee and the Capital Budget Committee (formed in 1971 to prioritize spending on capital projects) also opposed the purchase, and the town accordingly voted it down. Shortly thereafter, Thomas Chamberlain and Roger Pompeo bought the land for $135,000. They tested the land more thoroughly, and found that the area did perk after all. In 1979 the Planning Board approved a 33-lot subdivision for 70 of the acres. Pompeo kept most of his land undeveloped, classifying it as a tree farm. The other portion became a residential area called Fox Run.

CHURCHES AND TOWN ORGANIZATIONS

Three new pastors came to Cohasset in the seventies. In November 1970 the Reverend Richard D. Muir was installed as rector of St. Stephen's. A graduate of Miami University of Ohio and Bexley Hall Seminary, he had worked for eight years as a senior sales engineer for Honeywell, Inc., and later served as curate of St. Paul's Church in Akron, Ohio. At the Second Congregational Church, the Reverend John M. Benbow, a graduate of Iowa State University and Andover-Newton Theological Seminary, replaced Rev. Frank Chatterton, who retired in September 1976. And in March 1977 the Reverend John J. Keohane was appointed pastor of St. Anthony's, following the death of Rev. Joseph Brennan in November 1976.

Prior to coming to Cohasset, Father Keohane had served as chaplain of Florida State University and the federal penitentiary in Tallahassee, Florida. He was also chaplain of the U.S. Air Force in Vietnam and retired in 1976 with the rank of colonel.

After the activist years of the late 1960s, the churches in Cohasset entered a quieter phase. Nevertheless, many of the controversial issues of the sixties were still being debated. Reflecting on his years at St. Stephen's, Rev. Muir later wrote:

What an agenda we faced in those years between 1970 and 1984! Racism. Women's rights. An ominous, growing, spreading drug culture. The "quagmire" of the War in Vietnam. The Energy Crisis and the growing concern about the security of the Near East. Double-digit interest rates and economic depression. "Deflation."

And internally, the church wrestled with the changes in our worship brought about by the Liturgical Movement and the introduction of a new Prayer Book. Feelings were also strong as the issue of the ordination of women was debated and finally passed. The very role of the church, the ministry of the laity and of the clergy were . . . a source of passionate debate and disagreement.

[From *So Worship We God*, pp. 200–201]

He concluded by recalling the good times: "We had fun! We climbed mountains, went on bicycle and ski trips, had communion, marriages and picnics on beaches, in back yards, and on mountain-tops."

Clearly the character of worship had changed by the seventies. In the more liberal atmosphere of the period, the conventions of the past were shed as parishioners experimented with innovative forms of spritual expression. Marriages were held in unusual settings, folk masses became popular for young people, and Bible-inspired rock musicals such as *Jesus Christ Superstar* and *Godspell* were sellouts. In 1976 Cohasset High School gave its first production of *Godspell*, under the direction of drama coach Ron Emmons. Enjoying extraordinary success, the Drama Workshop presented the show eight more times over the next 25 years. The final performance, given in 2001 at

Emmons's retirement, featured both current and former students, including three members of the original cast.

Adapting to the decline in religious orders, St. Joseph Villa, a summer vacation home for the Sisters of St. Joseph, became a year-round retreat center for laypeople and religious alike in 1974. The lovely house on the shore at 339 Jerusalem Road is a haven for those seeking a "quiet space" for prayer, reflection, and spiritual renewal. Built before 1876 (no one knows the exact date), the building has an interesting history. It was originally called the Ahahden House, after a son of the sachem Chickataubut, who lived in the region before European settlement. Lacking the concept of property rights, Ahahden, with his brothers Wompatuck and Squmuck, deeded away the land of Hingham to the English in 1665. In 1904 Samuel S. Spaulding of Buffalo, New York, president of the Buffalo Street Railway, bought the house as a summer residence. The Sisters of Saint Joseph, a Boston-based order, have owned it since 1947. Although it used to accommodate 50 nuns a week during the summer, as a retreat center it now more comfortably houses 15 visitors.

Both churches and town organizations were struggling to attract the same level of support they had enjoyed earlier. During the seventies membership at St. Stephen's dropped from 180 to 70 parishioners. To counter that trend, Rev. Muir focused on expanding the adult education program, while his assistant, Rev. Roy Cederholm, a teacher at Cohasset High School, took charge of the youth ministry. Likewise, the Community Center found its once broadly based membership falling to 60 in 1976. There was even a debate over whether the center should continue to exist. Its popular nursery school, held at the center since 1953, was just breaking even. The programs for older children could not compete with street hockey, soccer, and other activities offered by the town's Recreation Commission under its first professional director, John M. Worley, appointed in 1976 (and still at the helm in 2000).

The directors considered selling the Community Center as housing for the elderly or for Town Hall office space and storage. But a group of loyal members urged reinvigorating the center instead. They formed a Concerned Citizens Committee and in 1978 proposed new, more forward-looking candidates to fill vacant slots on the board of directors. The reorganized board began an aggressive membership drive under the leadership of Martha Gjesteby and Edward Jacome. Simultaneously they designed a course program that would appeal to a range of ages and interests: gymnastics for young children, disco dancing for teens and adults, a "dancercise" program, ballroom dancing, beginner bridge, gourmet cooking, and a variety of crafts. With volunteer help from a Marine Corps reserve squadron, Building Committee director Rocco Laugelle renovated the bowling alleys and remodeled the building's six income-producing rental apartments. In the fall of 1978 the Program Committee, led by Jean Salvador, Regina Schultz, and Judy Volungis, held the center's first annual Oktoberfest, a lively festival with games, rides, prizes, crafts, carved pumpkins, and hearty German food and beer.

The campaign was a resounding success. The Oktoberfest put the Community Center "back on the map," and the new courses were so popular that many of them are still offered today. By the end of 1978, the center had acquired 525 dues-paying members. But that was only the beginning. In 1985 the board of directors expanded the center's facilities and gymnasium by tripling the size of McElwain Hall and adding nursery school classrooms below. The $550,000 project was funded primarily by a large grant from South Shore Playhouse Associates and matching grants from Jane (Steele) Cook. A year later Cohasset's new Senior Center opened on the first floor, drawing still more people to the facility. In 1990 the Community Center even offered to take over the town's Recreation Department programs—a stunning comeback for an organization that had nearly expired just 14 years earlier.

Another activity that went through a doldrums was Scouting. Strongly supported in the fifties and sixties, it was now hard pressed to recruit volunteers. Busy parents preferred to drop off their children at Little League and other organized sports instead of getting involved in Scouts. For older boys, peer pressure and anti-war sentiment made it "uncool" to appear in Scout uniform.

Scoutmaster Arthur Lehr recalls that even on the warmest summer days, boys would wear jackets to hide their distinctive Boy Scout shirts and familiar insignia.

For boys 14 and older, however, Explorer Scout Post 28 was an exception. Formed by Lehr in 1968, the Cohasset Explorers specialized in emergency medical training. They became proficient enough to assist at town emergencies and, in a pinch, drive the ambulance for Chief Feola, himself a former Eagle Scout. "About 10 boys between the ages of 16 and 18 had radio scanners and cars," explains Lehr. "When they heard about an accident, even at

2:00 in the morning, they would report to the scene. The chief would say to his patrolmen, 'Wait until the Boy Scouts get here.' As soon as the Scouts arrived, they would administer First Aid to the injured. Sometimes they even went to the police station to get the old Packard sedan that the town used as an ambulance. Then the police would take over." This practice continued until 1977, when the Fire Department

Longtime Scoutmaster Arthur Lehr and his son, Phil, about to leave for the 1969 National Scout Jamboree in Idaho.
Photo courtesy of Arthur Lehr

assumed operation of the town's EMT (emergency medical technician) and ambulance service. Two of Cohasset's Explorer Scouts became the first certified EMTs in Massachusetts. Explorer Scouts also assisted the harbormaster in policing the harbor. Assigned to night patrol in 1975 during a wave of vandalism and theft, they reduced the number of incidents by 18 percent.

Today Cohasset is particularly proud of its Eagle Scouts, youths who have fulfilled all the requirements of Scouting and completed a special project. The recyclables signs at the Cedar Street Transfer Station, the Dump Boutique, and the gateways and campsites at Wheelwright Park are some of their contributions. For younger children, the Boy Scouts and Girl Scouts also appear to be enjoying a comeback.

Membership was not a problem for the new Cohasset Swim Center. It opened in June 1974 with more than 500 children signed up for Red Cross swimming lessons and 125 on the Swim Team. The Swim Center was the idea of John H. Meyer, who believed Cohasset should have a pool not only for the Swim Team, which up to then relied on private pools, but for everyone in town who wanted to swim. In 1970 Meyer and six other citizens formed the Cohasset Swim and Recreation Trust for the purpose of raising $500,000 to construct a pool. The trustees included Meyer, Jane Cook and her sister Jessie Cox, Frederick Good, Herbert Hoefler, Richard Leggat, and Robert Sceery. Without the very generous funding provided by Cook and Cox in memory of their mother, Jane Bancroft, the facility, officially named the Bancroft Swim Center, could never have been built. The operating costs are covered by usage fees, but no resident is denied acess because of inability to pay. With its large six-lane pool and a smaller one for young children and beginners, the Swim Center is one of the most popular recreational facilities in town.

Cohasset Swim Center sign. Photo©Lynne Layman *Jessie Zerendow, member of the 1993 swim team and diving team, dives into the town pool.* Photo courtesy of Patriot Ledger/Rose Lincoln

In the mid-seventies a physical fitness craze swept the country, and jogging was one of its expressions. In Cohasset as elsewhere, runners took to the road. Drawing on this new enthusiasm, F. Roy Fitzsimmons, a member of the Cohasset Jaycees, organized and directed the town's first annual 10-kilometer (6.2-mile) Road Race by the Sea in April 1977. The Cohasset chapter of the Jaycees

(Junior Chamber of Commerce) had formed just the previous year. It had a brief but productive life. The Jaycees held several thrillingly scary Halloween Haunted Houses to raise money for their scholarship fund, conducted CPR (cardiopulmonary resuscitation) classes, and contributed funds to worthy causes. Although the Jaycees dissolved after a few years, the Road Race, still directed by Fitzsimmons, has continued to enjoy high success under the auspices of the Rotary Club, with nearly a thousand runners participating in recent years. In 1993 *New England* magazine named Cohasset's Road Race by the Sea the most scenic course in the six-state region.

In its heyday as a summer colony, Cohasset was host to nationally acclaimed horse shows that were held every year at the show grounds on Sohier Street, where the Music Circus now stands. Reviving the tradition, Sally Davenport organized the Cohasset Riding Club in the late 1970s. Nearly 60 entries participated in its first show in 1978. Under Sally's leadership, the club was active for about 10 years. Former members look back fondly on the riding lessons and weekly trail rides along the beautiful paths in Wheelwright Park and Whitney Woods.

THE ECOLOGICAL DECADE

Organized efforts to keep Cohasset beautiful began in the seventies. The first national Earth Day was held in April 1970. At "teach-ins" around the country, environmental activists raised people's awareness of how development could degrade the environment and urged them to clean up pollution. Cohasset High School seniors heeded the call by forming a Student Committee for a Cleaner Cohasset. Their project was Sandy Beach, a popular teen hangout. In the aftermath of a weekend, the parking lot and beach would be littered with beer cans, empty cigarette packs, and other trash. The committee's campaign to clean up the beach eventually succeeded, although it would take years of effort from many different groups before Cohasset was noticeably cleaner. Even in 1979, Reverend Atkinson complained that "the Common is a mess, littered almost daily . . . Where is our sense of civic pride?" (*Cohasset Mariner*, 3/15/79).

The public first became generally aware of environmental problems in 1962, when Rachel Carson published *Silent Spring.* Her landmark book warned of the dangers of insecticides such as DDT, which poisoned bird populations in North America. Carson's work, together with the passage of the Environmental Protection Act in 1970, inspired the formation of local action groups to protect the environment. In Cohasset the Gulf River Association was founded in 1971 by John Bleakie, Philip N. Bowditch, Albert M. Hunt, Irwin D. Matthew, and Louis A. Tonry to protect the marshes and channels of the Gulf River. Concerned about the loss of waterfowl and shellfish in the waterway, they identified the probable culprit as pollution from sewage that seeped into the river from two nearby restaurants, Hugo's Lighthouse and the Cocke 'n Kettle in North Scituate. It took the threat of court action for the restaurants to address this problem. The group still actively pursues its mission to protect the ecology of the Gulf River, one of our most scenic waterways.

In 1974 Cohasset resident Gerry Studds was elected to the U.S. Congress, the first Democrat ever to represent the Twelfth District. One plank of his platform was the need to protect the interests of our local fishermen. To this end he introduced a 200-mile-limit fishing bill, extending the exclusive fishing zone for U.S. fishermen from 12 miles to 200 miles from shore. This measure would prevent competition from foreign fishing fleets and conserve diminishing stocks of lobster and fish. In 1977 President Gerald Ford signed the bill into law.

Attention to the conservation of resources had officially begun in 1970 when President Nixon established the Environmental Protection Agency (EPA). Although many of its rules and regulations were necessary to stem pollution and protect human health, the EPA removed authority from the hands of local boards of health and vested it in either state or federal agencies. Control over our dump on Cedar Street was a case in point. Since the 1940s the Cohasset Board of Health had overseen the operation of what was then an open-burning dump. In 1970, in compliance with EPA directives aimed at the prevention of air pollution, the Commonwealth prohibited burning at

The old landfill operation on Cedar Street, complete with gulls. *Photo courtesy of Barbara Conte*

The transfer station and the first "take it or leave it" boutique. *Cartoon courtesy of James Hamilton/*Cohasset Mariner

The new "Boutique," constructed as an Eagle Scout project. *Photo © Lynne Layman*

town dumps and mandated their conversion to sanitary landfills.

The ban on burning hastened the end of life for the disposal area. It was rapidly filling up, and because it had to be capped daily with impermeable fill, it was also expensive to maintain. To extend its life, the Board of Health and a volunteer committee proposed a recycling program. In 1975 the committee launched a crusade to educate the public on the benefits of saving paper, glass, cans, and aluminum. Residents were instructed to deposit these materials in designated bins at the new Recycling Center at the landfill site. Led by Barbara Bliss, John Hubbard, Barbara Kern, and Elizabeth Stevenson, the committee's efforts were rewarded as Cohasset developed one of the most successful recycling programs in the Commonwealth. In 1988 the recycling of solid waste became mandatory in Cohasset. The following year the Cedar Street land-fill was converted to a modern, new recycling and transfer facility. Trash that could not be recycled would be transferred to SEMASS, a trash-to-energy plant in Rochester, Massachusetts, that would burn the rubbish and convert it to steam and electricity.

Cleanup and recycling campaigns drew attention to the wider need to preserve the quality of life in Cohasset. A watershed event was the construction of the motel at the harbor. This exemplified the kind of development that many believed threatened the very character of the town, particularly in the village and harbor areas. In response, the Planning Board initiated a program to identify and protect "critical areas" of the town. Assisting them was a subcom-mittee led by Mark S. Goodrich and Roberta K. Leary. The board hired a planning consultant, Anderson-Nichols & Company, to pre-pare a study of Cohasset's coastal zone and make recommenda-tions for preserving what they considered one of the most unique and diverse coastal environments in the Commonwealth. In their summary, published in 1976, the Coastal Zone Subcommittee defined the environmental values that contribute to that elusive quality, "character," in Cohasset:

- An identifiable center of interesting and historic character.
- A small, human-scale harbor of irregular dimensions.

- A pervading sense of the sea and easy access to water-oriented recreational opportunities.
- Uncrowded development.
- A combination of natural and manmade facilities.
- Winding, narrow streets.
- Unpolluted surroundings.

To preserve the character of the town, the study made specific proposals that were duly implemented: prohibit development in the new Flood Plain and Watershed Protection District; create a Waterfront Business District in the harbor area, limiting development to waterfront-related businesses only; establish a Design Review Board to "make advisory recommendations on all development in the village business district"; and institute a site-plan review process for developers in the business and light-industry districts. Finally, to preserve the architectural and historical character of the Common and its surrounding area, the town established a Historic District Commission in 1978.

The Historic District Commission is charged with maintaining the architectural integrity of the Cohasset Common Historic District and regulating proposed changes to the area. The Common itself is one of the town's most attractive historical assets, a green strip of land originally held "in common" by the property owners of Hingham in 1672. At that time the Common extended from Little Harbor to the Cove, filling the "Great Neck Plain." Cohasset's mariners and merchants built their homes in the surrounding area, particularly at the Cove and on the periphery of today's Common. Our first churches, school, and Town Hall were built on the Common. The Georgian, Federal, and Greek Revival style buildings and homes in the district are important historical assets today. The Common remains the center of community activity, the place where the town holds its art festivals and farmers' markets, listens to carillon concerts, and gathers for Memorial Day parades and other special events.

SEWER SAGA: PART II

Cohasset's wastewater treatment plant was built in 1968-69 to service the high school on Pond Street and the densely populated village and Elm Street areas. The sewer commissioners' ongoing plan was to expand the Jacob's Meadow plant and sewer progressively other critical areas of the town, beginning with Lincoln Hillside, the Pond Hill Veterans' area, Sohier Street, and the Route 3A business district. In 1974 town meeting authorized a study to determine the environmental impact of any sewerage expansion and a possible ocean outfall.

Meanwhile, the sewer commissioners confronted a growing bureaucracy. The federal Water Pollution Control Act Amendment of 1972 ("Clean Water Act") imposed a new set of stringent regulations on the discharge of pollutants into federal waters. All discharges were considered unlawful unless authorized by a permit. This act gave federal and state agencies broad jurisdiction over cities and towns. It also authorized federal grants for the construction of sewage treatment plants.

In 1975 Cohasset won the dubious distinction of being the first town in Massachusetts to receive a citation under the Clean Water Act for violating its discharge permit; at the same time, it became eligible for grant assistance to build a new plant. The commissioners therefore hired Metcalf & Eddy, a wastewater and environmental planning firm, to draw up plans for an expanded sewerage system. The M & E report, published in 1977, proposed that the town build a large-capacity treatment plant and install a central sewer system that would service the Hillside and Veterans' areas and portions of Route 3A, the three districts where soil conditions were so poor that septic systems regularly overflowed or failed. The cost was estimated to be $12.7 million; Cohasset's share would be $3.9 million, with state and federal funds picking up the remainder.

Despite numerous public meetings and the assurances of Metcalf & Eddy, many townspeople remained unconvinced that the M & E plan was appropriate for Cohasset, citing the expanded system's ultimate cost, controversies over the location of the new plant, the potential environmental damage of an ocean outfall pipe, and the system's impact on population growth. The expansion plans went nowhere. In 1978 the state banned additional tie-ins to the existing plant and mandated that the town build a new sewage treatment facility on a schedule that prescribed specific planning steps. If the town followed the schedule, it would be eligible for state and federal grants to fund plant design and construction. The EPA gave Cohasset a deadline of December 31, 1981, to comply.

In April 1979 voters at town meeting separated sewer responsibilities from the water commissioners and established a new, three-member Board of Sewer Commissioners. Indicative of the general resistance to the sewer-expansion project, town meeting then rejected the proposed site for a new treatment plant, a 10-acre parcel bounded by the Music Circus and Smith Place. Now the state Water Pollution Control Division of the Department of Environmental Quality Engineering stepped in. In September the agency threatened legal action against Cohasset for violating its discharge permit. It complained that not only had the town failed to vote funds for the mandated sewerage expansion, but it had also failed to submit a complete plan for new facilities and, in a continuing refrain, it was discharging unacceptably high levels of pollutants in the effluent from its Jacob's Meadow plant. In the opinion of later sewer commissioners, however, the violations of our discharge permit were only technical, with no impact on public health or the environment. As Commissioner Edward M. Guild put it, "It was like driving 35 miles per hour in a 30 mph zone."

At a special town meeting called in October, voters approved a resolution to fund a new plant, but again voted down proposed sites, leaving the project stalled. In November 1979 the ax fell on Cohasset. The attorney general's office sued the town for violating state and federal permits and the national Clean Water Act. Round one of a prolonged legal battle had begun.

AARON RIVER RESERVOIR

The population boom of the fifties and sixties created major headaches for the water/sewer commissioners. Too much wastewater was flowing out of homes and not enough fresh water was flowing in. Beginning in the mid-sixties, summer bans on out-door watering became commonplace. During severe droughts Lily Pond, our main source of water since 1913, would drop to such low levels that emergency pumps had to force water from the pond to the treatment plant. The town also depended on water from its old well field off Sohier Street and, at times, from wells in Ellms Meadow, east of Cushing Road.

The tubular wells in these fields, drilled by the Cohasset Water Company in 1886, were Cohasset's original source of public water. A distribution system consisting of a 1.5-million-gallon open reservoir atop Bear Hill and water mains throughout the town made it possible to build homes on rocks and ledges where residential wells were impractical. The town used the open reservoir until 1965, when it was replaced with a 2-million-gallon closed storage tank. (Edwin H. Pratt, who joined the Water Department in 1959, recalls that workers would ride around the reservoir in a little boat, throwing chlorine into the water to purify it.) In the 1930s the Hingham Water Company, which had served part of North Cohasset since 1881, acquired the small Cohasset company. On January 1, 1950, the town of Cohasset purchased the local system (except for the portion in North Cohasset, which remained in Hingham's service area) and set up a three-member Board of Water Commissioners to operate it.

Even under normal conditions, the old filtration plant and pumping station on Beechwood Street, built in 1913, could barely supply the needs of a burgeoning population. Cohasset clearly needed a new plant and a supplementary source of water. In 1965 the commissioners hired Sanitary Engineering Associates (SEA) to study the feasibility of using the Aaron River as a new source of water for the town. The Aaron River, whose watershed drains parts of Cohasset, Hingham, Scituate, and Norwell, flows from Wompatuck State Park into Bound Brook and finally into the Gulf River and out to the ocean. Bound Brook is connected to Lily Pond via Herring Brook. SEA proposed that the town create a new reservoir by damming the Aaron River at the west end of Beechwood Street. A small control structure across Bound Brook on the north side of Beechwood Street would control the water level at Lily Pond. Adjustable gates would allow the Water Department to direct most of the flow either into Lily Pond through Herring Brook or out to the ocean as needed.

The proposed Aaron River Reservoir was an immense undertaking for the water commissioners. The effort was led by Chairman Alan J. Murphy, Jr., with the assistance of Water Superintendent Edwin Pratt, Town Accountant William Signorelli, and Assistant Town Counsel Charles J. Humphreys. The commissioners negotiated with federal and state agencies, presented proposals at town meetings, and met repeatedly with different town boards. The first steps were to negotiate with the state Department of Natural Resources for permission to flood a portion of Wompatuck State Park

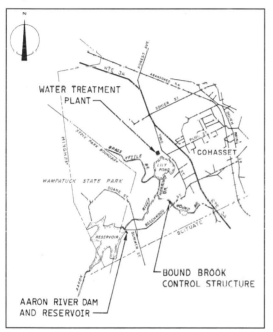

and to get the state legislature to pass an enabling act to impound the Aaron River. That done, the next move was to obtain funding.

The commissioners expected their project to cost about $2.5 million. The funding would come from two sources: a $994,000 federal grant from the Department of Housing and Urban Development and a loan of $1.5 million guaranteed by the Farmers Home Administration (FmHA). Pratt recalls driving up to the FmHA office in Montpelier, Vermont, with Bill Signorelli and Selectman Arthur Clark to negotiate the loan. They nervously loaded their car with boxes of documentation to support their request. The FmHA official must have been impressed by the delegation from Cohasset. To their surprise and relief, he never asked to see the data but immediately signed off on the loan. He supported the town throughout the project and attended the groundbreaking ceremony for the new treatment plant.

FmHA support was critical to the project. Costs rapidly escalated when the commissioners found they needed an environmental impact study. The study was expensive and took nearly a year to complete. It concluded with some bad news: the site they had selected for the treatment plant off Lily Pond was environmentally unsound. They would have to redesign the plant and place it in a more acceptable location—on private land off King Street, to be taken by eminent domain. Unfortunately, they would have to remove the old Couillard House on King Street, built in 1790, which had been vacant for several years. All these changes added costly delays, legal fees, and other unanticipated expenses to the project. This was also a period of double-digit inflation. By 1976 the estimated construction cost had increased by another $1.2 million.

To cover the shortfall, the commissioners went back to their FmHA friend in Vermont,who obligingly guaranteed another loan, for $1 million. The Water Department had to appropriate the balance of $206,000 from town funds, agreeing to pay it back over the years from water revenues. (Unlike other departments, the Water Department by state statute cannot be supported by taxation, because the citizens in North Cohasset would be taxed for a service not available to them.)

In July 1978 the water commissioners and the town celebrated the completion of Cohasset's new Aaron River Reservoir and water treatment plant. "This is a twelve-year dream come true," said Superintendent Pratt. Three times the size of Lily Pond, the reservoir brimmed with 323 million gallons of sparkling blue water, ensuring that Cohasset would never go short of water again. The King Street water treatment and pumping facility was capable of supplying residents with 3 million gallons of water a day, dwarfing the 800,000-gallon capacity of the old plant on Beechwood Street. Cohasset's summer watering bans were now a thing of the past.

BLIZZARD OF '78

Monday morning, February 6, 1978, dawned under gray skies. Cohasset resident Ralph S. Dormitzer vividly recalls what happened that day: "At lunchtime the first snow began to fall. Increasing in intensity with each hour, by 5:00 p.m., the commuter hour, the snow accumulation was over nine inches, and the storm of '78 was a blizzard. For South Shore drivers there were two major routes home, the Expressway and Route 128 north for those with downtown offices, and Route 128 south for the high-tech crowd who worked along that corridor. Both roads were inadequate for the traffic on them even in good weather, but this day was exceptional. When you finally reached the highway that evening and were able to merge into the traffic, you realized that you were locked in a fateful processional, one where your forward motion was dictated by the progress of thousands of other cars all packed together, and where with each passing minute the pace of the processional grew ever slower. By 7:00 p.m. the pace on Route 128 north and south had become zero. It was to remain zero for five days. Three thousand cars and trucks were trapped where they stood under mountains of snow. It took five days to clear the road. For all those drivers, refuge was the nearest place of shelter to which you could wade on your two feet. The blizzard is remembered for the generosity of the owners of nearby homes and restaurants who sheltered and fed the stranded commuters, sometimes for days."

The storm caused a massive power failure, leaving thousands of people without light or heat. By late Monday night Governor Michael Dukakis had declared a state of emergency and called in the National Guard. Commuters who made it back to Cohasset that night inched through the deep snow amid uprooted trees and downed power lines. Many did not reach home until after 11:00 p.m. Meanwhile their anxious families waited in houses that were growing colder by the hour. The streets became eerily silent and black. The only light you could see was the tiny, flickering glow of

candles and flashlights through windows. Along the shore fero-
cious winds drove towering 30-foot waves over seawalls, leaving in
their wake tons of sand and rock. Floods at high tide submerged
coastal roads under four feet of water.

Cohasset Civil Defense Director Lester Hiltz, the Red Cross, and
Cohasset firefighters were on alert to assist victims of the storm.
About 50 people were evacuated from their homes and took shelter
with friends or at Kimball's Motel. Worse off were neighboring Hull,
Scituate, and Marshfield, where the force of the blizzard ripped
houses off their foundations and washed away cars. A newspaper
photograher flying over the coastline described the incredible devastation: "Houses floating on the water—others reduced to match-
wood or piled atop one another—huge chunks carved out of beaches—This is the destruction all along the coast from Cape Cod to Hull
. . . When I got to Scituate . . . I saw that many of the big, beautiful
waterfront homes had been either destroyed or piled on top of one
another. There's nothing left of some but sticks . . . Almost every
waterfront town we flew over presented a . . . scene of devastation—
a crazy quilt of battered homes and wreckage, huge cliffs washed
away. The shoreline will never be the same" (*Boston Herald
American*, 2/9/78).

By Wednesday morning, February 8, the storm was over at last,
leaving a record snowfall of 30 inches on the ground. In Boston 14
military transport planes brought federal troops and heavy equipment
to assist the national guardsmen, state and local highway workers,
and rescue teams. Businesses and stores stayed closed for at least
five days, and driving was prohibited on state highways until February
10. To the delight of children, school was called off for a week. Many
in Cohasset remember seeing a wonderland of trees sparkling with
ice, roads blanketed in pure white snow, and huge drifts piled in fantastic shapes in front of their homes. But the beauty of the snow was
no consolation for the thousands of people elsewhere who lost their
homes and suffered millions of dollars worth of damage. In the South
Shore alone, 1,338 homes were destroyed and 5,538 damaged. Less
exposed than other towns, Cohasset nevertheless had $1.6 million of
damage. Fortunately no one was injured and no homes were lost.

The Blizzard of '78 was the final disaster in a trying decade, one in which optimism and consensus came to an end. Vietnam, Watergate, recession, inflation, the generation gap, drugs, crime— all took a toll on the spirit of the people. In Cohasset, friendliness and trust in local leaders gave way to confrontation and hostility. People formed groups to defend their interests and brought or threatened legal action against their offenders. The media exploit- ed the problems of the town, and critical articles began to appear— something unheard of in the fifties, a calmer, more conventional time. The state and federal governments also intervened more obtrusively in the affairs of the town, imposing rules and regula- tions that usurped local control.

Organizations that had thrived in the fifties struggled by the end of the seventies. The Community Center, once a model for the entire South Shore, managed to survive only by the dedicated effort of a few members. The Woman's Club no longer appealed in an age of women's liberation, and Subscription Club dances became passé. It was not cool to be a Scout. Only sports centered activi ties such as Little League, Sailing Club, and Swim Team flourished.

The Cohasset and national bicentennials were a welcome diversion. We came together with common purpose to celebrate our past and to share our hope for the future. And despite the polit- ical tensions, Cohasset was becoming a more homogenized com- munity. Not so long ago, oldtimers in the Beechwood area often spoke with a distinctive "down-Maine" type of accent and thought of themselves as living in a separate part of town. But now the social and economic differences that had distinguished the old neighborhoods were disappearing. Residents were rejecting labels such as "Beechwooders":

> [My neighbors and I] greatly resent being grouped as one, separate, and unfortunately, slightly lower class part of Cohasset, namely, "Beechwood." Beechwood is a street in Cohasset, just like any other. It has large homes and small, new and old, well-to-do and not so well-to-do . . . We have blue and white collar workers, laborers, farmers, older

families, and newcomers. I think we have a delightful
atmosphere in which to live and raise our children. I am
aware that in years past, this part of Cohasset was known
as the "disadvantaged" farming section of town, but I
assure you, it is a far cry from that stereotyped notion now.

[Letter to the Editor, *Cohasset Mariner*, 10/18/79]

Cohasset was changing in other ways too. It was becoming a
more expensive place in which to live. Parents who had hoped that
their sons and daughters would settle in the town realized that it
might not be possible. "People move here because Cohasset is a
beautiful town," commented Selectman Arthur Clark to a *Patriot
Ledger* reporter at the end of the decade. "We want to keep it that
way. Young people growing up in town can't afford to live here or
to buy here. Real estate is just too expensive." The costs of running the town were also rising. "Citizens' demand for public services continues unabated," wrote School Superintendent Maloney
in 1978, "yet the willingness to pay for such services through taxation is diminishing." The pressure was on for a limit to spending.

Cohasset in the 1980s:
BREAKING WITH
FOUR TRADITION

On Tuesday, January 20, 1981, Noel Ripley rang the bells of the First Parish Meeting House as he and other volunteers had for the past 444 days, only this time they pealed in jubilation. The 52 Americans held captive for 444 days by Iranian extremists had at last been set free. Seized at the American Embassy in Teheran during the final year of the Carter administration in retaliation for U.S. support of the shah of Iran, the hostages were now safely back on American soil. And on this day Ronald Reagan became our fortieth president. Reagan pledged to lower taxes, devolve more power to the states, ease the regulatory burden on business, and expand U.S. military strength. During his administration, federal income tax rates were cut by 25 percent and the inflation rate dropped from 12.4 percent to 4 percent. The nation's pride and spirit of optimism returned.

The robust economic recovery

Noel Ripley and Gilbert Tower ringing the First Parish Meeting House bell to remind the town of the 52 Americans held hostage in Iran for 444 days. Photo courtesy of Cohasset Mariner

Not everything changed in the 1980s

Vito Signorelli and George Calvi chat outside the still-popular West Corner Men's Club. Photo courtesy of Patriot Ledger/Fred Keenan

Former town moderator Bob James and Ozzie Ingram look natty at a tailgate party for the 1983 Harvard-Army football game. Photo courtesy of Osborne Ingram

that began in 1983 was accompanied by a relaxation of tensions both nationally and locally. Conflict among different political and cultural groups subsided, and the cold war began to wind down. In 1982 the United States and the Soviet Union conducted the first Strategic Arms Reduction Talks, and Mikhail Gorbachev, who became Communist party chairman in 1985, began to restructure the Soviet economy, introducing free-market policies and other reforms.

In Cohasset, too, changes were taking place. Although population growth came to a standstill—the population even shrank by about 100, from 7,174 in 1980 to 7,075 in 1990—the composition of the town was different. Newcomers began to outnumber natives as the sons and daughters of the original families moved away and the older generation died out. The first baby boomers were reaching middle age, and families were smaller, reflecting the national decline in size from an average of 3.14 per household in 1970 to 2.76

in 1980. The trend continued into the eighties, with fewer children per family, higher divorce rates, and single parenthood. In Cohasset the turnover of homes increased, and you no longer experienced the comfortable familiarity of knowing everyone on your street.

Among the recent arrivals were "yuppies" (*Young Urban Professionals*), riding the wave of economic prosperity generated by "Reaganomics," President Reagan's economic policies of tax cuts and smaller government. They were attracted to Cohasset by the beauty of its seacoast and harbor, by its recreational opportunities, by its reputation for good schools, and by its traditional, small-town New England atmosphere. But the more young professionals moved into town, the less traditional it became. Cohasset was now one of the most expensive communities on the South Shore. Realtor Christopher C. Ford recalls that a house on Fairoaks Lane which had sold for $70,000 in 1971 was offered for $400,000 in 1987. Wealthier people were buying these homes, and they boosted the median family income in Cohasset by 128 percent, from about $28,000 in 1980 to $63,000 in 1990.

The "old-money" residents disapproved of the way some of the newcomers seemed to flaunt their wealth. They drove status cars such as BMWs and Mercedes-Benzes and hired nannies to care for their children. Older homes were gutted, rebuilt, and expanded with Great Rooms for entertaining, professional kitchens, and recreational bathrooms. The median value of homes in this period more than tripled. Catering to upscale tastes, new stores such as Bildner's opened in Cushing Plaza, offering hand-selected produce, designer breads and bottled water, and gourmet specialties, from imported olives to herbed vinegars and expensive wines and cheese. Bildner's did not prosper, however, and closed after a few years. Cohasset was still a pretty conservative place, and the market for upscale stores was yet to develop.

Despite its solid conservative core, the town was more receptive to change than in previous years. Residents expected a higher level of efficiency and professionalism from town officials and were willing to modify years of tradition to achieve it. The town voted to give the Board of Selectmen direct hiring and firing authority over the then virtually autonomous chiefs of police and fire by removing the chiefs from Civil Service. (Voters had previously defeated an attempt to remove the entire Police Department from Civil Service.) Town meeting also voted a citizen-sponsored article to increase the Board of Selectmen from three to five members, altering two centuries of tradition. This change would foreshadow the shift in the balance of power from natives and longtime residents to relative newcomers. Finally, to ensure that town meetings could legally vote the articles in the warrant and to start the meetings on time, the town agreed to reduce the quorum from 200 to 100 registered voters, amending the 50-year-old rule.

For a town of 5,269 registered voters (in 1985), the reduction in the quorum would have major unintended consequences. Town meeting had long been deemed the purest form of democracy, giving citizens direct participation in their government. Now crucial decisions could be made by only 100 people, mostly the older generation and a smaller group of civic-minded citizens. The reduced quorum also enabled special-interest groups to form a majority with just 51 people, enough to push an article through if only 100 were present. Adding insult to injury, supporters would often exit the meeting after voting their issue. It seemed that the majority no longer cared about the well-being of the town as a whole.

By the early 1980s town meetings had become protracted affairs often extending from Saturday into Monday and sometimes Tuesday evenings. One or more special town meetings were also required during the year. You had to be a committed citizen to attend them all. The fall-off had already begun among the formerly active but now aging citizens of the postwar generation, while many of the younger and newer residents either lacked the interest or could not take time away from family or work to participate in town meeting. For similar reasons, fewer people were running for public office or volunteering to serve on town boards.

If newcomers to Cohasset were not as committed to traditional civic responsibility as their predecessors, they were also not as bound by the preexisting religious or geographic divisions in the town. After 40 years of exclusivity, the three churches on the

Common invited St. Anthony's and the new Greek Orthodox church to participate in their annual Village Fair. Congregations also joined in charitable work for the homeless in Boston. Families opened their homes to foreign students on cultural exchange programs, and Cohasset adopted a French town named Souppes-sur-Loing as its sister community. The town even assumed a new persona in the summer of 1986 when it became the setting for *The Witches of Eastwick*, starring Jack Nicholson, Cher, Susan Sarandon, and Michelle Pfeiffer. The filming of the movie right in downtown Cohasset reinforced the opinion that Cohasset was indeed a desirable place to live.

For the town the decade was also characterized by litigation, both public and private. The state cited us for violations of environmental codes and fair housing standards. We sued a private landfill for violating our health code. A homeowner sued the town over a tennis court on his property, and the Planning Board sued the Zoning Board over a variance regarding the Cox estate. Legal battles went on and on, and the rules and regulations we had to comply with seemed equally endless. One regulation that many people welcomed, however, was Proposition 2 1/2, a new law enacted in 1980 to limit local spending.

PROP 2 1/2

For many years taxes in Massachusetts had been rising at a faster rate than people's incomes. By the end of the 1970s they were among the highest in the nation, prompting critics to dub the state "Taxachusetts." Following the lead of California's Proposition 13, a group called Citizens for Limited Taxation launched a reform movement to limit property taxes. In 1980 they sponsored Proposition 2 1/2 , a citizens' initiative petition to restrict the total amount of tax revenue a city or town could raise to 2 1/2 percent of the full cash value of all its taxable property. This provision would set a tax cap of $25 per $1,000 of property valuation. It also would limit any increase in the tax levy to a maximum of 2 1/2 percent of the previous year's levy limit, unless citizens voted by secret ballot to override the tax cap. A hard-to-achieve two-thirds majority was required for an override.

"Prop 2 1/2" was presented to the voters of Massachusetts on the state ballot in November 1980. Fearing drastic cuts in town services, the Cohasset League of Women Voters rallied against it; the Board of Selectmen, the School Committee, and the Advisory Committee also opposed it. But beleaguered taxpayers felt that spending was out of control, particularly when activists and special-interest groups could and often did pack town meeting to get what they wanted. Prop 2 1/2 would put an end to that. To override the tax limit, you would have to persuade not just town meeting, but also the much larger number of voters at an election to spend more and raise their own taxes. And it was a lot easier to vote against spending when casting a secret ballot than when calling out your vote or raising your hand at town meeting. A full 84 percent of registered voters in Cohasset turned out for the November election. Prop 2 1/2 passed decisively, 2,482 to 1,651. Voters throughout the state supported the petition, and it became law in December 1980.

The new law not only placed a ceiling on property taxes but also reduced motor vehicle excise taxes. This double whammy would slash town revenues. Town Accountant William Signorelli figured that Cohasset would immediately lose $310,000 in excise taxes and nearly $1 million in property taxes. The problem was that property was currently assessed at only 42 percent of fair market value. Thus our tax base under Prop 2 1/2 would fall far below the maximum allowed at 100 percent valuation. The assessors had hired a professional appraiser to revaluate all property in Cohasset, but the work could not be completed by the state-imposed deadline. Determined to fight for a higher tax base, Bill Signorelli, Selectman Henry Ainslie, and Advisory Committee Chairman Jean Cotton appealed the town's case to the state and secured approval for an assessed valuation of $225 million, based on our appraiser's estimates. This was lower than the actual value, but higher than the $208 million originally assigned by the state.

Cotton worked diligently to understand the new law and its implications, attending conferences and spending hours with the town accountant. "She realized that not every budget could be cut by the same percentage," said Bill Signorelli, "and was extremely objective." Under her leadership, the Advisory Committee worked with department heads to keep the town budget within the limits of Prop 2 1/2. Many were asked to cut their expenses for the next fiscal year by 15 percent, and they dutifully complied. Town officials looked for more ways to save money and increase revenue. They turned off nearly a quarter of the town's street lights, closed the library on Wednesdays, made town buildings more energy efficient, and reduced personnel through attrition, leaving vacancies unfilled. They eliminated an outlying fire station and consolidated Fire Department services at the headquarters on Elm Street. They increased fines and fees and charged residents a new, combined fee for parking at Sandy Beach and depositing trash at the landfill.

Absorbing its proportionate cut, the School Department, which accounted for half the town's budget, took the biggest hit. To achieve their share of the reduction ($180,000), the School Committee eliminated 31 1/2 full and part-time positions, scheduled fewer schoolbus stops, and made the cafeteria self-supporting. Declining school enrollments softened the blow (the number of students dropped 26 percent in the 1980s, from 1,545 to 1,146), but cutting jobs and special programs was nonetheless painful. Adding to the committee's woes was that under Prop 2 1/2 the school lost its fiscal autonomy. From now on it would have to work with the Advisory Committee in setting its budget and seek town meeting approval for its spending.

Taxpayers should have been happy with the lean diet imposed on the town. Smaller budgets meant lower tax rates. Prop 2 1/2 also required, however, that all properties be assessed at 100 percent of full and fair market value, and some residents were in for a shock. Their assessments doubled or tripled, and their taxes were higher than ever. If you had lived in the same house for a long time, you were probably underassessed. Although many benefited from the reassessment, others suffered a one-time proportionate increase in taxes. A booming real estate market in the mid-1980s also increased the assessed value of many homes. The value of waterfront property in particular skyrocketed. The assessment on one house on Little Harbor, for example, doubled in the three years between 1986 and 1989, and the property tax rose 75 percent. After the stock market crash of October 1987, house values (except for waterfront property) dropped and did not fully recover until the late 1990s.

Revenue from property taxes alone was not enough to maintain town services. Cohasset also depended on state aid, federal revenue sharing, and growth in the tax base from new construction. In 1988, however, the state, suffering its own fiscal crisis, slashed aid to local communities, and the federal government phased out revenue sharing. For eight years the town had squeezed the departments to fit the Prop 2 1/2 revenue limits, but now no room was left to accommodate the new revenue shortfall. The only way to match expenses with revenue was to override Prop 2 1/2. Anticipating resistance from taxpayers, town officials led a media campaign to "educate" the public. Coming to their assistance, the *Mariner* (3/24/88) forbode disaster:

> The town's operating budget is in big trouble, and there's no disputing it. Town department heads agree there is an $800,000 hole created by a number of factors, but mostly because local revenues do not match budget estimates, state aid is leveling off and federal funds are drying up. These factors, coupled with a false tax base which began with Prop 2 1/2, have finally caught up with us . . . Rejecting an override will result in dire consequences for our community. There will be deep, harmful budget cuts in every department. The schools, which carry the largest budget load, will be forced to reduce supplies and personnel. Larger class sizes and less teaching materials do not produce quality, award-winning students. This is not a threat. This is reality. Other town departments will not be able to survive penetrating reductions, and they could be forced to shut down.

At town meeting voters approved the budget with the override, accepting the argument that to do otherwise would precipitate a fiscal crisis.

Final approval, however, was contingent on the election to be held in May. It was by secret ballot. Prop 2 1/2 had been amended by the state legislature in 1987 to allow operating budget overrides by a simple majority vote. This change would make the override easier to achieve. Yet for many people such a move was unthinkable. Advisory Committee Chairman Jane O. Goedecke pleaded with the electorate in her report to the town: "Please remember that the override is an integral part of the original Proposition 2 1/2 legislation, devised in order to keep control of a town's financial decision making in the hands of the people. It is not an attempt to get around the law. It is inevitable that in a society where costs are rising at a rate of 5 or 6% a year at least, a limit of only 2.5% plus new growth in increased taxes will eventually create a situation such as Cohasset faces today." The campaign succeeded. At the special election on May 14, 1988, Cohasset approved its first override, 1,021 to 808.

The following year the budget presented at town meeting again exceeded the limits of Prop 2 1/2. And again voters at town meeting approved the appropriation. At the election in May, however, the override failed by 141 votes. Now town departments would have to cut a total of $844,000 from their operating budgets. The schools alone would have to eliminate $400,000. Telephones began to ring as the Parent-School Organization mobilized its formidable network and lobbied for another try at the override. In an overwhelming show of support for the schools, 972 citizens at town meeting voted to place another general budget override question on the ballot at a special election. Town officials asked for a more modest and, they hoped, more acceptable override of $303,826. The ballot also included a yet smaller option of $203,000. On June 28, 1989, just two days before the end of the fiscal year, voters approved the smaller figure. Although many citizens complained about the unprecedented second election aimed at changing the outcome of the first one, Prop 2 1/2 had proved flexible. Overrides would become almost routine for Cohasset in the 1990s. In the 20 years since Prop 2 1/2 went into effect, Cohasset has overridden it 26 times (including 3 capital outlay, 7 general operating-budget, and 16 debt exclusion overrides). In comparison, Scituate has passed only 3 overrides; Norwell, 6; and Hingham, 14.

STRONG CHIEF/WEAK CHIEF

The police and fire chiefs enjoyed a long tradition of near-autonomy in Cohasset as a result of their protection under Civil Service. Former police officer Richard Barrow remembers a time back in the fifties when Chief Pelletier seemed to run the town. "The selectmen never went against him," he recalls. Nor did they have much control over Chief Feola. Now, however, the balance of power was shifting. In a judicial proceeding the Supreme Judicial Court ruled that selectmen could exercise direct authority over police and fire chiefs.

In 1978 the selectmen proposed to remove the position of police chief from Civil Service. Town meeting that year vigorously debated the merits of Civil Service versus local control and in the end voted to remove the chief's position from Civil Service, giving the selectmen discretionary power over the hiring (or firing) of the next chief. They would also have greater control over the management of the Police Department. Whereas the "strong" chief under Civil Service could set his own policies as well as manage the department, the "weak" chief would have to enforce the policies set by the Board of Selectmen. After Feola's retirement in 1980, the next chief would be a "weak" chief.

Chief DeBassio

The selectmen appointed a search committee to recruit the best possible candidate to replace Chief Feola. The committee's recommendation, and the unanimous choice of the selectmen, was John DeBassio, a police sergeant from Brockton. With degrees in criminal justice and public administration, DeBassio was recognized for his work in drug abuse and his administrative skills. He pledged to develop a police department in Cohasset that would be "the envy of all departments around" (*Mariner,* 9/11/80). He soon saw to it that his men were issued proper weapons and wore standard police uniforms (no more decals, slogan buttons, and Charlie Chan mustaches). Under DeBassio they received professional training. One officer remarked, "We've been to more schools in the last two years than in the past fifteen years" (*Mariner*, 6/23/82). By 1982 the department had clearly become more effective. After a spate of serious crimes, including one rape and two murders (committed by people from outside Cohasset), order returned to the town. The number of burglaries declined, and although vandalism continued for several more years, particularly in the village, people felt more secure.

When the townspeople voted for the "weak" chief position, they did so with the understanding that the selectmen would not interfere politically with the chief's work. The selectmen would act as policymakers, leaving the day-to-day administration of the Police Department to the chief. In June 1982, however, DeBassio received a note from the Board of Selectmen directing him not to overlook a particular "permanent intermittent" policeman when assigning men to special details. The individual in question happened to be the nephew of Henry Ainslie, chairman of the Board of Selectmen. DeBassio took offense at this directive, claiming it was political interference with his duties as chief. If he employed the young man for special details, no matter what his qualifications he would automatically be eligible for a full-time position. DeBassio faced a dilemma. As a "weak" chief, he no longer had Civil Service protection, but the men under him, including the nephew, were still Civil Service employees. The selectmen could fire the chief at their discretion, but the chief could not fire a patrolman without bringing charges against him and going through a long legal procedure.

The conflict became a public matter. Advisory Committee member James Lagrotteria commented that there hadn't been so much talk in town since the high school football team was undefeated (*Mariner*, 6/23/82). DeBassio had the support of the Cohasset Police Association and the search committee that recommended him. Selectman Mary Jane McArthur also brought before the board a petition in support of DeBassio signed by 450 citizens.

Heartened by the endorsement, the chief went forward and brought four charges against the nephew, including falsification of an official Police Department document, neglect of duty, conduct unbecoming a police officer, and unlawful and unnecessary exercise of authority. At the public hearing, however, he could not substantiate the charges, and the defendant was cleared. Overruled, DeBassio assigned the nephew to special details. He subsequently became a full-time patrolman.

Angered by the selectmen's handling of the "Ainslie issue," a grassroots committee of three — Tanna Kasperowicz, a reporter who later founded Cohasset's alternative newspaper, the *Tinytown Gazette* (1993); Richard Barrow, a police officer; and their friend Anthony Fasciano — circulated a petition to enlarge the Board of Selectmen from three to five members, as the Charter Commission had proposed in 1974. The town was now ready to make the change. One of the signers of the petition said, "Finally we've got a superb police chief. Frankly, we're a little worried he might not be around after his contract runs out. Obviously, if three new openings were to appear on the board in 1983, that freshly elected group would comprise the majority of the board. And hopefully that majority would be DeBassio supporters" *(Mariner,* 7/21/82). At a special town meeting in August 1982, 200 years of tradition were overturned, and the voters expanded the Board of Selectmen to five members.

Despite the support of the town, Chief DeBassio resigned in September 1982. Ironically, the following year he ran for a one-year term as selectman, and won. Now he would be in a position to determine the fate of the next chief. Before he could do so, however, the still three-person Board of Selectmen appointed Cohasset patrolman Joseph M. Kealy as acting police chief. This choice too was controversial, as they had passed over two higher-ranking officers. The selectmen declined to appoint a new search committee, and in February 1983 Kealy became the permanent chief. The Police Department quietly faded from the headlines.

Chief Dooley

The town also removed the position of fire chief from Civil Service, in 1981. The measure took effect in March 1982, after the retirement of Charles Piepenbrink, who had been chief for 28 years. During his last years of service, Piepenbrink saw his department shrink. In September 1980 he closed down the classic old Beechwood Fire Station because it was too small for his new

The old Beechwood Fire Station being readied for a move to Clapp Road in Scituate and a new life as a barn. Photo courtesy of Patriot Ledger/Bill Greene

The old North Cohasset Fire Station on Hull Street was closed in 1981 as a cost-cutting measure. It was finally razed in the 1990s. Photo courtesy of Hamilton Tewksbury

pumper, and in March 1981 the selectmen closed the North Cohasset Fire Station as a cost-saving measure. A family from Scituate bought the Beechwood building in 1983 and moved it to 55 Clapp Road. Its former site, across from the cemetery, was converted to a neighborhood basketball court.

Piepenbrink hoped that the town would purchase the defunct Cohasset Motors site on Route 3A for use as a combined fire station and Highway Department garage, but town officials, feeling pinched by Prop 2 1/2, turned down that option. (In 1988 a new Super Stop & Shop was built there instead.) When Piepenbrink retired, the Fire Department was left with two fire engines, a ladder truck, and an ambulance, all housed in the central headquarters on Elm Street. The staff was reduced from 28 men to 24.

Again the Board of Selectmen used a search committee to screen applicants for the chief's position. They first offered the job to fire captain Roger Lincoln, but he turned it down, preferring to keep his Civil Service protection. The selectmen then chose Martin W. Dooley, a firefighter from East Hartford, Connecticut. An outsider, Dooley had never held the position of chief. He had problems from the very beginning. After assuming his duties in January 1983, he set out to transform what had traditionally been an informally run small-town department into a quasi-military organization similar to the one he had known in Hartford. He wanted his men to follow a full set of rules and regulations and to work more productively (no more washing cars or painting lobster buoys while on duty). He also insisted on an uncustomary formality between officers and staff: "The respect for rank is something that I'm used to," he explained. "Cohasset's tradition is more of a personal relationship between the officers and men. An officer has to realize, and so do the men, that when a man becomes an officer, he steps above to a certain degree—he's automatically in a different league. You just can't be referring to them on duty on a first-name basis without the respect of giving them rank and title" (*Mariner*, 3/8/84).

The firefighters resisted this change. In fact, the men objected to almost everything the chief did, including changing the shape of their caps. Lowering morale even further was a tragic fire in August

1983 at a North Main Street home, which took the lives of three children, aged four, two, and one. Anguish over their deaths exacerbated the deteriorating relationship between the chief and his staff. During this period the firefighters' union filed 16 complaints against him and brought charges before the selectmen alleging that in November 1983 he misused fire equipment and endangered the lives of two of his men in a mutual aid call in Hull. The selectmen cleared him of the charges.

Then, joining the effort to comply with Prop 2 1/2, Dooley took the unusual step of asking for a decrease of six full-time firefighters in his budget for the fiscal year 1984-85. He reported to the Advisory Committee that Cohasset had more than the nationally recommended number of firefighters for a town its size. As there were more ambulance calls than fires in Cohasset, he felt that the department should develop its EMT (emergency medical technician) service and rely more heavily on its call force to answer fire alarms. He argued that a new law requiring smoke and heat detectors in homes made destructive fires less likely. In 1986 the detectors became mandatory in Cohasset for new construction. Although the staff remained at 24, four of the firefighters received training as EMTs. The 20 active members of the call force, including Denise Parsloe, Cohasset's first female firefighter, responded to more alarms than they had in many years. (The Police Department also hired its first female police officer, Maureen Healy, in 1983.)

Despite his accomplishments and the support of perhaps half the town, Dooley faced a demoralized force and a frustrated Board of Selectmen, including former chief of police John DeBassio, who had tried unsuccessfully to mediate

Maureen Healy, hired in 1983, suits up as the town's first female police officer. Photo courtesy of Patriot Ledger/Tom Tajima

between Dooley and the union. Exercising their prerogatives under the "weak" chief policy, the selectmen chose not to renew Dooley's contract. He subsequently decided to give up his career as a firefighter.

In November 1985 a new search committee recommended two candidates for the chief's position. Their first choice was a Cohasset fire captain; their second was Daniel Brock, a captain from Southborough, Massachusetts. Again the selectmen chose the outsider. Brock, they believed, had the experience and maturity to work with a close-knit brotherhood, a union strengthened by its affiliation, since 1981, with the International Association of Firefighters and the Professional Firefighters of Massachusetts. In January 1986 Brock assumed his duties as chief and restored calm to the department.

RESTRUCTURING TOWN GOVERNMENT

Changes in the structure of the Board of Selectmen had been proposed by the Charter Commission back in the mid-1970s. After the failure of the charter, town meeting voted in 1976 to create a Committee to Study Town Government. Chaired by former state senator (and future town moderator) William D. Weeks, the committee explored ways to improve both the structure of town government and the functions of officers, department heads, and boards. Taking a gradual approach, the committee recommended just one of the Charter Commission's proposals: creating the position of executive secretary to the Board of Selectmen. After long debate, the 1980 town meeting finally approved the measure.

Executive Secretary

Unexpectedly, the first person to apply for the job, and to be hired, was none other than Arthur L. Clark, a selectman and a zealous opponent of the Charter Commission. Now he would become Cohasset's first executive secretary. Clark had served on the board as a "full-time" selectman for 14 years and was chairman from 1971 to 1981. His new duties were to see that the selectmen's orders and policies were carried out, to provide information, to help prepare the Town Report, and to field citizens' complaints. Mary Jane E. McArthur was elected to replace him on the board.

The selectmen were hearing a growing number of complaints about a proposal to legalize casino gambling in Hull. In 1980 MGM Grand Hotels of Las Vegas purchased land and drew up plans to build a 350-room resort hotel and casino on a 64-acre parcel near Cohasset's West Corner. Although the site of the casino would be in Hull, it would nevertheless be just over the border from Cohasset, and people

Arthur L. Clark, a selectman for 14 years, resigned in 1981 to become the board's first executive secretary. Photo courtesy of Cohasset Mariner/Greg Derr

were alarmed about the spillover of traffic and the potential link to organized crime and corruption. The plan, however, was contingent on the passage of a bill before the state legislature to legalize the gambling. Hull, desperate to remedy its faltering economy, supported the bill. But people in Cohasset, particularly those in North Cohasset, vociferously objected to having a casino within walking distance of their homes. Maria Plante, who lived on Jerusalem Road less than a mile from the proposed site, organized a group called Citizens Against Casino Gambling. As a result of their lobbying, voters at a special town meeting directed Cohasset officials to oppose the legislation that would allow casino gambling in Hull. In February 1981 Clark testified against the bill before members of the state legislature.

He had an important ally in Mary Jeanette Murray, his former colleague on the Board of Selectmen. Following in the footsteps of her father, Nate Hurwitz, Mary Jeanette made a successful run for the legislature in 1976. (She also continued to serve as selectman until the end of her term in 1979.) As Republican representative for the Third Plymouth District, she was widely admired for her old-style dedication to her constituents. She took up the cause of "her people" and persuaded Governor Edward King to veto any bill

authorizing casino gam-
bling in Hull. The suc-
cessful lobbying of our
state "rep," as well as the
efforts of Arthur Clark
and other concerned citi-
zens, put an end to the

Mark J. Lanza, hired at age 27 to succeed Arthur
Clark as executive secretary in 1982. Photo courtesy of
Cohasset Mariner/Greg Derr

threat of crime and cor-
ruption at our border.

   In September 1982, after little more than a year as executive secretary, Clark handed in his resignation. The demands of the job were
too great for the 74-year-old public servant. He was replaced by
27-year-old Mark J. Lanza, former assistant executive secretary
in Yarmouth, Massachusetts. The position in Cohasset turned out to
be but a stepping stone for Lanza, who resigned in September 1984 to
take a higher-paying job elsewhere. In rapid succession, he was followed by Donald R. Andrew in 1985 and Gregory J. Doyon in 1988.

Five-Member Board

Gone were the days when the Board of Selectmen could run the
town with little scrutiny or complaint from the public. The Open
Meeting Law, passed in 1976, required all town committees to post
notices of their meetings 48 hours in advance and to open them to
anyone who wished to attend. The law also placed restrictions on
closed-door executive sessions. Further, in 1978 the Massachusetts
State Ethics Commission was established to enforce the state's con-
flict-of-interest and financial disclosure laws.

   The "first of many casualties" to come over the new laws, as
the *Mariner* put it, was Roger Pompeo, a five-year member of the
Board of Health and chairman since 1979. As a local physician and
developer, he had professional and business relationships with
many town residents. In 1980 Town Counsel Blake Thaxter advised
him to resign his position on the board, because under the current
law he would be "totally useless" 90 percent of the time. Citizens
paid attention to potential conflicts of interest, and local newspapers were quick to expose any perceived or real transgressions.

Publicity about the nepotism that tarnished an otherwise admirable selectman generated the successful move to increase the Board of Selectmen from three to five members. Stung by the "recent negative attitudes towards local officials" that erupted after the controversy over his nephew (*Mariner*, 2/23/83), Henry Ainslie, who had served the town ably and with dedication for 12 years,

The three-member Board of Selectmen at the April 1981 town meeting. Arthur Clark, Henry Ainslie, and Rocco Laugelle. Photo courtesy of Cohasset Mariner/Greg Derr

The first meeting of a five member Board of Selectmen in May 1983. Seated left to right: Frank England, John DeBassio, Chairman Mary Jane McArthur, Cliff Mitman, and Rocco Laugelle. Photo courtesy of Richard Barrow

declined to run for another term. Elected to serve on the first five-member board with Rocco Laugelle and Mary Jane McArthur were former police chief John A. DeBassio, Frank W. England, and Clifford Mitman, Jr.

Mitman, a 14-year resident of Cohasset, believed that "as long as you live in town, it is important to make a commitment to it" (*Mariner*, 5/11/83). The hope was that, with an executive secretary and an expanded board, more well-qualified local professionals would run for selectman. Mitman wanted to show that "a full-time businessperson-commuter might have a better perspective on issues, and [be] able to do the job well while holding down another demanding job."

Did the change from three to five selectmen make a significant difference? In the opinion of former treasurer-collector Gordon E. Flint, who served at Town Hall for 33 years until his retirement in 1984, the addition of two more members politicized the atmosphere. "Three was more like a close-knit family. There was not so much debate or dissension. They would talk things over and come to a consensus. With five, the political pot seemed to start boiling." For the first time you began to see political signs posted on front lawns before town elections. But Flint also acknowledges that the growth of the town and the profusion of state laws required a different level of performance from town officials.

Mary Jane McArthur, the new chairman of the Board of Selectmen, made the same point in her 1983 report to the town: "The Board has recognized the need for the adoption of administrative procedures and policies to promote more efficient and effective government . . . During the past year, the Board has established guidelines for the conduct of its meetings. We encourage participation by our citizens. We want each issue fully understood and each point of view fully explored." Members of the board were assigned as liaisons to town committees and departments, and new ad hoc committees were appointed to examine issues facing the selectmen.

Issues such as watershed protection, waste disposal, and transportation were not confined simply to Cohasset but involved neighboring towns as well. To deal with regional problems, the selectmen of Cohasset, Hingham, and Hull formed a Tri-Town Commission in 1983, comprising one selectman from each town. Taking another step toward regionalization, the selectmen appointed Martha Gjesteby to represent Cohasset on the Metropolitan Area Planning Council (MAPC), a planning agency for 101 cities and towns in the greater Boston region. Cohasset became a member of the South Shore Coalition, a subregional group working with MAPC staff to address issues of common concern such as affordable housing, solid waste disposal, water supply protection, and the proposed restoration of the Old Colony Railroad. Town government had grown enormously more complex than it had been in 1950.

Computerization

Town Hall entered the modern age in 1983 with the installation of its first central computer system. No one in the building knew much about computers. Cohasset residents Marilyn and John Keane, experts in the new technology, volunteered to train Town Accountant William Signorelli in the use of municipal accounting software. Though an authority in his own field—he was instrumental in developing the new Uniform Massachusetts Accounting

William Signorelli, left, town accountant 1967–1984; Gordon Flint, right, town treasurer-collector 1951–1984 These were the two on deck financially when computerization came to town.
Photos courtesy of Cohasset Mariner/Greg Derr

System—Signorelli was a novice when it came to computers. Nevertheless, he took on the thankless task of supervising all computer operations for Town Hall, spending long hours of his personal time trying to work out the bugs in the system. In 1984, after 17 years of service to the town, he decided it was time to retire.

Once the computer system was up and running smoothly, the daily functions of many departments were transformed. "The change in technology was the first big change in town government," in Gordon Flint's view. "During this period we went from the old way of doing things—writing ledgers by hand, typing out tax rolls and assessment records, hand proving totals—to computerized operations." Fewer people were required to perform routine tasks, information could be quickly retrieved and updated, and results were more accurate.

In 1985 the Paul Pratt Memorial Library became part of the Old Colony Library Network, a computerized regional network of libraries. "With the assistance of computers," reported the *Mariner*

(2/21/85), "access to about two million books will be available to Cohasset's library users. Although the Pratt Library currently contains about 40,000 volumes, the regional network will provide Cohasset readers with titles previously unattainable. With the touch of a computer keyboard, a Cohasset reader will know if a certain book is available and its location. An immediate request can be made for that title, and it will be transferred to the Pratt Library, usually within 24 hours." Card catalogues were soon to become obsolete. The library was one of several "wired" town departments, including the offices of the town clerk, the assessors, the treasurer-collector, the water and sewer departments, the police, and the schools.

Expanding Town Hall

Town Hall had run out of space by the 1980s, and some departments had become outliers. The Board of Health, the Conservation Commission, the Planning Board, and the Sewer Commission were all stationed in the old Bates Building at 43 Elm Street, once used by Philander Bates as a bootmaking shop in the nineteenth century. The selectmen wanted to put all departments under one roof again. The easiest way to create more room, they reasoned, would be to convert the large auditorium on the ground floor of Town Hall to office space. When the Cohasset Dramatic Club learned of this plan, they were aghast. The Town Hall auditorium had been their theater since 1921. If the auditorium goes, protested David Wadsworth, vice president of the club, "it will be a disaster, the end of the Cohasset Dramatic Club as we have known it for the past 63 years." It would also remove all traces of the building's colorful history.

Town Hall was built on the site of the old Cohasset Academy, a private school that became a town assembly hall and then Cohasset's public high school. In 1857 the building was moved "across the field" to what is now 29 Beach Street and converted to a home. Replacing it on the Common was the new two-story Town Hall. The first floor contained the high school, with an assembly hall and classrooms. The second floor included an "upper hall" for town meetings as well as offices for town departments. In 1879 the Cohasset Free Public Library was established in a room near the high school on the first floor. The high school remained at Town Hall until 1891, when the students were transferred to the new Osgood School on Elm Street. The library moved in 1903, when the Paul Pratt Memorial Library was built on South Main Street. Adding to the lore of Town Hall is an iron-barred door visible today in the corner of the cellar, where the town's first jail was located.

Town Hall was a festive place. Each year in February the annual Washington's Birthday Masquerade Ball was held there. Beginning in 1876 the townspeople, bedecked in their finery, would gather at the lower assembly hall to dance and admire one another's costumes and masks. Later a kitchen was installed, complete with dumbwaiter to a banquet hall on the second floor. In 1928 the Dramatic Club persuaded the town to combine the upper and lower assembly halls into one large auditorium, with a stage, dressing rooms beneath the stage, and storage for scenery. In addition, a movie projection booth was built in the mezzanine, and a ticket booth in the foyer. A new second floor was created for town offices. The auditorium was multifunctional, supporting the South

The 1988 wing of Town Hall. The addition brought most town departments under one roof while preserving the historic auditorium. Photo © Lynne Layman

Shore Players' summer theater productions, Dramatic Club plays, movies, minstrel shows, concerts, dances, basketball games, amateur boxing matches, and fairs.

The Dramatic Club's beloved auditorium was saved. The citizens of Cohasset listened to the club's entreaties. In April 1987 a supportive town meeting voted to appropriate $1,096,450 to build an addition to Town Hall rather than remove the auditorium. The following year the new wing, designed by architect Brett Donham, was completed. The town offices were consolidated in one building, and the Dramatic Club continued to delight its audiences in the historic old auditorium.

CHANGES IN THE SCHOOLS

The turnover of school superintendents that began in the seventies continued into the eighties. John Maloney left in 1980 to head the schools in Sharon. He was replaced by Eugene C. Crowell, from Danvers. When Crowell retired in 1986, Stephen Hart was appointed. Unlike the previous superintendents, however, Hart was an insider. He had entered the Cohasset school system in 1970 as a guidance counselor and went on to wear many hats, serving as assistant superintendent, director of special education, and financial manager. Personable and well-liked, he continued as superintendent until his retirement in 1998.

In 1986 High School Principal Richard Streeter was promoted to assistant superintendent, creating a vacancy in the position. The popular choice to replace him was Gino DiGirolamo, then assistant principal. But the search committee appointed to screen applicants for the job chose to bypass "Mr. Di." Parents wrote impassioned letters in his support and students talked of walking out in protest. It was a flashback to the Streeter crisis of the seventies. Unlike that period, however, the crisis was averted and no confrontation occurred. The episode ended sadly but quietly with DiGirolamo's decision to retire. It was a cooler, less passionate time. Mary Ellen Gallagher from Hingham became the new principal in a peaceful transition.

PSO

Controlling expenses under Prop 2 1/2 was a difficult problem for the schools. The School Committee even considered closing the Joseph Osgood School and housing all elementary grades at Deer Hill to save money. Enrollments at the Osgood School were in decline and consolidation was believed feasible. But parents liked the Osgood School. It seemed more suitable both in scale and in atmosphere for the younger children. Accordingly, the School Committee abandoned the idea.

Parents of school-aged children were now becoming aware of the pressure on school resources caused by Prop 2 1/2. Further, more mothers were working or pursuing interests outside the home and felt they were losing touch with the lives of their children. In 1982 a group of parents formed a new organization to address both those issues. The Parent-School Organization (PSO) evolved from the three Communication Councils established in 1975, one at each school. These councils were largely advisory and had limited goals. The PSO was designed as an umbrella organization to unify parents of children in all three schools, to inform them about school issues, to involve them in the schools, to raise funds for special programs, and to lobby for education.

The founding officers were Nancy Sandell, president, Rev. Edward Atkinson, John Conroy, and Marie McCarthy. Other board members included two representatives from each school, a student liaison, and parents representing special interests in the school. Several participants were former members of the League of Women Voters who wanted to remain actively involved in the community. The PSO gave them the opportunity to influence policy and help the schools.

The PSO became one of the most effective organizations in Cohasset. It supplemented the school budget by raising funds to provide grants for "enrichment" programs. Under the Arts Enrichment Program, teachers brought visiting artists, theatrical groups, authors, and illustrators into the schools. When the small senior class of 1982 could not produce the traditional annual school musical, the PSO helped fund the first all-school show, *Grease,* with students from every class in grades 7 through 12. It also backed the sports boosters clubs in supporting the junior high athletic program, a near-casualty of Prop 2 1/2. Most notably, the PSO was instrumental in building support for issues involving the schools. It collaborated with other town departments in lobbying for overrides to Prop 2 1/2 and called on parents to make their votes count at town meeting and town elections. And not least, it provided a training ground for future members of the School Committee and other town boards. The PSO remains an active organization dedicated to supporting the schools.

Other parent groups also made a difference. In September 1988 Osgood School parents collaborated to build a new play-

Volunteers built the nautically themed playpark on the grounds of the old Joseph Osgood School during a spring weekend in 1989. Photo courtesy of Patriot Ledger/Geoff Hansen

ground at the back of the schoolyard. Ann Whiteley did the research on the project, and Kevin Lewis raised funds. Whiteley engaged Customs Playground, Inc., to create the design in cooperation with interested parents. Together they agreed on a nautical theme for the playpark. The group raised $25,000 for the plans and materials, and volunteers provided free labor to construct it. On June 12, 1989, the beautiful new Osgood Playpark was opened to children. As Burt Pratt, chairman of the Board of Selectmen, commented at the dedication ceremony, "The Good Ship Osgood [the playpark] . . . stands as a model of the enthusiasm and determination of the people who made this happen." Addressing the children, Ann Whiteley added: "You should remember this playground when you are all grown up. And then you can think about how to do something nice for the community you are living in" (*Mariner*, 6/15/89).

Drug and Alcohol Program

Despite the best efforts of the community to help its youth, a small but troubling minority continued to binge on alcohol and to abuse drugs. The problem was not unique to Cohasset. To stem the spreading abuse of drugs and alcohol, the state required all public schools to develop health and drug education programs. In 1980 the School Committee hired Michael Gill to coordinate a health education program for Cohasset. The concept had strong support from many parents. To launch the program, a citizens' group raised $5,000 to sponsor a two-day presentation by David Toma, a police officer from Newark, New Jersey. Toma had developed his reputation by giving emotional lectures on the horrors of drug and alcohol abuse. He was a celebrity to many teenagers who had watched "Barretta," a television show based on his life as an undercover, drug-busting cop who used clever disguises to trap criminals. Hundreds of students and parents attended the lectures. Though controversial, Toma was a hit with his audience, eliciting tears and promises of reform from the teenagers.

The selectmen also appointed a nine-member Commission on Drug and Alcohol Abuse to follow up on the problem of substance abuse. After interviewing groups of students and adults, the commission reported the finding that alcohol abuse was a greater problem among young people than drugs. Alcohol was the most widely used and abused drug in the town. "While cocaine is very much present in Cohasset," the commissioners stated, "its use appears to be centered among adults. Young people and adults, both, abuse marijuana, again, in significantly smaller numbers . . . Alcohol, however, predominates as the community's drug of choice" (*Mariner*, 12/21/89). Alcohol abuse among teenagers remained a persistent problem for the Cohasset police.

High School Champions

Cohasset had more reasons to be proud of its students than to worry about them. In 1981 four Cohasset High School seniors were named National Merit Scholars, and the following year Cohasset ranked as one of the top academic high schools on the South Shore. It also boasted two undefeated seasons and league championships in hockey and gymnastics. In 1985 the girls' basketball team, coached by William Fallon, won 20 games in a single season and captured the title of South Shore Sectional Champions. The varsity team included Maria Cahill, Janet DiGirolamo, Tracy Fitzpatrick, Carla Lucas, Kerry O'Brien, Kristen O'Brien, Anne O'Leary, Maureen O'Leary, Sarah Seavey, Melissa Shea, Lisa Shumaker, Cindy Spooner, and Vicki Spooner. The boys' basketball team, coached by Edward Minelli, was number one in Division III in Massachusetts, ranking first for a high school its size in New England.

In 1986 Ed Minelli led his boys' team to an unprecedented second championship. "Eddie and the Cruisers," as they were affectionately called (after the title of a movie), "did what no other Massachusetts Division III team has ever done before," announced the *Mariner* (3/6/86). "They won their second straight state championship in a row." The team included Glenn Bernstein, Tony Bogarty, James Creed, Bryan Edwards, Tom

Tony Bogarty, a pivotal member of Cohasset High School's Division III championship team in 1985 and 1986. *Photo courtesy of* Cohasset Mariner/*Bill Quigley*

Larson, Matt Maloney, David Shumaker, Bob Shultz, David Shultz, Michael Smith, Andy Starmer, and Todd Trautwein. For this victory they won national recognition. The newspaper *USA Today* rated Cohasset as one of the top 35 high school basketball teams in the country.

Two years later town meeting unanimously approved a resolution recognizing the outstanding achievement of Cohasset High School students in extracurricular activities during the 1987-88 school year. The girls' basketball team won the Division III State Championship and the boys' team was a Division III State Finalist; the boys' hockey team was a Division III South Finalist; the boys' soccer team was a Division III State Finalist; the boys' wrestling team qualified for the State Wrestling Tournament; the drama workshop placed third among 77 schools statewide and was chosen as an alternate to the New England finals, and three Cohasset art students received regional awards at the State Scholastic Art Show.

The glory days for the basketball team, however, were nearing an end. In January 1989 Ed Minelli resigned as coach. School administrators and some parents were critical of the fact that he played his star Metco students, Bryan Edwards (who in 1988 set the state scoring record in basketball), James Creed, and Tony Bogarty, to the exclusion of local student athletes, who were left to warm the bench. He had an aggressive coaching style, always pushing his players, yelling at them, and manipulating them alternately with ridicule and praise. "Many argued that Minelli did not teach the basics," editorialized the *Mariner* (1/19/89), "that few of his brilliant star players have managed to stay in the sport beyond high school. But let's face it, we're talking about little Cohasset. He did his best with the limited amount of talent he had to work with . . . Minelli left a legacy in this town that will not likely be matched. For five years, the spotlight was turned on Cohasset and we reveled in it. Minelli helped bring that fleeting fame to Cohasset, and for that we owe him our gratitude. It was so much fun while it lasted." The year also ended with sad news for football fans. Because of declining enrollments, Cohasset would not have enough juniors and seniors to field a competitive football team. On Thanksgiving Day 1989, the varsity played its last football game for a while. In the 1990s the school was able to resume its varsity program.

CLUSTERS, CONDOS, AND DOCKOMINIUM

The town's population dropped by 1 percent during the 1980s while the number of housing units rose by 9 percent (from 2,488 to 2,724), reflecting a trend toward fewer people per household. The average age of the population was increasing, and the kids were moving out of their parents' home. Members of the senior generation were living longer and healthier lives, staying in their homes, if they could afford it, or moving to the new residential developments on Pond and Beechwood streets. New families moving into town were buying homes on Riverview Drive, a recent subdivision of Howard Bates's farm off Beechwood Street, on Heather Drive off Forest Avenue, or in one of several other developments. A number of luxury condominiums became available with the conversion of

Three of the mansions converted into luxury condominiums during the 1980s: **1.** *The Buckley at the corner of Jerusalem Road and Forest Avenue;* **2.** *Caravels by the Sea, overlooking Little Harbor; and* **3.** *Cohasset Condos, 646 Jerusalem Road.* Photos courtesy of Patriot Ledger

more old Victorian mansions. Cluster development was legalized in the early eighties, and developers took advantage of the opportunity to provide denser housing by building nearly 100 units of this type in the decade.

Cluster Development

The Residential Cluster Development District bylaw, passed in 1981, allowed developers to build several homes on smaller lots, provided that part of the land remained undisturbed. This was an attractive option now that buildable open land was scarce and the town wanted to preserve as much natural landscape as possible.

Cohasset's first cluster development, 100 Pond Street, was a planned community of 39 Contemporary Cape condominiums, designed by Claude Miquelle Associates of Melrose and built in 1984. The two-bedroom units were offered at a relatively affordable $165,000 to $168,000. Nearly half the 23-acre site was reserved as commonly held open space. In a country-club-like setting, residents could enjoy the amenities of a putting green, a tennis court, and footpaths meandering through landscaped grounds. It even included its own central sewage treatment and disposal plant. Like most cluster developments, 100 Pond Street was designed primarily for empty nesters who needed less space now that their children were gone. Widows and single women in particular appreciated the security of the clustered dwellings, the contracted maintenance, and the fact that they could remain in Cohasset among friends and family.

The two other cluster developments built in the 1980s were Cedar Ledge and Wheelwright Farm. Cedar Ledge, located near the Cedar Street landfill, soon to be capped and closed, consisted of 18 units on about 12 acres of land. Wheelwright Farm was a community of 35 homes on 22.5 acres off Beechwood Street. The site was the former pastureland of Frank Wheelwright's Walnut Grove Farm. The original intent of the developers was to build relatively affordable homes, but the costs of land and site preparation, as well as high interest rates, drove up the prices. In 1985 the developer of Cedar Ledge ran into financial difficulty. When his bank took over

Aerial view of Wheelwright Farm, one of three cluster developments built in the 1980s under a bylaw meant to preserve open space. Photo © Margot Cheel

the development, it raised the price of the unsold units by $50,000. Similarly, the developer of Wheelwright Farm raised the average price of his units to $212,000 from the original $135,000. Yet he, too, ran out of funds toward the end of his project, and his lender completed the development. Building in Cohasset on that scale was a risky proposition.

Affordable Housing

Property values continued to climb. Between 1984 and 1986 the average price of a home in Cohasset rose 65 percent, from $168,000 to $277,692. We were an expensive town and fewer people could afford to move here. Cohasset was evolving into a one-class community. The state, however, was interested in promoting socioeconomic diversity in suburbs like Cohasset and wanted the town to provide low-income and minority housing. To force the issue, the legislature mandated that towns set aside at least 10 percent of their housing stock as affordable housing.

To this end the selectmen appointed a Fair Housing Committee in September 1986, with Rev. E. Clifford Cutler of St. Stephen's Church, chairman, Daniel C. Cotton, Barbara Froio, James Gallagher, Leo J. Happenny, and Patrick Plante. The committee published a community profile of Cohasset, noting the "clear under-representation of minorities in this town" and the 26 percent increase in the number of elderly (over age 65) during the past decade.

Thus began a long and largely unsuccessful series of attempts to build affordable housing in Cohasset. The first attempt was on the Curtis estate, a 53-acre property off Black Rock Road. When George E. Curtis died in 1931, his will directed that his land be used to "operate a home and refuge, free of charge, for feeble, deformed, or invalid women." His trustees found these requirements unworkable. In the mid-1980s they petitioned the attorney general to release them from the terms of the will, permit them to develop the land for residential use, and add the income to the family's charitable foundation.

Enter the Curtis Estate Action Committee, led by Cohasset resident Joseph R. McElroy. They seized the opportunity to offer an alternative to the trustees' plan and petitioned the courts to allow the building of affordable housing on the estate. They later amended this petition to the building of a daycare center for victims of Alzheimer's disease, reflecting the spirit of Curtis's will. The Brockton District Court denied the committee's petition and ruled that the estate could be sold by the trustees for the benefit of the Curtis charitable foundation.

While this issue was tied up in the courts, high school manual arts teacher Patrick Plante organized volunteers to rehabilitate one of the long-neglected buildings on the estate for temporary use by a homeless family. The project received broad support. "Everyone I asked to help said yes—without question," said Plante. "All the town boards, all the businesses, and all the residents. I don't think most people realize the need out there for good housing, but once they realize it, they want to help" (*Mariner*, 12/8/88).

But good intentions were not enough. The state was impatient with the rate of Cohasset's progress, and in June 1987 the Executive Office of Communities and Development declared the town "unreasonably restrictive" and demanded a plan and a timetable for providing low- and moderate-income housing. It threatened to withhold all discretionary funding for our sewage treatment project and for the rehabilitation of our 100-year-old water distribution system if we did not comply. This is "coercion and blackmail," fumed Selectman Burt Pratt . "It is not a fair policy. We used to have home rule, and now the state mandates programs but they do not send the money to implement them" (*Mariner*, 6/25/87).

To review and examine affordable housing opportunities, the selectmen appointed a Housing Partnership Committee, chaired first by Israel M. Sanchez, Jr., and then by Chartis B. Langmaid. With the approval of both the partnership and the selectmen, developers could obtain state grants to build affordable homes. They were also aided by the "comprehensive permit process," the anti-snob zoning act that enabled developers to bypass the subdivision review of local planning boards and apply directly to zoning boards of appeals for variances from zoning restrictions.

In spite of these advantages, the only two attempts at large-scale low-income housing development failed, one by Deck Point, Inc., and the other by Crystal Land Development Corporation. Deck Point applied for a comprehensive permit to build 128 condominiums, of which 12 would be set aside for affordable housing, on Scituate Hill (at the site of the present Sunrise Assisted Living facility on Route 3A). Although the Housing Partnership, the selectmen, and the Chamber of Commerce opposed their plans, Deck Point nonetheless received a comprehensive permit from the Zoning Board of Appeals, with numerous conditions attached.   The project, however, failed to obtain affordable housing grants from the state and hence was abandoned.

The Crystal Land Development project, called Crystal Woods, also failed. The developer applied for a comprehensive permit to build 60 townhouse condominiums, a third of them affordable, on 20 acres of land off Route 3A behind Brewster Road, on the Scituate-Cohasset line.   Concerned about problems of sewage, drainage, high population density, and increased traffic, 100 residents signed a petition against the proposed development. They also complained that the owner of the land and the developer stood to make a "windfall profit by taking advantage of a state-funded program" (*Mariner*, 12/8/88), as they believed the value of the low-lying swampy land was overassessed. Again, the Cohasset Planning Board and the selectmen were against the proposal, but the Zoning Board of Appeals granted a comprehensive permit, with 32 restrictions, including a reduction in the number of units. This rendered the project uneconomical, and the developers abandoned it. By 1989 the state had run out of funds for affordable housing, bringing an end to the subsidized programs. The only affordable housing in Cohasset as of the year 2000 is Harborview and the Bates Building, which South Shore Habitat for Humanity converted to two condominium units in 1993.

The Bates Building on Elm Street, which once housed several town offices, was turned over to Habitat for Humanity in 1993 for conversion to affordable condos. Photo courtesy of Patriot Ledger/Fred Field

Cox Estate

At the high end of the housing market was the Cox estate. This prominent landmark was offered for sale in the early 1980s. Its disposition was a matter of great interest to the town. The history of the estate dated back to the town's Age of Sail:

> The large brick house at Cohasset's 49 Margin Street, long known as "The Oaks," and for years the home of Mr. and Mrs. William C. Cox (she was often called by her first name, Jessie), has been since its inception one of Cohasset's best known garden estates. Constructed in 1931, this spacious residence and its superbly landscaped yards reflect an era of gracious living now all but passed from the Cohasset scene.
>
> However, not everyone may realize that the beautiful grounds surrounding "The Oaks" once were the site of a thriving ship-building establishment whose produc-

tion included the largest sailing vessels ever built by Cohasset's 19th century shipwrights . . . Near the flourishing shipyard, Capt. Nichols Tower owned his wharf and store from which he conducted a fishing and marine salvage business . . .

By the 1850s, Richard Bourne, descendant of an early Cohasset family, had built his residence near the shipyard. Bourne's home soon was sold to the well-known dramatic actor Lawrence Barrett . . . Barrett enlarged the house, turning it into a Victorian estate-house of prominent size, then sold it in turn to Clarence W. Barron, the well-known financier . . .

By the second quarter of the [20th] century, "The Oaks" had passed to C. W. Barron's grand-daughter Mrs. William C. Cox. The Victorian mansion was razed, to be replaced by today's substantial brick structure. Thus the Cox family became the owners of one of Cohasset's newest—and finest—great estates. "The Oaks" soon became a focal point of attention, both for its handsome house and the tasteful beauty of its finely landscaped grounds. Carefully tended greenhouses displayed superb collections of flowers, and trees of numerous species were grown to shade the spacious lawns.

[David Wadsworth, article in *Cohasset Mariner*, 9/7/83]

During Jessie Cox's lifetime, The Oaks had hosted famous guests such as Bob Hope and Liberace, who stayed with her when they performed at the Music Circus. After her death in 1982, the family decided to sell the 55-room mansion and its nine acres of manicured landscaping. It was an anxious time for the town. With talk of casino gambling in Hull, would a Mafia-connected family make an offer?

Fortunately the new owner was a legitimate business, Yankee Oil and Gas Company. They purchased the estate in June 1983 for just under $900,000. Yankee's president, Paul Montle, received a variance from the Zoning Board of Appeals to use the residence as

his corporate headquarters, with office space for up to 18 employees. The Planning Board, however, had other ideas. Citing the
scarcity of public waterfront property in Cohasset, the chairman of
the Planning Board, John O'Toole, proposed that the town take the
estate by eminent domain, use the mansion for town offices, and
convert the rest of the property to a waterfront park. He formally
objected to the variance, and the Planning Board sued both Yankee
Oil and the ZBA. The suit was settled out of court when Montle
acceded to certain restrictions on the use of the property. He
agreed to leave the exterior intact and offered to lease to the town
a one-acre strip of land along the harbor, near Kimball's Motel, for
one dollar a year. The Oaks continued to function as a corporate
headquarters until Yankee Oil went bankrupt in 1987.

In December 1987 Oaks Realty Trust, a consortium of four
developers, bought the estate for $2.6 million in cash. Their mas-
ter plan was to build a "dockominium" on the harbor around the
periphery of the property. A dockominium was a condominium
arrangement for boats. They proposed taking the land occupied by
the tennis court and garages and dredging it to create enough
space for 109 private boat slips. To sweeten the deal, Oaks Realty
offered to donate 48 public slips to the town, as well as the acre of
waterfront property between Kimball's and The Oaks, which the
town could use for six floats. Most residents were appalled at the
thought of 109 more boats in the already crowded harbor, not to
mention the destruction of the grounds at The Oaks. Heaping more
sugar on the deal, Oaks Realty also offered to donate the mansion
to the town if the dockominium proposal were approved. The
town would have none of it. Voters at a special town meeting in
December 1988 passed a resolution against the proposal. The arguments were that the marina would ruin the appearance of the harbor, and the increased traffic and pollution would diminish the
value of the surrounding properties and increase costs to the town.
Two months later The Oaks was back on the market.

In August 1989 Cohasset resident Peter Roy purchased the
property for nearly $3 million. This was the largest residential real
estate transaction ever made in Cohasset. Roy's parents, who also

lived in Cohasset, owned Kimball's-by-the-Sea, which they purchased in 1981. Thus the motel that Jessie Cox so hated was now
held by members of the same family that would own her former
home. It was an ironic twist of fate and the conclusion to one of
the most bitter conflicts in Cohasset.

SEWER SAGA: PART III

Far from resolved was the battle over the sewer. Cohasset was the
defendant in a state suit brought in November 1979 for polluting
"the waters of the Commonwealth." Our small wastewater treatment plant off Elm Street had a permit to treat 72,000 gallons a day,
and the average daily flow into the plant was about 80,000 gallons.
Because of infiltration from groundwater and leaking sewage
pipes, however, flows during storms could peak at 200,000 gallons
or more. Under the threat of fines at the rate of $10,000 a day,
Cohasset signed an Agreement for Judgment in February 1980 to
settle the state's legal action. The terms of our judgment, or
obligation, required us (1) to pay a token penalty of $10,000 for
exceeding our discharge permit; (2) to design and construct a new,
large-capacity treatment plant, as proposed in 1977 by the engineering firm of Metcalf & Eddy; and (3) to follow a prescribed timetable.

The first step in our good-faith effort to build the plant was to
decide where to locate it, and where to route the ocean outfall pipe.
These issues were controversial but, spurred by the threat of fines,
voters at a special town meeting in February 1980 chose the Jones
conservation land between Sohier and North Main streets, east of
Fairoaks Lane, for the plant. The outfall pipe carrying treated
wastewater would run from the Sohier Street facility to Red Gate
Lane, down Jerusalem Road, and out Pleasant Beach several hundred yards into the ocean, less than a mile from Sandy Beach.

The plan proposed by Metcalf & Eddy entailed converting the
existing treatment plant into a pumping station to convey sewage
to the new plant. In Phase I of the project, the plant would have the
capacity to treat 500,000 gallons a day. About 500 new sewer connections would be installed in densely populated districts. With the
230 that already existed, about 30 percent of the town would be

sewered. In Phase II, plant capacity would be expanded to 700,000 gallons a day, and another 500 connections added to the system, sewering a total of about 55 percent of the town. The design would accommodate a possible Phase III, expanding capacity to 1 million gallons.

Townspeople expressed the concern that land unsuitable for septic systems would become buildable as a result of town sewerage, opening Cohasset to the potential for overdevelopment. They also objected to the cost of such a large system, an estimated $13.7 million for the design and construction of Phase I alone. Even though state and federal grants were expected to cover 90 percent of the cost, the town's share of the burden would cut into other needed services squeezed by Proposition 2 1/2. The environmental impacts of the facility and the ocean outfall, as well as unanticipated expenses down the road, were also matters of concern. Nevertheless, in May 1980 the sewer commissioners submitted the Metcalf & Eddy plan for approval to the federal Environmental Protection Agency and the state Department of Environmental Quality Engineering (DEQE). They also applied for a grant to design the system. We would wait three years to get an answer.

In late 1982, when the town learned that approval was imminent, resident Charles DeSantis, a vocal opponent of the "build 'em big" Metcalf & Eddy treatment facility, initiated countervailing action. Charlie was a full-time airline pilot. He had grown up in Cohasset in the forties and fifties, and his love for the town was unmistakable: "Cohasset is unique," he said, "and one of the most beautiful towns in America. I look back on my childhood as a happy experience, a marvelous experience . . . Cohasset is a natural island in a sea of rather intensely developed communities. If a town like Cohasset becomes overly developed, its natural assets can no longer be enjoyed by everybody. If utilized by so many, they will be appreciated and enjoyed by no one . . . Cohasset cannot be a community of 15,000 to 20,000 people and still be the Cohasset of a natural sense" (*Mariner*, 3/15/84). Determined to stop the proposed central sewer system, he led a petition drive to explore less expensive and smaller scale "innovative and alternative" solutions.

Charlie's efforts were rewarded at a special town meeting in November 1982. After intense debate voters, by a narrow margin

(184 to 173), authorized the town to suspend the Metcalf & Eddy plan and renegotiate the Agreement for Judgment so that the Sewer Commission could prepare an alternative plan. Commission Chairman Gerard Stanton and member Janet Daggett opposed the petition and immediately resigned. They had worked for three years to secure an approved plan, and just as they were about to receive the approval, the town killed the project. They felt they could not continue to serve as commissioners and face a contempt-of-court citation for violating the Agreement for Judgment. Charlie DeSantis and Maxwell Pounder were appointed to

Former sewer commissioner Charles DeSantis, who led the bruising fight for an alternative to a huge central sewer system proposed in the early 1980s.
Photo courtesy of Cohasset Mariner */ Rose Cundari*

replace them until the annual town election the following April.

The state was not pleased with Cohasset. The DEQE threatened to stop all funding for our sewer project unless we went forward with the M&E plan, as we had agreed to do in the settlement. In December 1982 the town hired an environmental attorney to renegotiate the Agreement for Judgment. State officials refused to renegotiate or to discuss funding for a new study. Instead, in March 1983 they awarded the town a grant of $1.1 million toward design and specifications for the M&E plan. Now that the plan was approved and backed with a grant, Manuel Salvador, operator of Cohasset's sewer plant, and other Cohasset residents who favored a central sewer system petitioned the selectmen to support an article rescinding the town's vote to suspend the M&E plan. At the annual town meeting in April, voters confirmed their previous decision and rejected the $1.1 million grant for the M&E plan. They also increased to $20,000 an appropriation for the study of "innovative and alternative approaches," to be conducted by Ward Engineering Associates.

Because we refused the grant for the M&E project and did not comply with the Agreement for Judgment, the DEQE brought a contempt-of-court citation against us. In August 1983 the DEQE imposed a fine of $2,000 a day, retroactive to April 11, 1983, until we either accepted the grant or appropriated town funds to correct our discharge violation. Shortly thereafter a special town meeting appropriated $86,000, with no grant assistance, to continue the Ward study. The selectmen also appointed a new special counsel, Goodwin, Proctor & Hoar, to fight the fine in court and to litigate for a modified Agreement for Judgment. In December the state decided to cooperate. The DEQE and town officials agreed to suspend all litigation until the Ward plan was completed and evaluated.

"Charlie fought the state and is still winning," read the headline of the *Cohasset Mariner* in March 1984. For his battle to preserve local autonomy in the spirit of Home Rule, the paper had named Charlie its first Person of the Year. One member of the panel that voted for him stated, "Over two years ago he alone mustered support for an alternative means to an expensive sewer project. We now have that study underway. Whether Mr. DeSantis is right or wrong, he did convince others to consider the cost, damage, impact, and loss of a lifestyle for which many residents live in Cohasset." Not everyone, of course, agreed with Charlie's solution. Opponents were skeptical about the alternative plans and critical of the delays that threatened to reduce state and federal funding.

The plan developed by Ward Engineering proposed converting the existing treatment plant to a pumping station, as in the M&E plan. But instead of constructing a large central sewer plant on Sohier Street, with an ocean outfall off Pleasant Beach, Cohasset would run a large sewer pipe from the Elm Street pumping station to Hull's new, oversized plant (designed for a daily capacity of 3 million gallons, it received an average of only 1 million gallons). Cohasset's sewer service would be expanded to the Veterans' and Hillside areas, as well as to the Deer Hill School–Fairoaks Lane areas. This expansion would involve "innovative, alternative" technology, in that a low-cost, small-diameter collector pipe would connect the homeowner's septic tank to the main sewer line in the street. The total amount of wastewater pumped to Hull would fall within the 300,000-gallon-a-day limit that Hull would allow. In addition, about 300 failing septic systems in Cohasset would be repaired. Total estimated cost: $8.6 million. Ninety percent of the cost of connecting our pumping station to Hull would be eligible for funding. In addition, DeSantis expected that 94 percent of the cost of both on-site system repairs and the small-diameter collector sewers recommended by Ward would also be eligible for funding.

In June 1984 the Ward proposal was brought before a special town meeting for approval. The plan was amended to expand sewering to the Route 3A business district and the adjacent Brewster Road neighborhood. The voters were asked to approve an appropriation of $1.1 million for the town's share of the cost to prepare design drawings and specifications for the Ward plan. All previous funding for the M&E plan would be rescinded. This was a critical moment for the success of the new plan. As a two-thirds majority vote was necessary, the moderator asked for a hand count. To the great joy of its proponents, the Ward plan won overwhelming support: the article passed 346 to 44. The *Mariner* (6/21/84) reported: "As the hand count vote was read aloud by Town Moderator William Weeks, the crowd erupted in unanimous jubilation. Backslaps, handshakes, and kisses were flowing freely as citizens finally approved a plan which has been promised to alleviate the town's wastewater discharge violation."

Feelings ran high on both sides of the sewerage issue. The town meeting vote was the last straw for Sewer Commissioner Joseph M. Gwinn, the only central-sewer supporter left on the board. He resigned, warning the town that the Ward plan would not receive adequate state and federal funding. R. Gary Vanderweil, Jr., was appointed to replace him. Gwinn's opposition to the Ward plan received strong backing from resident R. Murray Campbell, an engineer with Stone & Webster, who in July 1984 published an 80-page treatise titled "The Sewer Follies of Cohasset." Indeed, some of Charlie DeSantis's assumptions were unraveling. In June 1984 the director of the DEQE had informed the sewer commissioners that no funding was available for rehabilitation of on-site septic systems. The alternative sewer collectors, for which

Charlie had also hoped to receive a 94 percent state/federal grant, might be eligible for 50 percent funding. The only part of the Ward plan eligible to receive priority funding at 90 percent was the connection to Hull, pending the signing of an intermunicipal agreement.

Energized by the town's endorsement of the Ward plan, the sewer commissioners submitted a grant application for design and specifications in July 1984. A month later the DEQE rejected the application. But, in the words of Sewer Commissioner Edward ("Ted") Guild, who had been elected the previous year, "Charlie was a fighter. He was the kind of person who would pick up a broken sword from the field and lunge into battle." Charlie immediately appealed the DEQE decision to the regional office of the EPA. A year later, the EPA denied Cohasset's appeal—but it did authorize the town to investigate further the Cohasset-Hull connection.

In February 1987, after more than two years of rejections and delays, the state finally gave conditional approval to the Ward plan. Final approval required the signing of an intermunicipal agreement between Cohasset and Hull for the disposal of our wastewater into Hull's plant. By this time enthusiasm for the sewer project was cooling. At a special town meeting in May 1988, voters narrowly approved the Cohasset-Hull connection by a precise two-thirds majority. Both towns then signed the 30-year intermunicipal agreement.

At long last, everything was in place. We had all the necessary approvals and agreements. The town had appropriated almost $3 million toward the project. In May 1988 voters approved Cohasset's first override of Prop 2 1/2 to pay the bond issue. (They also passed a general levy override and approved various other debt and capital outlay exclusions.) Federal and state grants would cover the balance, about $5 million, of the $8-million project. But in July the sewer commissioners received bad news: Governor Michael Dukakis's so-called Massachusetts Miracle had collapsed. The state was in fiscal crisis, and no funds would be available for our project (the same was true for 45 other communities). All work would have to stop, at least temporarily. Alas, poor Charlie. He had to admit, this final blow left him feeling "a little bit empty." After two grueling terms as sewer commissioner, amid frequent bitter, personal attacks from Ward plan opponents, events beyond his control brought his leadership role to an end. In February 1989 his employer, Eastern Airlines, went bankrupt. Forced to relocate, Charlie moved away from Cohasset.

The good news was the successful privatization of the Elm Street treatment plant. All had not gone well with the previous operation of the plant. In 1987 the sewer commissioners had terminated the position of plant operator and hired a private contractor, York Water Consultants, to operate and maintain the facility. "Within a week," notes Ted Guild, "they had the plant operating like a Swiss watch." In contrast to the previous six years, the plant met state and federal discharge standards for 11 of 12 months in 1987. The following year it had a perfect record. The ultimate irony was that in September 1989 York Water Consultants merged with the firm of Metcalf & Eddy. Cohasset's sewer plant was now being run by M&E.

The year 1989 ended with the sewer commissioners "still awaiting word on state funding for the Hull intermunicipal project."

COHASSET HEIGHTS LIMITED

The most expensive and intractable legal problem in Cohasset was not the sewer issue but the controversy surrounding a private landfill on Route 3A. In September 1975 Cohasset resident James Tyeryar had purchased a 50-acre parcel of land off Crocker Lane on Scituate Hill, to the west of Route 3A. He paid $30,000 for the land and $15,000 to the town for back taxes owed on the property. His intention was to use 20 acres of the land as a dumping ground for stumps, brush, rocks, and demolition material.

As the property was near wetlands, Tyeryar asked the Conservation Commission to determine whether it was within the town's watershed area. The commission assured him that it was not. Joseph Rosano, an abutter to the site, had traced the flow of water. Examining the contours of the land, he concluded that the water flowed toward Hingham through the Great Swamp and out to the Weir River, not toward Lily Pond, our water supply. There was no opposition to Tyeryar's proposal. In June 1976 the Board of Health issued him a site assignment to use the site as a dumping facility for demolition material and brush. He developed the property, creating a 280,000-gallon pond to be used as a water source in the event of landfill fires. The fire chief, Charles Piepenbrink, told the Board of Health that the landfill would "aid the town immeasurably in taking some pressure off the town landfill" (*Patriot Ledger*, 6/24/76). Cohasset Heights Landfill opened for business, and in December 1978 the DEQE granted Tyeryar a permit to dispose of demolition waste over a 2.3-acre portion of his land.

Trouble began a year later. In December 1979 the DEQE, which periodically inspected the site, ordered Tyeryar to close his operation because he was dumping debris too close to wetlands and over a larger area than permitted. Using state approved drainage maps, he claimed, however, that his landfill did not drain into the watershed area. After he agreed to reduce his disposal area, the DEQE allowed him to continue operations. Nevertheless, Tyeryar decided to get out of the landfill business and offered to sell Cohasset Heights to the town for $5 million. The town needed an alternative to its Cedar Street landfill, which was in violation of the state's sanitary code and had to be closed. But the price was excessive, and town officials declined the offer. In January 1982 Tyeryar sold the property to trash haulers Barry Brothers, Inc., of Auburndale for $3.1 million.

Just 10 months later the Board of Health filed complaints in Quincy District Court against Paul and John Barry's Cohasset Heights Limited (CHL) for violating landfill regulations. The court closed the landfill for six weeks until CHL agreed to follow the health board's landfill regulations. Aggravating the situation, in 1983 the Barrys sold the rights to their trash-pickup routes to Browning-Ferris Industries (BFI), one of the nation's largest trash-hauling firms. Its routes covered all of southeastern Massachusetts. The town now confronted the possibility that BFI could unknowingly bring in refuse containing toxic industrial waste.

Taking steps to protect the water supply, the selectmen appointed a Watershed Protection Area Study Committee. Their task was to write a zoning bylaw creating a Water Resource District in Cohasset (adopted in 1986) and to investigate the drainage pattern of the area. Working with consultants Camp, Dresser & McKee, in 1985 the committee published the first professional engineering report on the site. The study concluded that contaminated leachate from the landfill did reach Lily Pond. "Had the previous owners of the landfill asked today for use of the land adjacent to the watershed," stated Water Commissioner Peter Pratt, "they would not have got it. The Water Commission feels this is an atrocious landuse of a public watershed" (*Mariner*, 11/14/85).

The Barrys maintained that the engineering study did not prove CHL was polluting the watershed. In fact they went ahead and applied to DEQE for permission to expand their operation. Then they filed a civil lawsuit against the town in Norfolk County Superior Court alleging that the Water Commission and the Board of Health had overstepped their authority and "misrepresented the true facts so as to create the false impression that the landfill operated by CHL has and is creating harm to the public water supply of the Town of Cohasset" (*Mariner*, 3/13/86). Paul Barry, who had moved to Cohasset in 1983, tried to assure his fellow townspeople that he, too, drank Cohasset water and would not allow his landfill to pollute the water supply. He was supervising his operation seven days a week. "My life has become this landfill," he told the *Mariner* (10/29/87). He also pointed out that CHL benefited the town by paying about $30,000 a year in disposal permit fees.

The conflict over the landfill had escalated into a costly legal battle. In the period from 1982 to 1987, the town's actions against CHL had already run up the highest tab for engineering and legal expenses in the town's history. (By 1995, when a specific figure was first given, the town had spent an estimated $450,000 in legal fees alone.) After still another year of litigation, the Land Court gave Cohasset a partial victory, ruling that the town could prohibit the dumping of any waste other than demolition debris into the landfill and that CHL had been illegally dumping general refuse in

Owner Paul Barry sits on his embattled landfill during one of the many legal contretemps between Cohasset Heights Ltd. and the town—a costly fight that lasted well into the 1990s. Photo courtesy of Patriot Ledger/Fred Field

violation of their special permit from 1980 to 1987 The resilient Paul Barry declared, "We are not out of business. The gates are still open and we're doing business. We spent a lot of money fighting this and there's been a lot of stress. It's something Cohasset doesn't want and they feel they made a mistake in allowing It [CHL] here. But you can't put people out of business from gut feelings" (*Mariner*, 6/16/88). In fact, there was some upside for the brothers. By confining CHL to demolition debris, they expected to be able to extend the life of the landfill site. The conflict between CHL and the town was to continue and intensify in the 1990s.

NEW TRADITIONS

Critics describe the eighties as a decade focusing on materialism, competition, success, and self-image. Yet for Cohasset what stands out is the spirit of unprecedented charitable and ecumenical generosity fostered by the churches. For the first time ever, in 1979 St. Stephen's Episcopal Church, the Second Congregational Church

Madeline Hargadon sells wreaths in Town Hall at the 43rd annual Village Fair in 1983. During the 1980s the fair grew to include five churches instead of the original three.
Photo courtesy of Patriot Ledger/Bob Stella

and the First Parish Unitarian-Universalist Church included St. Anthony's Catholic Church in their traditional annual Village Fair. In 1981 they were joined by the new Panagia Greek Orthodox Church, making the fair an ecumenical partnership of five denominations.

Welcoming a New Church

If you lived in Cohasset and belonged to the Greek Orthodox church, you attended services either in Quincy or in Boston. By 1980, however, the Orthodox community on the South Shore had grown large enough to support its own church. When the Pope Memorial Church in Cohasset became available in 1979, after the departure of the Methodist congregation, the South Shore Hellenic Church and Cultural Association signed an agreement to buy it from the Pope family, who still owned the building and the surrounding land. The association named its new Cohasset church the Nativity Assumption of the Virgin Mary Greek Orthodox Church.

To raise funds for the acquisition, the Hellenic group held the first of many Greek Tavernas (outdoor cafés) on the grounds of the church. Here you could sample an array of Greek delicacies—dolmathes (stuffed grape leaves), lamb roasted over charcoal, shish-ke-bob, moussaka (eggplant with ground beef), spanakopita (spinach pie), and flaky baklava drenched in honey. While enjoying the feast, guests were entertained by children in traditional dress performing Grecian dances. By December 1980 the Panagia Greek Orthodox Church at 811 Jerusalem Road belonged to its new congregation. (*Panagia* is the popular name for the Virgin Mary in Greek.) The Reverend John Maheras became pastor in 1985. A year later the membership of the church comprised more than 200 families from all over the South Shore. Consecrated on September 7, 1997, the Panagia Church has become an integral part of the Village Fair and a host at ecumenical Thanksgiving services. It is best known in Cohasset, however, for the festive Greek Taverna that signals the beginning of summer.

Reaching Out

Not everyone participated in the economic success of the Reagan years. The benefits of his policies did not extend to the poor. Poverty, and in particular homelessness, ballooned into a national problem as the deinstitutionalization of the mentally ill contributed to the numbers of men and women taking refuge at homeless shelters. People in Cohasset sought opportunities to help.

In 1982 Barbara M. Donahue and Sharon Becker decided to assist Rosie's Place, a shelter for homeless women founded in 1974. They placed notices in church bulletins around Cohasset inviting parishioners to attend a meeting at Donahue's home. About 80 people, including the pastors, responded. From this group Donahue and Becker organized 25 or 30 "regulars" to prepare food for Rosie's Place. Once a month they would drive into Boston with the donations and help serve a hot meal to 100 or more women and children. Some mothers would bring their children to Rosie's at the end of the month, when their welfare money ran out, to share in the meal. "The food is wonderful," commented the coordinator of volunteers at Rosie's. "There are lots of home-baked pies and breads. It's real home cooking, and that makes it special" (*Mariner*, 11/27/86). A personal touch was the contribution of a beautiful floral arrangement each month by a Cohasset woman, using flowers from her own garden. Still another volunteer group, organized by Nancy Anderson and drawn largely from St. Anthony's, provided and served hot meals each month to 60 to 80 women at the Pine Street Inn in Boston. In 1988 the volunteers received a Pine Street Humanitarian Award for their dedicated service. More than 10 years later, many of the same men and women still volunteer at Rosie's Place and the Pine Street Inn.

In 1981 and 1982 the Vedanta Centre held a summer fair to raise funds for the support of its two branches in Calcutta, India. Unknown to most Cohasset residents, the Vedanta group in India provides primary and secondary education to 6,000 underprivileged girls in each of two schools. The Calcutta ashramas also maintain an orphanage and housing for destitute girls, young widows, and abandoned wives left with no means of support. At the ashramas the women learn the practical skills they need to become self-sufficient. The schools are supported by the Indian government, but the other services depend on charitable donations.

At St. Stephen's Church the first priority of the Reverend E. Clifford Cutler, installed as rector in 1985 after the departure of Rev. Richard Muir, was the Sunday School program. In just 10 years he increased the enrollment from 6 to more than 100 children and teenagers. And by the year 2000, using an innovative curriculum called Godly Play, the program expanded to 160 students. Rev. Cutler also involved his adult parishioners in supporting a faith-based outreach agency in Quincy. Founded in 1978, the Quincy Crisis Center provides a 24-hour hotline, crisis counseling, emergency food supplies, hot meals, and shelter to poor and homeless people. Its Hingham branch, the Mary-Martha Learning Center, shelters and teaches skills to homeless women with children.

In 1987 the Reverend Gary A. Ritts became the Second Congregational Church's seventeenth full-time minister, after Rev. John Benbow moved to Milton. The charitable mission Rev. Ritts introduced to Cohasset was the Appalachia Service Project (ASP), a home-repair and home-building ministry founded in 1969 to help isolated and impoverished families in central Appalachia. According to Rev. Ritts, for many volunteers the project is "an eye-opening and possibly life-changing experience" (*Mariner*, 8/3/89). The growth of Cohasset's involvement has been phenomenal. In June 1989, 12 teenagers from the Second Congregational Church, St. Anthony's, St. Stephen's, and First Parish, accompanied by 6 adults, left the comfort of their homes in Cohasset to spend a week in Leslie County, Kentucky. There they toiled in the hot sun, repairing porches and rebuilding a roof to improve the lives of people who lacked the resources to help themselves.

In June 2001, 130 teenagers and 30 adult chaperones from Cohasset volunteered for ASP, a nearly tenfold increase in little more than a decade for this very successful program. High school junior David Ingber was one of those who traveled to the Kentucky-Virginia border, where he helped construct a working bathroom for a dilapidated home in a depressed coal-mining area. "It was an amazing experience," he said. "It doesn't seem that one week can change a

Cohasset volunteers for the Appalachia Service Project construct a deck and stairs for a home in Lincoln County, West Virginia, in 1999. Left to right: Evan Murphy, Alisha Suddath, Margot Cheel, Corinne Noering, Mary Lynn Cunningham, two ASP staff, Kevin DeVito. Photo courtesy of Margot Cheel

person, but it does . . . The people we met were probably the nicest people we had ever met, and they were so generous and giving, even though they didn't have as much" (*Mariner*, 7/12/01). He also proudly noted that Cohasset, with a population of less than 8,000, sent almost 200 people to Appalachia, whereas Columbia, Maryland, a city of about 90,000, sent only 80 there.

Caring for Seniors

Cohasset's population was aging. Those who had moved here after World War II were now the older generation. For many years they had been active members of the community, joining organizations, forming new ones, participating in town government—in short, creating the modern Cohasset. By the mid-1980s they were in their sixties and seventies, retired, their grown children off on their own. Many were alone and lonely.

The Council on Aging, the Social Service League, and various church groups provided services for the elderly, such as Meals on Wheels, shuttle bus transportation, and a drop-in center at First Parish for informal television watching and card games. These services, however, were poorly coordinated, and programs for the elderly were limited. To address the needs of seniors more fully, the Council on Aging (renamed Cohasset Elder Affairs in 1996) opened a new Senior Center at the Community Center in February 1986. They appointed a director, Kathleen R. Bryanton, to coordinate and expand activities for the over-60 population. This active and thriving organization, still under Bryanton's capable leadership, provides a well-attended hot lunch twice a week, often featuring guest speakers; tours to special attractions; trips to the theater, Symphony Hall, and museums in Boston; van transportation around Cohasset and to shopping malls; exercise, bridge, knitting, and gourmet cooking classes; and up-to-date information on insurance, health, taxes, and other matters of interest to seniors.

Chanticleers, a breakfast club for men 65 and over, is closely associated with the Senior Center. Alwin A. Merrill started the group in 1988, after inviting two elderly members of the center to

The Chanticleers, a peripatetic men's breakfast group associated with the Senior Center, descends on Kimball's in 1995. Photo courtesy of Dr. Alwin Merrill

breakfast in Hull. They enjoyed themselves so much that they decided to meet again — and again. Now about 25 to 30 men from all walks of life have breakfast together once a week. The comradeship is more important than the food. When asked why they all seemed to get along so well, Merrill made this broad observation: "We come from a different era. We grew up in a time where we trusted one another. We settled on a handshake and didn't need lawyers. We still work within that world" (*Mariner*, 11/12/98).

The same generation of civic-minded citizens formed the Cohasset Veterans of Foreign Wars Post 9146 in 1985. Charter members included Post Commander Ralph Perroncello, Vice Commander William Barnes, Adjunct Robert Jackson, Quartermaster William Higgins, Charter Committee Chairman Emilio Conte, Chaplain Louis Longo, and VFW State Commander Theodore R. Eaton. From 15 members in 1985, the post grew to a peak of 257 in the early 1990s. The membership has declined to about 175 now with the death of many of the older veterans. Nevertheless, the group is an active one, providing support to needy veterans and their widows and children. Each year they award $500 VFW scholarships to two or three high school graduates, donate American flags to organizations, make charitable contributions, and encourage patriotism in local schools.

Expanding the Arts

Since its founding in 1955, the South Shore Art Center has attracted newcomers. "When you moved to Cohasset, you either took a class at the Art Center or joined the Community Garden Club," recalls Christina ("Chris") Laney Rifkin. At a time when there were fewer activities, it was a place to make friends. More than this, however, the Art Center became a major facility for art education, attracting amateur artists from nearby towns as well as professionals from all over New England. Inevitably it outgrew its limited space in the "little red building with uneven floors" at 103 Ripley Road.

In 1985 the board of directors, chaired by Cohasset artist Eleanor ("Claffy") Williams, voted to construct a new art center. The site they chose was just down the street from the little red

For many years the South Shore Art Center was housed in the narrow "flatiron building" on Ripley Road. Photo courtesy of South Shore Art Center

The airy new South Shore Art Center opened in 1987 a few doors up Ripley Road from its predecessor. Photo © Lynne Layman

building, where Tantillo's Auto Body Shop stood at the original location of the railroad station. Designed by architect Vcevold Strekalovsky of Hingham and built by Travi Construction, the new center cost $950,000. Director Allen Weisenfluh led the capital campaign, while Thomas Hamilton and Chris Rifkin coordinated the planning of the building. The design included four large studio/classrooms, a dramatic two-story central gallery, a smaller gallery/members room, a lobby with space for a gift shop, and administrative offices. When the handsome new facility opened to the public in June 1987, membership and class enrollment doubled. As of the year 2000, the Art Center had over 900 members and 120 professional artist members. As the home of the South Shore Art Center, the Cohasset Dramatic Club, and the South Shore Music Circus, the small town of Cohasset has established itself as a dynamic cultural center for the region.

Exchanging Cultures

Cultural exchange programs in Cohasset, dormant since the controversy over "Claus's beard" in 1970, revived in the eighties. In 1980 Margot Cheel, who had just moved to Cohasset, became area coordinator for Cultural Homestay International, a nonprofit organization whose goal was to promote international understanding and friendship. That summer Cheel organized the first home visits for about 15 Japanese college students. During their three-week stay in Cohasset, the young people took English classes, went on

A Japanese student discusses her culture with local children during a Cultural Homestay International visit in 1988. Back row: Rob Buckley, Mark Whitman, Japanese visitor; middle row: Ely Kahn, Andrea Freeman, Jamie Kurtz; front row: Jessica Eaton-Bruce, Natalie Cheel. Photo © Margot Cheel

field trips, and became acquainted with the Cohasset community. The program developed into a rewarding experience for both guest and host family. "I feel very fortunate that we were able to do this," remarked host mother Jean Lennon. "I can't say enough about Atsumi. She gets along with my son and my daughter just fine. They do a lot together . . . [The students] are all very respectful and they appreciate everything so much . . . I have a new life-long friend" (*Mariner,* 8/20/87). Conversely, so impressed were the Japanese with Cohasset that one young man, when he got married, told Cheel that there were three places in North America he would like to show his new bride: Niagara Falls; Banff National Park in Canada; and Cohasset, Massachusetts. The Homestay program continues to thrive in Cohasset, 21 years after its introduction.

In 1981 Barbara and Alex Spooner initiated a new American Field Service (AFS) chapter for Cohasset, with the help of high school French teacher George Fortin and residents Jane Goedecke, Diana Kornet, Elizabeth O'Connell, Joanne Rossi, Nancy Sandell, and Brenda and James Urmson. The program was named after the American Ambulance Field Service drivers in World War I who wanted to give young Americans a chance to experience life overseas. The first year two students, one from Finland and one from Japan, stayed with Cohasset families and attended Cohasset High School. The following year five Cohasset students went abroad, some for the summer and some for the year. Paul Dormitzer, who spent his senior year in France, found that the AFS program "is like no other experience you can have. It is a chance to live in another culture—not as a tourist but as an actual member of that culture. During this year I have been going to a regular French high school, which is quite different from school in the U.S., and living with a French family as if I was one of their children rather than a guest" (*Mariner*, 6/15/83). In 1987 a record number of 11 students departed Cohasset for a summer in places as diverse as Turkey, the Mariana Islands, Indonesia, Germany, Portugal, Greece, Belgium, Malaysia, Brazil, and Finland. Over time, however, fewer and fewer students applied for AFS. American families were traveling widely on their own, other exchange programs competed with AFS, and families found it difficult to reciprocate by providing year-long opportunities for foreign students here. Around 1996 the program came to an end in Cohasset.

In 1984 Cohasset adopted the French town of Souppes-sur-Loing as its sister community. The link to Souppes came by way of Thomas Churchill, a Cohasset resident (and former selectman) who had led theTwelfth Tank Battalion of General Patton's Third Armored Division in World War II. During the Allied march to Paris in 1944, Churchill was ordered to penetrate to the east of France through the small rural town of Souppes. The Germans had other thoughts, namely, sabotaging the town's 13 bridges. In what would have been a heinous war crime, they also herded the women and children of Souppes into a church and surrounded it with hay, intending to set it on fire, when Churchill stormed in with his battalion and liberated the town. Forty years later, in June 1984, Churchill and other World War II veterans went to France on a pilgrimage to celebrate the fortieth anniversary of D-Day. Recalling the liberation of Souppes, Churchill visited the town and placed a garland of flowers on its War Memorial Monument. Profoundly moved by his gesture, Henri Grampré, a former Resistance fighter (volunteer "soldier without uniform"), suggested to the mayor that Souppes and Cohasset create a sister-city association. In Cohasset a Cultural Exchange Committee, chaired by Judith S. Keim, was appointed to work out the details. In 1986 delegations from Souppes and Cohasset visited each other's towns and were honored at townwide receptions.

The following year 13 French students stayed with Cohasset families, and 7 Cohasset students went to Souppes, whose residents "accepted them eagerly and with affection." Among the Cohasset students were Julia and Sarah Atkinson, daughters of Rev. Edward Atkinson at First Parish. The visit gave Julia a new perspective: "We showed [our French hosts] a picture of the First Parish and they said to us, 'Oh, a modern church.' To them, a 200-year-old church is modern. Their cathedrals date back to the eleventh and twelfth centuries. And they're magnificent buildings. When they're filled with hundreds of people singing and the organ playing, it's so inspiring. It's not like anything I've ever heard" (*Mariner*, 6/18/87)

Major Churchill died in April 1987. He had had the good fortune to fulfill his dream of building a bridge between Cohasset and Souppes. In commemoration of their hero, the citizens of Souppes designed a memorial made from their quarries. They shipped the stone to Cohasset, where it was dedicated at a ceremony on November 15, 1987, and placed on Churchill's grave at Woodside Cemetery.

A STROLL THROUGH THE PAST

In 1983 the Historical Commission unveiled the Captains' Walk, a walk around the harbor covering 10 historic sites. Francis Hagerty, who wanted townspeople to love Cohasset Harbor as much as the Common, came up with the idea. The five year project was headed by Noel Ripley, coordinated by Patricia Murphy, and supported by donations from individuals and businesses. Its purpose was to highlight the places and events that were important during the town's Age of Sail, from about 1750 to 1895, when the Cove was Cohasset's center of commerce, fishing, and shipbuilding. "From its earliest days," wrote David Wadsworth,

> the town's harbor was known as Ship Cove and was the center of a thriving maritime industry. Earliest ship-building records show that vessels were being constructed at Ship Cove about 1700, or shortly after the area now called Cohasset saw its first farms and homesteads.
>
> By the mid-18th century Samuel Bates had estab-

lished the town's first known fishing business at the harbor and had built the stone wharf that still carries his name. Not long after, Capt. Abraham Tower and the Doane family followed suit at Border Street to establish fishing wharves as well as fleets of cod and mackerel fishing schooners . . .

By the early 1800s Cohasset's Ship Cove had become a beehive of maritime-related industry, and by mid-century briefly ranked among the leading ports of Massachusetts in the size of its mackerel catch. Just before the Civil War more than 50 large two-masted mackerel schooners called Cohasset their home port, and the town's mercantile seafarers traveled to ports in all corners of the globe. The small ports of Massachusetts and their fishing industries went into decline in the latter 1800s when the once-plentiful schools of mackerel disappeared from traditional fishing grounds, and Cohasset's last mackerel schooner sailed its final fishing voyage to the Gulf of St. Lawrence in early summer of 1894, never to return home.

The mackerel schooners and shipyards now have vanished, but Cohasset's Ship Cove retains many remembrances of the great Age of Sail, when the ocean was the town's frontier.

[Wadsworth, article in *Cohasset Mariner*, 7/20/89]

Another local historian, Gilbert Tower, born in Cohasset in 1885 (near the end of the Age of Sail), described the town's maritime past from a more intimate perspective: "For years the principal occupation for Cohasset boys was going to sea and becoming sea captains. In the woods up in back of the town there were oak trees. In the winter they would be cut down and transported on sleds, drawn by oxen, to the shipyard at the cove. One can imagine what is now the Cox estate [as of 1989 the Roy estate] covered with oak wood to be fashioned into frames to be covered with planks. Eventually the supply of available oak became exhausted and that spelled the end of ship building in seashore towns like Cohasset. After 1862 steamships developed and there was little use for sailing ships, which resulted in many retired sea captains in Cohasset" (*Mariner*, 4/23/81).

If you have a vivid imagination, you can picture what Cohasset was like during its Great Age of Sail. Plaques at the 10 stations along the Captains' Walk describe the activities that took place at each site, and three porcelainized maps, drawn by artist Robert Sweeney, give the visitor an overview of the area. The route extends from Government Island to what was then known as the New Shipyard (now the Roy estate). At some of the following sites you can still see remnants of the original structures.

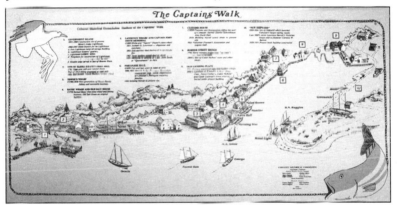

The Captains' Walk is a 10-station self-guided walking tour around the harbor. Plaques describe the historical activities that took place at each stop. Photo courtesy of Ralph Dormitzer

1. Government Island. Originally a part of Scituate, what is now Government Island was annexed by Cohasset in 1837. The federal government purchased this seven-acre peninsula from James Doane in the mid-1850s. It was used by the U.S. Lighthouse Service as a base of operations for building Minot's Ledge Lighthouse from 1855 to 1860. The two round templates for fitting the granite blocks of the 114-foot-high tower are prominently displayed at the site. Government Island served as a shore station reservation for the operation of the lighthouse until 1947, when the beacon became automated. A small brick shed used to store kerosene for the lighthouse lantern still exists on the property, as well as the former engineering office and one of the residences for the lightkeepers' families.

When the topmost portion of the lighthouse was renovated in 1987, the Historical Commission, under the leadership of Noel Ripley, constructed a replica of the tower's watch room using 42 of the original granite blocks that had fractured and were being replaced. Volunteers from town departments, supervised by Harold Litchfield, Anthony Sestito, and Peter Laugelle, reassembled them on Government Island to form the massive base of the watch room. The granite, donated by the U.S. Coast Guard, was transferred from the lighthouse to the site by helicopter. Many towns-

View of Government Island showing the old brick oil shed, the Sailing Club, and the 26-foot replica of the Minot's Light watchroom constructed after the Coast Guard repaired the light in 1987. Photo courtesy of Betty Maree

people and businesses contributed labor and funds to the reconstruction project, the principal benefactors being South Shore Playhouse Associates and Jane Cook. New England Steel Tank in Quincy fabricated the steel superstructure, with guidance from Joseph Lebherz of Scituate. Cohasset lobsterman and coppersmith Herbert L. Jason, assisted by his brother Kenneth, created the magnificent copper dome that crowns the beacon, as well as the brass railings around it. The replica also features the lighthouse's original rotating mechanism, the original fog bell, and a Fresnel lens used in the lighthouse for several years, which vandals had damaged in 1974. Hamilton Tewksbury obtained part of the original lens from the Coast Guard and, with the help of Nelson Pratt, reassembled the beacon. This historically significant project was largely completed by 1989.

2. Elisha Doane's Grist Mill. In 1792 Elisha Doane built his tidal grist mill over a natural sluice near Doane's (now Government) Island at the narrow passage to the Gulf River. During the War of 1812 the local militia encamped in this area. When the mill burned down in 1862, Tower Brothers used the site as their lumber wharf

and constructed a building, which still exists, to store lumber. Around 1900 the site became a boatyard.

The tumble-down marine railway building that sits on the site of Elisha Doane's tidal grist mill   Photo courtesy of Cohasset Mariner/Alan Chapman

3. Tower's Wharf. From 1790 to 1928 four generations of the Tower family conducted their fishing and mercantile business here. Built around 1790 by Abraham Tower (an "Indian" at the Boston Tea Party, as mentioned earlier, and a sergeant in the American Revolution), the stone wharf still lies there, under the present Atlantica Restaurant.

4. Bates's Wharf and Old Salt House. From 1750 to 1882 four generations of the Bates family conducted their fishing business from what is now Cohasset's oldest stone wharf, built around 1750 by shipowner Samuel Bates. The Old Salt House, now a restaurant of the same name, was used to store salt for fishpacking.

The Old Salt House, once used to store that commodity for fishpacking, sits on Bates Wharf. Photo courtesy of Barbara Conte

The refurbished Olde Salt House, now a restaurant associated with the neighboring Atlantica. Photo © Lynne Layman

266 *History of Cohasset*

5. Lawrence Wharf and Captain John Smith Memorial. Elisha and James ("Squire") Doane built this stone wharf in the early nineteenth century. In 1851 it was acquired by Josiah O. Lawrence, a shipowner and merchant who married the daughter of Squire Doane. The town purchased the wharf from the Lawrence family in 1907 for use as a public landing. On a granite boulder at the Town Landing is a bronze plaque erected in 1914 to commemorate Captain John Smith's landing in Quonahassit 300 years earlier.

6. Portuguese Hall. In 1896 the Minot's Ledge Portuguese Benevolent Association, a social organization for Cohasset's Portuguese seafaring families, purchased the site occupied by a fish and bait shop around 1870. Here the Benevolent Association installed their meeting place, known as "Portuguese Hall." In 1906 the building was moved from the head of the Cove to 84-86 Summer Street, where the Benevolent Association continued to function until 1941. The organization faded away, but the building still exists.

7. Customs House. The present American Legion Hall at 88 Summer Street once stood on the triangular piece of land nearby at the corner of Summer and Border streets. The building served as Cohasset's Customs and Immigration Office beginning around 1850, when Cohasset was an active fishing port and attracted many Portuguese families from the Azores. For several years the Harbor District School was on the second floor of the Customs House. Later the building became a meeting place for the Volunteer Veteran Firemen's Association and was known as Guild Hall, for the Guild Band that rehearsed there. It housed the *Konohasset*, the old hand-pumper used in firemen's musters. In 1916 the building was moved across the street to its present site. After World War I, it assumed its current function as the American Legion Hall for the George H. Mealy Post 118, named after a sergeant from Cohasset who lost his life in the war.

8. Cove, or Border Street, Bridge. In 1762 a wooden bridge was built over "ye creek" (James Brook) on the road to Scituate. Caleb Nichols's store and other shops lined the bridge in the 1800s. The bridge was later replaced by an underground culvert that now channels James Brook into the harbor.

9. **Old Landing Place.** Under Kimball's-by-the-Sea Motel lie three stone wharves. One was owned by clipper ship captain James Collier; the other two belonged to merchants Caleb Nichols and Caleb Lothrop. During the nineteenth century blacksmiths, carpenters, carriage makers, and shipbuilders operated their shops on "the old landing place." Kimball's Lobster Shop was built on one of the wharves in 1922, and in 1974 all three wharves were buried under the new motel.

10. **"New Shipyard."** Cohasset's largest sailing vessels were built between 1800 and 1866 at what was known as the New Shipyard, now the Roy estate. The history of this property was discussed earlier.

Another historical site that received attention during the 1980s was the small park on the northeast corner of Depot Court and Ripley Road. At this spot in the latter 1800s, Caleb Tilden had built a carriage shed and livery stable large enough for 50 horses. The facility included an elevator to lift carriages to the second floor for storage. In 1919, after the carriage business fell victim to the automobile, the Cohasset Improvement Association purchased the stable, razed it, and gave the land to the town for use as a public park.

Over the years the area was neglected. In 1987, however, a committee appointed to honor the Bicentennial of the U.S. Constitution, and chaired by David Wadsworth, gave the property a new life and a new name. The Highway and Tree and Park departments cleaned up the park, and the Community Garden Club and the Amateur Gardeners of Cohasset planted trees and shrubs. At a special ceremony on September 17, 1987, the Constitution Bicentennial Committee officially dedicated the lovely new greenspace as Constitution Park, fulfilling the Improvement Association's dream for the old Tilden property.

THE WITCHES OF EASTWICK

Celebrity fever swept over Cohasset with the filming of *The Witches of Eastwick* in the summer of 1986. Based on a novel of the same name by John Updike, the movie depicts the story of three modern-day witches whose lives are disrupted when Darryl Van Horne, a diabolical character, moves into their small town of Eastwick. He induces them to turn their mischievous but harmless witchcraft into black magic, resulting in the death of an Eastwickian. Although many Cohasset residents disapproved of the book's moral tone, the thrill of seeing famous movie stars — Jack Nicholson, Cher, Michelle Pfeiffer, and Susan Sarandon— stroll about town and pride in the choice of Cohasset as a location for the film compensated for any misgivings.

Cohasset was an ideal setting for the film. "I was attracted right from the start to Cohasset," said Samuel Mercer, the location manager. "We were looking for a charming, New England, picturesque town with an interesting architectural style. The town's shops and homes have the quintessential New England seaport look" (*Mariner*, 6/19/86). In fact, Cohasset was so perfect that the filmmakers feared it would not look real. To convince viewers, the film began with an aerial shot of the Common and village. The crew photographed local shopkeepers such as Sue Straley of Cards & Shards "to get an authentic feel for how Cohasset merchants dress." They painted wooden signs for downtown Cohasset that read "Eastwick Hardware Store," "Eastwick Central Market," and "Eastwick Historical Society." They set out planters filled with flowers and placed muntins on shop windows to make them look old-fashioned. Overnight Cohasset was transformed into the village of Eastwick. Straley recalls that out-of-town visitors would come into her store and ask for directions to Cohasset.

Crowds of townspeople and tourists gathered near the Common to see the movie stars and watch the filmmakers at work. Most of the time they waited around while the crew set up cameras and the actors went through numerous retakes. Occasionally there would be real excitement, such as when the witches caused hurricane-force winds to blow Darryl Van Horne (Jack Nicholson) down Main Street in front of the hardware store. James ("Benjie") Watson, operator of the store, noted that the film company had bought $1,500 worth of lawn furniture from him, only to wreck it all in the scene. According to Watson, "Jack Nicholson watched the stunt man being pulled by a cable attached to a truck, as if he were being blown down the street. He decided he would do it himself.

Cher and Michelle Pfeiffer relax between takes for The Witches of Eastwick. *Photo © Lynne Layman*

Eastwick *star Jack Nicholson in an informal mood near Sandy Beach.* *Photo © Lynne Layman*

Debris clutters South Main Street after the shooting of a windy sequence in Witches of Eastwick. *Note the track for the camera at right.* *Photo courtesy of A. J. Antoine*

He put on a leather vest, attached himself to the cable, and when the truck took off fast, he was 'blown' down the street along with the lawn furniture." Perhaps the biggest thrill for Cohasseters was seeing themselves in the film. Hundreds of local people were cast as "extras." Many appeared in scenes shot in the First Parish Meeting House, and about 20 Deer Hill School students became musicians in the Eastwick Elementary School Band. The filming of *Witches* left many indelible memories. Claire McDonough, a correspondent for the *Cohasset Mariner* (8/21/86), tells the story of one woman who will never forget that event:

> A Scituate resident sought relief from the heat last week by buying an ice cream cone in a Cohasset establishment. She gave her order and took a $10-bill out of her purse. As the waitress handed her her change, our heroine suddenly realized that the man standing next to her was actor Jack Nicholson.
>
> Overcome by awe and confusion, she felt her face redden and realized that her tongue was not functioning properly. She snatched up her change and ran out to her car, mentally planning phone calls to all her friends. She had, after all, stood next to a movie star.
>
> As she opened her car door, it occurred to her that she was holding her change but no ice cream. By this time she was close to incoherent, but she bravely reentered the store and confronted her waitress.
>
> "I have my change," she stated, "but I don't have my ice cream. You didn't give me my ice cream cone."
>
> Nicholson turned and touched her arm sympathetically. "Yes she did," the actor said helpfully. "It's in your purse."

Wayne Sawchuk, president of the Cohasset Chamber of Commerce, summed up the experience for many Cohasset residents: "It's been the highlight of our summer—seeing major movie stars up close. It's been a great experience to see just how much goes into making a movie. It's an incredible situation, to watch hours of rehearsing and shooting that will probably end up to be a minute in the movie" (*Mariner,* 8/21/86). When it was over, Warner Brothers gave the town $25,000 for permitting them to use town streets and property. They donated another $25,000 to First Parish for the three days of filming that took place in the Meeting House. Although the decision to allow the filming had been controversial, First Parish put the donation to good use. It funded the creation of a two-room homeless shelter on the second floor of the Parish House in 1989. Over the next 10 years the shelter would provide temporary housing for 17 people in crisis.

The evolution of Cohasset from a semirural village to an upscale bedroom community was essentially complete by the end of the 1980s. "The whole ambiance of the town has changed," reflected David Wadsworth in an interview with the *Cohasset Mariner* (5/29/86). "When I was young, it was still populated . . . by old families, the old residents of the town, many of whom are gone. The names have all but disappeared now . . . You tended to see the same faces every day on the street at the center, and you tended to know most of the people. You may have been related to many of them. And that is perhaps the biggest single change. It's a much prettier town now, because I don't think there was as much of an emphasis on attractiveness, preservation, and appearance. It was still a working town, where there were farms. I remember waking up and being able to hear the roosters crowing up at the dairy farm on North Main Street." Former selectman Arthur Clark put it more bluntly: "It's a Yuppie town now, I guess. The natives are a minority now."

Cohasset was indeed a more beautiful town than before. The old neighborhoods with dilapidated homes had been gentrified. By the end of the decade many of the houses had been remodeled or at least repainted, and new residential developments enhanced the outskirts of town. The neighborhoods were losing their distinctive character. With the closing of the Beechwood and North Cohasset fire stations, two of the last remaining village landmarks disappeared. The trend toward homogeneity and beautification would continue throughout the nineties.

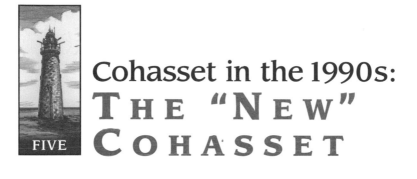

Cohasset in the 1990s:
THE "NEW"
FIVE # COHASSET

T his final chapter brings us up to date on Cohasset's history. We are much too close to the 1990s, however, to offer a valid historical perspective. What seems impor tant to us now may be insignificant in the long run Readers will have to judge for themselves the implications of the following account.

In August 1991 movie star Goldie Hawn stepped off a P&B bus at the Common and gazed in wonder at the picture perfect scene. Cohasset ("Dobbs Mill") was once again the setting for a film. The 22-second seg- ment of *Housesitter*, starring Hawn and comedian Steve Martin, required fall colors,

Cohasset Hardware in its Housesitter *persona for the 1991 film starring Steve Martin and Goldie Hawn.* Photo courtesy of A. J. Antoine

so the crew spray-painted the green foliage on the Common a more appropriate red, orange, and yellow. Over the next 10 years, civic groups and local businesses would add more permanent touches to the town. By the late 1990s Cohasset would be viewed as a small, quiet town with a lovely New England common surrounded by

273

historic buildings; a quaint village center with unique shops and small restaurants; a beautiful harbor; and a winding, rocky coastline bordered by elegant homes. Featured on the cover of *The Most Beautiful Villages of New England* (1997), Cohasset had become the quintessential New England town.

Many feel that Cohasset has not changed much over their lifetimes. William Park, who graduated from Cohasset High School in 1965, returned here in 1990 after an absence of 20 years and found it "remarkably the same town." In Cohasset people say hello to each other, and merchants in the stores recognize you.

"The more things change..."

The lobster fleet still plies Cohasset Harbor. Photo © Lynne Layman

Lobsterman Bill Stone on his boat, the Ida Jean, in 1996. Photo courtesy of Bill Stone

B. J. and Stephen Andrus take a friend for a ride along the coast in 1993. Pulling the wagon are their Morgan horses, Sebastian and Huntington. Photo courtesy of Patriot Ledger/Greg Derr

Skaters on the Common Pond, January 1, 2000.   Photo courtesy of Ann Pompeo

Little Leaguers wait for their turn at bat.   Photo © Lynne Layman

Steve Wigmore, commander of the American Legion Post, raising the flag at Veterans Park at the end of the 2000 Memorial Day observances. Father John Mulvehill looks on.   Photo © Lynne Layman

The Old Goats picnic in July 1998. Left to right rear: Lou Eaton, Bob Thompson, John O'Toole, Paul Donovan, John Coe, Charlie Ford, Steve Leighton, Lot Bates, Dave Whipple, Joe Wood, Russ Lennon, Jim Mullen; middle: Laurie MacLure, Ted Guild, Austin Ahearn, Ed Long, Murray Campbell, Dave Pottenger, Doug Peck, Ozzie Ingram, Jack Wilson; front: George Barunas, Jeff Howe, John Campbell, Dick Tousley, Ed Lincoln, John Mullett, Tom Williams.   Photo courtesy of Austin Ahearn

It is still heartwarming, he says, to see people around that he knew in high school. Another Cohasset High graduate, Karen Golden, moved to New York in 1974 and lived in a building with 3,600 other residents, about the same population as the entire town of Cohasset in 1950. When she came back in 1997, she was "thrilled to find that Cohasset is still a small town, where people know each other," a place with Little League parades and a central common.

Yet for oldtimers like Charlie Butman, Jr., a native of Cohasset who made his living as a lobster fisherman and woodworker, the town was very different from the days of his youth. Charlie used to know just about everybody. But when he attended his granddaughter's graduation in June 1999, he did not recognize anyone in

Cartoon courtesy of James Hamilton and Cohasset Mariner

the audience other than his own family. Older neighborhoods looked different now, and large new houses with beautifully land-scaped grounds were being built in areas he thought would never be developed.

In the 1950s strangers used to think that Cohasset was a town on the Cape. Now everyone seemed to know about our "Gold Coast" with its million-dollar homes. Mansions were also appearing on Lamberts Lane, once a neighborhood of modest homes, and on Cedar Street, which used to be known as the road to the dump. Even Cohasset village was going upscale, with the transformation of the Red Lion Inn into a first-class resort hotel. "It's beautiful," said Charlie," but it just isn't Cohasset." It was not the Cohasset Charlie knew back in the 1950s, when the village was where you shopped before Route 3A was developed, and people dropped in on their neighbors instead of watching TV in the evening. But to younger people, or to those who had lived elsewhere for a number of years, Cohasset in the 1990s was still a small, friendly town.

The graphs on page 278 show us how much the town has actually changed. Cohasset has doubled in size over the past half century. There are twice the number of people and more than twice the number of homes today than in 1950. The number of children enrolled in the Cohasset schools has also doubled. Most of this growth, however, occurred in the fifties and sixties. From 1970 to 2000 the population remained nearly constant, and school enrollment fell by about one-third. From a 50-year perspective, Cohasset is now a much larger town. But to those who grew up here in the mid-sixties and later, it is about the same size.

The most dramatic change has been the rise in the level of wealth. The median family income in Cohasset was 26 percent below the state median in 1950. In 1998 it was 68 percent above the median. In constant dollars family income is now six times higher than it was in 1950. The cost of housing has also soared. Cohasset now has the most expensive housing on

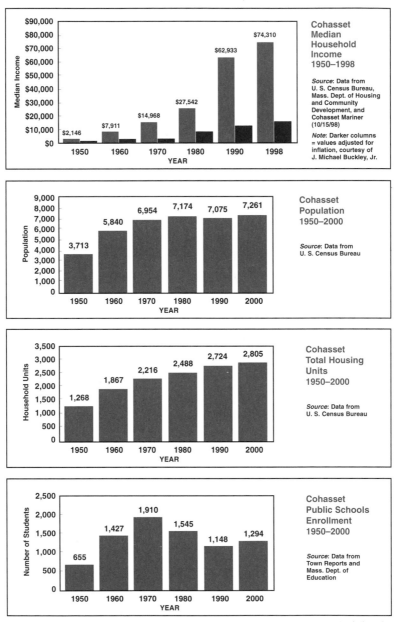

Cohasset
Median
Household
Income
1950–1998

Source: Data from
U. S. Census Bureau,
Mass. Dept. of Housing
and Community
Development, and
Cohasset Mariner
(10/15/98)

Note: Darker columns
= values adjusted for
inflation, courtesy of
J. Michael Buckley, Jr.

Cohasset
Population
1950–2000

Source: Data from
U. S. Census Bureau

Cohasset
Total Housing
Units
1950–2000

Source: Data from
U. S. Census Bureau

Cohasset
Public Schools
Enrollment
1950–2000

Source: Data from
Town Reports and
Mass. Dept. of
Education

Graphs by author

the South Shore. In just five years, from 1996 to 2001, the median sales price for a single-family home rose 109 percent, from $263,500 to $550,000. (Median price for the South Shore, $307,300.) To buy a typical home in Cohasset, and to pay the property taxes, it helps to be wealthy.

The town undertook an unprecedented number of large, expensive capital projects in the nineties. They included the construction of a new elementary school and plans to renovate and expand two other schools; the upgrading and expansion of athletic fields; the construction of a new Town Garage; the expansion of town sewerage; and the creation of a new park near the public landing on Parker Avenue. These projects reflected the wishes of a younger, more affluent population, and they would be costly to fund. As former town accountant Bill Signorelli points out, the town's real debt surged from $3.8 million in fiscal year 1982 to $47 million in FY 1999. The net result is that property taxes are rising far more rapidly than inflation and will continue to do so well into the future. Regrettably, the tax increases have made it difficult for moderate-income residents and the older, retired generation to remain here.

Besides building new facilities, the town also addressed several long-standing issues, aided in part by a new, more action-oriented town manager form of government. After a series of floods culminating in October 1996, when mail had to be ferried across Ripley Road to the post office, the town finally embarked on a James Brook flood control program, using funds from a federal emergency grant. (It was a bad decade for storms: in 1991 the Halloween, or No-Name, Storm, known more famously as the Perfect Storm, washed five cars off Atlantic Avenue and cost Cohasset fishermen $1.5 million in ruined gear; 1996 saw a record snowfall of more than 100 inches; and the April Fool's Day Storm of 1997 was second only to the Blizzard of '78 in the amount of snow that fell on the town.) The Water Department began an extensive upgrade of the town's antiquated water distribution system; Cohasset

Heights landfill was closed at last; and the town's 40-year struggle over sewerage came to an end. A debate over the restoration of Greenbush commuter rail service concluded with the expectation that the railroad would return to Cohasset.

Ben Bixby, 12, enjoys his fort, built with some of the record-breaking snowfall of winter 1995-96. Photo courtesy of Patriot Ledger/Tom Tajima

Surf from the No-Name Storm washes over Jerusalem Road. The October 30, 1991, storm was later immortalized in print and film as The Perfect Storm. Photo courtesy of Carol Riley

A cabin cruiser pulled from its moorings in Cohasset Harbor during the No-Name Storm of October 30, 1991. Photo courtesy of Patriot Ledger/Tom Tajima

Ted Goff, Stephen Kovach, and Brian Donovan paddle past a fleet of post office trucks swamped by the October 1996 flood. Photo courtesy of Patriot Ledger/Fred Field

As the town improved its physical infrastructure, it also participated in a massive modernization of its communication infrastructure, financed by private capital, with cell phone towers, a
cable network, connection to the Internet "information highway,"
and choice among long-distance carriers. The telecommunication
revolution of the 1980s and 1990s was remarkably liberating. In the
1950s you thought twice before making long-distance phone calls
because they were expensive. Financial records were scribed by
hand into bound books, and letters printed on typewriters, with the
use of carbon paper for copies. The new communication is cheap
and instantaneous. One can make calls from anywhere on cell
phones, page people on electronic beepers, obtain information
instantly via the Internet, and send information virtually free of
charge by fax and electronic mail. We can attend Board of
Selectmen meetings, town meetings, and special events in spirit, if
not in person, on cable television, introduced to Cohasset in 1984.

For a 10-
year period,
from 1987 to
1997, Cohasset
had its own
award-win-
ning talk show
on cable TV.
Host Wigmore
A. Pierson kept
us informed on
local, regional,
and national
issues through
his entertain-

*Former Governor William Weld happily accepts a T-shirt from
talk-show host Wigmore Pierson. Weld was a guest on the cable
television show during the primary campaign.* Photo © Fred Robertson

ing interviews with experts and officials. In January 1991 he presented a two-hour special on an impending war in the Persian Gulf.
The show was dedicated to the men and women of Massachusetts,
including several Cohasset citizens, who formed part of the post-
Vietnam all-volunteer American military forces. The popular sup-

port for this war stood in marked contrast to the bitter protests of the Vietnam War era.

A HEROES' WELCOME

On August 2, 1990, Iraq invaded the tiny oil-rich country of Kuwait on its southeastern border. This act of war threatened the entire Persian Gulf region, and in particular Saudi Arabia, immediately to the south of Kuwait. Unless checked, Iraq potentially could take control of the entire oil-producing region and cut off oil supplies to the United States and Europe. The United Nations Security Council condemned the invasion and demanded the immediate withdrawal of Iraqi troops. They were given until January 15, 1991, to comply or be forcibly expelled. In the meantime an overwhelming force of nearly 540,000 troops from the United States and 270,000 from other U.N. countries was deployed to the Persian Gulf.

The deadline passed, with half a million Iraqi soldiers still occupying Kuwait. On January 16 the United States and its U.N. allies launched a massive assault on Iraq. Cruise missiles and laser-guided bombs blasted command-and-control centers in Baghdad and established air superiority for the allies. After 37 days of air strikes, the ground action began. On February 24 several divisions of the allied forces engaged Iraqi front-line troops in Kuwait, while fast mobile units raced north through Iraq to flank the enemy on the west. The land war, called Operation Desert Storm, was over in four days. On February 27, 1991, Saddam Hussein, the president of Iraq, agreed to a cease-fire. The occupying forces evacuated Kuwait, and in the spring and summer of 1991 American soldiers came home to a heroes' welcome.

Unlike the Vietnam War, this conflict was short and ended decisively. Antiwar protests never had time to materialize, and American casualties were low: 383 dead, 458 wounded. The allied forces suffered a total of 510 casualties. An estimated tens of thousands of Iraqi soldiers were killed. All 18 Cohasset volunteers who served in the war came home safely. As listed in the 1991 Town Report, Cohasset's Operation Desert Storm Honor Roll includes three brothers: Pfc Brian E. Curran, Cpl. Daniel W. Curran, and Pfc

Timothy M. Curran, as well as Sgt. David D. Cuddahy, Jr., Pfc Glenn E. Dukes, Lt. Col. Edward M. Guild, Jr., Pfc Prescott Hobson, Sgt. Lawrence Hoogeveen, Hm 1 Arthur B. Howe, A l c Garrett A. Hunt, Sgt. Robert M. Kierce, Sgt. Scott A. Muir, Cpl. Gary Parziale, Ad2 Gordon Ricketts, S. Sgt. James J. Smith, Comdr. Daniel J. Sullivan, M.D., S. Sgt. Joseph Tolini, and Capt. Stephen Winn.

To show support for our troops, Deer Hill School students wrote to Cohasset servicemen. Among the letters was this admiring tribute from a sixth grader, published in the *Mariner* (3/7/91):

> Dear Sgt. Lawrence Hoogeveen,
>
> My name is Ely Kahn and I'm twelve years old. I'm in Mr. Shultz's sixth grade homeroom.
>
> I wanted to say to you congratulations for defeating the Iraqi army and liberating Kuwait. You are very brave to be defending Kuwait and putting your life in danger to make sure justice prevails.
>
> I am proud to know that ruthless leaders will think twice before invading a country because of you and the other men and women of 28 nations.
>
> Come home safe and sound!
>
> > Best wishes,
> >
> > Ely Kahn

In the words of Lt. Col. Edward Graham, Jr., the guest speaker at Cohasset's 1991 Memorial Day celebration, "When the war was over, Saddam's military [the fourth largest army in the world] was no longer a threat to the world, and America had purged itself of the ghost of Vietnam" *(Mariner, 5/30/91)*.

By the end of 1991 America and other democratic nations were also free from the threat of communist aggression. Communist governments in Eastern Europe had collapsed in 1989 and the Berlin Wall that divided East from West Germany was torn down. In October 1990 the two Germanies were reunited. Then in December 1991 Soviet president Mikhail Gorbachev resigned and the Soviet Union dissolved into 15 independent noncommunist republics. The cold war that had lasted nearly half a century was finally over.

At home, the conflict in the Persian Gulf was accompanied by rising oil prices, which, coupled with tight credit, tipped the U.S. economy into recession. President George H. W. Bush lost his bid for a second term, and Democratic candidate William Clinton was elected president in 1992. The economy boomed during his first term, even though (or perhaps because) he signed one of the largest tax increases in U.S. history. In 1996 he was elected to a second term. Two years later he was impeached, and later acquitted, by the Congress on charges of perjury and obstruction of justice related to his affairs with a White House intern and other women. Despite the impeachment, during his administrations the country enjoyed the longest economic expansion in its history.

VILLAGE BEAUTIFICATION

Local enterprises followed the national business cycle, struggling in the early 1990s and prospering as the decade closed. In cooperation with merchants, Cohasset citizens mounted grass-roots efforts to improve the appearance of the village and attract more people to its restaurants and shops.

Village Renaissance

The Village Renaissance was a response to the decline of small downtown businesses, a trend that had begun decades earlier. It was conceived by Philip H. Smith, owner of Designers' Creations on Ripley Road, and sponsored by the Village and Harbor Association, an organization of merchants formed in 1974. Smith declared 1990 to be the year of Cohasset's Village Renaissance, a time when merchants and townspeople would work together to beautify and invigorate the village. Two residents of the town, Elizabeth Christoffel and I, volunteered to coordinate the effort. We remembered better years for the village. Now we saw tattered awnings, peeling paint, dirty sidewalks, and empty storefronts. We wanted to help, and asked for suggestions from shopkeepers and residents. Jane White, who ran a needlework shop, asked us to renovate the weed-infested walkway between Cards & Shards and the Texaco station; Philip Smith thought we should create a pocket park in the vacant lot once occupied by Delory's Drugstore; and Noel Ripley came up with the most creative idea of all: replicate the nineteenth-century pump that once stood in the heart of the village.

The Village Renaissance Committee, consisting of Dormitzer, chairman, Christoffel, and longtime Cohasset resident Ann Whelan, took on those three projects. In the fall of 1990 the selectmen approved our plan to install a working replica of the old town pump at the corner of Main and Elm streets. Many members of the

Replica of the old town pump, installed in spring 1991. This was the beginning of beautification efforts by the Village Renaissance Committee. Photo courtesy of Jacqueline Dormitzer

Cohasset community pitched in. Local architect Benjamin Blake drew the initial design for the pump based on a historical photograph. Architect and urban designer James Sandell created the final architectural drawings and designed a brick and cobblestone site for the pump. Ralph Dormitzer produced the engineering drawings and designed the mechanism that made the pump work. And Charlie Butman crafted the pump enclosure from cypress, using a custom lathe he assembled from parts in his workshop. "I never throw anything away," he said, living by the old Yankee adage, Use it up, wear it out, make it do, or do without.

As soon as we publicized our plans, resident Phyllis Leslie came forward with a generous contribution. We also received donations from the Cohasset Police Department, local businesses, and individuals. The pump slowly took shape in Charlie Butman's barn while town employees and others prepared the site. Norfolk County engineer Wayne Simpson surveyed and supervised the site-work. Highway Department head Harold Litchfield and his assistants Anthony and Carl Sestito excavated and prepared the site and set the granite curbing. Kevin and Raymond Sargent laid the bricks and cobblestone, and Robert Leonard, Jr., connected the plumbing to the water system. In the spring of 1991 the pump was installed on the site in the center of a large, round granite slab. A section of a granite steeple salvaged from a church in New Hampshire served as a basin to drain the water. Tina Watson, who ran the hardware store next to the pump, planted flowers in two cast-stone planters. What had once been a nondescript patch of bare asphalt was now the village centerpiece. The pump was dedicated in May 1991, and Noel Ripley's pony Cimmaron was the first to drink from it. Since then, countless children and adults have pumped the handle just for fun or to refresh themselves on a hot summer day.

The James Brook Walkway project, named for the infamous (over-flowing) brook that runs under the village through a culvert, involved many of the same people. Phyllis Leslie was again the major donor, and Jim Sandell the designer. The Highway Department tore up the old, uneven, cracked asphalt, Wayne Simpson graded the underlayment, and the highway workers laid smooth, new pavement. Then they installed a stockade fence and neat wooden posts along one side of the path from the town parking lot to Main Street. The Tree and Park Department pulled out the bamboo grass that had invaded the other side and planted a privet

Designer James Sandell cuts the ribbon to open the James Brook Walkway in 1993. This was another project of the Village Renaissance Committee. Photo courtesy of Hubert van der Lugt

hedge, and Georgine Butman and her Girl Scout troop planted flowers. The finishing touches were two handsome wooden signs carved by signmaker David Hassan and three tall cast-iron street lamps provided at cost by Mark and Zeena Forent. In June 1993 Jim Sandell cut the ribbon to the new James Brook Walkway, now a safe and attractive path from the parking lot to the village.

Our final task was to convert a derelict vacant lot into a small park. It was bordered on the north by a large brick wall that loomed above weeds and dirt in the empty space between Tedeschi's Food Shop and the old Central Market (French Memories Bakery as of 1992). In 1990 town resident Virginia Ferenz volunteered to plant flowers in the lot, and the Village Renaissance Committee asked high school art teacher Colleen Lucas to create a mural for the wall. Lucas designed the first of four scenes, a beautiful "Public Garden," for her students to paint. In 1995 Cohasset students painted three more murals, depicting different seasons, and transformed the wall into an art gallery. Hubert van der Lugt, president of Hub Shipping on Elm Street, directed the landscaping of the lot based on a design by Jim Sandell. A winding gravel path, ornamental trees, a wooden bench, and granite seats completed the project. The new greenspace, dedicated in September 1995, was dubbed Ship Cove Park after the historic name for Elm Street, Ship Cove Lane. Since then, the Village Renaissance Committee has continued its beautification campaign by planting flowerboxes every spring outside shops on Main Street.

Farmers' Market

In 1996 the Cohasset Chamber of Commerce launched yet another "village revitalization" effort. Chamber vice president Dean Rizzo, a newcomer to Cohasset, invited business owners and interested citizens to a brainstorming session. At the meeting Village Renaissance member Anna Abbruzzese suggested hosting a weekly Farmers' Market to draw people to the village. Subsequently Abbruzzese, Rizzo, and Rizzo's wife, Barbara Anglin, organized what has become one of the most successful farmers' markets on the South Shore. Every Thursday afternoon during the summer, vendors sell fresh-picked herbs, flowers, fruits, vegetables, and home-baked breads on the Common. Most of the produce comes from local New England farms, two of them in Cohasset. Alix White and her husband, David Bigley, sell fresh raspberries picked from their White Cedar Farm on Jerusalem Road. From neighboring Holly Hill Farm, Frank and Jean White bring in a bountiful harvest of tomatoes, lettuces, potatoes, broccoli, and many other fresh vegetables. While mothers shop, children can have their faces painted, ride ponies, listen to storytellers, and sing along with musicians. The Farmers' Market is a new tradition that recalls Cohasset's rural past and old-fashioned neighborliness.

Tina Watson, right, mans the soup pot at the Farmers' Market. Photo © Lynne Layman

Cohasset Revitalization Corporation

Rizzo's efforts to revitalize Cohasset village mushroomed into a town-appointed task force. The group focused on obtaining state grants for large-scale projects such as widening the sidewalk below St. Stephen's Church, creating a "harborwalk" around the harbor, burying utility lines, and installing new sidewalks and streetlights in the village. Their proposals gained momentum in 2000 when resident Peter Roy, owner of Kimball's-by-the-Sea Motor Inn and Atlantica Restaurant, and Gerd Ordelheide, owner of the Red Lion Inn, funded the development of engineering designs and plans for village and harbor improvements. To carry the projects forward, Roy and Ordelheide incorporated the Cohasset Revitalization Corporation (CRC) and invited the support of other contributors. Roy hired Dean Rizzo as executive director and the Cecil Group, an urban landscape architectural firm, as design consultants. Rizzo and the Cecil Group held numerous public meetings to discuss the plans. At first many townspeople resisted what they thought were efforts to bring in tourists by "Nantucketizing" Cohasset. After the plans were scaled down, however, the CRC won wider public acceptance. Their proposals, if implemented, will turn worn pavement and curbless, asphalt sidewalks into a stylish new village "streetscape."

Loss and Restoration

Beautification efforts, however, could not save Colonial Pharmacy, a small, independent drugstore with a reputation for personalized service and quality merchandise. Ralph Harrison had owned it since 1959. Originally located on the corner of South Main Street and Depot Court, where Call's Drugstore used to be, it now occupied the site of the old A&P. His business prospered for 34 years. Then in March 1993 Bay State Health Care, the insurance provider for town employees, required clients to fill their prescriptions at high-volume chain stores such as CVS (on Route 3A) and Osco. As a result Harrison lost nearly a third of his business. Six months later he closed his doors, and the village was left with another empty storefront. Subsequently it was occupied by a fitness center, and then by Coldwell Banker Hunneman Realtors, which expanded their offices from next door.

As the economy improved, other downtown businesses picked up, sparking a village renewal. Some of the oldest buildings underwent striking transformations. The Cohasset Savings Bank building on Elm Street, an elegant brick structure designed by local architect Edward Nichols, had been a town landmark since 1898.

The bank converted from private to public ownership in the 1980s and was nearly swallowed up in a merger with regional giant Shawmut National Corporation in 1994, but a year later it was sold to Hingham Institution for Savings and again became a community bank. The directors of Hingham Institution ordered the restoration of many of its original Classical Revival features. They exposed the old nineteenth-century ceiling, with its beautiful, ornate decorative plaster molding; removed the concrete steps at the front entry and replaced them with granite replicas of the originals; and restored the hand-carved portico above the columns on the facade. "The bank has never looked better," said town historian David Wadsworth, a descendant of the architect, Edward Nichols.

In 1997 Cohasset resident Gerd Ordelheide bought the village's most historic building, the Red Lion Inn on South Main Street. Two years later, after a long permitting process, he began a $4-million renovation of the badly deteriorated hostelry. Although making the building much larger and grander than before, Ordelheide preserved or replicated many of its original features. As reporter Molly Hochkeppel observed, "Anyone who had not seen the Red Lion Inn's renovation and expansion over the past year would glance around the interior, with its low-

The historic Red Lion Inn as it appeared in the 1970s. The inn has been a hostelry for nearly 300 years. Photo courtesy of Ann Pompeo

The renovated and expanded Red Lion, the vision of owner Gerd Ordelheide in the late 1990s. Photo © Lynne Layman

beamed ceilings, wide-plank floors, and fat candles burning in iron
wall sconces, and swear that everything must be as it was when the
original building went up in 1704. Some of it is" (*Patriot Ledger*,
4/21/00). Ordelheide reused much of the original wood and some
of the ovens, including the Dutch brick oven that was used both to
heat the building and to cook. With its elegant rooms, gourmet dining, French bakery, and blues club, the Red Lion Inn has become an
icon of the new Cohasset while preserving the best of the old.

The oldest municipal building
in Cohasset was also restored. The
Independence Building, near the corner
of South Main and Elm streets, was first
a fire station, then a police station, and
then a gown museum. It was converted
to a teen center in 1995, several years
after The Depot on Depot Court failed to
hold the interest of Cohasset youth.
When the new center did not succeed
either, the building was abandoned.
Considered a liability and slated to be
demolished, this historic structure was

The Independence Building
in its latest incarnation as a
flower shop. Photo © Lynne Layman

saved by Cohasset resident Thomas
Koncius, who bought it in June 2000. He
exposed the original brick facade and
renovated the interior. It is now the
attractive home of Cohasset Greenery, a
flower shop and antiques showroom.
The two jail cells that survive from its
days as a police station are still on the
first floor. Meanwhile, a larger and more
appealing teen center, called The Garage,

Tony Bramblett and Jodi
Butman, both 17 in 1998 when
they spearheaded the effort to
transform the old highway
garage into a teen center. Photo
courtesy of Patriot Ledger/Fred Field

has been created from the former Highway Department garage in
the town parking lot, behind the Red Lion Inn.

Cohasset village is a blend of the old and the new. Its ambiance
is notably more upscale today than in the 1950s. Then you had coffee and doughnuts at Joe's Coffee Shop; now you order a cappucci-

no and croissants at French Memories or Chez Jean-Claude. The "woodies" and old sedans at the curb have been replaced by luxury cars and sport utility vehicles. Youths in "hip-hop" clothing on skateboards and joggers in spandex shorts, pushing infants in three-wheeled strollers, pass you by. Yet a few things remain the same. You can still find vintage faucet repair parts at Cohasset Hardware and dine at the Red Lion Inn amid hand-hewn beams and old Dutch ovens.

HARBOR RENEWAL

Francis Hagerty used to wonder why Cohasset did not love its harbor as much as its Common. Government Island and other harbor sites were some of the town's most underappreciated resources. In the 1990s that changed with the implementation of several

Atlantica Restaurant, formerly Hugo's, and the Olde Salt House, formerly the Old Salt House.

The refurbished patio in back of Kimball's-by-the-Sea. Photos © Lynne Layman

renewal projects. Cohasset Harbor is one of the few undeveloped, sheltered harbors on the East Coast, crowded with boats mostly secured at moorings instead of slips. The vibrant commercial activity of earlier decades had been indifferently sustained by the businesses remaining along the waterfront—Kimball's Motel, the Old Salt House, the Chart House Restaurant, and Mill River Marine.

But Peter Roy saw the possibilities and acquired each of the properties. Kimball's received a face-lift, the Old Salt House was restored and expanded with an outdoor patio, and the Chart House Restaurant (formerly Hugo's) was renamed Atlantica, renovated, and taken upscale. Roy also plans to

"Motif #2," Mill River Marine Railway, in a picturesque but dilapidated state in 2000. Photo © Lynne Layman

restore "Motif #2," the building at Mill River Marine (second only to Rockport's Motif #1 in artistic appeal), rebuild the railway, and enhance the complex with attractive condominiums on the wharf

Lightkeepers' Residence

Not far from Atlantica, across the Mill River Bridge, is Government Island, a town-owned property where the Sailing Club, the harbormaster's office, and the Minot's Light watch room replica are located. It is also the site of the Minot Lightkeepers' Residence, an inspiring example of what community teamwork can accomplish. The historic duplex building on the hill, dating back to the mid-1800s, had housed the assistant keepers of Minot's Ledge Lighthouse and their families. Robert Thompson, son of former lightkeeper Winfield Scott Thompson, recalls that at dusk his father would point the beacon toward the house and flash the famous 1-4 3, "I Love You," signal to his family. When the beacon became automated in 1947, the federal government sold the residence and the land, including a second residence, used by the head lighthouse keeper, back to the town. Cohasset citizen Ralph Scripture is credited with having had the vision, at a 1946 town meeting, to recommend the purchase of Government Island for the enjoyment of town residents.

After World War II the buildings were used as temporary housing for returning veterans. The head lighthouse keeper's residence, however, was so dilapidated that the town ultimately tore it down. For many years the other house was rented out at bargain rates to Cohasset families. In 1991, with the economy in recession, the town stopped maintaining it. Some officials wanted to demolish the building, but Joseph R. McElroy, who had moved to Cohasset just six years earlier, and Herbert R. Towle, founder of the Cohasset Sailing Club, proposed renovating it for the benefit of the public. At that time there was a forbidding aspect to the residence, and the site felt like private property. Yet it commanded a sweeping view of the harbor and the Atlantic beyond, and just behind the building was Beacon Rock, a granite pinnacle offering a beautiful panorama of the harbor. Why not open the site to the community and provide a hall for meetings, receptions, and parties? said McElroy and Towle.

The selectmen agreed, and a corporation was formed to work on the project. McElroy believed that since the community would benefit, the community should be involved, and he expanded the corporation from 17 members to 30. George Kovach was named chairman of the Architecture and Construction Committee. His group donated thousands of hours of labor to the restoration of the house. Richard T. Grinnell, an architect, provided detailed drawings based on sketches contributed by the Boston Architectural Center. Ira Stoughton, Jr., served as clerk of the works with Herb Towle. He contracted with the Braintree Alternative Center (part of the Norfolk County Prison system) to use low-risk inmates for the heavy demolition work on the interior of the building. Other key members of the committee were William Higgins, Patrick Plante, and Steven Weber.

After overcoming many obstacles, financial and political, McElroy and his group completed the job. The final stage was to beautify the grounds. Barbara L. Dillon enlisted the support of the garden clubs. The Community Garden Club landscaped the front of the house and donated a stone wall. They also planted the oval at the Edwin A. Young Parking Lot, named in memory of a Cohasset civil engineer who had devoted many years to the improvement of the harbor and Government Island. The Cohasset Garden Club landscaped the back and side of the house, and the Amateur Gardeners of Cohasset planted wildflowers. "In all my years in Cohasset," said Dillon, "I've never before seen the community come together and work so hard on a project." Newcomers and natives, town officials and department heads, businesses and organizations, all worked together.

Ribbon cutting for the Minot Lightkeepers' Residence, May 15, 1994. Members of the Cohasset Lightkeepers' Corporation—rear: Betty Maree, Bill Higgins, Ira Stoughton, Bob Silvia, Paul Pattison, Arne Gjesteby, Arthur Lehr, Jr., Herb Towle, Bob Martin; middle: Nancy Snowdale, Merle Brown, Brian Noonan, Richard Barrow, Wayne Sawchuk, Gerard Keating, Barbara Dillon, Kit Bryant, Patrick Plante; front: Joe McElroy, George Kovach, Steve Weber, Michelle Buckley, Glenn Pratt. Photo courtesy of Richard Barrow

A cookout on the grounds of the renovated Lightkeepers' Residence after the 2000 Memorial Day parade. Photo © Lynne Layman

The community also contributed funds. "The money demands of the project were insatiable," says McElroy. With major contributions from Jane Cook, the Cohasset Conservation Trust, and the Rotary Club, supplemented by donations from hundreds of individuals, the Lightkeepers' Corporation raised about $250,000. Polly Logan assisted with fund-raising brunches at her house and at the home of Jane and Peter Goedecke. "Who could say no to Joe?" she said.

The grand opening of the beautifully renovated Minot

Lightkeepers' Residence was held on May 15, 1994, three years
after the project began. More than 300 people gathered to celebrate
at the residence's new Bancroft Hall, complete with chandeliers and
an inlaid oak compass rose created by Patrick Plante. Among the
speakers was special guest Jane Bancroft Cook, who shared her joy
with the crowd. "I feel fortunate to have been born in Cohasset," she
said. "I've always loved it." She had been born in Cohasset on that
very day 82 years ago, in 1912. As told by her friend Louise G.
Littlehale, Jane was lucky to survive. She weighed only three
pounds at birth. Her incubator was a warming oven near the family's big stove. The improvisation worked, and Jane and her sister
Jessie grew up to be Cohasset's most generous benefactors. Among
the projects that Jane supported were not only the Lightkeepers'
Residence but also the Swim Center, the expansion of the
Community Center, and the reconstruction of the Minot's Light
watch room.

Today Bancroft Hall is used for Rotary Club and VFW Post 9146
meetings, Historical Society functions, special events, and private
parties and receptions. The Lightkeepers' Corporation leases the
building from the town for a dollar a year and charges Cohasset residents a modest fee for private use of the hall. Two small rental units
on the second floor help to cover maintenance costs. The superb
view of the harbor from the front porch is open to everyone, and the
corporation invites townspeople to a free cookout each year following the Memorial Day parade. The Lightkeepers' Residence is a historical treasure and a proud testimony to what private individuals
with vision, energy, and commitment can achieve.

Mariners Park

From Government Island, it is but a short stroll on a boardwalk to
the new waterfront park at the end of Parker Avenue. In 1993 the
town bought what was then known as the Hagerty Property, a two-
acre site that once housed Francis Hagerty's Cohasset Colonials furniture factory and showroom. Among the buildings was an old
boathouse where Hagerty crafted rowing shells and skiffs. It had
originally been located on Government Island and was used by the

Humane Society to launch lifeboats.

The selectmen appointed a 15-member committee, chaired first by Alfred S. Moore, Jr., and then by James Russell Bonetti, to determine the best use for the site and to develop it accordingly. Private acquisition of waterfront property had, over many years, reduced both physical and visual access to the water, and a priority was to open the harbor to the townspeople. Hence the committee recommended that the Hagerty Property be converted to a community park and boating area.

The committee tore down most of the buildings, but the boathouse was turned over to the Cohasset Maritime Institute (CMI), an organization founded by Cohasset High School history teacher John C. Buckley, Jr., to promote local maritime history and traditional rowing. In 1991 Buckley and his students had restored an old wooden rowing surfboat, the *John Warren*, formerly used by lifesavers. The historic boathouse, restored to its original use and leased to CMI, now houses the surfboat and racing shells.

Renovation of the rest of the property took several years of diligent work by committee member Veneta P. Roebuck just to obtain environmental and construction permits. At a special town meeting in October 2000, the committee sought $175,000 to construct a 32-space parking lot, a 100-foot pier, and a wooden boardwalk linking the site to Government Island. The town had already spent $485,000 to purchase the property, partially offset by an anonymous donation of $50,000 and a $50,000 matching grant from the Cohasset Conservation Trust. The $175,000 was approved, and by the summer of 2001 the new Mariners Park was largely complete.

Antoine and Wilson Memorial

On May 21, 2000, 86-year-old Herb Jason realized a boyhood dream with the unveiling of a monument to Joseph Antoine and Joseph Wilson, the two young assistant lighthouse keepers who lost their lives on April 17, 1851, when the first Minot's Ledge Lighthouse was swept into the sea during a violent storm. They were only 21 and 23 years old. Jason had been haunted by the image of their last hours on duty: "The lighthouse bell was ringing furiously around

11:00 p.m.," he recounts. "The lighthouse was swaying two feet from center on either side. Antoine and Wilson put a message in a bottle which said that the lighthouse would not last the night and put their initials, J.A. and J.W., on it" *(Mariner, 7/1/99)*. Both perished after desperately struggling to swim ashore that fatal night.

To honor their courageous dedication to duty, Jason proposed that a memorial be erected on Government Island. With his grandson John Small and his brother Kenneth, he sketched a design for a granite monument and began to raise funds in 1996. There was some resistance from town officials who would have preferred a simple bronze plaque, but Jason and his supporters persuaded the Board of Selectmen to accept the project. They chose a site for the monument that had an unobstructed view of Minot's Light. The base of the memorial is a beautiful 12-foot-diameter compass rose of gray granite and tapestry brick created by Anthony ("Scout") Barbuto. At its center is a 3,300-pound slab of polished black granite imported from India. On one side engravers from Romania

Ken and Herb Jason stand tall just after unveiling the Antoine and Wilson Memorial.
Photo © Lynne Layman

At the May 21, 2000, dedication of the Antoine and Wilson Memorial. U.S. Coast Guard Capt. Blaine Horrocks honors Herb Jason for his untiring effort to honor the lost lighthouse keepers. From left: Town Manager Mark Haddad, State Senator Bob Hedlund, event Chairman Wigmore Pierson, Horrocks, and Jason. Photo © Lynne Layman

etched a finely rendered image of the first Minot's Ledge Lighthouse and an inscription memorializing Antoine and Wilson. On the other side is a small ethereal image of the lighthouse crashing into the sea.

Jason's friend Wigmore Pierson, a staunch supporter of the project, organized a stirring dedication ceremony at the unveiling of the monument on May 21, 2000. Keynote speaker Douglas Bingham of the American Lighthouse Foundation gave the following tribute to the two brave lightkeepers: "These were men of character, true heroes in American history. They kept a good light, they served with pride under the most adverse of conditions and they died with honor. May they never be forgotten." And thanks to Herb Jason, they never will be.

HIGHWAY IMPROVEMENT

Unlike the village and harbor, Route 3A received little civic attention during the project-oriented 1990s. Certainly no attempt was made by citizen groups to beautify the highway. Yet it too experienced a renaissance of sorts with new business and residential development.

Cushing Plaza, once a successful shopping mall with a dozen small businesses, retail stores, and restaurants, anchored by a large A&P supermarket, had been slowly deteriorating since the 1980s. Vacancies increased after the A&P closed in December 1981, followed by the bankruptcy in 1983 of J. Bildner's & Sons, the upscale grocery chain that owned the plaza. Later the receiver bank also failed, creating a vacuum in the plaza's management. To add insult to injury, even the septic system failed.

In 1993 the giant Shaw's Supermarket chain bought Cushing Plaza from Resolution Trust Corporation, a federal agency set up to liquidate the assets of failed savings-and-loan institutions. Two years later Shaw's terminated the leases of the surrounding shops, including the popular Sea 'n Cheese, there since 1983, as it prepared to construct its new supermarket. All the buildings were demolished except for Bergson's Ice Cream Shop and Restaurant (later replaced by Newport Creamery). Shaw's built retail space for new stores and former tenants such as Walgreen's and Buttonwood Books & Toys,

History of Cohasset

landscaped the plaza, and installed a new sewage-disposal system.
By August 1997, when Shaw's opened, Cushing Plaza had meta-
morphosed from a decaying strip mall into an attractive new shopping center, now called Shaw's Plaza.

The old Cushing Plaza at its foreclosure auction in October 1991. Photo courtesy of Patriot
Ledger/Mary Lee

*Shaw's Supermarket chain bought Cushing Plaza in 1993, razed the buildings, rebuilt,
and opened in 1997.* Photo © Lynne Layman

Farther north on Route 3A, developer Donald Staszko had converted (in 1988-89) an unimproved stretch of highway and an abandoned car dealership into the tastefully designed Cohasset Plaza,
with a new Super Stop & Shop and several small stores. Diagonally
across 3A from Cohasset Plaza is a 62-acre site on Scituate (or
Whitney, or Town) Hill. Now vacant, it was the home of Webb-
Norfolk Conveyor Company until 1994. At that time the firm was the
fourth largest employer in Cohasset, after the town itself, Stop &
Shop, and the Chart House Restaurant. Although the land is now
zoned for technology business, a developer from Virginia has
applied for a comprehensive permit to bypass the zoning restriction
and build a 254-unit rental apartment complex, including about 50
units of affordable housing. It is not a popular project, as the cost
of town services to support several hundred new residents in high-
density housing would significantly exceed their contribution to the
tax base. Many townspeople would prefer to broaden the tax base,
which is already 93 percent residential, with business development.
    Adjacent to the Norfolk Conveyor site is Sunrise Assisted
Living, one of 66 assisted-living communities operated by
Sunrise. Opened in 1998, it is a residential facility for senior citizens who need help with activities of daily living and for those
impaired by Alzheimer's disease. Coincidentally, a plan by Deck
Point, Inc., to develop an affordable housing complex on the site
had been proposed in the 1980s, and failed. Sunrise is a large, tur-
reted Victorian-style building. Local developer Wayne Sawchuk,
who brokered the sale of the four-acre site, commented, "We are
constantly talking about Route 3A as if it was a blighted landscape. This will be the most beautiful building on 3A" (*Mariner*,
7/3/97).
    Shortly after Sunrise was built, a residential development fea-
turing large single-family homes opened on the east side of Route
3A, with an entry on the King Street portion of the highway.
Completed in 1998, the 25-acre, 14-home subdivision was developed on land formerly owned by Charles and Rose Pape. Rose,
who had been a schoolbus driver for many years, died just after the
land was sold. In her memory the attractive development, nestled

on a hill behind her home, was called Rose Hill. Families in the Colonial-style homes on Rose Hill enjoy proximity to Sanctuary Pond and the densely wooded Bancroft Bird Sanctuary.

Hundreds of acres of unspoiled natural landscape have been preserved to the west of the highway, across from Cohasset Plaza. Extending toward Hingham is a greenbelt consisting of the 819-acre Whitney and Thayer Woods reservation and 2,900-acre Wompatuck State Park. Whitney and Thayer Woods includes Turkey Hill and Weir River Farm (in Hingham), added in 1997 and 1999, respectively. Turkey Hill is a 187-foot-high drumlin deposited when the glaciers retreated some 12,000 years ago. From its summit you can enjoy a panoramic view from the Boston skyline to the Atlantic Ocean off Scituate. During the 1950s Turkey Hill was the radar control site for a Nike missile launching station located to the south on Scituate Hill in Cohasset. Decommissioned in 1965, the Turkey Hill site returned to private ownership. In 1996 the owner, Joseph Saponaro, agreed to sell his parcel at the bargain price of $810,000, less than half the market value, to a five-member coalition headed by the Trustees of Reservations. The other partners were Hingham and Cohasset and their respective conservation trusts. Each town was to acquire the portion of the land that fell within its boundaries. The October 1996 special town meeting authorized an appropriation of $125,000 for Cohasset's 20-acre share of the 55-acre acquisition.

In November 1997 Turkey Hill was opened to the public. When you climb the gently rising path to the summit, you will see a granite bench dedicated to Cohasset conservationist Jack Hubbard, with the inscription: "In tribute to Jack Hubbard and his work to preserve this special place." Wild turkeys, reintroduced after disappearing from New England in the 1800s, might be roosting in the woods nearby. History is all around you. During the War of 1812, local residents gathered at the crest of the hill to watch a naval battle between the British warship *Shannon* and the American ship *Chesapeake* raging off the coast of Scituate. The battle is famous for the words spoken by the dying Captain Lawrence to his crew: "Don't give up the ship!" Ancient cart paths and foot paths crisscross the woods, and remnants of old stone walls mark the boundaries of bygone farms and pastures. The Trustees of Reservations, which holds a conservation restriction over Turkey Hill and the adjacent Whitney and Thayer Woods, will preserve this scenic and historic resource for all time.

SAFE AND CHL

Just out of sight on Route 3A, up Crocker Lane on Scituate Hill and one mile north of Lily Pond, is a dump. Developed by Paul and John Barry, Cohasset Heights Limited (CHL) is a private landfill. In February 1991 the Barrys proposed to expand their operation by 27.5 acres into Area 5 of their 50-acre property, and accordingly filed an environmental impact report with the state. Massachusetts needed more landfill space, and CHL was one of the few dumps that could still grow. Other landfills were at capacity and converting to recycling-transfer facilities. The Barrys hoped to use their dump as a regional landfill for general municipal trash.

The dump was not popular. Earlier, in October 1987 six protesters had been arrested for blocking the gate to CHL in an attempt to prevent refuse trucks from entering in violation of a cease-and-desist order from the Board of Health. They were concerned about odors emanating from the landfill and the potential for pollution from liquefied garbage leaching into the watershed of Lily Pond, the town's source of drinking water. The Barrys' new proposal mobilized the already alarmed Concerned Citizens of Cohasset, who formed a new organization in 1991 called SAFE (Stop Any Further Expansion). Founding members were John K. McNabb, Jr., legislative liaison officer for the Massachusetts Department of Environmental Protection from 1983 to 1989; Alix P. White, organic farmer and president of the Concerned Citizens group; attorney Kevin F. O'Donnell, who would devote thousands of hours over the next several years representing SAFE at no cost; Martha K. Gjesteby, selectman; Peter J. Pratt, former water commissioner; and residents Constance Afshar, David Bigley, Charles and Mary Gainor, Ronald Goodwin, Linda Keller, and

Peter Whittemore. From these modest beginnings in February 1991, SAFE grew to more than 700 members by 1998.

Shortly after filing for expansion, the owners of CHL offered to sell their landfill to the Massachusetts Water Resources Authority for $20 million. Cohasset Heights would make a fine dump, they thought, for sludge, grit, and screenings (much of it contaminated) from the Boston Harbor Cleanup. SAFE's first victory occurred in June 1991, when town meeting resoundingly defeated that proposal. SAFE also succeeded in pointing out the inadequacies of CHL's environmental report, forcing the Barrys to revise it five times between 1991 and 1995. In July 1995, however, the Massachusetts Department of Environmental Protection (DEP) approved the expansion. Meanwhile, in 1996 Cohasset Board of Health Chairman Thomas C. Cook began to hold hearings on the site assignment that would permit CHL to expand into Area 5. After 19 grueling sessions of testimony from CHL's experts, SAFE, and the landfill's opponents, the health board denied the permit for expansion on the grounds that it would pose a potential public health risk. Immediately CHL filed an appeal to Norfolk Superior Court.

CHL was now blocked, at least temporarily, from expanding outward—but not upward. So in 1997 Paul Barry applied for a 20-foot vertical expansion over the landfill. If the DEP allowed this move, the landfill mound would be clearly visible from Route 3A. "This was a bogus plan to add space to the landfill," SAFE leader John McNabb later explained. "They saw the Board of Health couldn't stop them [from expanding vertically], and DEP was going to approve it, and I just got mad. I needed a strategy to stop them, and I finally looked to DEP's regulations, which said they shall not approve vertical expansions unless the site assignment is in good order" (*Mariner*, 8/6/98).

McNabb had just discovered CHL's Achilles' heel. The landfill had committed two violations. In November 1997 McNabb found that they had dumped more than 7,800 square feet of trash illegally into an area not approved for landfilling. Taken by surprise, CHL checked with their engineer, who said the violation did indeed occur but was unintentional. This violation stopped the vertical expansion; environmental secretary Trudy Cox directed DEP not to approve any expansion until the waste was removed. The second violation proved the undoing of CHL: in January 1998 McNabb uncovered the fact that James Tyeryar, the original owner of the property, had never filed his landfill permit, granted in 1976, with the Norfolk County Registry of Deeds. Nor did Paul and John Barry when they bought the landfill in 1982. Therefore CHL was operating illegally in the Water Resource District that Cohasset had created in 1986. It could not be "grandfathered" in as a preexisting use, because the 1976 permit would have had to be filed with the registry to be effective.

In response to the permit violation, Cohasset building inspector Robert M. Egan ordered the landfill to close. CHL immediately appealed the decision and declared that it would remain open until all legal avenues were exhausted. Their lawyer asserted: "That interpretation [illegal operation because of an unfiled permit] is a hypertechnicality that has been concocted by a group that has sworn to close the landfill. This group has had members elected or appointed to the Board of Health and the Water Commission in an attempt to be in the position of judge and jury. They are a small but vocal minority that have pushed responsible town authorities so those authorities defer to their every statement and demand" (*Mariner*, 2/5/98). McNabb insisted that CHL's violations were more than technical, charging that

> evidence does show that contaminants have traveled from CHL toward Lily Pond, and that this can occur every time it rains . . . CHL has been improperly managing landfill gases and has inadequately managed erosion control . . . The mismanagement has damaged more than 10 acres of wetlands, more than 6 acres of groundwater, and is regularly discharging large amounts of explosive methane gas underground. CHL has also illegally dumped more than 2,000 tons of waste in area IV-B, which does not have a site assignment and is located in the town water resource district, where all landfilling is prohibited . . . CHL's numerous violations of law and their

proven damage to the air and water resources of the town
of Cohasset are by themselves sufficient legal grounds that
not only allow the Board of Health, but compel the board—
today—to shut CHL down.

[Letter to the Editor, *Cohasset Mariner*, 5/14/98]

In May 1998 town officials filed a criminal complaint against CHL
for its refusal to shut down.

Two months later, just as CHL and the town began negotiations
to end all disputes, CHL abruptly closed. The Superior Court had
upheld the Board of Health's denial of CHL's request for expansion
and, because SAFE had stopped the expansions, the landfill was
at capacity. The Barrys had run out of space and alternatives.
Nonetheless McNabb and his colleagues were not satisfied. To
close CHL permanently, the town had to rescind the site assignment
that allowed it to operate on Scituate Hill. Weary from 15 years of
litigation, at a cost of about $1.5 million for the town and for CHL,
Paul Barry unexpectedly conceded. He agreed to relinquish his site
assignment.

Leaving no stone unturned, McNabb wanted to ensure that
CHL could never open another landfill operation nearby. He pro-
posed changing the zoning bylaws to rezone the area from "light
industry" to "technology business," thereby prohibiting landfills. At
the March 2000 town meeting, voters approved the zoning change.
SAFE could now declare victory. In April McNabb wrote to the
Mariner that the new designation "will protect the future of
Cohasset from the adverse effects of any new solid waste landfills
or transfer stations along Route 3A, which could have turned
Cohasset into the trash capital of the South Shore. This ends the
10-year fight by SAFE to stop any further expansion of the Cohasset
Heights landfill."

The Water Department continues to monitor the area between
CHL and Lily Pond for traces of leachate that may still threaten our
water supply. The commissioners estimate that it will take another 20 to 30 years before the landfill site will cease to produce contaminated leachate.

CHANGES IN THE WATER DEPARTMENT

The Water Department took several initiatives to protect Lily Pond from pollution and to improve Cohasset's water distribution system. In 1990 the department acquired a 37-acre parcel of land abutting Lily Pond that would have been developed for the construction of 11 houses. Town meeting authorized the borrowing of $1.9 million to take Lily Pond Estates by eminent domain. Generous contributions from the Cohasset Conservation Trust and Jane Cook helped to repay the loan within a few years. At Cook's request, the land was renamed the Robert S. Pape Reservation, in memory of a highly regarded citizen of the town

In the summer of 1994, residents of the Jerusalem Road and Linden Drive neighborhoods complained of unacceptably low water pressure. The summer had been dry, and increased demand created by underground watering systems and new residential development had reduced water supply in some homes to a trickle. At the root of the problem were the town's narrow, aging water mains. In response to this emergency, the Water Commission, chaired by Frederick R. Koed, hired Tutela Engineering, Inc., to conduct a study of the water distribution system and recommend improvements. The result was a 10-year program to repair leaking pipes, replace or reline old water mains throughout town, and add new mains where necessary. The town approved $2.5 million for the project, as well as a 30 percent increase in water rates to pay for it.

In 1997 the commissioners asked town meeting to approve construction of a second water storage tank on Bear Hill to supplement the existing one. The new tank would ensure an adequate fire reserve and enable the department to clean each tank alternately while maintaining service. Because of citizen opposition to the Bear Hill location, the commissioners looked for another site. In April 2000 ground was broken on Scituate Hill for the new tank, the Water Department's most significant new construction since 1978, when the Lily Pond Water Treatment Plant was built. To further upgrade their service, the Water Commission privatized the department by contracting for operation and maintenance.

Thanks to the foresight of water commissioners past and present, Cohasset has an abundant water supply. The commission,
chaired by SAFE leader John McNabb as of 1999, could look back
with satisfaction on its considerable achievements. By July 1998 the
department had paid off all its loans from the town and become fully
self-supporting. In 1999, owing to the capacity of the Aaron River
Reservoir and the recent systemwide improvements, Cohasset was
the only town in the Southeast that did not have to impose an outdoor watering ban during a severe summer drought. And in 2000
the Cohasset Water Department received national recognition for its
annual Water Quality Report and for its public-private partnership
with professional management services. In fact, the Environmental
Protection Agency was now using the department as a model in
seminars on how to run small water systems.

Sewer Saga: Part IV

Cohasset's interminable battle over compliance with the federal
Clean Water Act was finally resolved in this decade. The town had
been under a court order since 1980 to expand, upgrade, and modernize its sewage-treatment system. In 1988 the state agreed that
instead of building a large central sewer plant with an ocean outfall, Cohasset could rehabilitate failed septic systems, expand sewer
service to critical areas by using inexpensive small-diameter collector pipes, convert the small treatment plant off Elm Street to a
pumping station, and pump Cohasset's wastewater to Hull's large-
capacity treatment plant. The sewer commissioners expected that
state grants would fund most of the cost of the Hull connection. But
the state ran out of money in late 1988, and by 1991 it was clear
that no state funding would be available. Cohasset would have to
pay the entire amount, about $5 million, itself.

The Sewer Commission was forced to reconsider the Hull connection. Time, however, had worked in favor of the embattled
commissioners. In the early 1990s membrane technology, a
method of using ultra-filtration to treat wastewater, had become
feasible. It offered Cohasset the possibility of upgrading its existing
treatment plant. Used in combination with traditional technology,

Above: Harking back to the town's bucolic roots. Holly Hill, a working organic farm off Jerusalem Road, is owned by a sixth generation of the White family.

Right: First Parish Unitarian Meeting House, built in 1747, still stands on the town's classic common. The first town meeting was held here after Cohasset split from Hingham in 1770

Below: Blissful summer afternoon at Sandy Beach, Atlantic Avenue.

Paul Pratt Memorial Library, dedicated in 1903. By the end of the century, the town had outgrown the graceful Greek Revival building, but could not expand it for environmental reasons. Operations will soon move to the former Joseph Osgood School building on Ripley Road.

The 1857 section of Town Hall, renovated in 1925 and again in 1988. The new wing, also built in 1988, is unseen to the right.

The rundown, but picturesque, boatyard/marine railway complex near Border Street Bridge. The site was originally a grist mill and later a lumberyard. It is soon to be renovated by new owner Peter Roy.

The private Central Cemetery on Joy Place overlooking Little Harbor.

Boaters take advantage of low tide to stroll the sandbar off the Cohasset Harbor breakwater.

The historic Elisha Doane House has been home to the Community Center since 1949, expanding several times to accommodate a growing number of programs and the town's Senior Center.

A working replica of the old town pump refreshes local children as well as the occasional horse. The pump, crafted by Charlie Butman, was installed in 1991 by the Village Renaissance Committee.

The Historical Society's two Elm Street museums, the Capt. John Wilson House and the Maritime Museum, are open to the public during the summer.

At Veterans' Memorial Park on the harbor, stone monuments honor all Cohasset residents who died in the nation's wars as well as all those who served in World War II. Other memorials are planned.

Cohasset Troop 28 of the Boy Scouts of America relaxing after the 2000 Memorial Day parade.

Motor inn at the head of the Cove built by John Carzis amid a firestorm of controversy in the 1970s, now owned by the Roy family.

View from Government Island toward Mariners' Park showing the sailing club, the boathouse for the Cohasset Marine Institute and the former showhouse for the Cohasset Colonial furniture kit company.

Top: Strawberry Parfait on Pleasant Street has been the town's take-out place of choice since 1978. The building formerly housed the Lincoln Coal Co. office.

Above: Possibly the world's best known storefront, Cohasset Hardware was featured in two major movies, "The Witches of Eastwick" and "Housesitter"—under stage names, of course.

Left: The surest sign of summer in Cohasset is the opening of JJ's Dairy Hut on Route 3A.

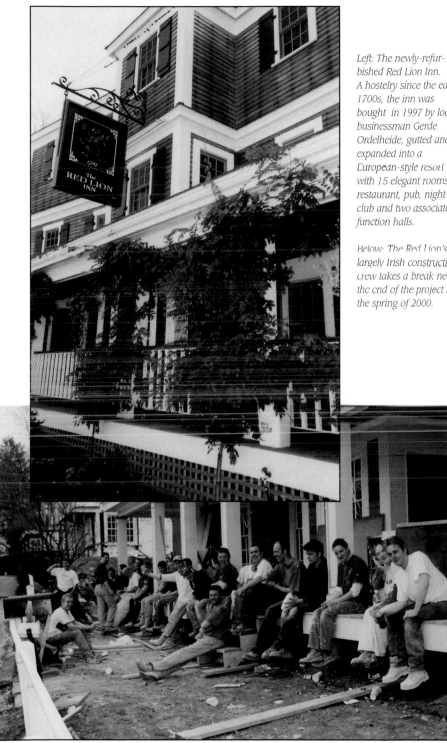

Left: The newly-refur-bished Red Lion Inn. A hostelry since the early 1700s, the inn was bought in 1997 by local businessman Gerde Ordelheide, gutted and expanded into a European-style resort with 15 elegant rooms, restaurant, pub, night-club and two associated function halls.

Below: The Red Lion's largely Irish construction crew takes a break near the end of the project in the spring of 2000.

French Memories, an upscale bakery and coffee shop, occupies the village space once filled by Central Market.

The new Joseph Osgood School, opened in September 1998. The $9.9 million school was the subject of tumultuous town meeting battles that culminated with a record throng of 1,574 voters at the South Shore Music Circus reaffirming the vote to build it.

South Shore Art Center's Festival on the Common, a summer tradition since 1953, now draws artists, craftspeople and musicians from all over New England.

The Parish Center at St. Anthony's Roman Catholic Church, completed in 1999, offers a roomy and handsome hall for community functions as well as parish activities.

New age transportation for three small spectators at the Memorial Day parade.

Sunrise Assisted Living on Route 3A, opened in 1998, offers a homelike option for senior citizens who need help with daily activities.

The Flying Scotts race on a sparkling August day off Cohasset Harbor.

The new face of the Village. Handsome gilded wooden signs identify refurbished storefronts.

Young cyclists proudly display their colors at the 2000 Memorial Day Parade.

This polished granite memorial to two young lighthouse keepers who died when the first Minot Light toppled into the sea in a fierce gale in April 1851 was a longtime dream of fisherman Herb Jason. It was dedicated in May 2000.

The flower-bedecked façade of Circa, an upscale home furnishings boutique that now thrives in the Village.

Above: At the opening gun of the April 2000 Cohasset Roadrace by the Sea. The popular 10k event was begun by the Jaycees in 1977 and continues under Rotary Club sponsorship.

Right: John Roland of Kingston finishes first in a time of 33:12. The field averages about 1,000 runners from all over New England who often use it as a tune-up for the Boston Marathon.

Local veterans snap to attention at Central Cemetery to honor fallen comrades during the 2000 Memorial Day parade. In foreground left to right: Tom Wigmore, commander of the Sons of the American Legion post, Steve Wigmore, commander of the American Legion Post, and Ralph Perroncello, commander of the Veterans of Foreign Wars Post.

A vendor at Cohasset's popular Farmers' Market, a June-October fixture on the Common since 1997.

South Shore Art Center board member Eleanor Bleakie and Red Lion Inn owner Gerd Ordelheide in western getup for the grand opening of The Barn function hall at the inn. The event served as a fundraiser for the Art Center.

Above: Contemporary interior of the South Shore Music Circus with its graduated seating and bank of lights.

Right: New carved wooden sign for the Music Circus, which replaced a lighted plastic version in time for the venue's 50th anniversary.

Computer lab at the Middle School. In foreground, Daniel Sullivan.

David Wadsworth, longtime town archivist, historian for the Cohasset Historical Society and former curator of the society's museums.

Mary Jeanette Murray, former Cohasset selectman and beloved 12-term State Representative for Cohasset, Hingham and Hull. The World War II Marine corporal proudly wears her vintage uniform to march every Memorial Day.

The slope in front of the Lighthouse Keepers' Residence blooms each year thanks to the Community Garden Club. Other areas around the facility were landscaped by the Cohasset Garden Club and the Amateur Gardeners of Cohasset.

Brass section of the Deer Hill marching band.

Children rehearse at Town Hall for the Cohasset Dramatic Club's December 2001 production of "The Best Christmas Pageant Ever."

Cub Scouts head for the harbor on the last leg of the 2000 Memorial Day Parade.

Girl Scouts and Brownies march along Elm Street during the 2000 Memorial Day Parade.

Two boys try different techniques to nab a donut during the harvest festival that ends the Farmers' Market season.

Judy Stavis propels her sleeping tots in a jogging stroller.

Signs of the Times

Skateboard skeptic.

Belt and suspenders; helmet and training wheels.

Razor scooting.

Backpacks are now de rigeur for schoolchildren of all ages.

The newly ubiquitous cell phone.

That steely-eyed Little League batter isn't always a boy these days.

it would produce cleaner wastewater and allow the plant to handle far greater flow rates than before. Moreover, the plant itself could be expanded in the future by adding modular components. Building a new, larger plant would not be necessary. Sewer Commission Chairman Ted Guild, highly knowledgeable in membrane technology used in water desalinization, championed the method for Cohasset. It looked like the answer to our need for higher-capacity treatment, cleaner discharge, expandability, and affordable cost.

The state cooperated in September 1994 by amending its Agreement for Judgment, giving Cohasset five more years to solve its sewage problems. For homes dependent on septic systems, however, the new Title V regulations of the state environmental code were to make on-site sewage treatment a costly and often unsightly problem. Cohasset added still more stringent provisions to the regulations with respect to nitrogen performance and setbacks from bodies of water. The impact of Title V was to fall heavily on sellers of existing homes. As of spring 1995, homeowners were required to pass new, rigorous standards based on a detailed inspection of their septic system and to repair or replace the system, if necessary, before completing the sale. Title V was in effect a full-employment act for disposal system installers. Repairs or replacement in Cohasset's impermeable terrain could cost in the range of $25,000 to $70,000. Between 1995 and 1998 about 50 homes failed inspection, forcing owners to install innovative/alternative systems based on mechanical aeration of wastewater, pumps, and traditional leaching fields. People joked about their new "Mount Flushmores," elevated leaching fields forming prominent mounds of earth.

The homes around Straits Pond in North Cohasset had an exceptionally difficult problem. As they were located far from the Elm Street treatment plant and built on mostly impermeable soil, replacing failed systems was difficult and often prohibitively expensive. The town of Hull, on the other side of the pond, blamed Cohasset for polluting the water and contributing to the proliferation of midges, tiny flies that at times grew so thick you seemed to be breathing them in. The state declared Straits Pond an area of critical environmental concern, and Hull threatened to sue unless we sewered our side of the pond.

After decades of indecision, the town took action. In 1996 the Sewer Commission embarked on two major projects: one to triple the size of the sewered area in central Cohasset, and the other to sewer homes around Straits Pond. The central Cohasset project entailed upgrading the existing sewer plant and sewering about 45 streets, the Deer Hill School, and the proposed new elementary school. The plant would adopt the new membrane technology, making Cohasset the first municipal system in the United States to use it. The treated wastewater would be clean enough to discharge into Cohasset Harbor. The Straits Pond project involved sewering North Cohasset and pumping the wastewater to Hull's underutilized treatment plant. When these two projects were complete, about 40 percent of the town, the most densely populated districts, would be sewered, and Cohasset's obligation to the state would be met. The estimated price tag for both projects was $18 million, in 1996 the town's largest capital outlay ever. Property owners connected to the system would be charged a betterment fee, payable over 20 years, for their proportionate share, plus an annual usage charge of about $400 for the operation and maintenance of their sewer connections.

Initially homeowners in the North Cohasset district were asked to pay the full cost of the Hull connection, about $16,000 per household. They protested vehemently. The state was forcing sewerage on them, they said, whether they wanted it or not. Moreover, they were still angry over a recent 155 percent increase in water rates charged by the Massachusetts-American Water Company. Overwhelmed by unexpected expenses, they demanded that the town pay half the capital costs of the Straits Pond project.

The issue was brought up in an article that came before the March 1996 town meeting. Residents who lived in unsewered areas and opposed sharing argued that they would have to bear the full cost of upgrading their septic systems at an average cost of $30,000, with no subsidy from the town. After heated debate, voters finally agreed that the town (all taxpayers) should pay half the

projected $6.3 million cost. The proposal required a Prop 2 1/2 over-
ride, however, and voters at a special election in May narrowly
defeated it. The article was reintroduced in March 1997, with residents in central Cohasset now joining the call for sharing the cost
of their project, estimated at $13.5 million. This time, with the sup-
port of the sewer commissioners, voters at both the town meeting
and the election approved the 50 percent subsidy for the two districts. At the same time, a $5-million loan fund was established to
help nonsewered residents upgrade their systems.

Sewer rage, however, was not entirely quelled. In November
1997 residents around Lily Pond and Little Harbor learned that their
neighborhoods had been targeted as priority districts for mandated
septic system inspections every seven years, whether or not their
homes were for sale. The state had ordered the Sewer Commission
to create two special inspection districts in unsewered areas of
town as part of a second amended Agreement for Judgment. This
nearly caused a citizen uprising. Lily Pond and Little Harbor residents organized to fight the Sewer Commission. In an effective
campaign, the Citizens for Equitable Environmental Solutions
(CEES), under the leadership of Lisa L. Bumstead, persuaded the
Sewer Commission to expand the central Cohasset sewerage district to include the 36 homes on Lily Pond. The commission also
agreed to conduct a study to determine the best methods of wastewater management for homes in the Little Harbor district.

After 16 years of service, more than half of them as chairman,
Ted Guild decided not to run for reelection as sewer commissioner
in 1999. He could say with pride that he and his colleagues had
achieved their goals: "We've handed the citizens something that is
still a lovely New England town, while at the same time protecting
the environment" (*Mariner*, 4/29/99). Through Guild's initiative, in
September 2000 the sewer plant began to use the innovative membrane technology to treat wastewater. So effective is the system that
state and federal environmental agencies have increased Cohasset's
discharge permit from 72,000 gallons to 300,000 gallons per day.

Over a thousand homes in Cohasset have been sewered—at a
final cost of nearly $25 million. The North Cohasset sewer system,

completed at a cost of $9.3 million, serves 295 homes (using the Hull treatment plant). The expanded central Cohasset (and Lily Pond) sewer system cost $15.6 million and serves 827 homes (using the Elm Street treatment plant). Would the town have been better off had it implemented the M&E proposal back in 1983, with the 90 percent federal and state reimbursement available at that time? The number of houses served by M&E's Phase I would have been similar to the number served by our current plant, and the town would have saved a few million dollars. But we benefited by waiting for the new technology. We have gained significantly cleaner wastewater and the ability to upgrade the plant through staged expansion We have also avoided an ocean outfall pipe whose cost and environmental impact were unknown at the time.

Moreover, the state ban on additional sewer connections in the 1980s had restrained growth at a time when developers wanted to build hundreds of new units in marginal areas under the comprehensive permit process. The additional capacity of the upgraded plant may enable development, but at the sewer commissioners' discretion. Current requests for connections, particularly in the Little Harbor area, are likely to absorb most of the anticipated excess capacity, and it will be up to the town to decide whether to expand the plant one more time. The state is pushing affordable housing and using the comprehensive permit process to override local zoning ordinances. An unintended consequence of the town's innovative solution to its wastewater problem is the potential for large-scale affordable housing. Seen as a benefit to some, particularly senior citizens and people of moderate means, most residents believe that housing development needs to be balanced with the equally desirable goal of maintaining the quality of life in Cohasset in all its many dimensions.

REVIVING THE RAILROAD

The future of Cohasset will also very likely be influenced by the return of the commuter railroad, which ceased operation in 1959. When the Old Colony rail line was first built in the mid-nineteenth century, it had a profound impact on the character of the town. The train improved access to and from Boston, making it easier for families to travel here. Large estates developed along the shore, and Cohasset became a summer colony for city dwellers. The head of the family could commute to Boston by train and return to his "cottage" in the evening or on weekends. Not only was a new social and economic element woven into the fabric of the town, but the center of activity shifted from the Cove to the village, where the station was located.

In the 1950s, however, commuters favored driving to Boston rather than riding the train. When the Southeast Expressway opened in 1959, passenger rail service on the South Shore ended and the Cohasset station closed. By the mid-1970s the expressway had twice the traffic load it was designed to carry. A proposed Southwest Expressway, which would have diverted some of the traffic, was never built. As congestion increased and the expressway deteriorated, the trip into and out of Boston grew longer and more frustrating. To reduce automobile traffic during reconstruction of the expressway in 1984-85, the Massachusetts Bay Transportation Authority (MBTA) began to subsidize the existing commuter boat service from Hewitt's Cove in the Hingham Shipyard.

At the same time, the state directed the MBTA to study the feasibility of returning commuter rail service to the South Shore, the only region in the Greater Boston area not served by mass transit. The legislature appropriated $10 million for a detailed plan and an environmental impact report. The proposal was to reactivate passenger service on the two branches of the Old Colony Railroad that terminated in Plymouth and Middleboro. It also called for rebuilding the abandoned Greenbush branch that passed through Braintree, Weymouth, Hingham, and Cohasset and ended in the Greenbush district of Scituate.

Initially most Cohasset residents were in favor of restoring the Greenbush line. A referendum question in the April 1985 town election showed overwhelming support, 1,192 to 266. In 1986 a 22-member Citizens Advisory Committee was appointed to review the proposal for restoration of the Greenbush line and the environmental impact statement. While some members believed that restored rail service would benefit the local economy, others questioned its cost-effectiveness and impact on the environment.

As the debate progressed, antitrain sentiment gained momentum. Opponents pointed out that most rail passengers would likely be those who already commuted by bus or boat; hence relatively few cars would be pulled off the road. Moreover, in Cohasset the tracks would run through wetlands and densely populated neighborhoods. In Hingham they would cut through historic Lincoln Square. People were concerned about noise, vibration, pollution from diesel engines, and the high costs of construction and maintenance. Many Cohasset and Hingham residents felt that the MBTA should enhance commuter boat service instead of rebuilding the rail line. In 1990 Cohasset selectmen voted unanimously to join Hingham in requesting a delay of the comment period on the Greenbush project.

The state, however, became increasingly committed to restoring the train. The entire Old Colony Railroad restoration was mitigation for the "Big Dig," Boston's Central Artery/Tunnel project. Begun in 1991, the Big Dig was designed to reduce traffic congestion through the city and to open up access to the waterfront by replacing the Central Artery elevated highway with a wider underground expressway and by extending the Massachusetts Turnpike through a tunnel under Boston Harbor to Logan Airport. But the Conservation Law Foundation (CLF), a self-appointed, nonprofit environmental advocacy organization, asserted that air pollution would increase as more cars used the improved routes through and around the city. In August 1991 the CLF sued to stop the Big Dig under the federal Clean Air Act. The negotiation that followed resulted in an agreement to withdraw the suit if, among other things, all three lines of the Old Colony Railroad, including Greenbush, were restored. Service on the Plymouth and Middleboro lines was popular with the affected communities, but Greenbush was controversial. If not completed or if a suitable alternative was not found, the CLF vowed to reinstate its suit blocking the Big Dig.

By the mid-1990s sentiment in Cohasset for or against the train was evenly split. At the May 1995 election, a referendum question on the restoration of Greenbush was approved by a paper-thin margin of 3 votes: 1,383 to 1,380. Arguments in favor of the train were summarized in a letter to the *Mariner* (5/25/95) by resident Jacqueline Whipple, who responded to parents' fears about the rail crossings planned for 12 streets and the safety of their children:

> Parents should worry if trains don't come back. Only 22 percent of Cohasset's population (persons over 18) has children in school Young managerial and executive families who support good schools will continue to prefer Weston, Lincoln, Concord, North Shore with their reliable commuter rail. We will continue to have an aging population with other priorities, empty store fronts, degradation of 3A in pursuit of taxable enterprises, shortfalls in school financing, and a long, lonely mosquito-breeding right of way.

To rebuild the tracks through Cohasset, the MBTA needed to purchase our right-of-way. We had bought the abandoned rail bed in 1982 from Penn Central and were using it as open space for jogging, hiking, and bicycling — when it was not too muddy. Now we had a bargaining chip. If the MBTA wanted the land, it would have to pay not only for the property but also to mitigate the adverse effects of restoring the railroad. Among the environmental impacts were noise from warning signals, vibration, air pollution from diesel engines, and increased flooding of James Brook. In 1997 the selectmen appointed a Greenbush Mitigation Committee, chaired by Thomas L. Gruber, to address these issues. The committee was directed to assume that the rail line would be restored and to negotiate for the best possible "deal" for Cohasset. The selectmen also picked a site for the station. After debating the merits of a village versus Route 3A location, they chose the 3A alternative. The site is the former Winter Garden skating rink property, now occupied by Graham Waste Services, Inc. (owned by Paul Barry).

The mitigation committee spent nearly four frustrating years negotiating with the MBTA. At the end they were offered a package of mitigations totaling more than $5 million. The MBTA agreed to pay $1.6 million for our 3.4-mile-long right-of-way. In addition, we would receive $250,000 to relocate a Sohier Street well that was too close to the rail bed; $500,000 to replace lost open space; $1.2 million to complete the James Brook Flood Abatement project; and a promise to endorse a $1.5 million Public Works Economic Development grant. The MBTA also agreed to expand and repave the village parking lot, built over the former turntable of the old roundhouse that existed when Cohasset was the terminal for the Old Colony Railroad.

In 1997 the cost of the Greenbush project was estimated at about $215 million. But as of 2001, with mitigation for all the communities along the line, including the construction of a tunnel under Hingham's historic district, the price tag has ballooned to an estimated $408 million or more. Despite the high cost, the railroad is on track to be rebuilt. The train will have an impact if for no other reason than making it easier to travel to and from Boston. This should attract more business to Route 3A and perhaps residential development as well. To anticipate and plan for the future, voters at the March 2000 town meeting created the position of town planner. Elizabeth Harrington, our first town planner, is working with the Growth and Development Committee to design a master plan for Cohasset, the first new vision for the future since the Benjamin Report was published 40 years ago. Expanded sewerage and the return of the railroad will no doubt be two of the most potent forces for change in Cohasset.

Upgrading the Schools

Cohasset did not have to wait for population growth to build new schools. A priority for the town in the 1990s was to upgrade the school system. The desire of parents for smaller classes and better facilities for their children drove energetic campaigns to improve and expand athletic fields, construct a new elementary school, and renovate and expand the Deer Hill and high schools. These were major capital projects that required overrides of Prop 2 1/2. School-based parent organizations also raised funds privately to support educational projects that could not be funded within the school budget.

Fiscal restraints did not affect some cherished traditions

Tuxedo shorts were "in" in 1992. Dave Cullinane, Matt Marks, and Ollie Nivaud prepare to board a corporate yacht for their senior prom. Photo courtesy of Patriot Ledger/Gary Higgins

For the 1997 prom, a trolley took seniors and their dates to a pre-prom reception. From left: Robert Stansell, Emily Henderson, Karen Niessink, John Lonborg, and Nichole Santoro. Photo © Margot Cheel

Cohasset Education Foundation

In 1992 the Cohasset Education Foundation (CEF) was formed under the auspices of the PSO to conduct serious fundraising. Founding members were Brian McKenney, chairman; Elaine Coyne, treasurer; Holly Holway, secretary; and 20 other men and women. The CEF held corporate-sponsored spelling bees, sold tickets to special Music Circus performances and Art Center receptions, and sought donations from individuals and grants from local groups such as the Cohasset Conservation Trust and the South Shore Playhouse Associates. In 1992-93 they raised $22,000 for a computer center at the Osgood School and the following year $15,000 for professional development programs for teachers as well as art and science programs for students. The most impressive gift of all was $110,000 in 1997 to construct a World Language Laboratory at the Cohasset Middle-High School.

The efforts of the CEF and of Cohasset teachers were rewarded by the outstanding performance of the students. In 1995 Cohasset ranked number one in the state for the percentage of seniors who went on to college (63 of 64 students). The school has also performed well under the standards of the Massachusetts Education Reform Act of 1993. In 1999, the second year of required testing, our tenth graders were the top scorers among all their counterparts statewide on the MCAS (Massachusetts Comprehensive Assessment System) test.

Milliken/Alumni Field Complex

In sports as in academics, Cohasset students excelled. "People really marvel at what we do with our size," beamed Athletic Director Clark Chatterton (*Mariner*, 5/23/96). With the smallest enrollment of any squad in Massachusetts, the lacrosse team was a perennial qualifier for tournament competition. The varsity basketball team won several Division III South Sectional championships, the sailing team ranked second in the state in 1992, and the gymnastic squad won South Shore League titles three years in a row from 1994 to 1996. Under Coach Torin Sweeney the wrestling team produced a star performer, Kevin Duffy, who won Cohasset's first All-State individual title in 1997.

Field sports were played on Milliken-Bancroft and Lillard fields. Milliken, on Bancroft Road, contained a track, a baseball diamond,

The 1992 high school sailing team was ranked second in the state. From left: Joe Menis, Nikki Peterson, John Murphy, and Chloe Chittick. Photo courtesy of Robert Davenport

The 1993 high school Homecoming Court. Rear: David Leahy, Julie Good, Courtney Schultz, Brian Pattison, Brooke Sheerin, Jack DeLorenzo; front: Melinda Cheel, Chris Rolandelli. Photo © Margot Cheel

an all purpose athletic field, and two tennis courts. Adjacent to the high school were four other tennis courts. Over the years these facilities had become overused and downright shabby. In 1989 a few of the school's alumni and sports boosters decided to do something about it. Charlie DeSantis and Wayne Sawchuk placed an article in the town meeting warrant that year to fund the development of new fields. The article passed, but then failed to win town support at the override election.

Five years later Gary Vanderweil and Wayne Sawchuk spearheaded a new effort to create and fund a sports complex the town could be proud of. With the support of a broad-based committee, they prepared plans and a proposal for the March 1994 town meeting. The timing was right and the plans well presented. The article, and subsequent override, was approved. It authorized the town to borrow $775,000 to build a new, lighted sports field and an all-weather track at what was then a parking lot and tennis courts next to the high school. Milliken-Bancroft Field would also be improved and expanded, with a new baseball diamond and practice fields and four new tennis courts. Jane Cook, whose mother, Jane Bancroft, had donated the land for Milliken Field in 1938, contributed the lights for the sports and track field, and Pilgrim Co-operative Bank funded the new electronic scoreboard. Ground was broken in May 1995. In September 1996 the town's new Alumni Field was dedicated, and alumni from as far back as 1936 joined the varsity teams for a celebratory lap around the all-weather track.

A year later, in 1997, High School Athletic Director Clark Chatterton was among the first organizers of Cohasset's Relay for Life around the new Charles R. Davis Track, named in memory of a popular track coach and teacher who died in 1985. Part of a nation-

The Charles R. Davis Track was dedicated in 1996 to the memory of this popular coach and teacher. The entire athletic complex was named for longtime Athletic Director Clark Chatterton, who died in 2000. Photos © Lynne Layman

Welcome to the
Clark Chatterton
★ ATHLETIC COMPLEX ★

wide fundraiser for the American Cancer Society, the relay involves teams of walkers who keep a representative moving around the track for 24 hours. Each participant has a sponsor who pledges a donation for the relay. No one knew in the first year of the relay that Cohasset teams would next be rounding the track for Clark Chatterton's own fight against cancer. This much-admired and beloved director died in July 2000. In his honor the new high school athletic fields were named the Clark Chatterton Athletic Complex.

Work at Milliken Field was completed in 1997. The practice fields present a lively scene on weekends. Every Saturday morning in the spring and fall, hundreds of children in vivid team colors gather to play soccer. They are members of the Cohasset Soccer Club, founded in 1982 by Charles DeSantis, John S. Duncombe, and Russell J. Reidy. Under the energetic leadership of longtime organizer Lawrence R. Shultz, a teacher at Deer Hill, this popular club has expanded from 2 teams to about 40. Parents enjoy it too, some volunteering to coach and others content to stand in the sun and cheer for their children or socialize with their neighbors.

New and Better School Buildings

The athletic field project enjoyed broad popular support. Much more divisive was the proposal to build a new elementary school, brought before town meeting in 1996. In fact, it was the most bitterly contested issue of the decade.

By the mid-nineties the school population was beginning to grow again as a result of the baby "boomlet" that had occurred in the late 1980s. As more children entered the system, pressure was felt at the elementary schools, particularly the Osgood School, which housed kindergarten through grade 3. Constructed in 1927, the building was showing its age, made worse by spotty maintenance. The Deer Hill School, grades 4–6, was also becoming crowded. Concerned about the condition and capacity of the buildings, and aware that state grants were available for school construction, the School Facilities Committee hired a Boston architectural firm in the summer of 1995 to conduct a study. The architects, Earl R. Flansburgh and Associates, concluded that the capacity of the Osgood and Deer Hill schools was "inadequate to serve the needs of our current student population and [was] substantially below minimum state standards" (*Mariner*, 10/19/95). As the state would reimburse 60 percent of improvements to Deer Hill, but would fund only new construction at Osgood, the proposal was to upgrade Deer Hill and replace the Osgood School with a new building.

Enthusiastic supporters attended the special town meeting in January 1996 to vote on a $14-million school building and renovation program. They gave one of the proponents "a standing ovation and thunderous applause when he stated the Osgood School was in a deplorable state" (*Mariner*, 1/25/96). But when a selectman warned of prohibitive costs and proposed increasing class size to 30 instead, they responded with boos and hisses. Many town meeting regulars deplored the behavior of the crowd. But when the vote was taken, the article won overwhelming support. At the override election, however, the debt exclusion for the school project was narrowly defeated, 1,162 to 1,134.

At the annual town meeting in March 1996, the School Department proposed a smaller amount, $9.9 million, to replace the Osgood School only. This time some parents even brought children to garner support for their cause. After an hour-long presentation, including a film of the Osgood School at its worst, impatient proponents called the question, attempting to stop debate before it started. School officials realized that this would turn public opinion against them at the override election. They called for a recess and spent the next 45 minutes persuading the ringleaders to allow further discussion. But when debate began and an opponent spoke, the din was so loud that few could hear him. Shortly thereafter a vote was taken and the measure passed, 419 to 49. At the election in April, however, the debt exclusion override was approved by a much narrower margin, 1,574 to 1,494.

Angered by the lack of open debate, a group of Concerned Cohasset Taxpayers had gathered 500 signatures requesting a special town meeting in August to reconsider the vote on the school. Anticipating an enormous crowd, the selectmen asked South Shore Playhouse Associates for the use of the Music Circus tent. A record 1,589 voters assembled under the tent on August 12, 1996, for what became another loud, rowdy town meeting. In contrast to the previous meetings, however, both sides of the issue were debated at length. At the second session a vote was taken, and the motion to reconsider failed. Cohasset would get its new $10-million school.

These turbulent town meetings exposed the widening gap

The nearly 1,600 voters who crowded
the South Shore Music Circus tent in
August 1996 refused to rescind a
controversial earlier vote to replace
the old Osgood School. *Cartoons courtesy
of James Hamilton and* Cohasset Mariner. *Photo
courtesy of* Patriot Ledger/Derick Pruitt.

The new Joseph Osgood School, opened in September 1998. Renovation under way at Deer Hill School and Cohasset Middle-High School in 2000. Photos © Lynne Layman

between relatively affluent residents, many of them young newcomers, and others who were struggling just to remain in Cohasset.
Marilyn Previte, who runs a daycare business from her home, artic-
ulated the concerns of many local families: "Young people with
money who move here raise our taxes to build this or that in town;
then they transfer out and leave others to pay the bill. This leaves
middle-class townies struggling to live here. The newcomers have
big ideas on changing this little town. They don't care about others, and they move on. Where is it all going?" The battle over the
Osgood School was a watershed event. After it was over, older,
more conservative town meeting members seemed to give up.
Voices that typically spoke out against spending fell silent, and
some left the town altogether. It was a new Cohasset.

On September 8, 1998, the new Osgood School, designed by
Flansburgh and Associates, opened for the first time. The sturdy
brick building contained spacious, air-conditioned classrooms, a
large gymnasium, a computer lab, art and music rooms, a library, a
cafeteria, and a wide carpeted stairway that doubled as seating for
school assemblies. At the opening was the schools' new superintendent, Dr. Edward Malvey, from Griswold, Connecticut He
replaced Stephen Hart, who retired after 11 years as head of the
school system.

Edward ("Ted") Malvey would oversee the development of the
second major school project, the most expensive capital project in
the town's history, a $41 million renovation and expansion pro-
gram (60 percent reimbursable) for the Deer Hill School and
Cohasset Middle-Senior High School. Unlike the fight over the
Osgood School, the plans for this project were readily approved by
town meeting, in March 2000, and the subsequent override election. The design called for the construction of two new classrooms
for Deer Hill, as well as two computer labs, a gymnasium, and an
expanded library, cafeteria, and administrative area. The middle-
high school would get a new double gymnasium and cafeteria, with
separate entrances for each wing of the now separated schools. (In
1997, as part of a nationwide "middle-school movement," grades 7
and 8 were separated from the high school and given their

own faculty and athletic and extracurricular programs.)

The abandoned Osgood School on Ripley Road, so recently condemned as a fire trap and a "major hindrance to our children's education" (School Committee letter to *Mariner*, 7/25/96), was touched by a magic wand. The trustees of the Paul Pratt Memorial Library saw it as a beautiful brick-and-slate building with "excellent space and a central, visible location"—ideal for a new public library. The Paul Pratt library on South Main Street was a town landmark, a classical Greek Revival building with a cupola topped by a mackerel weathervane, a clipper ship clock, and a rotunda painted with murals depicting scenes of early Cohasset. But it lacked space for additional collections and computers, and parking was inadequate. Remodeling the building would cost about $3 million, nearly the same as the cost of converting the old Osgood School into a library. But the latter would qualify for state grants and the former would not, nor would it meet all the library's needs. The trustees believed they could raise the funds for a new library through the combination of a state grant, private donations, and the sale of the Paul Pratt library. Although some town officials wished to convert the Osgood School into senior housing, voters at the October 1998 special town meeting approved the proposal to convert the school into a library. The town looks forward to the construction of its new state-of-the-art library sometime in 2002.

RESHAPING TOWN GOVERNMENT

For nearly 40 years town study committees had recommended combining departments and hiring professional managers to improve the efficiency and effectiveness of town government. Many of these ideas would be realized in the nineties. In 1995 the town merged the Highway, Tree and Park, and Recycling/Transfer departments into a single Department of Public Works, headed by longtime highway surveyor Harold W. Litchfield. Bringing to closure a 20-year campaign for a new town garage, the town also built a 13,000-square-foot corrugated-metal DPW garage near the Recycling/Transfer Facility on Cedar Street. With air-conditioned offices and ample space for vehicles and equipment, the new

Harold W. Litchfield, longtime highway surveyor, became the town's first public works direc- tor in 1995. Photo courtesy of Cohasset Mariner/Greg Derr

garage was a vast improvement over the old Highway Department garage behind the Red Lion Inn. But passersby in the village could no longer drop in for a casual chat with Harold.

In 1996 the selectmen replaced our local town counsel with an entire Boston law firm. When Richard Henderson stepped down from his posi- tion in 1996, after serving as a dedicated and accessible town counsel for 14 years, the selectmen hired the firm of Deutsch Williams Brooks DeRensis Holland & Drachman, a 40-member team, to handle all the town's litigation and labor negotiations. Legal issues had proliferated. The firefighters and police officers had organized into unions for collective bargaining back in 1974. In 1990 workers at Town Hall formed the Konohasset Clerical and Custodial Union, and library employees the CLASS Union in 1991. The law firm was expected to save the town money by eliminating the need for spe- cial counsel to represent the town when legal issues became too numerous or specialized for a single attorney to handle.

A sense that the system might not be in control was reinforced by various overruns in town budgets. Town meeting had approved $752,000 for the design and construction of the new DPW garage, but the actual cost turned out to be $982,000, and another $60,000 was needed to extend a water main to the garage. Legal expenses to fight Cohasset Heights landfill were mounting, and Cohasset Water Department customers were paying a 30 percent rate increase for long-deferred improvements to the water system. Critical of these unanticipated expenditures and generally dissatis- fied with other issues, townspeople faulted the selectmen and the executive secretary for poor management.

In 1997 a group of frustrated citizens petitioned town meeting to replace the selectmen/executive-secretary form of government with a selectmen/town-manager system. Perhaps not fully appreciated by some at the time, this change would concentrate significant power in a single position. The town manager would run the day-to-day operations of Town Hall and appoint all municipal employees under the Board of Selectmen, except for the town clerk (still an elected position) and town counsel (appointed by the selectmen). The town accountant, the treasurer-collector, the building inspector, the DPW superintendent, the harbormaster, and the police and fire chiefs, all of whom previously reported to the selectmen, would now report to the manager. As the chief administrative and financial officer, the town manager would set the agenda for Board of Selectmen meetings, prepare warrants for town meeting, and develop and propose the annual town budget.

There were serious objections to the petition. Among them were that the position concentrated too much power in the hands of a single individual and that it would diminish the roles of the Board of Selectmen and the Advisory Committee. Proponents, however, argued that the selectmen would still be in charge. They hired and could fire the town manager, and they could veto his or her appointments. After lengthy debate at town meeting, the question came to a vote late at night, with barely a quorum present. The proposal was approved, 75 to 61. "It was too important an issue to do it in that manner," admonishes former moderator William Weeks.

The change required state approval, and the legislature passed a special act that allowed Cohasset to create the position. In August 1997 the selectmen hired our first town manager, 33-year-old Mark W. Haddad. Cohasset "went from a situation where boards and committees had direct control over departments," says Haddad, to one in which he was the appointing authority. This was unsettling to many boards. The library trustees, for example, could now only recommend that Janet Husband replace Richard Hayes as library director. The final decision was Haddad's.

The town manager usually endorsed the recommendations of elected officials, but not always. As chief procurement officer, he canceled a contract awarded by the sewer commissioners because

it exceeded the amount appropriated at town meeting. The commissioners sued him for overstepping his authority. Represented by
town counsel, Haddad won the case. "Everytime there's been a challenge to the town manager's authority and it gets clarified," he calmly points out, "it provides a better understanding of my position."

Although he stepped on
some toes in the process,
Haddad succeeded in
streamlining town govern-
ment. He created a single
finance department by
combining the depart-
ments of the treasurer-collector, the deputy assessor,
and the town accountant
under Director of Finance/
Town Accountant J. Michael
Buckley, Jr. Town Hall
offices now share secretar-
ial and other support staff,
eliminating redundancy and improving coordination among
departments. And, because they can get an immediate anwer or
decision without having to go through the Board of Selectmen,
department heads like the efficiency of the town-manager
system, says Haddad. He has saved the town money by producing long-range financial plans that have improved our bond
rating and by directly negotiating police, fire, and clerical
contracts himself. As for concerns that he has too much
authority, he is quick to point out that the selectmen still set
policies for the town, which he must carry out: "They are still
my bosses, and I still report to them."

*Town Manager Mark Haddad confers with Town
Moderator George Marlette during the March
2000 annual town meeting. Photo © Lynne Layman*

PROTECTING THE PUBLIC

New initiatives in the Fire and Police departments focused on the
needs of older citizens and young people, respectively. In 1998
nearly a quarter of Cohasset's population was over age 60. The Fire

Department improved its ability to handle the medical emergencies of this age group, and the police dealt with the problems of unsupervised teenagers.

Significant changes in the Fire Department began when the selectmen did not renew Chief Daniel Brock's contract in 1991. They replaced him with John Nadeau, deputy chief in Sanford, Maine. Nadeau set out on a mission, unpopular with the permanent firefighters, to rebuild the department's call-firefighter division. It had dwindled from 20 members in 1985 to only 13 by the end of 1991. Within a year he had 24 call firefighters ready to assist the permanent staff. Although several were longtime volunteers, such as Clifford J. Dickson, a 51-year veteran when he retired in 1993, many of the others were rookies and needed training. The permanent firefighters refused to train them, fearing it would result in a reduction in staff. Some of the call force did get trained, however, when Nadeau persuaded the Plymouth County Training School to take a few of the novices.

Midway through his three-year contract, the chief submitted a letter of resignation to the selectmen. "Unlike my professional transition to Cohasset," Nadeau wrote, "my personal transition has not been successful; my personal goals are beyond reach in Cohasset" (*Mariner*, 6/17/93). During his brief tenure here, he restored the call force, increased ambulance billing collections (neglected by the previous chief) sevenfold, obtained a new $90,000 ambulance and a rescue boat for the department, and reduced sick leave from 72 to 58 hours a week.

In October 1993 Cohasset native Roger W. Lincoln, a firefighter with the Cohasset department since 1969, accepted the top position and became the town's first local fire chief since 1982, when Charles Piepenbrink retired. He improved the response of the department to fire and medical emergencies and in 1995 introduced Enhanced 911 service. The latter replaced the town's obsolete alarm boxes, installed in 1912 when many houses lacked telephones. The 911 service is available from any phone, including cell phones. From a home phone the caller's name, address, and telephone number automatically appear on a computer screen, enabling firefighters to gain precious response time. More recently, the department's eight call firefighters and many contributors donated a thermal imaging camera, which enables firefighters to locate victims obscured by smoke in burning buildings.

The Fire Department had provided emergency medical services since 1983. The firefighter/EMTs could perform basic life-support services. In 1999 the department's life-saving capability was expanded by the addition of six firefighter/paramedics. Paramedics can administer advanced life-support (ALS) services such as cardiac monitor-defibrillators, IVs, and airway-passage intubation. The following year ALS equipment was installed in the town's ambulance, allowing a wider range of treatments. As a result, paramedics can treat serious injuries at the scene of an accident and stabilize victims more adequately before transporting them to the hospital. The ALS-equipped ambulance serves as a portable emergency room and in effect brings the hospital to the victim, saving time and lives.

In 1993, the same year Roger Lincoln became fire chief, Brian W. Noonan replaced Joseph Kealey as police chief. Noonan had been a member of the Cohasset Police Department since 1974 and was appointed sergeant in 1986. He reminisced to a *Mariner* reporter (10/16/86) that when he first applied for a job on the force at age 29, Chief Feola asked him, "If you got on the department, what job would you want?" Noonan replied, "Yours." Then, Noonan said, "he laughed. A little."

As the saying goes, Be careful what you wish for. Chief Noonan faced the perennial challenge of dealing with alcohol abuse among teenagers. Kids had binged on alchohol for decades—that had not changed. What had changed drastically was the attitude of parents. In the 1980s parents wanted enforcement. They complained to the selectmen that some police officers were ignoring the problem of alcohol possession by minors; that they failed to notify parents when youths were caught breaking the law; and that in general they were "too soft on the kids" (*Mariner*, 6/12/80). By 1995 the tables had turned: it was the police who were complaining that parents either did not want to know or did not care what their teenagers were up to. When eight youths were arrested for under-aged drinking in November 1998, the parents berated the chief.

Since the late 1980s citizens and town officials had coordinat-ed a series of interventions to prevent drug and alcohol abuse among teenagers. The Cohasset Drug and Alcohol Committee, formed in 1989 and chaired by Keith Knowles, organized a Safe Homes program sponsored by the Board of Selectmen, the Police Department, the school system, the clergy, and the PSO. Its pur-pose was to help parents form a network of homes where all par-ties would be supervised and no alcohol served. In 1994 Michael Gill, the school's health coordinator, and Chief Noonan developed a program for Cohasset children called PALS (Police Assisting Local Schools) for Wellness. Under the PALS program, police officer Lisa Matos and safety officer Clifton Jones taught children at all age lev-els about substance abuse, violence prevention, and conflict man-agement.

Behavior did not improve. On Halloween night in 1995, local youths went on a rampage. They threw eggs at police cars and offi-cers, vandalized property, fought, and used "the foulest language imaginable when confronted" (*Mariner*, 11/16/95). In 1996 and again in 1999 they repeated the behavior and reportedly intimidat-ed some children by stealing their candy. Underaged drinking con-tributed to the mayhem and violence.

Despite the campaigns against substance abuse, a particular incident of teenage drinking in Cohasset was to have fatal conse-quences and to result in legislation aimed at avoiding similar tragedies in the future. In June 1996 a Marshfield youth died when his car crashed into a tree after he became inebriated at a party held in Cohasset. The teenager's parents believed that their son's drink-ing had been condoned, if not encouraged, by adults at the party. Criminal charges lodged by the Cohasset police against the hosts for providing alcohol to minors were dismissed, and a subsequent civil suit brought by the parents for wrongful death was settled out of court. Dissatisfied with these outcomes, the grief-stricken family appealed to the state legislature to enact a bill that would hold adults accountable for providing alcohol to teenagers. In

August 2000 the state passed the Social Host Responsibility Act: adults who knowingly and intentionally supply alcohol to guests under the age of 21 or allow them to possess alcohol on their premises can be prosecuted and punished by a fine of up to $2,000 or a year in prison.

Shortly after the "Social Host" tragedy, Cohasset again figured in the news. On April 25, 1997, the front page of the *Boston Globe* headlined a scandalous story about two prominent Cohasset families. Thirty-nine-year-old Michael Kennedy, son of the late Senator Robert Kennedy, had allegedly had an affair over several years with his children's teenaged babysitter, the daughter of close friends who also lived in Cohasset. Michael and his wife, Victoria, had lived in Cohasset since 1985, residing first on Stevens Lane and later on Atlantic Avenue. He was the first of the Kennedy clan to live in Cohasset since the early 1920s, when his grandparents, Rose and Joe, rented a summer home near Sandy Beach. After receiving a cold reception here, the senior Kennedys left for Hyannis Port. Until the "Babysitter Scandal" broke out, Michael had led an apparently quiet life in Cohasset, contributed to good causes, coached youth soccer, and attended church regularly with his three children. Good works notwithstanding, the Cohasset police and the Norfolk County district attorney began to investigate the allegations of statutory rape. The media descended on Cohasset, and the story was publicized around the world. Although Kennedy never denied the relationship, the babysitter refused to testify and the investigation was eventually dropped. The story ended tragically on December 31, 1997. Skiing down a mountain in Aspen, Colorado, while tossing a football to companions, Michael Kennedy ran headlong into a tree and was killed instantly.

COMMUNITY LIFE

The sensational stories of the 1990s will fade over time. What will endure in memory are the community gatherings and celebrations—church suppers and blueberry festivals at Beechwood Congregational, Saturday morning soccer games, Memorial Day and Little League parades, art festivals, village fairs, regattas and

road races, carillon concerts on the Common—ordinary events
that collectively form the life of the town.

Churches and Church Events

The churches in the nineties contributed to community life while
also serving the needs of their own congregations. Rev. Edward
Atkinson—or Ed, as everyone called him—the pastor at First
Parish, was as involved in the community as he was in his parish.
He had served as vice president of the Parent-School Organization,
trustee of the Paul Pratt Memorial Library, commodore of the
Sailing Club, chairman of the Council on Aging, and chairman of
the Cohasset Metco program.

In 1995 Ed fulfilled a lifelong desire to lead a marching band.
The high school had earlier eliminated its band, and he missed it,
he said. So he organized his own. He called for volunteers, recruit-

*The Rusty Skippers, a hometown marching band organized by Rev. Edward Atkinson
for the 1995 Harborfest parade, made great strides in skill and coordination over the
next several years.* Photo © Lynne Layman

ed 14 musicians (some a bit rusty, but all enthusiastic), and organized a marching band for the 1995 Harborfest parade. Now
known as the Rusty Skippers, the band continues to play in
Memorial Day parades and other town events. On July 24, 1995,
Ed died suddenly. He was 60 years old and had been pastor of First

Parish for 26 years. Ed's involvement in the town reflected his love for Cohasset. Parishioner Iri Bloomfield recalled that after he spent a sabbatical year traveling around the country, "he happily returned to Cohasset and told people that everything he ever wanted was here" (*Mariner*, 7/27/95).

Two years after Ed passed away, First Parish welcomed the Reverend Elizabeth Tarbox, its first woman minister. Born in England and raised as an Anglican, Rev. Tarbox was committed to the principles of Unitarian Universalism. She was an inspiring speaker, and the congregation was devoted to her. In early 1998, however, her parishioners were devastated to learn that she had been diagnosed with cancer. She retired from her duties in May 1999 and died in October.

The Reverend Jennifer Justice was installed at First Parish in November 2000. She brings to her congregation of more than 250 adults and children a unique background in the performing arts and storytelling, which preceded her ministries in Provincetown and in York, Pennsylvania.

Ongoing is a $750,000 renovation and expansion program for the Parish House and Trueblood Hall, partially funded by "Cabaret," the church's annual variety show. Cabaret has become a popular event starring talented parishioners who can sing, dance, play instruments, and do an awesome imitation of the Blues Brothers.

Across the Common, Rev. Gary Ritts, pastor of the Second Congregational Church, continues his highly successful Appalachia Service Project. The church also donates space in its basement for the Cohasset Food Pantry. This townwide program, founded in 1993 by Cohasset resident Stuart Pratt, provides food and household supplies to about 30 needy local families. It is supported by contributions from Cohasset churches, individuals, businesses, and supermarkets. During a food drive in 1996, Cohasset mail carriers collected more than two tons of donated items from customers on their routes. The Pantry also receives grants from Project Bread that enable it to purchase surplus food through the Boston Food Bank.

In July 1990 the church broke ground for a new addition.

Designed by Cohasset architect James Shipsky, the two-story wing contains a chapel and administrative offices, Sunday School classrooms, and a nursery. Not to be outdone by First Parish, the Second Congo Church, as it is informally called, holds an annual song-and-dance show called Congo Capers. Held at the high school auditorium and directed by parishioner Jo Ann Fichtner, the show is open to the whole community.

Like Second Congregational, St. Stephen's Church, led by Rev. Clifford Cutler, also makes space available for civic organizations. Since 1981 the Social Service League has operated from offices in the parish hall. During the nineties the league sponsored programs to help residents of Cohasset and neighboring communities cope with problems such as Internet addiction, college-application stress, end-of-life care, and the "speeded-up, overloaded" family. As it has since its founding, the league still delivers Thanksgiving and Christmas dinners to needy families; it also provides Meals on Wheels and the services of a social worker. In 2001 the nursing service formerly administered by the league moved into Town Hall, and the public health nurse, Judith E. Fitzsimmons, became an employee of the town under the direction of the Board of Health.

In August 1999 St. Stephen's celebrated the seventy-fifth anniversary of its famous carillon. The townspeople were invited to share in the festivities. The celebration featured a dramatic reenactment of President Calvin Coolidge's visit to Cohasset back in August 1925, when he enjoyed a carillon concert on the Common. Assistant carilloneur Mary Kennedy described the historic occasion:

> President Coolidge and his wife arrived in Cohasset at the invitation of his friend Clarence Barron. In the interests of historical accuracy we must report that his main intent was not to enjoy the music of the bells. Rather, as he announced to Barron, "I should certainly like to see your cows." After lunch at the Barron estate on Cohasset Harbor, the President and his party made their way to Cohasset Common for the afternoon recital. After listening to the first two pieces, "Old Folks at Home" and "Annie Laurie,"

the group left for an inspection of cows, including a prize
bull worth some $25,000.

[From a brochure on the Carillon,
75th Anniversary Year, 1999]

On the day of the celebration, historical impersonator Jim
Cooke arrived at the Common in a green 1928 Model A Ford to
address the crowd. "Calvin Coolidge" delighted his audience with
Silent Cal's terse witticisms, delivered in the president's halting
speech and New England accent. Cooke's performance was followed by a recital of music from the 1920s played on the recently
renovated carillon. In 1990, 35 of the original 51 bells were
replaced, and 6 new ones added, for a grand total of 57. These bells
range in weight from 29 pounds to a colossal 11,280 pounds.

In October 1999 the community was invited to St. Anthony's
Church to commemorate the 150th anniversary of the sinking of the
brig *St. John*, the worst shipwreck in Cohasset's history. On Sunday,
October 7, 1849, the *St. John*, carrying more than 120 Irish immigrants fleeing the Great Hunger, was wrecked on the Grampus
Ledge off Cohasset during a violent nor'easter. An estimated 99
people were drowned, and about 22 survived. Forty-five of the victims were recovered and buried in a mass grave at Central
Cemetery. David Wadsworth describes the tragic events that
occurred after the *St. John* struck the Grampuses:

Attempts to free the vessel failed and the pounding waves
began to split open its hull. In desperation, *St. John*'s crew
cut aways masts and rigging in an attempt to lighten the
ship, but to no avail. A ship's boat was launched only to be
smashed by the raging seas, and some drowned.

Within an hour, the vessel's hull itself had broken into
fragments and no longer was visible from the shore.
Horrified watchers could see only great raftlike sections of
the ship rising and falling with the waves as they drifted
slowly toward the shore. Upon one of these sections, there
huddled a pitifully few half-drowned persons who eventually would be counted among the survivors. Of the rest,
only the ship's Captain Oliver, a few crew members and a

handful of passengers were able to launch the vessel's longboat and gain safety upon dry land.

Ashore, a 19-year-old girl named Elizabeth Lothrop witnessed the entire tragedy in shocked dismay. But then she calmly began to prepare her parents' home to receive whatever survivors there might be. The family home, near Cohasset's Sandy Cove, was a summer hotel, one of the many which lined our shores during the mid-nineteenth century . . . Elizabeth's father, Capt. Daniel Tower Lothrop, a Cohasset seafarer, had departed earlier for Cohasset Harbor to assist the Humane Society's volunteer lifeboat crew in an attempt to reach the site of the disaster . . . Struggling through tumultuous seas into the teeth of the gale, the big rowboat headed for the Grampuses . . . When part of the way there, they saw the *St. John*'s longboat with Capt. Oliver and the survivors heading past them for the shore. No attempt was made by the longboat's occupants to inform the lifesavers of the presence of others at the site of the wreck .

Soon seeing the other drifting brig *Kathleen*, which was flying distress signals, the exhausted lifesavers veered off to assist that vessel, unaware that scores of persons may still have been clinging to the wreckage of *St. John* . . . In the appalling disaster which befell the brig from Galway, entire families were wiped out . . . For the victims, a service was conducted by Father Roddan of Quincy, and about 45 unidentified victims were buried in a grave at Cohasset's Central Cemetery . . . Some time after the shipwreck, the girl Elizabeth Lothrop, in a saddened, somber train of thought, confided to her diary that, having witnessed the awful event from beginning to end that day, she feared her life could never be as happy and carefree as it had been before. She wrote of a sense of profound sadness that seemed never to depart.

[David Wadsworth, article in *Cohasset Mariner*, 9/1/94]

The events planned by the local chapter of the Ancient Order of Hibernians, the largest and oldest Irish Catholic fraternal organization in the United States, included a Mass celebrated at St. Anthony's by Bernard Cardinal Law, a procession to Central Cemetery, and the laying of a wreath at the foot of the 20-foot-high Celtic cross erected in 1914 to honor the victims. The ceremonies ended with a memorial program held at St. Anthony's new Parish Center.

The Parish Center had been the dream of Rev. John Keohane. He began to make plans and raise funds to build it, but when he retired in 1995, after 18 years as pastor, the center was still a dream. The Reverend John R. Mulvehill, assigned to St. Anthony's in 1995, would turn that dream into reality. Before serving in Cohasset, Father Mulvehill had been president of Cardinal Cushing College in Brookline, director of religious education for the Archdiocese of Boston, and pastor of St. Francis Xavier Church in Weymouth.

By 1998 St. Anthony's parish, the largest in Cohasset, had more than 1,200 members. With 650 children enrolled in the religious education program, and no central place for classes and social activities, the need for a new building was clear. Town boards and

The new Parish Center at St. Anthony's Roman Catholic Church was dedicated in September 1999. Photo © Lynne Layman

the Archdiocese of Boston approved plans designed by architect Joseph Donahue for a hall large enough to seat 355 people, as well as a fully equipped kitchen, eight classrooms, and two administrative offices. Ground was broken in October 1998 and construction began at the edge of the church parking lot near Sankey Road. The $2.5 million project was funded through individual gifts and a highly successful capital campaign led by John P. Reardon, Jr., and Andrea and John Wade. One of the most generous gifts was a bequest from Father Keohane, who, regrettably, died on May 31, 1996, without seeing the new building. Under the watchful eye of James Lagrotteria, clerk of the works, the handsome brick structure, mirroring the style of St. Anthony's Church, was completed on time and on budget. The Parish Center was dedicated by Bishop Joseph Maguire on September 19, 1999. Offering the largest hall in town, with plenty of parking space, the center accommodates not only parish activities but the Red Cross bloodmobile and many other community functions.

St. Anthony's, First Parish, and the Vedanta Centre all experienced loss and change in leadership during the nineties. In September 1995 the Reverend Mother Gayatri Devi, spiritual leader of the Vedanta Centre since 1940, passed away. The first woman ordained to teach Vedanta in the Western world, she had represented her faith at the 1975 Conference of World Religions at the United Nations, where she appeared with Mother Teresa, founder of the Missionaries of Charity in Calcutta, India, and a Nobel Peace Prize winner. Gayatri Devi had appointed as her successor Dr. Susan Schrager, an educational psychologist and teacher from California and longtime student of Vedanta and other world religions. In 1995 Dr. Schrager, now Reverend Mother Sudha Puri, became the first American woman to be spiritual leader of the Vedanta centers. She continues the ashrama's tradition of openness, prayer, meditation, and selfless service.

Contributing to the cultural diversity of the South Shore, the Panagia Greek Orthodox Church on Jerusalem Road continues to promote the Greek culture and heritage through its annual Taverna. From small beginnings in 1980, the Cohasset Taverna has become the largest Greek fair in the region and attracts busloads of tourists. The church, led by Father John Maheras, now has a membership of about 225 families, a new church choir, and an enhanced youth program.

Community Activities

Church and town events create a sense of solidarity among people, a feeling of belonging to the community. One of the best examples of this social dynamic is the Cohasset Bicentennial celebration of 1970, when townspeople worked together for a common purpose. To recapture the camaraderie of the past, James Lagrotteria proposed a new celebration, a harbor festival, in 1991. Lagrotteria and Robert Martin, representing the Cohasset Chamber of Commerce, planned "Harborfest" for the same weekend as the South Shore Art Festival. Its aim was to boost morale in the economic downturn of the early 1990s and to link the harbor to the Common through a variety of activities.

The first Harborfest was a hit. Children and adults flocked to

Model sailboat builders at the 1992 Harborfest. In the lead, Steve and Danielle Hajjar.
Photo courtesy of Patriot Ledger/John Simpson

A float in the 1995 Harborfest parade. At attention next to the flag, State Representative Mary Jeanette Murray. Photo © Lynne Layman

the parade of boats and the blessing of the fleet at the harbor. They followed the marching parade from the harbor to the Common, cheering the color guards, the floats, the antique cars and fire engines, the marching bands, and the Marching Mermaids twirling colorful streamers. Harborfest became an annual tradition, with parades, chowder competitions, baseball tosses, pancake break-fasts, lighting of luminaria on the Common, and, in 1998, a special celebration for the soon-to-be-closed Osgood School.

The art festival, now called the Festival on the Common, also thrived, adding new attractions and more vendors to its program. But the transient crowds were eroding the small-town character of the accompanying Harborfest, and out-of-town vendors competed with local merchants, defeating the purpose of the harbor celebra-tion. In 1998 the Harborfest Committee decided to separate from the art festival and hold their activities on a different weekend. To their chagrin, however, they found that the Festival on the Common had become the draw, and residents lost interest in Harborfest. Unable to stand on its own, the new tradition sadly came to an end.

The three-day Festival on the Common continued to attract over 10,000 people a day from towns all around Massachusetts, and from Connecticut and Rhode Island as well. Festival Chairman Rhonda Corey Myers deftly coordinated about 400 volunteers to create a spectacular celebration of the arts. *Mariner* correspondent Robert Ziff described what you might see on a typical day at the festival:

> Festival-goers congregated on the town's common bring-ing droves of children. The ones too young to fend for themselves could be found in baby backpacks, in tradition-al four-wheeled strollers, or in state-of-the-art three-wheeled buggies that looked like they belonged to the moon . . . Much of the green grass on the town's common was covered by a conglomeration of white tents that housed the array of arts and crafts, entertainment, and cui-sine that was being offered to the thousands who were at the Festival on the Common. People strolled from one tent to the next, either browsing or purchasing the scarves and clothes, handcrafted jewelry, hats, artwork, ceramics,

hand-painted bird houses, homemade gourmet vinegars packaged in fancy bottles, and virtually every other art or craft you could imagine . . . In addition to vendors, there was food galore. You could have everything from fried dough to Middle Eastern cuisine to the traditional and mouth-watering strawberry shortcake. You could also just relax on the grass in front of the stage and listen to the music and watch the performers.

[*Cohasset Mariner*, 6/26/97]

Another town organization that had shed its purely local character was Cohasset's Community Center, renamed the South Shore Community Center of Cohasset in 1994. In addition to Cohasset,

A fire juggler performs at the 1992 Cohasset First Night celebration, sponsored by the Community Center. Photo courtesy of Patriot Ledger/Carey Marden

the Community Center attracts people from Hingham, Hull, Norwell, and Scituate. During the 1990s it sponsored a number of popular events such as First Night entertainment on New Year's Eve, a firemen's muster, and an annual Jingle Bell Walk from the harbor to the village. On the day of the Walk, held in December, Santa and his elves arrive by boat at the harbor and disembark, distributing bells to the children. Hundreds of children and adults, whose jingling bells are joined by the bells of St. Stephen's, follow Santa and Mrs. Claus, seated in Glenn Pratt's antique fire truck, to the Community Center. There everyone gathers for cookies and hot chocolate and a sing-a-long led by Cohasset High School music director Bryan Marks. At the end of the day, the crowd reassembles at the Common for the first lighting of the outdoor Christmas tree. The Community Center Halloween Fair has also become an annual tradition. Children are invited to display their best Halloween costumes, and the center provides amusements. For a nominal charge, children can enjoy bouncing on a "moon walk" in a giant inflatable giraffe or win prizes at games of skill and chance.

Once-in-a-century events occurred at the Cohasset Yacht Club

Both the Cohasset Yacht Club and the Cohasset Golf Club hit the century mark in 1994.
Photos © Margot Cheel

and Golf Club. Both turned 100 in 1994. The highlight of the Yacht Club's celebration was the Adams Cup U.S. Women's National Sailing Championship. Ten of the nation's best all-woman crews raced International 210s out of Cohasset Harbor for top honors.

This marked the seventh time in 70 years that Cohasset hosted the competition; the last time was in 1956. The event has long been associated with Cohasset. The cup itself had been donated in 1925 by Cohasset Yacht Club member and Secretary of the Navy Charles Francis Adams, in honor of his wife. The winner of the race an unprecedented four years in a row, from 1935 to 1938, was Cohasset resident Frances McElwain Wakeman. And the 30-foot International 210 keelboat class that competed for the 1994 Adams Cup was designed in 1945 by Cohasset Yacht Club member C. Raymond Hunt.

The Cohasset Golf Club, one of the oldest clubs in the country, celebrated its one hundredth anniversary in 1994 with a Centennial Golf Tournament and a Tri-Sport Championship (golf, tennis, and basketball), dinner dances, and other social events. The club has undergone a major upgrade since then with a $6-million renovation of the clubhouse and golf course, "probably the largest single private investment in the town's history," according to club president Clifford Mitman, Jr.

With so many activities to support, Cohasset had to tap other communities for volunteers. Working couples hardly had time for their own families. As Marilyn Previte notes, "Today, for working mothers, the pace of life is insane; there is no time for nurturing children." With the exception of the garden clubs, the more successful organizations, such as the Art Center, the Community Center, and the Social Service League, depend on members and volunteers from surrounding towns as well as from Cohasset. They also pay salaries to key personnel.

An organization that struggled despite a long tradition of inclusiveness was the Cohasset Dramatic Club. The club had always attracted a large membership from neighboring communities. Being a member meant that you participated in at least one production or play-reading a year. If you were not an actor, you could paint scenery, pull curtains, or collect props. As a patron member, you could simply give financial support and enjoy the three or four plays the club produced annually. Everyone was invited to club beach parties, cast parties, and other social events.

Membership was typically as high as 200. Revenue from dues and advertising covered most of the expenses. The talent base enabled the club to present challenging plays such as Lillian Hellman's *Children's Hour* and Anton Chekhov's *Uncle Vanya*. Starting in the early 1980s, however, competition from new amateur theaters on the South Shore began to divert audiences and actors away from Cohasset, and membership declined. Fewer businesses bought advertising space in the playbills. It became difficult to find enough men, now working longer hours, to fill male roles.

By 1994 the club had only 50 members. To promote ticket sales, it abandoned serious theater and began to present familiar, popular plays. *Little Women* and *Best Christmas Pageant Ever*, for example, featured lots of children, guaranteeing an audience of admiring friends and relatives. The 1994 production of the musical *Annie* was a smash hit, packing the Town Hall auditorium. A new informality, with the audience seated around tables instead of in rows, made the theater even more appealing. The change in format appears to have worked, and the Dramatic Club is once again drawing crowds to community theater.

Another Cohasset fixture is the South Shore Music Circus. You know summer is here when you see the big green tent go up on Sohier Street. Though the Music Circus is a regional attraction, its staff is mostly local. Many Cohasset residents held summer jobs at the Circus as teenagers, some as far back as 1951, when the tent first opened. Most began as ushers and returned season after season, working their way up in the ranks, becoming stagehands and box office help. Clark Chatterton met his wife, Sallyann, when they both starting working there in 1960. Until his death in 2000, Clark ran the concessions stand, hiring his students to assist him. Ron Rawson, executive director from 1968 to 1988, commented on the family atmosphere that still prevails at the Music Circus: the local youths "are really the ones who have stabilized this operation. Without all these local people who work and who enjoy the performances here, the South Shore Music Circus would cease to exist" (*Mariner*, 8/16/84).

Since the late 1980s the South Shore Playhouse Associates,

parent company of the Music Circus, has been generous in its support of local and regional nonprofit organizations. It has donated more than a million dollars to various groups, including the Cohasset Dramatic Club and the South Shore Art Center. It has also made its tent available for Cohasset High School graduation exercises and other special events. As Ron Rawson observed, Cohasset and the Music Circus "have been good for each other. Cohasset brings a certain panache to this theater—the physical location, the beauty, and the ambiance of this area. It lends itself to make this an atmosphere people want to return to."

The closing years of the twentieth century seemed like a golden age of peace, prosperity, and security. The cold war was over and the economy was booming. Life in Cohasset reflected these good times. We had confidence in our ability to solve problems and, to some extent at least, control our future. Not everything was perfect, of course. The older and less affluent population worried about rising property taxes and whether they could afford to stay here. The pace of life was frenetic for young working couples with children. Developers seemed intent on maximizing the use of any available open space. Nevertheless, residents of Cohasset enjoyed a particularly agreeable quality of life.

But on September 11, 2001, life as we knew it changed. Two jets hijacked by terrorists ripped into the World Trade Center in New York. They exploded, and the giant twin towers collapsed into the ground. Another plane struck the Pentagon in Washington, D.C., and a fourth crashed into an open field in Pennsylvania. More than 3,000 innocent civilians were killed. These horrendous attacks affected the American psyche as powerfully as the fear of nuclear war had in the fifties and sixties. In Cohasset they brought an end to complacency. Our new vulnerability made us realize how much we had taken for granted.

Eleven days after the attacks, the George H. Mealy Post 118 of the American Legion held a prayer and remembrance service at Veterans Memorial Park. U.S. Navy veteran Robert W. Jackson, a sergeant on the Cohasset police force, spoke to citizens gathered for the ceremony. His reflections on the catastrophic events of September 11 mark the beginning of a new chapter in the history of Cohasset:

> *Eleven days ago on a beautiful clear morning, the clouds of war rose over New York, Washington, D.C., and Pennsylvania. Innocent civilians were slaughtered in the thousands, our military nerve center took a heavy hit, and the country was shaken to its very foundations.*
>
> *Immediately the country united and watched in awe and reverence as new heroes struggled to deal with these horrific events. We all wept as the enormity of the events became clear. We took pride in the actions of our fellow citizens. American flags were proudly and defiantly flown as a quiet resolve settled in.*
>
> *These events had in a sense made all Americans veterans and united us with a dogged determination to eradicate the evil that has caused these events. The conflict we now find ourselves in will not be short and it certainly will not be pretty. Further sacrifices will be demanded, but the American people in their collective strength will prevail.*

SOURCES
INTERVIEWS AND DISCUSSIONS
SELECTED TOWN OFFICIALS
INDEX

SOURCES

Epigraph by Van Wyck Brooks quoted in B. A. Botkin, ed., A *Treasury of New England Folklore*, rev. ed. (New York: Bonanza Books, 1947 and 1965)

COHASSET IN THE 1950s
Opening Portait
Data from U.S. Census Bureau; *Cohasset Mariner,* 10/15/98; Town of
   Cohasset Annual Reports; Michael Barone, *The Shaping of America
   from Roosevelt to Reagan* (New York: Free Press, 1990)
George Lyman Davenport and Elizabeth Osgood Davenport, *Genealogies
   of the Families of Cohasset Massachusetts* [and historical addendum],
   1909; reprinted 1984
Alfred G. Odermatt interview, 11/5/98
David H. Wadsworth note, 9/99
Louis F. Eaton, Jr., interview, 10/29/98
Marion Coulter Bowditch interview, 11/13/98
Henry A. Rattenbury interview, 11/11/98
Frances Chatterton interview, 3/2/99
Louis N. Simeone interview, 11/4/98
Noel A. Ripley interview, 11/19/98
Virginia I. Najmi discussion, 5/25/00
John Bishop, "St. Stephen's Church: An Historical Profile," in *So Worship
   We God: Essays on the History of Saint Stephen's Episcopal Church,
   Cohasset, Massachusetts,* ed. David H. Pottenger (Cohasset, Mass.: Saint
   Stephen's Episcopal Church, 1998)
Elaine Tyler May, *Homeward Bound: American Families in the Cold War Era*
   (New York: Basic Books, 1988)
On number of families who summered in Cohasset: *South Shore Mirror*, 4/4/57

Rural Cohasset
Merle S. Brown interview, 11/23/98
Leo J. Fiori interview, 1/4/99
Oliver H. Howe, "Chronological Outline History of the Town of Cohasset,
   Massachusetts, 1886-1949"
National Grange pamphlet
Jeanette C. and Arthur Somerville interview, 6/6/01
Thomas C. Stoddard discussion, 11/30/98
Raymond C. Sargent interview, 1/30/99
Frank S. Wheelwright interview, 11/30/98
Rebecca Bates-McArthur interview, 1/30/99
On turtle races stopped by minister: *Patriot Ledger,* 2/7/92
"The Beechwood Improvement Association, 1909-1979," pamphlet,
   Cohasset Historical Society
James W. Lagrotteria interview, 1/29/99
Katherine E. Mayo, "A History of the Nantasket Library Incorporated,
   1890-1970," Feb. 1970

351

"History of the Oaks Farm," videotape, Living History Series, Cohasset
    Historical Society
Pauline A. Keating interview, 11/30/98
Burtram J. Pratt, *A Narrative History of the Town of Cohasset, Massachusetts,*
    Vol. II (Cohasset, Mass.: Committee on Town History, 1956)
Edward F. Goff interview, 9/8/98
Frank H. White interview, 12/7/98
"The Story of Holly Hill Farm," *Bulletin of the Trustees of Reservations,*
    Winter/Spring 1981
Harold W. Litchfield discussion, 1/99
List of Persons Residing in the Town of Cohasset, 1950, 1959

Lobster Fishing

A. J. Antoine, Jr., interview, 11/12/98
Kenneth R. Jason and Herbert L. Jason interview, 1/25/99
Charles E. Butman, Jr., interview, 12/31/98
"Covering the Waterfront," videotape, Living History Series, Cohasset
    Historical Society
Dino Drudi, "Fishing for a Living is Dangerous Work," excerpted from
    Compensation and Working Conditions, Bureau of Labor Statistics,
    Summer 1998
William G. Stone interview, 12/31/98
On Irish mossing: information from Scituate Historical Society's Maritime
    and Irish Mossing Museum
On overfishing: "Biologists Say Lobster Level in a Pinch," *Boston Globe,*
    7/24/98; *Cohasset Mariner,* 6/15/00

The Cove

Richard P. Barrow interview, 11/18/98
A. J. Antoine, Jr., interview, 11/12/98
Gilbert S. Tower, unpublished article, 5/31/75
Clark Chatterton interview, 12/11/98
Cohasset Mariner, 2/9/83, 8/25/88
Advertisements and notices in various issues of the *South Shore Mirror*
    and *South Shore News*
Edward F. Goff interview, 9/8/98
Pratt, *Narrative History*
E. Victor Bigelow, *A Narrative History of the Town of Cohasset, Massachusetts*
    (Cohasset. Mass.: Committee on Town History, 1898; reprint, 1970)

The Village

Louis N. Simeone interview, 11/4/98
Town Reports, various years
Pauline A. Keating interview, 11/30/98
Frank H. White interview, 12/7/98

Burtram J. Pratt, "Entertainment for Man and Beast Still Available at
    Cohasset's Red Lion Inn Celebrating 250th Anniversary This Summer,"
    unpublished article, 8/17/54
Robert N. Fraser discussion, 8/5/99
On Cohasset Hardware Store: *South Shore Mirror,* 6/2/66; James Watson
    interview, 11/28/00
Anna A. Abbruzzese discussion, 11/17/98
Louis F. Eaton, Jr., interview, 10/29/98
David Wadsworth, article in *Cohasset Mirror,* 12/17/80
On Village Shopping Center: *South Shore Mirror,* 3/21/57

The Highway

Francis L. Mitchell discussion, 11/23/98; *Cohasset Mariner,* 2/18/88
Edward F. Goff interview, 9/8/98
On Cushing Plaza: *South Shore Mirror,* 4/11/57, 8/25/60; *South Shore
    News,* 5/12/60
D.S. Kennedy and Company Profile
D.S. Kennedy Notes, communication from John M. Seavey, 9/22/01
Merle S. Brown interview, 11/23/8
David Wadsworth, "A Brief History of the Hagerty Company of Cohasset,
    Mass.," pamphlet
South Shore News, 5/12/60; *South Look/* Mariner Newspapers, 7/7-8/99

Demise of the Railroad

Louis F. Eaton, Jr., interview, 10/29/98
Boston Herald Sunday rotogravure section, Jan. 1949
On problems of the railroad: *South Shore Mirror,* 9/19/57, 7/2/59,
    2/4/01, *South Shore News,* 4/16/84
David Wadsworth note, 9/99
James A. Henretta et al., *America's History since 1865* (Chicago: Dorsey
    Press, 1987)

New Faces, New Homes, New Streets

List of Persons 1950, 1959
John J. Rowlands, *Spindrift from a House by the Sea* (New York: W.W.
    Norton, 1960)
Henry A. Rattenbury interview, 11/11/98
On postwar optimism: *Cohasset Mariner,* 10/24/91
David Wadsworth, "Curator's corner: Victorian Summer Estates Mirrored a
    Lifestyle," *Historical Highlights,* Fall 1998; also his list of houses built in
    the 1950s
On Diab development: *Patriot Ledger,* 10/31/97
George E. Buckley correspondence, 12/2/98
Cohasset Mariner, 5/5/88
Frank H. White interview, 12/7/98

Harold W. Litchfield discussion, 1/99
David H. Wadsworth discussion, 11/11/98
Edward F. Goff interview, 9/8/98
Richard P. Barrow and Jean F. Higgins discussion, 11/17/99
Cohasset U.S.A. 200 Years, 1970
Town Reports, various years

New Schools

Town Reports, 1950-1959
Anna A. Abbruzzese discussion, 11/17/98
Report of the School Study Committee
Osborne F. Ingram interview, 11/9/98
Henry A. Rattenbury interview, 11/11/98
On new high school: *South Shore News,* 9/28/51
On Walter Sweeney: *South Shore Mirror,* 12/25/58; *Brockton Enterprise,*
    9/20/85; CHS Class of 1959 25th Reunion Directory, 1984
On need for new high school wing: *South Shore Mirror,* 8/30/56
Robert G. Ripley and Elizabeth B. Ripley interview, 12/3/98
On Deer Hill School land: *South Shore News,* 9/25/53
On AFS program, Science Fairs, AP program: *South Shore Mirror,* 4/12/56;
    3/28/57; 1/23/58

Churches

Pratt, *Narrative History*
Marion Bowditch interview, 11/13/98
Roscoe Trueblood, "Say I Was Glad," reprinted with permission of the
    Parish Committee, First Parish
Epilogue to "Historical Sketch of the First Parish Church and Its Meeting
    House," 6/15/86
South Shore Mirror, 6/17/71
Brochure for Chatterton retirement reception, June 1972
South Shore Mirror, 5/9/63, 5/11/72, 9/21/72
Cohasset Mariner, 5/2/91, 9/4/97
Frances Chatterton interview, 3/2/99
Osborne F. Ingram interview, 11/9/98
Beechwood Congregational Church Centennial Anniversary
    pamphlet, 1967
On Portuguese and Italian confessors: bulletins from St. Anthony's Church,
    May and June 1957
Cohasset Mariner, 8/10/89
Roger Leonard, *We Protect: An Historical Account and Social Study of the
    Portuguese in Cohasset, Massachusetts,* privately printed, 1994
Robert Leonard and Roger Leonard interview, 2/21/99
"Our Future, Our Faith: Saint Anthony Parish," pamphlet, 1999
So Worship We God, ed. Pottenger

On new St. Stephen's Parish House: *South Shore Mirror*, 4/11/57
Tree of Shelter, Vedanta Center, Cohasset, Mass., 1979
Program for Dedication of the New Temple of the Universal Spirit, 10/4/59
Dr. Susan Schrager communication, 2/6/99; interview, 9/1/99
On Pope Memorial Church: *Cohasset Mariner*, 9/13/79, 10/28/81, 7/7/94

Town Organizations

On Little League: *South Shore News*, 3/21/52, 4/18/52; Cohasset Little
    League banquet program,1952; *South Shore Mirror*, 4/28/57; *Cohasset
    Mariner*, 5/2/96; Robert Leonard and Roger Leonard interview,
    2/21/99; Albert Sencabaugh discussion, 5/01
Gordon Flint interview, 12/4/98
Clark Chatterton interview, 12/11/98
Arthur L. Lehr, Jr., interview, 12/11/98
On Dorothy Bates: *South Shore Mirror*, 3/21/57; Rebecca Bates-McArthur
    interview, 1/30/99
On Red Cross programs: *South Shore News*, 3/7/52, 8/7/53; *South Shore
    Mirror*, 8/27/59; *Cohasset Mariner*, 5/9/91; Alfred G. Odermatt inter-
    view, 11/5/98
Pratt, *Narrative History*
On Community Center: *South Shore Mirror*, 5/14/59; Eleanor G. Bleakie
    interview, 9/27/99
On Nathaniel Hurwitz: *South Shore Mirror*, 1/12/61, 3/9/61
On Town Hall: David H. Wadsworth, article in *Cohasset Mariner*, 8/2/84
On Cohasset Dramatic Club and South Shore Music Circus: writing con
    tributed by Molly Hochkeppel Pierson
On South Shore Art Center. *South Shore Mirror*, 2/9/56, 9/27/56,
    4/25/57; *South Look*/Mariner Newspapers, 6/17/98; information from
    a 1959 art festival program; Thomas Lucas interview, 1/18/99
On Community Garden Club: *South Shore News*, 2/5/59; Mildred P.
    Grinnell discussion, 3/5/99; Rita Morgan discussion, 12/8/01
On Social Service League: Susan Higginson McVeigh, research notes on
    Social Service League; *South Shore News*, 6/26/53, 12/4/53; *South
    Shore Mirror*, 5/17/56, 8/8/57; Motoko T. Deane communication,
    11/15/01
Konohassett Lodge, A.F. & A.M., Cohasset, Massachusetts, "One Hundred
    Years of Light," pamphlet, 1965; Nelson C. Pratt, Jr., interview, 2/9/99
On Rotary Club: *South Shore News*, 10/27/50; "Brief Facts about Rotary,"
    pamphlet, 1953; *South Shore Mirror*, 10/23/51, 8/30/56
Cohasset Golf Club: The First 100 Years, ed. Ronald P. Hobson, 1994;
    Laurence Leamer, *The Kennedy Women* (New York: Villard Books, 1994)
Cohasset Yacht Club: A Centennial History: 1894-1994; Rowlands, *Spindrift*

Town Government

Nancy S. Garrison interview, 11/13/98
Town Reports, 1950-1959, 1997

Louis C. Bailey discussion, 9/30/99
George E. Buckley correspondence, 12/2/98
Louis F. Eaton, Jr., interview, 12/3/98
Ira Stoughton, Jr., discussion, 2/11/02
On Norman Card: *Tinytown Gazette,* 12/19/95
Philip N. Bowditch interview, 11/9/98
Marcia C. Carthaus and Philip M. James interview, 4/30/99
Henry A. Rattenbury interview, 11/11/98
On drive-in movie theater: *South Shore Mirror,* 11/10/55
On zoning Route 3A for light industry: *Cohasset Mariner,* 4/24/97

Natural Disasters
On Hurricane Carol: *Boston Sunday Globe,* 9/19/54
On Dutch elm disease: *South Shore Life,* 12/10/54; *South Shore Mirror,*
   11/13/58

War and the Threat of War
Henretta, *America's History*
Col. Harry G. Summers, Jr., "The Korean War: A Fresh Perspective,"
   Military History, April 1996
Nelson C. Pratt, Jr., interview 2/9/99
On Clifford Strout: *South Shore News,* 2/22/52, 4/11/52
On Joseph Salvador: *South Shore News,* 1/5/51
On Barron Salvador: *South Shore News,* 7/24/53
Town Reports, 1950, 1952, 1954, 1957, 1959, 1991
On Civil Defense: *South Shore Mirror,* 2/14/57
Arthur L. Lehr, Jr., interview, 12/11/98
Clifford J. Dickson and David R. Marks, Jr., discussion, 7/15/99
Edwin H. Pratt discussion, 6/28/00

COHASSET IN THE 1960s
Portrait
Henretta., *America's History*
David Farber, *The Age of Great Dreams: America in the 1960s* (New York:
   Hill and Wang, 1994)
On the 1960 presidential election: *South Shore Mirror,* 11/10/60
Louis F. Eaton, Jr., interview, 9/30/99
David H. Wadsworth discussion, 6/13/98
Lincoln P. Bloomfield and Irirangi C. Bloomfield interview, 9/7/99
Sheila S. Evans interview, 9/23/99
Genevieve G. Good interview, 9/8/99

Preserving the Past
South Shore Mirror, 8/9/56, 4/18/57, 7/2/64, 8/6/64, 6/20/68
Information compiled by Henry F. Howe and displayed at the Maritime
   Museum, 1960

Cohasset Historical Society, "Highlights," May 1972
On Robert Fraser: *South Shore News*, 6/10/65
Cohasset Historical Society, "Cohasset Maritime Museum (Samuel Bates'
Ship Chandlery): An Historical Profile"
On the ancient anchor: *Quincy Patriot Ledger*, 6/5/60
David Wadsworth, "Cohasset's Maritime Museum was Host to a Ghost,"
Cohasset Historical Society pamphlet
Robert N. Fraser discussion, 8/5/99
Marjorie Ladd discussion, 10/22/99
On Minot's Light construction site: *South Shore Mirror*, 8/29/68; Harry H.
Ritter discussion, 11/29/99

Coping with Growth

Allen Benjamin, *Long-Range General Plan for Cohasset*, Dec. 1961
On Route 3A and village: *South Shore News*, 5/12/60, 11/7/65, 2/25/65,
2/11/65, *South Shore Mirror*, 8/4/60, 8/18/60, 1/4/62, 5/23/63,
1/2/64, 4/28/66; *Cohasset Mariner*, 3/17/82, 8/6/98; *Boston Sunday
Globe*, 5/10/64; Henry Rattenbury interview, 11/11/98
On new homes: Town Reports, 1963, 1965, 1966, 1968; *South Shore
Mirror*, 9/11/69, 4/23/64, Harold Litchfield discussion, 10/20/99;
Joseph Peroncello interview, 9/28/99; Evelyn Prescott discussion,
6/28/99; Francis L. Mitchell discussion, 11/23/98; Richard P. Barrow
interview,11/18/98

Sewer Saga: Part I

Pratt, *Narrative History*, pp. 98-100
South Shore Mirror, 8/2/62, 10/11/62, 12/2/62
Town Reports, 1957, 1960, 1965, 1969
Joseph Perroncello interview, 9/28/99
Sheila S. Evans interview, 9/23/99
Philip Bowditch interview, 11/9/98
Henry Rattenbury interview, 11/11/98
Boston Sunday Globe, 5/10/64

Out with the Old, In with the New

On Fire-Police Headquarters: Town Reports, 1950, 1960, 1962; Benjamin
Report, 1961; *South Shore Mirror*, 3/8/62, 6/15/67, 6/29/67; Tom
Finegan discussion, 11/11/99; Richard P. Barrow interview, 11/18/98
On libraries: Benjamin Report, 1961; library pamphlet, 1970; *South Shore
Mirror*, 9/17/64, 4/25/68, 4/24/69
On St. Anthony's: *Cohasset Mariner*, 8/10/89; *South Shore News*, 7/8/65;
Patriot Ledger, 7/8/65 and undated article; Leonard, *We Protect*
On Black Rock House: "Cohasset's Seashore Hotels of the 19th Century,"
Cohasset Historical Society pamphlet; Pratt, *Narrative History;* Oliver H.
Howe, "Two Old-Time Cohasset Inns," *Cohasset Cottager*, 7/4/30; *South
Shore News*, 10/29/64; *Patriot Ledger* article, 1964; *South Shore Mirror*
article, 1969; Charles Higginson discussion, 8/5/00

Youth Days, Sailing Club, and More

Boston Sunday Globe, 5/10/64
On CYAA: *South Shore Mirror,* 5/5/60, 8/31/61, 11/7/63, 6/18/64,
4/28/66, 6/2/66, 6/9/66, 7/21/66; *South Shore News,* 7/8/65
On Boosters Club and Hot Sullivan: *South Shore Mirror,* 5/16/64, 10/1/64;
Patriot Ledger, 10/1/64; Jeanne Sullivan discussion, 9/4/99
On Sailing Club: 1960 newspaper clipping posted at club; *South Shore
News,* 8/6/64; *South Shore Mirror,* 9/8/60t
On Tennis : Anna Abbruzzese discussion, 10/30/98; J. Blake Thaxter dis-
cussion, 5/24/99; *South Shore Mirror,* 8/18/60, 8/17/61, 11/2/61;
South Shore News, 3/12/64; *Cohasset Mariner,* 8/2/01
On Slalom: *South Shore News,* 9/30/65
On LWV: Margaret A. Lynch discussion, 8/11/99; Ann Whelan discussion,
9/1/99; *South Shore Mirror,* 2/1/62, 2/14/63, 2/23/67
On Newcomers Club: *South Shore News,* 1/23/64; Department of Defense
publication, 1961
On Lions and Goats: *Patriot Ledger,* 11/25/57; *South Shore News,* 2/18/65,
8/12/65; *South Shore Mirror,* 11/17/66, 1/27/66; Joseph S. Laugelle
discussion, 11/22/99

Changes in Town Government

Richard D. Leggat interview, 9/26/99
Philip Bowditch interview, 11/9/98
Joseph Perroncello interview, 9/28/99
Louis F. Eaton, Jr., interview, 9/30/99
On selectmen: *South Shore Mirror,* 3/9/61, 3/14/63, 10/6/66, 9/14/67,
1/11/68; Town Reports, 1962, 1968; Oliver H. Howe,"Chronological
History of Cohasset"; Mary Jeanette Murray interview, 9/7/99; *Patriot
Ledger,* 3/8/77, 5/29/81
On conservation: Town Reports, 1958, 1961, 1964; *Boston Sunday Globe,*
5/10/64; "Town of Cohasset Open Space and Recreation Plan, 1997-
2001," 1996 publication of the Open Space Advisory Committee; *South
Shore Mirror,* 2/16/61, 5/16/68, 7/4/68; *Cohasset Mariner,* 7/23/98
On end-of-decade business: Town Report, 1968; *South Shore Mirror,*
2/26/70, 5/6/71, 5/20/71, 9/20/73; Harry H. Ritter discussion,
11/29/99

Changes in the Schools

Town Reports, 1960-1969
South Shore Mirror, 2/18/60, 9/29/60, 7/23/63, 4/13/67,
8/2/68,11/28/68, 2/6/69, 5/1/69, 5/15/69
Sheila S. Evans interview, 9/23/99
Boston Traveler, 6/11/64
William W. Park interview, 9/4/99
Marilyn C. Previte interview, 9/21/99

South Shore News, 2/18/65, 9/2/65, 12/23/65
Henretta, *America's History*
Gregory P. Dormitzer discussion, 8/9/99
Irirangi C. and Lincoln P. Bloomfield interview, 9/7/99
Cohasset Mariner, 11/12/98
Louis F. Eaton, Jr., interview, 9/30/99

The "Sixties" in Cohasset
William W. Park interview, 9/4/99
Sheila S Evans interview, 9/23/99
South Shore Mirror, 8/11/60, 1/9/64, 11/10/66, 6/67, 7/6/67, 8/10/67,
    1/30/69, 5/22/69, 8/7/69
Bishop, "Saint Stephen's Church"
South Shore News, 1/14/65, 1/28/65, 8/26/65
Corinne H. Cahill discussion, 12/12/99
Dr. Susan Schrager interview, 9/1/99
Marilyn C. Previte interview, 9/21/99
Thomas D. Corrigan discussion, 8/14/99

A Town Divided
Henretta, *America's History*
Farber, *The Age of Great Dreams*
Robert K. Brigham, "Battlefield Vietnam: A Brief History"
Barone, *Our Country*
James Gilbert, *Another Chance: Postwar America, 1945-1968* (Philadelphia:
    Temple University Press, 1981)
Irirangi C. and Lincoln P. Bloomfield interview, 9/7/99
Peter J. Pratt discussion, 4/26/00
South Shore Mirror, 10/23/69, 11/13/69, 11/20/69, 12/11/69
South Shore News, 9/26/65
Bishop, "Saint Stephen's Church"

In Memoriam
Cohasset Mariner, 8/26/99
Patriot Ledger, 11/11/96
South Shore Mirror, 7/6/67, 5/15/69
Information from citation for Bronze Star Medal of Craig Michael Simeone
Information from Glenn A. Pratt and Robert W. Jackson
Cohasset Veterans Day, 1996, video

COHASSET IN THE 1970s
Portrait
Henretta, *America's History*
Peter N. Carroll, *It Seemed Like Nothing Happened: America in the 1970s*
    (New Brunswick: Rutgers University Press, 1982, 1990)
Patriot Ledger, 6/11/74, 2/18/75
Genevieve G. Good interview, 9/8/99

Celebrating the Past

On Cohassset Bicentennial: article by Burtram J. Pratt in *Massachusetts Selectman*, January 1970; Bicentennial Schedule of Events pamphlet; *South Shore News* article, n.d.; *South Shore Mirror*, 6/25/70, 7/16/70; *Patriot Ledger*, 7/11/70, 7/13/70, 8/10/70; Bicentennial brochure on Tour of Historic Houses; *Cohasset Mariner*, 5/27/81; *Boston Herald Traveler*, 7/20/70; script for *Town Meeting: 1770*

On historical assets: Town Report, 1973; article by David Wadsworth, *Cohasset Mariner*, 1/29/87; D. Wadsworth interview, 7/13/00

On Lothrop House: *Patriot Ledger*, 8/2/79; Cohasset Historical Society pamphlet, "Cohasset Historical Society: A Brief History of the Society from 1928"; Frances (Tower) Maroni discussion, 12/2/00

On National Bicentennial: *Patriot Ledger*, various issues 2/17/76 to 7/12/76

On archives: David Wadsworth interview, 7/5/00; article by D. Wadsworth, *Cohasset Mariner*, 11/8/79

Facing the Present

On school controversy: *Patriot Ledger*, various issues 11/3/71 to 6/11/75; *South Shore Mirror*, various issues 4/8/71 to 12/6/73; Town Report, 1973; Margaret R. Charles discussion, 5/6/00; Peter J. Pratt discussion, 4/26/00; John P. Reardon, Jr., discussion, 4/29/00

On other school issues: Town Reports, 1970, 1971,1974, 1979; *Patriot Ledger*, various issues 5/13/74 to 7/14/78; "Cohasset Through the Spyglass," Cohasset League of Women Voters, 1976; Clark Chatterton interview, 12/11/98; Katherine F. Stanton discussion, 6/7/00; *Cohasset Mariner*, 2/8/79, 3/22/79, 4/5/79

On Cove confrontation: *Patriot Ledger*, various issues 8/11/71 to 3/4/77; *South Shore News*, 3/4/65; Barbara Power discussion, 4/28/00; letter from W. Chester Browne and Associates, Inc., 7/22/71; *Cohasset Mirror*, 1/12/78; *Cohasset Mariner*, 1/4/79, 10/7/93; *South Shore Mirror*, 6/18/64; *Boston Globe*, 5/26/75, 4/22/82; *Horse Show* magazine, Nov. 1998

On Charter fight: Town Reports, 1972, 1973; 1974 Charter of the Town of Cohasset; information published by the Friends of the Charter; information published by the Committee for Responsive and Accountable Government in Cohasset; *Patriot Ledger*, 2/24/75, 4/4/75, 5/12/75; *Boston Globe*, 8/9/98, 9/11/00

On Citizens v. Music Circus: *Patriot Ledger*, various issues 8/4/77 to 7/3/78; Mary E. Gainor discussion, 5/17/00

On law and disorder: *Boston* magazine, June 1977; *Cohasset Mariner*, various issues 11/9/78 to 8/2/79, 7/29/81, 8/12/81; *Patriot Ledger*, various issues 12/17/70 to 5/30/78; *Boston Globe*, 12/25/79, 9/24/89

Life Goes On

On Log & Line: *Cohasset Mariner*, 3/15/79

On Target Industries, *Patriot Ledger*, 8/26/76; Osborne F. Ingram interview, 11/9/98

On Strawberry Parfait, *Patriot Ledger*, 3/30/78
On Logan estate: *Patriot Ledger*, 8/20/75; Paula F. Logan interview,
  8/10/99; written communication from P. Logan, n.d.; *Conway Country
  Citizen*, 9/73; *Cohasset Mariner*, 2/14/80; *Boston Globe*, 9/12/00
On Black Rock highrise: *Patriot Ledger*, 10/12/71, 8/10/76; Albert
  Sencabaugh discussion, 5/01
On Harborview: *Cohasset Through the Spyglass*, Cohasset League of
  Women Voters, 1976; Town Reports, 1969, 1999
On Legion Land: *Patriot Ledger*, 3/7/77, 8/2/77; *Cohasset Mariner*, 8/2/79

Churches and Town Organizations

On churches: *South Shore Mirror*, 11/19/70; *So Worship We God*, ed.,
  Pottenger; *Patriot Ledger*, 1/2/74; *Cohasset Mariner*, 9/13/79, 4/17/86,
  8/6/98; David Pottenger discussion, 9/30/99
On Community Center: information published for special town meeting,
  12/6/76; *Patriot Ledger*, various issues 11/4/76 to 2/15/79;
  Community Center "History," 1990; *Cohasset Mariner*, 7/4/85; Glenn A.
  Pratt discussion, 6/26/01
On other organizations: *Patriot Ledger*, various issues 6/17/71 to 8/14/78;
  Arthur L. Lehr, Jr., interview, 12/11/98; Clark Chatterton Interview,
  12/11/98; *Cohasset Mariner*, 10/78, 4/8/93, 6/22/00

The Ecological Decade

South Shore Mirror, 4/9/70
Patriot Ledger, 11/12/71, various issues 6/18/75 to 2/28/77
Cohasset Mariner, 3/15/79, 1/28/88, 4/13/89
Town Reports, 1970, 1972
Town of Cohasset Open Space and Recreation Plan, 1997-2001, Oct. 1996
Cohasset Coastal Zone Study, 1976
"An Old New England Town Common," Cohasset Historical Society

Sewer Saga: Part II

Town Reports, 1973, 1975, 1979
Claudia Copeland, "Clean Water Act: A Summary of the Law,"
  Congressional Research Service Issue Brief, Jan. 20, 1999
Patriot Ledger, various issues 12/18/75 to 6/29/78
Cohasset Mariner, 4/12/79, 9/6/79, 11/29/79, 2/12/98
Edward M. Guild discussion, 3/7/01

Aaron River Reservoir

Benjamin Report, 1961
Patriot Ledger, various issues 1/6/72 to 6/11/79
Town Report, 1965
Cohasset Mariner, 10/5/78, 12/15/82
Town of Cohasset Open Space and Recreation Plan, 1997-2001, Oct. 1996
Edwin H. Pratt interview, 6/28/00
Cohasset Water Supply Improvement Program, 1978-79 (brochure)

Blizzard of '78
Ralph S. Dormitzer communication, 10/12/00
Boston Herald American, 2/9/78, 2/12/78
South Shore Mirror, 2/9/78
Patriot Ledger, 2/17/78, 2/23/78

COHASSET IN THE 1980s
Portrait
Cohasset Mariner, 5/29/86, 10/20/83
Data from U.S. Census and Department of Housing and Community
  Development; Town Reports
Thomas A. Bailey and David M. Kennedy, *The American Pageant*, 10th ed.
  (Lexington, Mass.: D.C. Heath , 1970)

Prop 2 1/2
What Is Prop 2 1/2?" Official Town of Wellesley Web Site, Board of
  Assessors, www.ci.wellesley.ma
Susanne Tompkins, "Proposition 2 1/2," www.mccormack.umb.edu
Cohasset Mariner, 10/16/80, 11/8/80, 12/11/80,12/1/83, 3/24/88,
  6/1/89,6/29/89, letter to editor 5/20/99, 7/26/01
Patriot Ledger, 11/14/80
William S. Signorelli interview, 11/6/00
Advisory Committee Reports, warrants for 1981,1988 town meetings
Town Reports, 1981,1985, 1988, 1989
Boston Globe, 12/31/89

Strong Chief/Weak Chief
Richard P. Barrow interview, 11/18/98
Cohasset Mariner, various issues 8/14/80 to 1/9/86
Patriot Ledger, 5/1/81, 12/2/82
Boston Globe, 11/24/81
Town Reports, 1982, 1983
Tinytown Gazette, 2/20/96, 1/10/01
Rocco F. Laugelle interview, 1/19/01
Mary Jane E. McArthur discussion, 3/29/01

Restructuring Town Government
Cohasset Mariner, various issues 3/6/80 to 2/21/85
William D. Weeks interview, 11/10/00
Town Reports, 1980, 1983, 1985, 1987
Gordon E. Flint interview, 12/4/98
William S. Signorelli interview, 11/6/00
Bigelow, *Narrative History*
Pratt, *Narrative History*
Cohasset Mariner, 1/11/79, 5/11/83, 7/5/84, 7/12/84, 8/2/84, 3/20/97
South Look/Cohasset Mariner, 4/14-16/87
Town Reports, 1987, 1988

Changes in the Schools

Cohasset Mariner, various issues 11/20/80 to 12/21/89
Town Reports, 1981, 1982, 1983, 1988, 1989
Boston Globe, 3/12/88
Norma J. Grassey discussion, 1/15/01

Clusters, Condos, and Dockominium

Town Reports, 1981, 1985
Cohasset Mariner, various issues 8/7/80 to 12/21/89, 5/14/98
Boston Globe, 6/18/84, 10/2/87
Patriot Ledger, 11/4/83, 11/2/90
Chartis L. Tebbetts discussion, 11/12/00
Rev. E. Clifford Cutler discussion, 2/16/01

Sewer Saga: Part III

Town Reports, 1980-1989
Cohasset Mariner, various issues 2/21/80 to 2/16/89
R. M. Campbell, "The Sewer Follies of Cohasset," July 1984
Henry A. Rattenbury, Jr., interview, 11/11/98
Edward M. Guild interview, 1/9/01
Joseph M. Gwinn discussion, 1/10/01
Janet M. Daggett discussion, 1/12/01

Cohasset Heights Limited

Patriot Ledger, 6/24/76, 12/16/76
Cohasset Mariner, various issues 12/21/78 to 6/16/88, 4/6/95
Board of Health files

New Traditions

On the Panagia Greek Orthodox Church: *Cohasset Mariner*, 6/26/80,
    12/25/80, 5/15/86, 9/4/97
On reaching out: *Cohasset Mariner*, 7/4/82, 3/27/86, 11/27/86, 6/23/88,
    8/3/89, 3/15/01, 7/12/01; Dr. Susan Schrager interview, 9/1/99; *So
    Worship We God*, ed. Pottenger; Rev. E. Clifford Cutler discussion,
    2/16/01; Web Home Sites: Rosie's Place, Pine Street Inn, Quincy Crisis
    Center, Appalachia Service Project; Barbara Donahue discussion,
    3/17/01; Nancy Anderson discussion, 3/19/01
On seniors: *Cohasset Mariner*, 1/23/86, 10/16/86, 11/12/98; *Senior Vista
    News*, Dec. 2000; Ralph Perroncello discussion, 11/27/00
On Art Center: *Cohasset Mariner*, 7/2/87, 7/10/87, 11/26/87
On cultural exchange: *Cohasset Mariner*, various issues 6/17/81 to
    8/20/87, 5/28/92; Town Reports, 1986, 1987; Margot Cheel discus-
    sion, 3/13/ 01; Jane Goedecke discussion, 3/13/01; David M. Kennedy,
    Over Here: The First World War and American Society (New York: Oxford
    University Press, 1980)

A Stroll through the Past

Town Reports, 1983, 1989
Cohasset Mariner, various issues 4/23/81 to 8/17/00
Information from plaques on Captains' Walk
Leonard, *We Protect*
Pratt, *Narrative History*
Hamilton T. Tewskbury discussion, 8/23/01

The Witches of Eastwick

Cohasset Mariner, 6/19/86, 6/26/86, 8/21/86, 10/9/86
Patriot Ledger, 6/14/86
James Watson interview, 11/28/00

COHASSET IN THE 1990s

Portrait

Charles Butman, Jr., discussion, 11/6/99
Data from Massachusetts Department of Housing and Community
  Development, Community Profiles
Cohasset Mariner, 1/10/91, 4/18/91, 5/5/94, 7/26/01
Patriot Ledger, 10/15/01, 10/17/01
Karen Golden discussion, 12/18/99
William W. Park interview, 9/4/99
William S. Signorelli interview, 11/6/00
Mark W. Haddad interview, 8/8/01
Robert D. Putnam, *Bowling Alone: The Collapse and Revival of American
  Community* (New York: Simon & Schuster, 2000)

A Heroes' Welcome

Bailey and Kennedy, *American Pageant*
Roger J. Spiller, "A War against History," *American Heritage,* Feb./March 2001
Town Report, 1991
Cohasset Mariner, 3/7/91

Village Beautification

Cohasset Mariner, various issues 3/1/90 to 1/27/00
Alix White communication, 5/10/01
Boston Globe, 8/6/00
Gordon E. Flint interview, 12/4/98
Patriot Ledger, 4/21/00

Harbor Renewal

On Lightkeepers' Residence: *Cohasset Mariner*, various issues 6/21/90 to
  7/16/98; *Boston Globe*, 10/4/92; Joseph R. McElroy interview, 8/23/01;
  videotape of Grand Opening, 5/15/94; Louise G. Littlehale discussion,
  8/25/01

On Mariners Park: *Patriot Ledger*, 2/4/93; Town Report, 1993; *Cohasset Mariner*, 4/25/96, 9/11/97,10/22/98,12/24/98, 8/28/00, 7/19/01; John C. Buckley discussion, 8/22/01; James R. Bonetti discussion, 9/5/01
On Antoine and Wilson Memorial: *Cohasset Mariner*, 7/1/99, 10/28/99, 5/25/00; *Lighthouse Digest*, July 2000

Highway Improvement
Cohasset Mariner, various issues 10/24/91 to 4/9/98
Town of Cohasset Open Space and Recreation Plan, 1997-2001, Oct. 1996
A Guide to the Properties of the Trustees of Reservations, 1992

SAFE and CHL
Cohasset Mariner, various issues 7/4/91 to 4/13/00
Boston Globe, 5/5/96, 9/6/98
Patriot Ledger, 7/20/98, 3/27/00
Town Report, 2000

Changes in the Water Department
Cohasset Mariner, various issues 5/16/91 to 4/20/00
Town Reports, 1994 to 2000
Town of Cohasset Open Space and Recreation Plan, 1997-2001, Oct. 1996

Sewer Saga: Part IV
Cohasset Mariner, various issues 5/16/91 to 11/16/00
Town Reports, 1995 to 2000
Boston Globe, 1/7/96, 3/30/96
Henry A. Rattenbury, Jr., interview, 11/11/98
Edward M. Guild interview, 1/9/01

Reviving the Railroad
Cohasset Mariner, 12/20/84, 4/18/85; various issues 3/15/90 to 8/30/01
www.bigdig.com
Patriot Ledger, 8/21/76, 9/29/98
Boston Globe, 8/5/86, 11/15/90, 5/14/95
Town Manager Report, March 6, 2000

Upgrading the Schools
Cohasset Mariner, various issues 12/6/90 to 3/27/00
Lawrence R. Shultz discussion, 7/14/01
Town Reports, 1993, 1996, 1997, 1998
Marilyn C. Previte interview, 9/21/99
Mary Jane E. McArthur discussion, 3/29/01

Reshaping Town Government
William D. Weeks interview, 11/10/00
William S. Signorelli interview, 11/6/00

Cohasset Mariner, various issues 11/9/95 to 1/14/99
Town Reports, 1995 to 1998
Mark W. Haddad interview, 8/8/01

Protecting the Public

On Fire Department: *Cohasset Mariner*, various issues 7/12/90 to
    10/7/93, 10/23/97, 8/2/01; Town Reports, 1992,1993, 2000; Roger W.
    Lincoln discussion, 9/24/01
On Police Department: *Cohasset Mariner*, 10/16/86, 10/4/90, various
    issues 1/21/93 to 12/28/00; *Boston Globe*,12/01/95, 8/11/96; Brian
    W. Noonan discussion, 8/6/01
On Kennedy scandal: *Cohasset Mariner*, 3/22/84, various issues 4/14/92
    to 1/8/98; *Boston* magazine, Sept. 1997; *Time* magazine, July 26, 1999

Community Life

On churches: *Cohasset Mariner*, various issues 6/28/90 to 9/7/00;
    "Taking Our Heritage to the Future," First Parish, Feb. 1999; *Patriot
    Ledger*, 12/2-3/95; brochure on St. Stephen's carillon, 1999; *Boston
    Globe*, 8/30/99,10/3/99; "Our Future, Our Faith," St. Anthony
    brochure, 1999; Rev. John R. Mulvehill discussion, 9/28/01; "A Brief
    Overview of Vedanta Centre and Ananda Ashrama"; Dr. Susan
    Schrager interview, 9/1/99; Motoko Deane communication, 10/18/01;
    Rev. John Maheras discussion, 2/1/01
On community activities: *Cohasset Mariner*, 8/16/84 and various issues,
    6/27/91 to 5/3/01; *Boston Globe*, 6/17/90, 8/28/94; *Cohasset Yacht
    Club: Centennial History*; *Cohasset Golf Club: First 100 Years*, ed. Hobson;
    Clifford Mitman, Jr., communication, 10/3/01; Marilyn C. Previte inter-
    view, 9/21/99
Robert W. Jackson speech, 9/22/01

Interviews and Discussions

R. Murray Campbell
Margaret R. Charles
Margot P. Cheel
Christine P. Collins
Thomas D. Corrigan
Rev. E. Clifford Cutler
Janet M. Daggett
Motoko T. Deane
Clifford J. Dickson and
    David R. Marks, Jr.
Barbara Donahue
Gregory P. Dormitzer
Ralph S. Dormitzer
Thomas Finegan
F. Roy Fitzsimmons
Christopher C. Ford
Robert N. Fraser
Mary E. Gainor
Lawrence Gates
Jane O. Goedecke
Karen Golden
Norma J. Grassey
Mildred P. Grinnell
Thomas L. Gruber
Joseph M. Gwinn
Jean F. Higgins
Charles Higginson
Robert W. Jackson
Marjorie Ladd
Joseph S. Laugelle
Roger W. Lincoln
Harold W. Litchfield
Louise G. Littlehale
Edward B. Long
Margaret A. Lynch
Rev. John Maheras
Frances Maroni
Mary Jane E. McArthur
John K. McNabb, Jr.
Francis L. Mitchell

Clifford Mitman, Jr.
Anne Montague
Robert Montague
Rita Morgan
Rev. John R. Mulvehill
Edward T. Mulvey
Virginia L. Najmi
Brian W. Noonan
Margaret M. O'Donnell
Ralph Perroncello
David H. Pottenger
Barbara M. Power
Glenn A. Pratt
Peter J. Pratt
Evelyn Prescott
John P. Reardon, Jr.
Harry H. Ritter
Rev. Gary A. Ritts
Nancy L. Sandell
John M. Seavey
Albert M. Sencabaugh
Ross Sherbrooke
Lawrence R. Shultz
Lisa D. Smith
Nancy C. Snowdale
Katherine F. Stanton
Thomas C. Stoddard
Ira Stoughton, Jr.
Ernest J. Sullivan
Jeanne Sullivan
Chartis L. Tebbetts
Hamilton T. Tewskbury
J. Blake Thaxter
Robert M. Thompson
Herbert R. Towle
Raimund G. Vanderweil, Jr.
Ann K. Whelan
Alix P. White
Frank Wunschel
Sally Young

SELECTED TOWN OFFICIALS
1950 – 2000

Selectmen (chairmen listed first)

1950	Norman Card Ira B. P. Stoughton Everett W. Wheelwright	1961	George W. McLaughlin Helen E. Scripture Ira B. P. Stoughton
1951	Norman Card Ira B. P. Stoughton Everett W. Wheelwright	1962	George W. McLaughlin Thomas G. Churchill Helen E. Scripture Ira B. P. Stoughton (died Jan. 4, 1962)
1952	Norman Card Helen E. Scripture Ira B. P. Stoughton	1963	George W. McLaughlin Nathaniel Hurwitz Helen E. Scripture
1953	Norman Card Helen E. Scripture Ira B. P. Stoughton	1964	George W. McLaughlin Nathaniel Hurwitz Helen E. Scripture
1954	Norman Card Helen E. Scripture Ira B. P. Stoughton	1965	George W. McLaughlin Nathaniel Hurwitz Helen E. Scripture
1955	Norman Card Helen E. Scripture Ira B. P. Stoughton	1966	George W. McLaughlin Nathaniel Hurwitz (died Oct. 4, 1966) Helen E. Scripture
1956	Norman Card Helen E. Scripture Ira B. P. Stoughton	1967	George W. McLaughlin Arthur L. Clark Helen E. Scripture
1957	Norman Card Helen E. Scripture Ira B. P. Stoughton	1968	George W. McLaughlin Arthur L. Clark Helen E. Scripture
1958	Norman Card Helen E. Scripture Ira B. P. Stoughton	1969	Arthur L. Clark George W. McLaughlin Helen E. Scripture
1959	Norman Card Helen E. Scripture Ira B. P. Stoughton	1970	George W. McLaughlin Arthur L. Clark Mary Jeanette Murray
1960	Norman Card (died Dec. 24, 1960) Helen E. Scripture Ira B. P. Stoughton	1971	Arthur L. Clark Henry W. Ainslie, Jr. Mary Jeanette Murray

1972	Arthur L. Clark Henry W. Ainslie, Jr. Mary Jeanette Murray	1984	Clifford J. Mitman, Jr. John A. DeBassio Frank W. England Rocco F. Laugelle
1973	Arthur L. Clark Henry W. Ainslie, Jr. Mary Jeanette Murray		Mary Jane E. McArthur
1974	Arthur L. Clark Henry W. Ainslie, Jr. Mary Jeanette Murray	1985	Frank W. England Rocco F. Laugelle Mary Jane E. McArthur Clifford J. Mitman, Jr. Diane C. Sullivan
1975	Arthur L. Clark Henry W. Ainslie, Jr. Mary Jeanette Murray	1986	Diane C. Sullivan James L. Gallagher Rocco F. Laugelle Mary Jane E. McArthur Clifford J. Mitman, Jr.
1976	Arthur L. Clark Henry W. Ainslie, Jr. Mary Jeanette Murray	1987	Rocco F. Laugelle James L. Gallagher Martha K. Gjesteby Clifford J. Mitman, Jr. Burtram J. Pratt
1977	Arthur L. Clark Henry W. Ainslie, Jr. Mary Jeanette Murray		
1978	Arthur L. Clark Henry W. Ainslie, Jr. Mary Jeanette Murray	1988	Clifford J. Mitman, Jr. James L. Gallagher Martha K. Gjesteby Rocco F. Laugelle Burtram J. Pratt
1979	Arthur L. Clark Henry W. Ainslie, Jr. Rocco F. Laugelle	1989	Burtram J. Pratt James L. Gallagher Martha K. Gjesteby Rocco F. Laugelle Clifford Mitman, Jr.
1980	Arthur L. Clark Henry W. Ainslie, Jr. Rocco F. Laugelle		
1981	Henry W. Ainslie, Jr. Rocco F. Laugelle Mary Jane E. McArthur	1990	Rocco F. Laugelle Martha K. Gjesteby Jane O. Goedecke Diana D. Kornet Edwin H. Tebbetts
1982	Henry W. Ainslie, Jr. Rocco F. Laugelle Mary Jane E. McArthur	1991	Edwin H. Tebbetts Martha K. Gjesteby Jane O. Goedecke Diana D. Kornet Rocco F. Laugelle
1983	Mary Jane E. McArthur John A. DeBassio Frank W. England Rocco F. Laugelle Clifford J. Mitman, Jr.		

1992	Jane O. Goedecke	1997	Michael H. Sullivan
	Merle S. Brown		Merle S. Brown
	Martha K. Gjesteby		Roseanne M. McMorris
	Rocco F. Laugelle		Nancy A. Roth
	Michael H. Sullivan		Diane C. Sullivan
1993	Martha K. Gjesteby	1998	Roseanne M. McMorris
	Merle S. Brown		Merle S. Brown
	Jane O. Goedecke		Thomas J. Callahan
	Rocco F. Laugelle		Nancy A. Roth
	Michael H. Sullivan		Diane C. Sullivan
1994	Michael H. Sullivan	1999	Merle S. Brown
	Merle S. Brown		Thomas J. Callahan
	Martha K. Gjesteby		Frederick R. Koed
	Jane O. Goedecke		Roseanne M. McMorris
	Peter J. Pratt		Diane C. Sullivan
1995	Merle S. Brown	2000	Thomas J. Callahan
	Martha K. Gjesteby		Merle S. Brown
	Jane O. Goedecke		Frederick R. Koed
	Peter J. Pratt		Roseanne M. McMorris
	Michael H. Sullivan		Michael H. Sullivan
1996	Merle S. Brown		
	Roseanne M. McMorris		
	Peter J. Pratt		
	Michael H. Sullivan		
	Nancy A. Roth		

School Committee Chairmen

1950-1952	Harry H. Reed, Jr.	1984-1988	Joseph R. Nedrow
1952-1954	John H. Dean	1988-1989	Diana D. Kornet
1954-1965	Osborne F. Ingram	1989-1993	Barbara W. Bliss
1965-1968	Sumner Smith, Jr.	1993-1995	Nancy L. Sandell
1968-1969	T. Gerard Keating	1995-1997	Ralph D. Kidder
1969-1971	Sumner Smith, Jr.	1997-1988	Maureen E. Jerz
1971-1974	John P. Reardon	1998-1999	Richard Shea
1974-1979	Doris C. Golden	1999-2000	Mark G. DeGiacomo
1979-1980	John Langmaid III	2000-	Patricia C. Martin
1980-1982	Frank W. England		
1982-1983	Diana D. Kornet		
1983-1984	Richard M. Conley		

Advisory Committee Chairmen

1950-1951	Elmer H. Pratt	1974-1977	Joseph R. Barresi
1951-1953	Jerome F.	1977-1978	Brian R. Wilkin
	Wadsworth	1978-1979	John J. Wilson
1953-1956	G. Prescott Low	1979-1980	Patrick J. Hurley
1956-1958	Louis F. Eaton, Jr.	1980-1983	Jean B. Cotton
1958-1960	George W.	1983-1986	Jacqueline M.
	McLaughlin		Dormitzer
1960-1961	Louis F. Eaton, Jr.	1986-1987	Frederick H. Koed
1961-1963	Charles J. Fox	1987-1990	Jane O. Goedecke
1963-1964	Philip N. Bowditch	1990	Raymond
1964-1965	Louis F. Eaton, Jr.		Kasperowicz
1965-1967	Richard D. Leggat	1990-1991	Arne K. Gjesteby
1967-1969	Daniel C. Cotton	1991-1995	Nancy A. Roth
1969-1971	Joseph Peroncello	1995-1999	Roger S. Whitley
1971-1972	Danforth B. Lincoln	1999-	Richard J. Avery
1972-1974	L. Emmett Holt		

Police Chief

1950-1967	Hector J. Pelletier	1982-1992	Joseph A. Kealey
1967-1980	Randolph A. Feola	1993-	Brian W. Noonan
1980-1982	John A. DeBassio		

Fire Chief

1950-1954	Joseph L. Oliver	1983-1985	Martin W. Dooley
1954-1982	Charles Piepenbrink	1986-1992	Daniel F. Brock
1982	Roger W. Lincoln	1992-1993	John R. Nadeau
	(acting chief)	1993-	Roger W. Lincoln

Town Moderator

1950-1969	Robert B. James	1981-1992	William D. Weeks
1969-1981	David E. Place	1992-	George L. Marlette

Town Clerk

1950-1957	William B. Morris	1958-1984	Charles A. Marks
1957-1958	Walter R. Lillard	1984-1991	Frances L. Marks
	(temporary)	1991-	Marion L. Douglas

Town Executive Secretary

1981	Arthur L. Clark	1988-1997	Gregory J. Doyon
1982-1984	Mark J. Lanza	1997	Edward G. McCann
1985-1988	Donald R. Andrew		(temporary)

Town Manager

1997	Edward G. McCann	1997-	Mark W. Haddad
	(acting)		

INDEX

Index

387

Town Hall, 52-53, 226-227
Town Home, 43, 36
Town manager, 328-329
Town meeting quorum change, 208
Town planner, 316
Town pump, 285-286
Townsend, Rev. J. David, 47
Trainor, David L., 172, 179
Trautwein, Todd, 233
Treat's Pond, 117
Tri-Town Commission, 224
Trueblood, Rev. Roscoe E., 40, 128, 130
  poem by, 40
Tupelo Road, 33, 35
Turkey Hill, 302-303
Tutela Engineering, Inc., 307
Tyeryar, James, 248-249, 305

Unionization
  of school personnel, 125
  of town department personnel, 327
Urmson, Brenda and James, 259
U.S. Post Office, 6, 87

Van der Lugt, Hubert, 287
Vanderweil, R. Gary, Jr., 39, 246, 319
VanDuzer, Rev. John, 48
Vedanta Centre, 46-47, 129-130, 254, 340
Veterans Development, Pond Hill, 33-34
Veterans of Foreign Wars, 257
Veterans Memorial Park, 96, 135, 166
Vietnam War
  and Cohasset, 131-139
  dedication ceremonies, 135-136
  heroes, 136-139
Village. See Cohasset village
Village Fair, 43, 252
Village and Harbor Association, 284
Village Renaissance, 284-287
Volpe, John A., 36, 103
Volungis, Judy, 188
Vosoff, Helen Howes, 53
Vosoff Archives, 154

Wade, Andrea and John, 340
Wadsworth, David, 29, 54-55, 156, 226, 267, 271, 290
  and brig St. John, 337-338
  and Maritime Museum ghost, 80
  and The Oaks, 239-240

and Ship Cove, 261-262
and survey of historical assets, 152
and town archives, 156
and Town Hall in 1950s, 52
Wadsworth, Dorothy, 151
Wakeman
  Frances McElwain, 345
  Samuel, 105
Walgreen's Drugstore, 299
Water Commissioners, Board of, 93, 198-200
Water Department, 65, 306-308
Water distribution system, 198-201, 307-308
Water Resource District, 250, 305
Water supply, pollution of, 303-306
Watson
  James, 21, 268
  Louis and Helen, 21
  Robert, 77
  Tina, 21, 286
Webb-Norfolk Conveyor Company, 6, 301
Weber, Steven, 294
Weeks, William D., 75, 246, 328
Weisenfluh, Allen, 258
Welch, Helen, 35
We Protect (Leonard), 45
wheelwright
  Everett W., 64
  Frank, 7
Wheelwright Farm development, 235-236
Wheelwright Park, 185
Whelan
  Ann K., 31, 109, 285
  James, 31
  Robert, 106
Whipple, Jacqueline, 315
White
  Alix P., 288, 303
  Cornelia, 82, 119
  Frank H., 12, 19, 288
  Jane, 284
  Jean, 288
  Richardson, 12-13, 19, 82
Whiteley, Ann, 230, 231
Whitney and Thayer Woods, 302-303
Whittemore, Peter, 304
Whittington, William, 148
Wilder, Thornton, 100

Typeface is ITC Leawood Book, Medium, Bold, & Italic

Color separations by Quebecor World Universal Press, Westwood, Massachusetts

Black-and-white photos scanned by Ralph S. Dormitzer and Harold E. Coughlin

Designed and composed on Macintosh(OS 9.2.2) using QuarkXPress 4.1 by Harold E. Coughlin

Offset printed by Sheridan Books, Fredericksburg, Virginia

Stock is 60 lb. Finch Opaque text and 80 lb. Sterling Ultra Gloss text

Bound by Sheridan Books, Fredericksburg, Virginia

Endleaves are Rainbow Parchment Natural B

Binding cloth is Arrestok/Roxite Linen

Margaret B. Rose   Carol A. Riley   Shirley Marten   Robert F. Johnston   W
Anthony Fasciano   Denise Parsloe   Maureen Healy   Maria Plante   Louis
Crowell   Stephen Hart   Richard Streeter   Gino DiGirolamo   Rev. John K
Kevin Lewis   Michael Gill   David Toma   William Fallon   Maria Cahill   J
Anne O'Leary   Sarah Seavey   Melissa Shea   Edward Minelli   Lisa Shumaker
Bogarty   James Creed   Bryan Edwards   Tom Larson   Matt Maloney   Maur
Andy Starmer   Todd Trautwein   Barbara Froio   Leo J. Happenny   Kriste
O'Toole   Israel M. Sanchez, Jr.   Harold E. Coughlin   Maxwell Pounder   M
M. Donahue   Sharon Becker   Nancy Anderson   Michael Smith   Rev. John
Ralph Perroncello   William Barnes   Emilio Conte   Theodore R. Eaton
Thomas Hamilton   Jean Lennon   Barbara and Alex Spooner   George Fortin
Judith S. Keim   Julia and Sarah Atkinson   Patricia Murphy   Gilbert Tower
Tewksbury   Samuel Mercer   Sue Straley   James Watson   Prescott T. Cum
Marjorie F. Ritter   Jean M. Salvador   Maria Jason   Charles B. Wood   Lawre
Helen Howes Vosoff   Henry Dormitzer   Nelson Megna   Claus Guggenber
Douglas James   John F. Maloney   Gia Baressi   Michael Christopher Gurnis
Chester Browne   Jane W. Bancroft   Michael Abbruzzese   William C. Cox
Ruth S. Payne   Lester Hiltz   David Trainor   Arthur C. Herrington   Peter
Edward Logan   John Murphy   John Riley   Margaret A. Lynch   Samuel Ha
Chatterton   John M. Worley   Edward Jacome   Judy Volungis   Regina Schu
Bleakie   Albert M. Hunt   Irwin D. Matthew   Louis A. Tonry   Gerry Stud
Mark S. Goodrich   Roberta K. Leary   Alan J. Murphy, Jr.   Charles J. Hum
Richardson White   Harry Ritter   Sheldon Sladen   Joe Figueiredo   George V
H. Pratt   Martha E. Smith   Eleanor Stoddard Marsh   Michael O'Connell
Samuel Baugh   D. J. Buckley   Eleanor Collins   Royal Barry Wills   Richard
Eastman Studds   George Jednick   Randy Feola, Jr.   J. Edward Younie   Mon
Richards   Helen Pratt   Lawrence S. Gates   Michael Joseph ("Hot") Sulliva
Hagerty   Annie Abbruzzese   Joy Pratt   Robert Whelan   J. Blake Thaxter   Jo
John J. Hayes, Jr.   William M. Hunt   Louis F. Eaton, Jr.   Newell W. Rogers
Burbridge   Arlene S. Cline   James E. Carroll   Robert Arndt   Charles J. Fo:
Rev. Richard Brady   Parker Schofield   Cornelia H. White   Harry H. Reed, J.
Roscoe Trueblood   Rev. William H. Mullin   Andrea Parker   Herbert She
Laidlaw   Peter Cogill   John Paul Lyon   Craig M. Simeone   R. Edward Mare
E. Oliver   Howard Bates   Percival M. James   Charles R. Stoddard   Herbert
G. Erickson   William T. Barnes   Parker Malley   Rev. Hubert Desmond   Ra
Lean   John Pattison   Arnold and Alonzo Pearson   Bernard and Manuel Sal
Lynne Pape   Ken Boylston   Murray and Grace Cone   Edward, John, and M
Kealey   Robert Cowdrie   Kenneth Souther   Peter Cappazoli   Claude L. Rici
Diab   Asa Potter   Colonel Albert A. Pope   Grenville Temple Winthrop Bra
Charles Howe   Clarence Patrolia   Edward Goff   Henry B. Perry   Frank C
Bates   Reverend Fred V. Stanley   Rev. Gordon Goodfellow   Marjorie E. Cr
Campbell   May Merritt   Rev. Stephen Hall   Flossie Cogill   Rev. Dr. Bran
Blanchard   Mercie Nichols   Rev. J. David Townsend   Marian Keith Harris
Charles Linder Pope   Isobel Grassie   Rev. Franklin E. Blanchard   Kitty M
Leach   Edith Metcalf   Rev. John VanDuzer   Rev. Earl Luscombe   Penelope
Potter   Martha Ann Selph   Lucia R. Woods   Barbara R. Blackett   Lydia
P. Hobson   Philip Benson   F. Gregg Bemis   Richard A. Sullivan   Edwin A